EUROPE BEFORE ROME

EUROPE BEFORE ROME

A Site-by-Site Tour of the Stone,
Bronze, and Iron Ages

T. DOUGLAS PRICE

OXFORD
UNIVERSITY PRESS

Oxford University Press is a department of the University of Oxford.
It furthers the University's objective of excellence in research,
scholarship, and education by publishing worldwide.

Oxford New York
Auckland   Cape Town   Dar es Salaam   Hong Kong   Karachi
Kuala Lumpur   Madrid   Melbourne   Mexico City   Nairobi
New Delhi   Shanghai   Taipei   Toronto

With offices in
Argentina   Austria   Brazil   Chile   Czech Republic   France   Greece
Guatemala   Hungary   Italy   Japan   Poland   Portugal   Singapore
South Korea   Switzerland   Thailand   Turkey   Ukraine   Vietnam

Oxford is a registered trade mark of Oxford University Press
in the UK and certain other countries.

Published in the United States of America by
Oxford University Press
198 Madison Avenue, New York, NY 10016

Library of Congress Cataloging-in-Publication Data
Price, T. Douglas (Theron Douglas)
Europe before Rome: a site-by-site tour of the stone, bronze, and iron ages / T. Douglas Price.
p. cm.
Includes bibliographical references and index.
ISBN 978–0–19–991470–8
1. Antiquities, Prehistoric—Europe—Guidebooks.
2. Europe—Antiquities—Guidebooks.   I. Title.
GN803.P757 2012
936 – dc23
2011044145

ISBN 978–0–19–991470–8

1 3 5 7 9 8 6 4 2
Printed in China
on acid-free paper

CONTENTS

CHAPTER FOUR   The First Farmers

CHAPTER FIVE   Bronze Age Warriors

BIOGRAPHICAL NOTE

DOUG PRICE (Ph.D., 1975, University of Michigan) is Weinstein Professor of European Archaeology Emeritus and former director of the Laboratory for Archaeological Chemistry at the University of Wisconsin-Madison, where he served on the faculty for more than thirty-seven years. He was also Sixth Century Chair in Archaeological Science at the University of Aberdeen until his retirement. His current research at the Laboratory for Archaeological Chemistry concerns the use of strontium isotopes in human tooth enamel to look at questions of prehistoric migration. The laboratory is involved in the chemical analysis of ceramics, bone, soils, and other archaeological materials. His archaeological fieldwork has focused on the beginnings of agriculture on the island of Zealand, Denmark. He is the author or editor of more than 150 scientific articles and fifteen books, the most recent of which include *Principles of Archaeology* (2006); *An Introduction to Archaeological Chemistry* (with James Burton, 2010); *Pathways to Power* (edited with Gary Feinman, 2010); *The Origins of Agriculture: New Data, New Ideas* (edited with Ofer Bar-Yosef, 2011), and *Images of the Past* 7th ed. (with Gary Feinman, 2012).

PREFACE

I HAVE wanted to write this book for a number of years, but other demands, duties, and procrastination got in the way. The delay was probably a good thing. I recently retired as Weinstein Professor of European Archaeology at the University of Wisconsin-Madison after thirty-seven years. I now have a little more time to pursue my dreams and a bit more knowledge and experience with which to do it.

I have been studying European archaeology since 1970. My Ph.D. focused on the last hunter-gatherers in the Stone Age of the Netherlands. Since 1978 I have conducted archaeological surveys and excavations at a series of sites in Denmark, focused on the last hunters and first farmers, driven by an interest in the beginnings of agriculture.

I am currently an honorary professor in the Section for Prehistoric Archaeology, Department of Anthropology, Archaeology and Linguistics at Aarhus University in Denmark. Other hats I have worn were as director of the Laboratory for Archaeological Chemistry in Madison and as Sixth Century Chair in Archaeological Science at the University of Aberdeen. In the lab, we analyze various archaeological materials to learn about their composition, technology of manufacture, and place of origin. A major part of that research in recent years has involved the use of isotopes to study questions about human mobility in the past.

My career has taken me to a variety of archaeological places in Europe in the last forty years. Research trips, conferences, and touring have allowed me to visit many of the sites I write about here and to experience firsthand some of the places, the finds, and the ambience.

It has been a remarkable journey and left indelible impressions of the abilities and achievements of our distant relatives. It is a story I want to tell others, to share some of the fascinating things that archaeologists have learned about our past and about ourselves. Europe is an extraordinary place for archaeology, for a number of reasons. Interest in the past arose early here and has continued, in large part because of fascination with ancestors and the rise of nationalism. A long history of research in Europe is accompanied by an exceptionally rich body of evidence. The prehistory of Europe contains a long record of human existence, beginning with our early and very different ancestors, culminating in the achievements of Greece and Rome.

Our understanding of the archaeology of Europe has been almost completely rewritten in the last twenty-five years with a series of major discoveries from virtually every time period. Vibrant economic growth (until recently) associated with the expansion of the European Union and the development of infrastructure across the continent resulted in the revelation of many new archaeological objects and places that have profoundly revised our picture of the past. Chance finds and basic archaeological research—survey and excavation—have also provided much new information. Ötzi the Iceman, the renewed investigations at Stonehenge, the discoveries at Atapuerca, the Bronze Age Pompeii at Croce de Papa...the list goes on and on. The finds and discoveries about Europe's past have more than doubled in the last two and a half decades alone. This information is slowly becoming public; fascination with the past can only be enhanced. These discoveries have essentially rewritten large parts of European prehistory.

The archaeology of Europe then is a rich and fascinating body of things and places and information. The path in this book winds through important archaeological sites, the stepping stones through Europe's past that have been uncovered and investigated. There are tens of thousands of archaeological places in Europe. I have included some of those that have provided major, new, and exciting insights into Europe's prehistory, both recent discoveries and long-famous places. The focus is on archaeological sites, but there are also important landscapes of features such as tombs and rock art. Shipwrecks are exceptionally important archaeological sites as well.

This book then is about archaeological places. These places are ordered in a series of chapters according to the archaeological divisions of time: the Stone Age, Bronze Age, and Iron Age. To make sense of the time and significance of these places, the chapters are introduced with some facts, thoughts, and comments about the events that have made us more human and that mark changes in society and behavior. The chapters end with an overview of the time, some remaining questions, and a few controversies. The concluding chapter is a brief essay on the relevance of archaeology and Europe's past to our lives and to the future.

Europe's prehistory is an enormous subject and simply impossible to review in anything other than an encyclopedic format. This book is not that. There are tens of thousands of archaeological places in Europe, many more than can be mentioned in this book. I have chosen a site-by-site approach deliberately because I believe it is a more effective way to understand the past. This format provides a better view of what archaeology is actually about and leaves lasting impressions of places and things from the past. I believe that detailed examination of these archaeological places carries more of the flavor and excitement of the subject than a comprehensive survey of what is known.

There are many things I don't write about, or note only in passing. There are any number of specialist books on specific archaeological cultures, places, and things that never appear in *Europe before Rome*. Selecting the sites and places to include has not been easy. There is clearly emphasis on what I know best and where I have been, and that means a bias toward western Europe. In fact, for this book I have drawn the boundaries of Europe rather tightly; Russia, Belarus, Moldova, and the Ukraine are not included. There are other biases as well. Language is a barrier, and I have certainly spent more time with information published in English. There are more pages and sites in the

Neolithic chapter than the others, no doubt a reflection of my own interests in the origins of agriculture. My geographic bias is even more pronounced. I have spent more than thirty years studying the Stone Age of Denmark and remain fascinated by the archaeology of Scandinavia. There are eight sites each from Germany and England, seven from France, six from Italy and Denmark, five from Spain, and four from Greece. The remaining countries have three or fewer.

I take a somewhat cautious approach to archaeological finds and interpretations of the past. Controversial or unverified finds and findings are generally not included in this book. I hesitate to put in print "spectacular" discoveries that later turn out to be fraudulent or too eagerly interpreted; there are already too many examples in the archaeological literature. To make the chapters more of a narrative and less of an academic text, I have avoided certain formalities. Complicated militarylike maps with large arrows stretching across the continent and verbose tables combining time, geography, and culture history have been used to describe European prehistory for many years. These are not used here, for the most part.

I have not provided detailed chronologies and culture histories of Europe's prehistory. There must be 10,000 named archaeological cultures in Europe. The terminology is often more confusing than clarifying. The Early Neolithic in southeastern Europe, for example, is called Starçevo/Vinça in Serbia, Karanovo in Bulgaria, Gumelniţa in Romania, and Körös in Hungary— different terms for what is largely the same phenomenon. My emphasis is on broader patterns of change and less on the details that can be found in reference books. I have not included citations for information and facts within sentences. I mention some of the scholars involved in the various investigations described herein. Relevant literature is arranged by chapter at the end of the book.

I put emphasis on illustration. Every figure in a book should easily be worth a thousand, hopefully more, words. I have chosen the photos, plans, maps, and drawings with care. I very much hope they will provide you with pleasure and enlightenment in your passage through this book.

Archaeology is the study of past human behavior. I have also tried to place less emphasis on artifacts and more on the varied evidence for changes in behavior and society that took place in the past. That evidence comes from a wide variety of archaeological information—structures, animal bones, plant remains, site distributions, exotic materials, among other things—in addition to the artifacts themselves. My goal is to provide a clear overview of what is happening across more than one million years of Europe's past.

I frequently write about "our ancestors" in this book, and I want to be clear that I refer not to Europeans, or any other specific group of people. One of the things I have learned from archaeology is that we are one, all part of humanity. Archaeology allows us to see our place in the diversity of human societies and gain some appreciation for how much alike, in fact, we all are. Archaeology is the history of us. Perhaps more than any other field of study, archaeology tells us that we are all members of the human family, traveling together on a miraculous journey through time.

I want to gratefully acknowledge the many individuals and institutions that have assisted in one way or another with this volume. A book is never just the work of a single author. Contributions come in many forms—photographs, copies of articles, advice, information, editing, fact checking, oral traditions, permissions, contacts—and from many organizations and people. Sincere and heartfelt thanks to Pedro Alvim, Niels H. Andersen, Søren H. Andersen, David Anthony, Juan Luis Arsuaga, Pauline Asingh, Françoise Audouze, Dominique Baffier, José M. Bermúdez de Castro, Nuno Bicho, Herve Bocherens, Karen M. Boe, Dusan Boriç, Gerhard Bosinski, Dory Brown, Jean-Louis Brunaux, Miha Budja, Jill Capps, Eudald Carbonell, Nick Card, Ian Cartwright, Bob Chapman, John Chapman, Carolyn Chenery, Daniel Cilia, John Coles, Barry Cunliffe, Andras Czene, Francine David, William Davies, Mauro Antonio Di Vito, James Enloe, Berit Eriksen, Jane Evans, Joseph Fenwick, Fiamma Fulgenzi, Anders Fischer, Andrew Fitzpatrick, Harry Fokkens, David Frayer, Vince Gaffney, Sabine Gaudzinski-Windheuser, Anne Birgitte Gebauer, Patrice Gérard, Mircea Gherase, Michel Girard, Detlef Groenenborn, Jean Guilaine, Attila Gyucha, Fredrik Hallgren, Svend Hansen, Debi Harlan, Knut Helskog, Don Hitchcock, Jan Holmes, Mads Holst, Noah V. Honch, Mary Jackes, Stefanie Jacomet, Simon James, Michele Julien, Adrie Kennis, Richard Klein, Jan Kolen, Rüdiger Krause, Kristian Kristiansen, Lucy Kubiak-Marten, Rudolf Kuper, Lars Larsson, Walter Leitner, Domingo Leiva, Urs Leuzinger, Johan Ling, Leendert Louwe Kooijmanns, Trond Lødøen, Blaine Maley, Torben Malm, Sturt Manning, Sarah McClure, Vincent Megaw, Egil Mikkelsen, Nicky Milner, Gerhard Milstreu, Michèle Monnier, Elisa Naumann, Tamara Norton, Welmoed Out, Mike Parker Pearson, Bill Parkinson, Clemens Pasda, Stig A. Schack Pedersen, Catherine Perlés, Andrea Pessina, Wojciech Piotrowski, Mike Pitts, B. W. Roberts, Antonio Rosas, Peter Rowley-Conwy, Hannes Schroeder, Helga Schütze, Michel Sheridan, Adam Stanford, Jiří Svoboda, Josep Tarrús, Nenad Tasić, Thomas Terberger, Hartmut Thieme, Julian Thomas, Carlos Tornero, Robert Tykot, Antonis Vasilakis, Jean-Denis Vigne, Boudewijn Voormolen, Randy White, Caroline Wickham-Jones, Andrea Zeeb-Lanz, Joao Zilhao, and the University of Wisconsin-Madison InterLibrary Loan Department. Their help and generosity with advice, information, or illustrations is greatly appreciated and witness to the collegial rapport among archaeologists. I have undoubtedly missed a few names—my apologies in advance. You are much appreciated in spite of my fallible memory.

Several folks expended their time and energy, and probably their patience, reading and checking various chapters for me—Peter Bogucki, Mike Galaty, Jonathan Haws, Mike Jochim, Tina Thurston, Peter Wells, and Peter Woodman. I am filled with thanks and overwhelmed by the kind help of these friends and colleagues. I should also state immediately, according to protocol, that any errors or omissions are my responsibility alone.

My good friend Peter Woodman and I have traveled together to a number of the places in this book; those have been delightful journeys, and I hope they continue for many years. Thanks for your company, Peter! I would also like to extend my appreciation to the founder of and contributors to Wikipedia for several of the maps and illustrations in this volume. Such communal sharing of resources is truly commendable. In turn, my editor at Oxford University Press, Stefan Vranka, lent a guiding hand that has been an important part of the project and made the editorial connection for this book a pleasure. Sarah Pirovitz at Oxford has also provided much appreciated editorial assistance herding all the details. The copy editor, Thomas Finnegan, did a really excellent job fine-tuning my prose.

I would like to gratefully acknowledge the hospitable support of the Alexander von Humboldt Foundation, which made 2010 a very good year in which to write this book. The Carlsberg Foundation has made available a delightful home for my wife and me in their Akademi in Copenhagen, where most of this was written. It is not possible to adequately express my gratitude to these foundations.

Archaeology is a passion. I decided to become an archaeologist when I was ten years old, standing in front of an ancient Roman tomb along a roadside in northeastern Spain. This passion has focused on Europe for the last forty years. This book is dedicated to another major passion—Anne Birgitte Gebauer—without whom life could not be so sweet.

Carlsberg Akademi
Copenhagen 2011

CHAPTER ONE

Frameworks for Europe's Past

Geography and environment

Geology

Past climate

Raw materials

Time and chronology

A very short history of European archaeology

THIS BOOK is about the prehistoric archaeology of Europe—the lives and deaths of peoples and cultures—about how we became human; the rise of hunters; the birth and growth of society; the emergence of art; the beginnings of agriculture, villages, towns and cities, wars and conquest, peace and trade—the plans and ideas, achievements and failures, of our ancestors across hundreds of thousands of years. It is a story of humanity on planet Earth. It's also about the study of the past—how archaeologists have dug into the ground, uncovered the remaining traces of these ancient peoples, and begun to make sense of that past through painstaking detective work.

This book is about prehistoric societies from the Stone Age into the Iron Age. The story of European prehistory is one of spectacular growth and change. It begins more than a million years ago with the first inhabitants. The endpoint of this journey through the continent's past is marked by the emergence of the literate societies of classical Greece and Rome.

Because of a long history of archaeological research and the richness of the prehistoric remains, we know more about the past of Europe than almost anywhere else. The prehistory of Europe is, in fact, one model of the evolution of society, from small groups of early human ancestors to bands of hunter-gatherers, through the arrival of the first farmers to the emergence of hierarchical societies and powerful states in the Bronze and Iron Ages.

The chapters of our story are the major ages of prehistoric time (Stone, Bronze, and Iron). The content involves the places, events, and changes of those ages from ancient to more recent times. The focus of the chapters is on exceptional archaeological sites that provide the background for much of this story. Before we can begin, however, it is essential to review the larger context in which these developments took place.

This chapter is concerned with the time and space setting of the archaeology of Europe. Specifically, I discuss the continent: its geography, environment, and climate. I examine the concept of time as archaeologists and geologists use it to organize and understand the past. I review the history of archaeology in Europe for some perspective on how archaeologists view and explore the past. With this background, we can turn to the arrival of the first human inhabitants, in Chapter 2.

GEOGRAPHY AND ENVIRONMENT

Maybe the easiest way to first consider the geography of Europe is in two parts: north and south of the Alps. The Alps and the highlands to their east and west stand as a substantial barrier to movement. Of course olive oil, wine consumption, renowned cuisines, and darker complexions contrast dramatically with butter, beer, and pale blonds, but other distinctions between the Mediterranean south and the colder north are significant—and have been for millennia. Technologies and lifestyles differ. Europe was (and is) two contrasting places between north and south.

The movement of trade goods, resources, people, and ideas across the Alpine wall was very limited until the Bronze Age. The relatively calm waters of the Mediterranean made travel by sea preferable. Southern Europe—particularly southeastern Europe—is also closer to southwest Asia, the region sometimes called the Near East, where the origins of agriculture and the rise of cities heralded major transformations in human society. Environmentally, southeastern Europe is not greatly different from Anatolia and parts of the Near East. Fundamental changes in food production and the organization of society spread first from the Near East to southeastern Europe. Major civilizations in Europe—Minoan, Mykenean (also written Mycenaean), Athenian Greece, and the Roman Empire—appeared first in the south along the Mediterranean and had profound influences across the remainder of the continent.

Technically speaking, Europe is not a continent, but a peninsula or subcontinent of the Eurasian landmass, joined completely with Asia (Fig. 1.1). However, for historic reasons—largely because European cartographers defined many of the earth's landforms—it is usually treated as a separate continent. Europe is really a collection of peninsulas. The largest of these is Scandinavia to the north, demarcated by the Baltic Sea. Three other large peninsulas—Iberia, Italy, and the Balkans—extend from the mainland south into the Mediterranean. Europe is also islands—large ones, notably Britain and Ireland, Sardinia and Corsica, Sicily and Crete—and smaller ones in the Aegean, western Mediterranean, Baltic, and elsewhere. A consequence of the peninsular nature of the European continent is the enormous extent of coastline, an estimated 37,000 km (23,000 mi) in length, roughly equivalent to the circumference of the earth.

The Ural Mountains are conventionally taken as the eastern border of Europe. For the purposes of this book, however, the eastern boundary has been moved to the west and excludes Russia, Belarus, Ukraine, and points east in the discussion. The south of Europe is bounded by the Mediterranean and

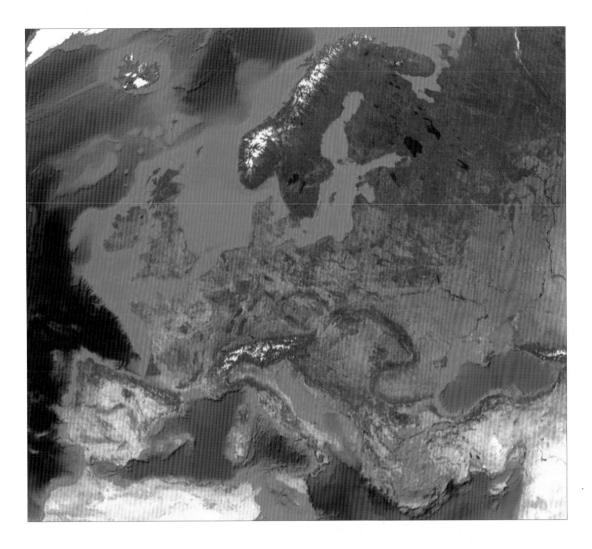

the western shores by the Atlantic and North Sea. Iceland is often included as part of Europe by geographers but is not a concern here because its first inhabitants, the Vikings, did not arrive until the ninth century AD, much too late in our story.

Major rivers of Europe include the Danube, Rhine, and Rhône, all originating within 150 km (100 mi) of one another in and around the Alps. The Danube, the longest, starts in the Black Forest of Germany and flows across Central and Eastern Europe, entering the Black Sea at the Romanian-Bulgarian border. On the way, the Danube runs through Austria, Slovakia, Hungary, Croatia, and Serbia. The Rhine flows north from Switzerland between Germany and France and empties into the North Sea in the southern Netherlands. The Rhône rises in a Swiss glacier and runs through southern France to the Mediterranean. These rivers act as corridors, cutting across the continent. Other important rivers from west to east are the Shannon, Thames, Tagus, Seine, Loire, Po, Elbe, Oder, and Vistula.

Fig. 1.1.
The outline and topography of Europe.

Europe at present is made up of about fifty countries, monarchies, and dependencies (a number that changes frequently), not including Russia, Belarus, Ukraine, and points east. The total landmass is just over 6 million km², with a population of 600 million people. In comparison, the continental United States is about 8 million km² and holds about 300 million people. The largest country in Europe (outside of Russia and the Ukraine) is France, about the same size as the state of Texas. Distances across Europe are not great. London to Paris is about the same as New York to Washington, 325 km (200 mi). Oslo to Rome is ca. 2,000 km (1,250 mi), the same as Boston to Miami.

If you ask most people where a line drawn straight east from New York City would intersect the continent, they will often say England or France. In fact that line from New York City crosses the coast of Portugal and runs near Madrid, Rome, and Istanbul. Europe is much further to the north than the continental United States. The northern part of Europe (northern Norway, Sweden, and Finland) lies north of the Arctic Circle, like the northern third of Alaska.

The climate of Europe is more temperate, however, than other regions at similar latitudes. The Gulf Stream provides for a milder and damper climate, warming the waters of Europe's west coast, as well as the prevailing westerly winds that blow across the continent. Average annual temperatures are higher than should be expected given the northern latitude of the continent. Temperatures increase from north to south and west to east in Europe and range from arctic to subtropical, but extremes are rare and observed only at the margins of the continent. For the most part, *temperate* best describes the climate. Of course, climate has changed substantially in Europe over the last million years, and these changes are part of the context of human evolution. More details on Europe's past climate appear in a section below.

GEOLOGY

The varied landforms of Europe, a contrast of mountains and plains, are a reflection of its geology. Southern Europe is more mountainous than the north, which, except for the Scottish Highlands and Scandinavian Mountains, is largely lowlands. Other major mountain ranges are the Pyrenees, the Alps, the Ore Mountains, the Carpathians, the Dinaric Alps, the Apennines, and the Balkans. The North European Plain defines northern Europe south of Scandinavia, stretching from the English Channel to the Russian marshes. The Po River plain and the Hungarian Basin are also notable large, level, low areas.

A brief geology of Europe as described here starts with the oldest rocks and moves to more recent deposits overlying them. A geological map of Europe is shown in Figure 1.2. The unusual map projection emphasizes Europe as a peninsula, and the simplified geology at this large scale provides a useful view of the important rock formations and their ages. The major geological divisions of time are used in this map. Cenozoic rocks are the youngest. The oldest rocks

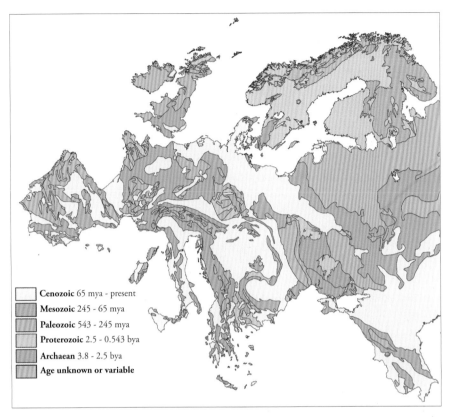

Cenozoic 65 mya - present
Mesozoic 245 - 65 mya
Paleozoic 543 - 245 mya
Proterozoic 2.5 - 0.543 bya
Archaean 3.8 - 2.5 bya
Age unknown or variable

Fig. 1.2.
The geology of Europe
as a peninsula.

in Europe come from the early Proterozoic and Archaean periods, between 4 and 2.5 billion years ago (bya), and are found largely in Scandinavia. The more recent geological periods are the Paleozoic (543–245 million year ago, mya), the Mesozoic (245–65 mya, which is the age of dinosaurs), and the Cenozoic, the last 65 million years of the earth's history.

Continents are composed of cratons and platforms. Cratons are old igneous and metamorphic rocks that make up the basement of the continents—remains of the original crust, dating more than 500 million years in age. Platforms are extensive sedimentary layers covering some areas of the craton and filling in lower places on the surface. Geologists define three major types of rock. Igneous rocks make up the majority of the earth's crust and are formed from the cooling of magma, the molten rock from the earth's interior. Sedimentary rocks are made up normally of small pieces of other rocks created by the processes of erosion and deposition—gravel, sand, silt, and clay. These sediments accumulate in layers and are compacted and cemented over time into rock. Metamorphic rocks are igneous, sedimentary, or other metamorphic rocks that are changed to a new form by heat or pressure during burial.

Shields are large areas where the cratons are exposed on the surface. The Scandinavia Shield dominates the northernmost part of Europe, across Norway, central and northern Sweden, and Finland. These rocks also extend across the North Sea to the highlands of Scotland. Ancient rock is found as well in smaller pieces in the Bohemian Massif of the Czech Republic, the

Massif Central in southeastern France, the Meseta region of western Iberia, and parts of the Balkan Peninsula. These terms—massif, meseta—refer to a group or mass of connected mountains independent of a larger range. Somewhat younger, but still ancient, rocks are found in these same areas as well as the Alps and further east into the Carpathians.

On top of these old rocks, sedimentary basins developed in the lower topography. Seas formed in these basins at various times, giving rise in some areas to thick, marine sedimentary rock layers of Paleozoic, Mesozoic, and Cenozoic age such as limestone, chalk, sandstone, shales, and many more. For example, the Paleozoic and Mesozoic sedimentary units of the Northern European Plain mark the southern boundary of the Scandinavia Shield. Large areas of western Europe have surface deposits of such materials. In eastern Europe, the Hungarian Plain marks the center of a large basin that extends far to the east. Elsewhere in Europe, the limestone landscapes of southwestern France, riddled with the caves that hold the remarkable art of the Upper Paleolithic, are a classic example of such sedimentary units.

More recent geological activity in Europe in the last 2 million years is largely a result of tectonics and glaciation. Tectonics refers to the geological forces associated with movements of the earth's crust and mountain building. Tectonic and volcanic activity have broken through the ancient rocks and platforms of Europe in limited areas. Outside of Iceland and the Canary Islands, the major region of modern volcanic activity in Europe lies in the central and eastern Mediterranean. The famous volcanoes of southern Italy (Vesuvius), Sicily (Etna), and the islands of the Aegean (e.g., Melos, Santorini) are well-known examples. Remnants of older tectonic activity show up in parts of Germany, France, and the Balkans, among other places.

This epoch of geological time—the last 2 million years—is the Pleistocene, known colloquially as the Ice Age. The Pleistocene was in fact a series of ice ages, perhaps as many as twenty cycles of warmer and colder climate. Warmer periods, known as interglacials, were like today or slightly warmer. Cold episodes, known as glacial periods, were characterized by a significant drop in the earth's atmospheric temperature, on the order of 8–10 °C (14–18 °F) from today's average. These colder temperatures fostered the accumulation of snow and ice in northern latitudes and higher elevations. Huge mountains of ice formed, 2–3 km (1–1½ mi) in thickness, and expanded over large areas under the pressure of their own weight. Glaciation refers to the processes involved in the formation, expansion, and retreat of such ice sheets.

PAST CLIMATE

During the Pleistocene, huge ice sheets covered northern Europe, originating in the northern Baltic Sea, and expanding across Scandinavia and the northern part of the continent and over the North Sea floor to most of Britain and Ireland. Another major consequence of these cold episodes was the lowering of sea level. So much of the earth's water was tied up in ice sheets that sea levels fell as much as 120 m (almost 400 ft) or more during the periods of maximum cold. The lowering of sea level greatly changed the outline of the continent and left the North Sea floor, for example, as dry land. The British Isles were connected to the continent, as were some of the islands of the Mediterranean. Huge ice sheets also formed in the Alps, Pyrenees, and other high altitudes in Europe. A map of Europe showing the extent of Pleistocene glaciation appears as Figure 3.1. The glaciers that sit in the Alps and Scandinavian mountains today are the remnants of that last glaciation.

As the last ice sheets began to melt about 16,000 years ago, a number of processes took place. Retreating ice left deposits of ground-up rock and sediment tens of meters deep that the ice had picked up and pulverized during its expansion (Figure 3.31). This undulating surface of ground moraine covers large areas of northern Europe and is found in remnants around the Alps and Pyrenees. Thicker deposits, known as end moraine, piled up at the edges of the ice sheet when melting slowed, leaving the hills and higher places of southern Scandinavia. Enormous amounts of melt water were released as the ice shrank back toward its place of origin, and that water carried a huge load of sands and gravels that were deposited at the margins of the ice. The fine silt sediments, known as loess, from the retreating ice were picked up by the prevailing westerly winds. Tens of meters of this loess were deposited across large parts of Central Europe and remain as the primary surface today.

The meltwaters eventually found their way to the oceans, and the sea began to climb back to levels that are present today, once again redrawing the outline of the European continent. Ancient humans living along the coast of Europe during the Pleistocene were pushed inland and their former living places submerged by the sea. Many of the archaeological remains of Pleistocene Europe have been covered by the waters of the Atlantic, North Sea, and Mediterranean.

As the ice melted, its unimaginable weight disappeared. That weight had depressed the earth's surface by hundreds of meters in some cases. Slowly the earth began to recover, or rebound as geologists say, returning toward its earlier position. There are archaeological sites from 8,000 years ago on the northeastern coast of Sweden that today are 200 m (650 ft) above modern sea level, lifted by the rebound of the earth's crust. This process is still ongoing in northern Europe; the uplift continues in the Bay of Bothnia in the upper Baltic Sea today, at a rate of almost 1 cm (about a half-inch) per year. The low-lying coastline is expanding, and large areas of the former sea floor are now dry land.

RAW MATERIALS

Geology is also important in terms of mineral raw materials and their sources. Stone, not surprisingly, was a critical resource during the Stone Age. Materials for producing sharp-edged tools were indispensable. As humans we lack biological equipment (such as sharp teeth and claws) for cutting or tearing to obtain food, or for defense. Although several types of hard rock were

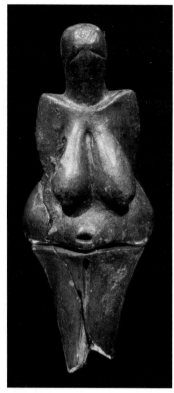

Fig. 1.3.
A fired clay Venus figurine from Dolni Věstonice. 11 cm high.

used to make stone tools, flint and obsidian were favored because breaking these materials produced sharp edges in a predictable way. Flint is a very fine-grained form of quartz, found primarily as nodules and globular masses in sedimentary rocks, such as chalks and limestones. Flint is found in many, but not all, parts of Europe, especially in areas of ancient marine deposits or glacial till. Obsidian is a black natural glass, produced from molten sands that are sometimes created by volcanic activity. Obsidian is rare and found almost exclusively on a few islands in the central and eastern Mediterranean.

With the arrival of the Neolithic and the advent of pottery, clay became another important resource for human existence. Ceramic is a remarkable material; it's basically a rock made by people. Firing soft clay to create a hard ceramic was an important discovery, permitting the invention of fireproof containers—cooking and storage vessels— and other objects. The earliest known use of fired clay was in the form of small human and animal figurines dating from about 25,000 years ago in the Upper Paleolithic in Europe (Fig. 1.3). The first ceramic containers, actual pottery, appeared more than 15,000 years ago in the Far East. Fired-clay pottery comes to Europe about the time of the first farmers, more than 8,000 years ago.

Clay is necessary for the manufacture of pottery. Natural sources of clay are found in most of the landscapes of Europe, wherever slow-moving water deposited accumulations of this very fine sediment. Natural deposits of pure clay are rarely suitable for making ceramics, however. A mix of clay and another material is normally required. This other material—known as temper—is a substance intentionally added to reduce breakage caused by shrinkage during drying and firing. The temper allows more even distribution of heat during the firing process. Prehistoric ceramics are typically about 70–80 percent clay and 20–30 percent temper. A variety of materials have been used as temper in the past, including sand, shell, volcanic ash, pulverized sherds (known as grog), or small pieces of rock, and even organic materials such as bone, straw, and other fibers.

In addition to stone and clay, metals are an important part of later European prehistory. Copper, then bronze, and then iron appear as the primary metallurgies in Europe after 5000 BC. Gold and silver appear after 4000 BC, largely in the form of jewelry. The Bronze Age begins in southern Europe after 3000 BC, and the Iron Age begins shortly after 1000 BC. Bronze has several advantages over copper. It can be recycled repeatedly, whereas copper loses its tensile strength in recasting. Bronze holds an edge much better than copper. Most of the early bronze objects were weapons: swords, daggers, spearheads, and arrowheads.

A map of ore sources in Europe offers clues to the beginnings of metallurgy on the continent (Fig. 1.4). Iron is not shown on the map because of the numerous sources present and the different kinds of iron ore available, to be discussed in Chapter 6. Native metals and ores normally occur as veins in faults and cracks through older rocks, which appear largely in the south of Europe.

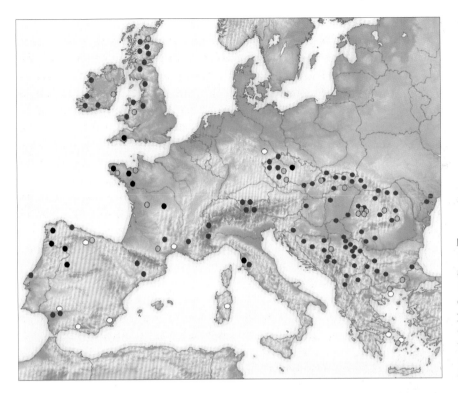

Fig. 1.4.
Metal ore sources in prehistoric Europe. Black dots = tin, red = copper, white = silver, yellow = gold. Iron ores are not shown on the map as they are common in many parts of the continent.

As can be seen on the map, the majority of sources of copper are in eastern Europe, particularly the Balkans and Carpathian Mountains. A few additional sources are known in the Alps, the British Isles, and Spain. Tin is rare; a few scattered outcrops yielded this important metal for the production of high-quality bronze. The precious metals—silver and gold—are also available from a limited number of sources. Eastern Europe is a primary region for gold.

TIME AND CHRONOLOGY

Time, as Woody Allen once noted, is what keeps everything from happening at once. Time is one of those concepts that we take for granted, in part because it is difficult to comprehend. Time can be defined as a continuum in which events occur in succession from the past through the present to the future. There are in fact two time scales of significance for understanding the past: geological time and archaeological time. These time scales or chronologies are the frameworks that geologists and archaeologists create to subdivide time into manageable units.

Archaeological time developed early in the nineteenth century. A Danish naturalist named Christian Jürgensen Thomsen was given the responsibility for organizing the royal antiquarian collections. Thomsen found a simple solution, dividing up objects in the collections according to the material from which they were made: stone, bronze, or iron. His formulation became the standard chronology for European prehistory, dividing the archaeological periods into the Stone Age, Bronze Age, and Iron Age.

Thomsen's original scheme has evolved over time, but the basic framework remains. The Stone Age is the period of hunters and early farmers, when stone tools were predominant, before the discovery of metals. A subsequent subdivision parted the Stone Age into the Paleolithic (Old Stone Age) and Neolithic (New Stone Age) to distinguish the arrival of agriculture, farmers, and pottery after 7000 BC. The Mesolithic was later added to recognize the period of more recent hunter-gatherers in Europe just before the arrival of the farmers. The Paleolithic has been subdivided into three major segments—Lower, Middle, and Upper—to reflect significant changes that occurred during this time span of more than a million years. More details on these divisions are presented in the following chapters.

The nature of archaeological sites and their contents change through these periods. Paleolithic archaeology is dominated by caves and tools made by breaking stone. The Neolithic is characterized by open-air villages, large tombs, pottery, and artifacts made by grinding stone. The Bronze Age is best known from Aegean states, earthen mounds, rich burials, long-distance trade, and rarer and more exotic materials, including early metals. The Iron Age is fortresses and towns, cemeteries, and iron weapons and tools. The prehistory of Europe is a story of increasing local and regional differentiation along with the growth of population, settlement, development of technology, and increasing social, economic, and political complexity.

The archaeological periods of Europe's past take place within the framework of geological time. Geologists have partitioned the 4.5 billion years of the Earth's history into units reflecting major changes and life forms. The Cenozoic is the last 65 million years, the age of mammals. Geological time in terms of humans in Europe includes the last two epochs of the Cenozoic: the Pleistocene, which began 2.6 million years ago, and our current geological epoch, the Holocene, which began almost 12,000 years ago. More on this in the next section.

The Pleistocene was the time of the Ice Ages. It may be surprising to learn that the evidence for the dramatic changes in temperature and glaciation in the Pleistocene has come from underwater in the Caribbean Sea and from the ice cap on Greenland. Scientists have made deep corings of marine sediments and glacial ice respectively in these places. Oxygen isotopes are the key. Oxygen isotope ratios vary with the temperature of ocean water or the atmosphere and can thus indicate temperature change over time. The amount of the ^{18}O isotope relative to the ^{16}O isotope decreases with increasing temperature. The small animal shells (foraminifera) that make up much of the sediment on the ocean floor contain oxygen isotopes in the carbonate of the shell. On Greenland, oxygen isotopes from the Pleistocene are preserved in the kilometers-thick layer of glacial ice that covers the huge island. These layers of shell and ice go from youngest on top and oldest on the bottom and cover hundreds of thousands of years.

During the Pleistocene, alternations between warmer and cooler periods defined by oxygen isotopes have been numbered sequentially and are defined as marine isotope stages (MIS). These stages today are used for the chronology of the Paleolithic. Figure 1.5 shows years before present, changes in isotopes and temperature, stage numbers, and divisions of the Pleistocene. The major cold and warm periods can be seen, as well as the great variation in temperatures that occurred. In addition, the warming episode that began toward the end of the Pleistocene is recorded, along with the present interglacial period, the Holocene.

In this book I follow standard archaeological reporting of time. Several conventions are used. The oldest human remains are usually described as millions of years in age (mya). Many of the dates for the Paleolithic inhabitants of Europe are estimates based on various methods and are reported as hundreds of thousands of years before present (BP). Dates before 10,000 years ago are often reported as BP. As we come closer in time to the present, methods and dates become more precise. The last 10,000 years or so are usually described using the Christian calendar with BC and AD as the suffix.

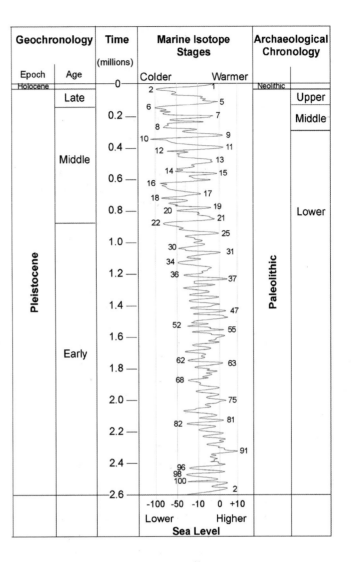

Fig. 1.5.
A chart of the Pleistocene and the Paleolithic. Major subdivisions in both time scales are provided along with the Marine Isotope Stages, an indicator of atmospheric temperature for the last 2.6 million years.

I have listed an age for every site that is discussed in this book. In most cases this date is for the earliest occupation of the site. Sometimes sites are inhabited for very long periods of time and only some of that time span is of special interest. In such an instance, the date for the site reflects the period of most importance. The locations of sites are shown on a map of Europe at the beginning of the chapter, along with a timeline to provide an indication of their age.

A VERY SHORT HISTORY OF EUROPEAN ARCHAEOLOGY

Like many academic disciplines today, archaeology did not really exist as a separate branch of study until the nineteenth century. The history of archaeology follows closely the path that we all take to learn almost any subject—from awareness to interest to questioning to exploration and—eventually—to investigation and understanding. Archaeology is also a product of its times in the sense that current issues and concerns influence the development of the discipline. The period of exploration that accompanied the European colonization of large parts of the world was one of discovery; many new archaeological regions and sites were recognized and new questions were asked. The period after World War II was generally one of optimism and a sense that everything could be known and done using modern technology and ideas. Growing awareness that too many people threatened the environment led to greater concern with population and environment in archaeological thinking. Today in archaeology there is rising concern with globalization, ethical issues, climate change, and preserving the past.

Modern archaeology began in Europe with antiquarians in the sixteenth century. This phase included the celebrated example of the early work of William Stukeley (1687–1765) at Stonehenge in Britain (Fig. 1.6), published between 1740 and 1743. The period after 1800 was marked by creation of museums of antiquity, appointment of the first university chairs in archaeology, and initiation of more systematic fieldwork in various parts of Europe. The very first professor of archaeology was probably Caspar Reuvens, appointed at the University of Leiden in the Netherlands in 1818.

By the beginning of the nineteenth century, the museums of Europe were filling with strange objects from antiquity and collections of exotic souvenirs assembled by ship captains and wealthy dilettantes from colonies and ports of call around the world. Thomsen in Denmark had created the categories—stone, bronze, and iron—for organizing the Danish past. The search for human antiquity began in earnest. Jacques Boucher de Perthes, excavating in his native France in the 1830s to 1850s, uncovered the bones of extinct animals in association with handaxes and argued that humanity was clearly older than the orthodox date of 6,000 years, dictated by the church. Matyáš Kalina and Václav Krolmus published *Pagan Sacrificial Places, Graves and Antiquities in Bohemia* in 1836, based on fieldwork and the study of museum collections.

Fig. 1.6.
A drawing of Stonehenge by William Stukeley, 1722.

Across the continent, intrepid individuals were investigating local prehistory. Ferdinand Keller described the discovery of Swiss lake dwellings during a period of extremely low water levels in the winter of 1853–54. The Italian archaeologist Giuseppe Fiorelli directed excavations at Pompeii in the 1860s, excavating entire room blocks and recording stratigraphic layers. Working in England, Augustus Henry Lane-Fox Pitt-Rivers—"the father of scientific excavation"—stressed the significance of simple artifacts for understanding the past. In the 1870s Heinrich Schliemann popularized his finds at Troy and Mykene with dramatic newspaper accounts that captivated the public. Arthur Evans uncovered and reconstructed the home of the Minoan civilization at Knossos on Crete around the turn of the century.

A century ago the field of archaeology was unknown to most people. During the first decades of the twentieth century, spectacular new sites were revealed as archaeologists visited distant lands in search of the origins of civilization. Archaeology gained an interested public. Those years also were a time of large-scale public works projects in Europe; excavations produced mountains of artifacts and information, revealing the richness of the archaeological record.

The years from 1900 to the Second World War were a classic stage of exploration and investigation of culture history. Culture history focused on the questions of when and where major changes and innovations happened, and on the origins of those changes. Primary sources for change were thought to be either innovation or diffusion. New artifacts and ideas were either local inventions or borrowed from elsewhere.

The years following the Second World War saw dramatic changes in the scale and perspectives of European archaeology. These changes involved enormous growth in the number of archaeologists, museums, and excavations. This period also saw dramatic developments in the nature of archaeological research, in archaeological theory and new orientations to understanding the past. Archaeological investigations have become larger, and the kinds of analyses required much more sophisticated.

These changes in the second half of the twentieth century embraced new theoretical orientations toward understanding the past. Theoretically, archaeology has explored several perspectives, across the gamut from culture history to a positivist, processual view and a postmodern, subjective outlook. Positivists regarded the past world as objectively real and observable with the right methods and instruments. Processual archaeologists wanted to explain cultural change over time in a scientific manner, searching for cultural process and generalizations. Postprocessual archaeologists often took a relativistic perspective that led some to argue that archaeology cannot have an objective view of the past, that our own biases and perceptions determine how we interpret the archaeological record. Postprocessualists rejected evolutionary arguments that suggested progressive change, and they generally avoided generalizations. Today these perspectives have largely melded into a more cohesive and coherent perspective on the past.

During this same period, there was an enormous increase in the number of archaeologists, along with growth in the number and scale of archaeological projects. Many countries established new, or expanded existing, heritage agencies to reduce the impact of construction and development on historical and archaeological places. Rescue archaeology has become a major theme. Multimillion-dollar archaeological projects were undertaken in various places around the continent. An example of such a project is the investigations at the site of Polderweg, described in Chapter 3.

There is no pan-European archaeology. Although most archaeologists are interested in understanding the past through investigation of material remains, there are many ways to do this. There are substantial differences in how archaeology is done and how the past is viewed in Europe (and elsewhere). Certainly there are divergent approaches and goals at the national level. Italian archaeology is focused primarily on the classical period of Rome; Greek archaeology has concentrated on the Archaic and Classical periods (800–300 BC), the time of city-states and Homer, Socrates, and other heroes of the past. British archaeology tends to be more theoretical, perhaps in response to a somewhat less abundant archaeological record on the island. German archaeology is known for meticulous excavations and compendiumlike reports of investigations. Scandinavian archaeology concentrates on more on local issues and rarely reaches the rest of the continent. These are gross generalizations, of course, but they serve to highlight some of the variation.

There are large differences as well between schools of thought that cross-cut national boundaries, and even more dissimilarities between east and west. Archaeology was part of the cold war. Soviet archaeology and a Marxist perspective dominated Eastern Europe until the 1990s, while the West was pursuing a range of theoretical orientations and was perhaps somewhat less dogmatic in approaches to the past. Technological innovations were incorporated much more rapidly into the archaeology of the West. These differences are shrinking but still apparent.

The economic realities of the last few years have slowed change and growth in European archaeology and provided some space for reflection. Theoretical perspectives are no longer viewed as competitive, but rather more compatible. Multidisciplinary archaeology is the norm today, combining the skills and knowledge of many specialists in the investigation of the past. Before 1950 almost everyone was simply an archaeologist; today there are archaeological chemists, archaeometrists, archaeozoologists, archaeobotanists, archaeogeneticists, bioarchaeologists, geoarchaeologists, theoretical archaeologists, and many others. The huge amount of information uncovered and analyzed in recent decades has completely rewritten our understanding of European prehistory and, along with myriad exciting discoveries, is painting a fascinating picture of Europe before Rome. The first part of this story begins with the next chapter.

CHAPTER TWO

The First Europeans

EARLY EUROPEANS

The story of our human ancestors is a fascinating, but fragmentary, tale. There are lots of missing pages in the book. The further back we go in time, the less evidence is available and the more conjecture is required to fill in the gaps. Our oldest arguably human ancestors are found mostly in East and South Africa, resemble our ape family relatives, and date to more than 6 mya (million years ago). These individuals walked on two feet, the first step on the path to becoming human.

Fossils of our ancient ancestors are diagnosed as to genus and species, a dual scientific designation in Latin; a wide range of names have been applied. We modern humans are *Homo sapiens*. Some of our earliest relatives have species names such as *Ardipithecus ramidus*, *Australopithecus afarensis*, and many others. These names are often more confusing than enlightening for anyone but the experts. To make a long story short, there appear to have been several early humanlike ancestors and the exact relationships among them are not

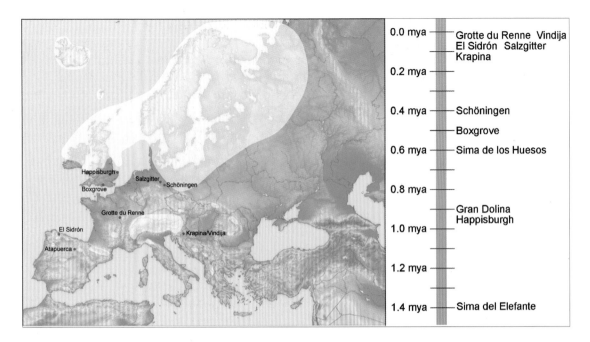

0.0 mya	Grotte du Renne Vindija El Sidrón Salzgitter Krapina
0.2 mya	
0.4 mya	Schöningen
	Boxgrove
0.6 mya	Sima de los Huesos
0.8 mya	
	Gran Dolina Happisburgh
1.0 mya	
1.2 mya	
1.4 mya	Sima del Elefante

Fig. 2.1.
The location and time scale for sites mentioned in this chapter. The white areas mark the maximum extent of glacial ice during the last major cold phase of the Pleistocene.

clear. These individuals walked on two legs, had relatively small brains, did not use tools, and were largely vegetarian.

Sometime around 2.5 mya, however, a clearer line of human evolution emerged with the appearance of the first members of our own genus, *Homo*, again in East Africa. This area is the center for most of the current research on early human ancestors. There are fossil-containing geological deposits from the appropriate time periods. Many of the earliest human remains have been found in this region. The first *Homo* is subtitled *habilis*, or tool-using human. At about this same time, the first evidence for the manufacture of simple stone tools comes to light. These so-called pebble tools provided a cutting edge for a creature that lacked sharp teeth and claws. Stone tools may have afforded better access to meat for these individuals, whose brains began to grow from ape toward human in size.

Shortly after 2 mya a new species, *Homo ergaster,* emerged in Africa and our evolutionary story started to change dramatically. For the first time, fossils of our ancient human ancestors are found outside Africa—in Asia, around 1.8 mya. Shortly thereafter, by 1.3 mya, these early human ancestors spread into Europe. In this nomenclature, there are three variants of *Homo* during the earlier Pleistocene: *ergaster* in Africa, *erectus* in Asia, and *antecessor* in Europe. In Europe the early *antecessor* form evolves into *heidelbergensis* and eventually becomes *neanderthalensis*.

The expansion of early human ancestors out of Africa is surprising, given that the cold climate of Pleistocene Europe and Asia made for a much more difficult habitat than the benign warmth of the African continent. In fact, with only a few exceptions, almost all the sites in Europe earlier than 500,000 years ago—and there are not a large number—are found south of the Alps. Interestingly a dramatic increase in archaeological sites in Europe younger than

500,000 years corresponds closely with the disappearance of large predatory lions, tigers, and the giant hyena.

Early humans in Europe had to adapt to the more northerly conditions of harsher winters, an absence of vegetable foods for parts of the year, and the availability of large herds of migratory animals. Evidence for the first use of fire appears around 800,000 years ago in the Near East, and this new technology eventually arrives in Europe apparently much later, perhaps around 400,000 years ago. Humans became hunters. Long, wooden throwing spears for hunting have been found amid the bones of ancient horses at Schöningen in Germany from some 400,000 years ago, documenting both large-game hunting and early use of wood for making tools and equipment.

Homo erectus appears to have continued in Asia until it was replaced by *Homo sapiens*. In Europe, however, perhaps under conditions of extreme cold and genetic isolation, the Neanderthals (*Homo neanderthalensis*) evolved from *heidelbergensis*, as a rather specialized form. Early Neanderthals are recognizably distinct by ca. 250,000 years ago, and then, by 30,000 years ago at the latest, they were gone from the earth, replaced by expanding populations of anatomically modern humans (AMH) as they are known, early *Homo sapiens*. This species, our own, likely evolved in East Africa around 200,000 years ago. The first *Homo sapiens* fossils appear outside of Africa by 90,000 years ago in the Near East and slightly later in south and east Asia. The first *sapiens* creatures in Europe arrive around 40,000 years ago and completely replace Neanderthals over a period of 10,000 years.

One of the major questions concerning the appearance of anatomically modern humans and the emergence of late Paleolithic cultures has been, What happened to the Neanderthals? This issue has dominated debate in Paleolithic archaeology for more than fifty years, but resolution appears closer today. New evidence from a variety of sources seems to indicate that the Neanderthals were gradually replaced—absorbed might be a good word—by anatomically modern humans in Europe. More discussion of this question continues in the sections on Neanderthals in this chapter, including Arcy-sur-Cure, El Sidrón, and Vindija Cave. The evidence from ancient DNA is reviewed in regard to Vindija.

Thus, the first 4–5 million years of the evolution of the human lineage took place in Africa. It is only during the Pleistocene epoch, the last 2 million years, that our ancestors ventured outside of Africa, into Asia and Europe. We begin the story of European prehistory at that point, with the arrival of *Homo antecessor*. Intriguingly, some of the earliest evidence comes from northern Spain—a place called Atapuerca, in the westernmost part of Europe, far from the presumed entry point through the Near Eastern corridor. This chapter on the first inhabitants covers more than 1 million years of European prehistory and takes us to the appearance of early *Homo sapiens*.

There are several issues to keep in mind when considering the evidence for the oldest human ancestors in Europe. There are problems with understanding the context of the materials, with preservation, and with dating these remains. In this chapter, we visit a series of archaeological sites as much as 1.3 million years of age. This is very old stuff. A lot has happened in terms of disturbances, erosion and deposition, and other biological and geological processes in that period of time. It is often difficult to determine if archaeological materials are in their original place of deposit (*in situ*) or if they have been moved by stream action, mudslides, frozen ground phenomena, animal activity, and the like. Time has faded the edges of the layers and muted the colors of earth and soil. Strata are difficult to distinguish. Because of the time that has passed, it is often impossible to determine if the archaeological materials at a site are the result of one episode of human activity or a palimpsest of repeated visits and returns.

The age of these sites also means that preservation is usually very poor. The further back we go in time, the more likely the disappearance or degradation of all but the hardest materials. Stone tools are the hallmark of the Paleolithic because they survive under most conditions of burial. But other materials—bone, wood, skin, plant remains—usually disappear quickly from the archaeological record. Sites with preserved organic remains from the earlier part of the Paleolithic are extremely rare and thus vitally important to helping us understand that part of the past.

The terminology for the earlier part of the Paleolithic in Europe is fairly straightforward (Fig. 2.2). The Lower Paleolithic begins with the earliest inhabitants, ca. 1.3 mya, with the individuals known as *Homo antecessor* and stone tools referred to as Oldowan or Pebble Tools. The handaxe appears shortly thereafter and defines the Acheulean archaeological culture of the Lower Paleolithic. *Homo neanderthalensis* evolves from *heidelbergensis* after 250,000 years ago and is associated with what are called Mousterian stone tools, dominated by flake tools and smaller handaxes.

It is difficult to date archaeological materials older than about 40,000 years ago, the outer limit of radiocarbon dating. The use of accelerator mass spectrometers (AMS) in radiocarbon dating has been a major advance in the

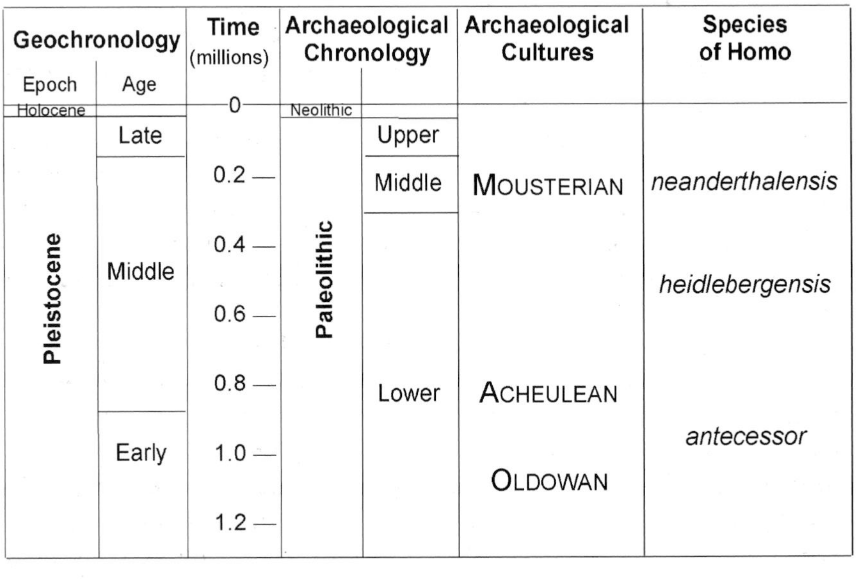

Fig. 2.2.
Time and terminology for the Lower and Middle Paleolithic.

Geochronology		Time (millions)	Archaeological Chronology		Archaeological Cultures	Species of Homo
Epoch	Age					
Holocene		0	Neolithic			
Pleistocene	Late		Paleolithic	Upper		
		0.2		Middle	MOUSTERIAN	*neanderthalensis*
	Middle	0.4				*heidlebergensis*
		0.6				
		0.8		Lower	ACHEULEAN	
	Early	1.0				*antecessor*
					OLDOWAN	
		1.2				

last twenty-five years. AMS dating can accurately estimate the age of very small samples of organic materials, often within a few decades. However, after 40,000 years or so, since there is so little radioactive carbon left in a sample it is almost impossible to measure. For older periods, there is no reliable technique available for directly dating archaeological materials themselves.

Other radiometric techniques can be used, such as argon-argon dating, but these methods depend on the presence of rare kinds of geological materials (volcanic ash, basalt) associated with the archaeological remains. Only a few early archaeological sites can be dated with these techniques. Moreover, the error of such methods is quite high, in the thousands of years, so that age estimates are very approximate. Earlier sites are often dated by association, relying on the types of stone tools present or the species of animals found, where these tools or bones have known dates from other places. This is a useful way to estimate the antiquity of a site, but again it offers only an approximate indication of the age of the materials.

ATAPUERCA, SPAIN, 1.3 MILLION YEARS AGO

Atapuerca holds a treasure trove of ancient archaeology, a bevy of highly significant archaeological sites all in one location. It contains some of the first Europeans and has more of the oldest human remains, more mystery, and more information than any Paleolithic place previously known in Europe. At the same time, there is a space-age feel at the site, with helmeted archaeologists climbing bright steel scaffolding several stories high, covered by plastic roofs, while colorful chutes for removing sediment and rock hang on the cliffs like great yellow vines.

A ridge of limestone hills marks the horizon to the east of the city of Burgos in northern Spain. Limestone is soft and is gradually dissolved by rain and groundwater, which cut channels, caves, and underground streams through the hills. Human remains and artifacts from the early to late Paleolithic are hidden in the many caves of this porous rock mass. The entrances to many of these caverns collapsed over time, closing and hiding the chambers and entombing the materials within.

In the 1890s, a railroad was built through the area known as Atapuerca. Because of the elevation and the need to maintain a reasonably level grade, several deep cuts or trenches were hacked through the limestone for the rail line. This railroad trench exposed a number of caverns and chambers that had been hidden inside the hills for hundreds of thousands of years (Fig. 2.3).

Major excavations to uncover the richness of their contents began in the 1990s. These include archaeological materials from the oldest Europeans to the Bronze Age. The geology of the place has been divided into 11 stratigraphic levels, which contain an important record of the Lower and Middle Pleistocene, between 1.3 million and 150,000 years ago. There are at least seven sites being investigated simultaneously within the caves and crevices of Atapuerca. It's a bit like an anthill, with large crews of diggers working at the top of high scaffolding,

Fig. 2.3.
The railroad cut at Atapuerca with the excavation scaffolding at Gran Dolina in the distance.

digging into the cliff, and other groups near the base, exploring very deep deposits exposed there. Passages and channels lead off the exposed parts of these caves into the interior of the limestone. There is international interest, large amounts of funding, and a fascinating group of scientists working devotedly to uncover the secrets of the area. It is a special place indeed.

The major sites at Atapuerca are each given a name. The most important for our Paleolithic story here are known as Sima del Elefante, Gran Dolina, and Sima de los Huesos (Fig. 2.4). The remains from Sima del Elefante and Gran Dolina are immediately relevant to the first Europeans. Gran Dolina held the record for the oldest human remains in Europe from 1999 until 2008, when the new discoveries from Sima del Elefante were dated and made public. The finds from Sima de los Huesos are equally fascinating, are also early, and yield some information on the beginnings of the Neanderthals.

The three sites together constitute a marvelous introduction to the arrival and evolution of early human ancestors in Europe. The human remains from Elefante and Gran Dolina belong to the species *Homo antecessor*. The abundant fossil materials from Sima de los Huesos come from *Homo heidelbergensis*, the intermediary between *antecessor* and *neanderthalensis*. There is still substantial disagreement about the classification and relatives of *ergaster*, but the species is now widely accepted as the direct ancestor of later hominins such as *Homo heidelbergensis* and *Homo neanderthalensis* rather than the Asian version, *Homo erectus*.

Atapuerca may hold the answers to many questions about our early ancestors. The human remains from these three sites at Atapuerca are the largest collection of fossils of our early ancestors anywhere. As such, Atapuerca is one of the most important archaeological sites in the world. It is also extraordinary that this important place of so many early finds lies in the far reaches of western Europe. The Straits of Gibraltar in southern Spain were always a barrier of open sea waters to passage from Africa. *Homo ergaster* individuals are assumed to have traveled from northwest Africa through the Near East in order to reach the European continent. The first human remains in Europe would have been expected in southeastern Europe, but they are not found there.

Atapuerca, Spain: Sima del Elefante, 1.3 mya

It is in terms of the early *Homo* remains that Sima del Elefante (Cave of the Elephant) is most important, the oldest humans yet discovered on the continent of Europe. The Sima del Elefante is a cave 18 m (60 ft) deep and up to 15 m (50 ft) wide at the base of the Atapuerca railroad cut, filled with washed-in deposits of coarse sediment. The excavations go very slowly, as the sediments are strongly consolidated. Hammers, fine chisels, and small picks are used to remove the layer in the search for stone and bone from the Lower Paleolithic. From this deposit there are human remains, stone tools, and animal bones with cut marks that very clearly indicate a human presence here dated to 1.3 mya. This is the best current evidence for the oldest human ancestor in Europe. The human remains include the frontal portion of a mandible with several teeth in place. *Homo antecessor* is estimated to have been a 1.6–1.8 m (5'3"–5'10" ft) tall male who probably weighed around 90 kg (200 lb). Brain size was roughly three-quarters that of anatomically modern humans. Along with the mandible, there are thirty-two simple stone flakes and other artifacts, made from local stone. These tools are typical of the oldest stone assemblages in Europe.

The list of animals identified among the bones at Sima del Elefante is extensive and includes a number of warm-climate species that indicate the human presence here was during an interglacial, or warmer, period of the Pleistocene. Among the larger mammals are extinct forms of macaque monkeys, wild boar, bison, several types of deer, rhinoceros, horse, wild cat, panther, bear, fox, wolf, beaver, squirrel, hare, rabbit, hedgehog, and some weasel species. Microfauna (species with small bones, mouse-size) are numerous and include various species of voles, lemmings, dormouse, shrews, and moles. The large mammals are primarily represented by long bones; rabbits and birds are found in complete anatomical segments, mainly limbs, suggesting they may have been eaten. Some bones of the large mammals show definite evidence of marrow extraction, such as percussion marks on long bones (Fig. 2.5) and cut marks to remove meat made by stone tools on other bones.

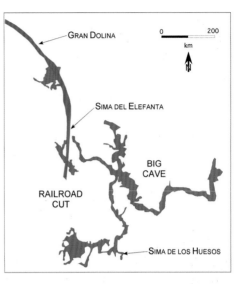

Fig. 2.4.
Location of the sites at Atapuerca. The green band is the railroad cut; the caves are shown in brown.

Atapuerca, Spain: Gran Dolina, 900,000 years ago

The deposits at Gran Dolina accumulated at the mouth of a cave or rock shelter that has largely disappeared. The original entrance near the top of the hill of

Fig. 2.5.

Long bone from a large mammal from Sima del Elefante, intentionally fractured (arrows show the impact points) to extract marrow.

Atapuerca was exposed when the deep railroad cut was made through this area. High scaffolding is necessary to reach the deposits where the excavations take place. The site is only 200 m (600 ft) from Sima de Elefante.

There are many layers at Gran Dolina but the most important is layer 6, which has been dated to approximately 900,000 years ago. This layer is one of the richest in terms of bone remains, with more than twenty-five animal species such as horse, deer, bison, rhinoceros, wildcat, hyena, and wolf. Several hundred stone artifacts have been found among the bones, for the most part simple pebble tools and flakes along with a few handaxes. In addition, approximately a hundred human fossil fragments, representing at least six individuals, have been found to date. These bones belong to *Homo antecessor*. The best-preserved specimens include a maxilla (upper jaw) and a partial frontal portion of the cranium including the right eye socket (Fig. 2.6). The human remains from Gran Dolina were the oldest in Europe until the discoveries at Sima del Elefante.

These human bones exhibit a pattern of breakage, cutting, and chopping by stone tools that clearly indicates that the humans who butchered the animals whose bones are in the cave also must have butchered and consumed these folks. Gran Dolina documents the fact that these early Europeans were cannibals.

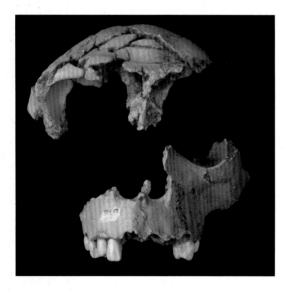

Fig. 2.6.

The skull of *Homo antecessor* from Gran Dolina.

Atapuerca, Spain: Sima de los Huesos, 530,000 years ago

Both Elefante and Dolina were exposed when the railroad was cut through the hills of Atapuerca. Sima de los Huesos ("pit of bones"), however, lies deep inside the hill and was found by spelunkers and zoologists collecting the bones of bears that had died while hibernating in the cave during the Pleistocene.

The Pit of Bones is an extraordinary crevice deep in one of the largest caves in the Atapuerca region. The "pit" lies 55 m (180 ft) below ground surface and 500 m (1,650 ft) from the nearest modern entrance to the cave. The pit is "sock-shaped," a small depression at the end of a sloping passage entered from a 13 m vertical shaft. Just to reach this crevice is a difficult journey for the excavators. The passage is narrow and slippery, and part of the trip into the site requires traversing a deep shaft. Only one or two individuals at a time can work in this nook; it is warm and has a low level of oxygen.

The excavations, however difficult, have produced spectacular results and the largest set of human remains from the Paleolithic ever recovered. The remains of humans and bears are mixed together at the bottom of the shaft in a red clay layer that has preserved the bone. There are an especially large number of teeth and finger bones at the site. The human remains in Sima de los Huesos have been designated as *Homo heidelbergensis* and represent the ancestors of the Neanderthals discussed later in this chapter. These remains have recently been dated to a minimum age of 530,000 years.

Parts of the skeletons of at least thirty-two individuals have been found (Fig. 2.7), a remarkably large number. Nine are male, nine are female (the sex of fourteen could not be determined on the basis of the bones). The largest number, eleven individuals, were between thirteen and seventeen years of age. There are four children between three and thirteen. Only three people were older than thirty when they died, and no one had reached the age of forty. These individuals were of normal height; males averaged 1.75 m (5'9"), females 1.7 m (5'6"). The tallest person was 1.8 m (5'9") and probably weighed 90 kg (200 lbs). The cause of death is unknown. Several of the individuals had suffered from disease or injury.

The Sima de los Huesos remains account for more than 80 percent of all known Middle Pleistocene fossils for the genus *Homo* and furnish an

Fig. 2.7.
An artist's reconstruction of the individuals from Sima de los Huesos.

unprecedented collection for study. Excavations at the site continue every year, and the project scientists believe there are likely forty more individuals in the pit. The remains are an extraordinary sample of a human population living during the Lower Paleolithic. As a result, we know more about these early hominins than about almost any others.

It is also important to think about the context of the human remains at Sima de los Huesos, at the bottom of a four-story shaft in the back of a cave more than half a kilometer from the nearest entrance and sunlight. The bodies of these *heidelbergensis* individuals were intentionally put into the pit. Their cadavers must have been carried into the cave, through the difficult passage, and dropped into the shaft. Perhaps this behavior foreshadows the practice of intentional burial that is first seen among Neanderthals in the Middle Paleolithic. The question of course is, Why? It appears there was no health or sanitary reason for the long and arduous journey though the cave. We may be witnessing here some of the first evidence for a "human" awareness of death and special treatment of the dead. Of course, there may be very different reasons these individuals were placed or somehow ended up in the shaft, but they are not known.

Fig. 2.8.
The handaxe from Sima de los Huesos. Length approximately 16 cm.

New discoveries turn up regularly. Recently the hallmark stone tool of the Lower Paleolithic, a handaxe, was found among the bones (Fig. 2.8). Although the earliest stone tools do have a cutting edge, they are extremely simple and unwieldy. These early tools evolved and improved over time as early hominins began to remove more and more flakes from the core of raw material, reshaping it and creating longer, straighter edges for cutting. When such a core tool assumes a distinctive teardrop shape—pointed at one end, rounded at the other, retouched to a desired size, shape, and heft—it is known as a handaxe, the signature tool of *Homo ergaster*, *erectus*, and *antecessor*. The handaxe is truly an all-purpose piece of equipment that was used for cutting, sawing, digging, bashing, and boring large holes, among other things. This tool was the Swiss army knife of the Paleolithic and must have been used by everyone, since hundreds of thousands of examples have been found at Lower Paleolithic sites throughout Europe, Africa, and large areas of Asia.

The handaxe is a more complex tool than it first appears. Its final form is a shape inside a piece of stone, and so it is in the mind of the maker; a cobble must be heavily modified for the handaxe to emerge. Moreover, the handaxe is symmetrical in outline, reflecting purpose, skill, and foresight in manufacture. Handaxes are often made from small cobbles 10–15 cm (4–6 in) long. A number of much larger examples, however, also exist, some more than 30 cm (1 ft) in length. The oldest Acheulean handaxes are known from a site in Ethiopia and date to 1.9 mya. The oldest known handaxes in Europe come from southern Spain and date to about 900,000 years ago.

BOXGROVE, ENGLAND, 500,000 YEARS AGO

The relatively few archaeological sites in Europe older than 500,000 years, like Atapuerca, are usually found south of the Alps. The general consensus has been that northern Europe was a hostile and difficult climate in the Pleistocene and early hominin groups stayed closer to the warmer zone of the Mediterranean. This picture has changed a bit with major recent discoveries in the British Isles. Early Paleolithic materials have been found at Happisburgh, Pakefield, and Boxgrove. The first two sites have been reported only in the last few years and are still under investigation. Pakefield, in county Suffolk on the east coast of England, dates to ca. 700,000 years ago, and Happisburgh, in Norfolk, also along the east coast, is perhaps 950,000 years old.

The site of Boxgrove has been known for some time and is one of the best-documented Paleolithic sites in Europe. The name of the site comes from the large parish in which it is located, not far from Brighton on the coast of England, about 80 km (50 mi) directly south of London. Today the site lies 12 km (7.5 mi) from the sea, but 500,000 years ago it was part of the Atlantic coast of Britain. The site here is in an area of buried chalk cliff that overlooked a wide, level beach with a water hole or small stream.

The Eartham Quarry Company has been removing sand and gravel from the deposits at Boxgrove for decades. The quarries go deeper and deeper into the old seashore and move along the base of the chalk cliffs where these materials formed half a million years ago. Many years ago, the workmen at the gravel quarry began finding the bones of ancient animals and stone tools in some of the layers they were digging up. Eventually archaeologists got involved, and a long-term program of investigations was begun and continues here today (Fig. 2.9).

The quarry work has exposed these old surfaces over large areas. Boxgrove is important for many reasons, notably the degree of preservation of the landscape, the impressive size of the undisturbed ancient land surface, and the quantity of well-preserved animal bones—even bird and fish bones are in excellent condition. Many fine Paleolithic flint artifacts and the bones of *Homo heidelbergensis* also found at the site. The combination of geology and bones and stone artifacts found *in situ* gives a detailed picture of the coastal plain of southern Britain half a million years ago.

The region around Boxgrove contains one of the largest preserved Paleolithic land surfaces in Europe, buried beneath several meters of more recent sediments (Fig. 2.10). More than ninety separate excavation areas have been opened by the Boxgrove archaeological project since the 1980s, many producing exceptionally well-preserved scatters of flint artifacts and mammalian fauna. This unique record is allowing aspects of past human life such as tool manufacture, subsistence, butchery patterns, and land use to be studied in detail.

Fig. 2.9.
Excavations at Boxgrove exposing the Lower Paleolithic surface.

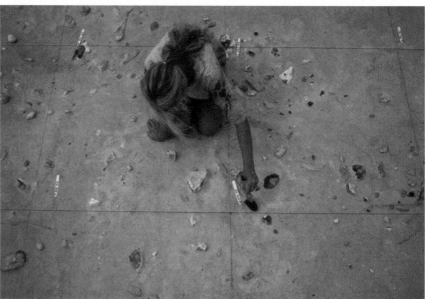

Fig. 2.10.
Cleaning stone artifacts on the Lower Paleolithic surface at Boxgrove.

The archaeological materials have been found in a deposit known as the Slindon formation, sands and silts deposited at the junction of the chalk cliff and the coastal plain (Fig. 2.11). Geological investigation of these deposits has documented that this was a terrestrial environment surrounding a small, shallow lake or pond, fed by spring water from the chalk cliffs. Isotopic analyses of shells from the deposits indicate that summer temperatures were similar to present day, while winters were probably colder.

The human activity at Boxgrove took place during an interglacial period, a warm episode between the major cold spells of the Pleistocene. The best-preserved remains had been buried in fine silt near the bottom of the high chalk cliff,

Fig. 2.11.
The sequence of
deposits at Boxgrove.
The Paleolithic
materials are near
the bottom of the
stratigraphy.

deposited in still water around the water hole, close to the high-tide mark. The lack of in-ground features such as pits, postholes, or hearths suggests that this was not an area of residence, but rather involved hunting and butchering activities.

At the excavation area designated as Q1/B, freshwater deposits next to the chalk preserved the remains of butchered animal bones along with quantities of handaxes, a few flake tools, and many sharp waste flakes. The flint was available in the nearby chalk cliffs. The few flake tools were standard forms, mostly scrapers. A large number of very fine handaxes have been found at this location. This site appears to have been repeatedly used by early humans. Herbivores such as rhinoceros, horse, bison, giant deer, and red deer may have been attracted to the water hole, an excellent location for intercepting game. It was also here that a tibia and two teeth belonging to *Homo heidelbergensis* were found.

Many of the animal bones exhibit cut marks from the flint tools used to butcher the carcasses of the large game animals. There were no cut marks observed on small animals found at the site, suggesting that the large game were the primary prey. Cut marks from butchering occur in places on the skeleton where large sections of meat were available and suggest that the animals were hunted rather than scavenged. Cut marks were always found beneath the later gnawing marks from scavengers. The whole spectrum of butchery-related traces has been identified by the researchers, including cut marks created during skinning, dismemberment, filleting, and scraping of long bones along with impact scars resulting from breaking bones to remove the marrow.

At another site in the huge quarry at Boxgrove, the fragmentary bones of a large horse were surrounded by small heaps of flint debris, left where a group of human ancestors had made some new handaxes before butchering the meat. You can almost imagine the stone waste materials piling up between the legs of the flint worker as the handaxes took shape. The hunters here brought six large nodules of flint to the site to make stone tools. A hole in a shoulder blade of the horse has

Fig. 2.12.
Four views of an
Acheulean handaxe
from a Lower
Paleolithic site in
France. 27 cm long.

been interpreted as a sign that the animal was killed with a wooden spear. Such spears, found at Schöningen, Germany, dating from 400,000 years ago, strongly support this suggestion. (Schöningen is discussed in the next section.)

The flint tools at the site, including the handaxes, appear to have been made rather quickly, used for butchering the animal prey and then discarded (Fig. 2.12). Archaeologists spent many hours refitting the pieces of flaked stone back into their original "unbroken" nodules. It's a three-dimensional jigsaw puzzle with very similar pieces. The information gained, however, is invaluable. By mapping the location of the pieces that fit together it is possible to see all the places associated with the making and use of the stone artifacts. At Boxgrove, the distribution of refitted pieces was usually very tight, indicating that the manufacture, use, and discarding of the products of tool making took place in the same immediate area and that it was not substantially disturbed in the last 500,000 years.

The Boxgrove quarry was purchased by English Heritage in 2003 for preservation and future research. Boxgrove has been declared a Site of Special Scientific Interest in Britain; almost 10 hectares (25 acres) have been protected for the future by reburying the deposits of a part of the site with inert waste.

SCHÖNINGEN, GERMANY, 400,000 YEARS AGO

There is an important debate among the scientists studying our early human ancestors about what we ate and how we obtained our food. The early human diet is difficult to determine because the remains of meals are generally not well preserved. The wild plants of Africa probably provided a ready source of food for early humans, but plant materials do not survive from so long ago. The importance of fruits, nuts, and other plant foods in the diet is unknown. Longer, colder winters in more northern latitudes must have put a premium on successful predation. Meat would have been the source of sustenance during winter when roots, nuts, leaves, and other edible plants were not readily available. Meat became essential to the human way of life in colder climates.

plant materials that are on their way to becoming coal. Lignite is used as a fuel for electric power generation; Germany is the world's largest producer of lignite.

Around Schöningen, the deposits of lignite are up to 30 m (100 ft) in depth. Hartmut Thieme, an archaeologist from Hannover, has been visiting the strip mines there since 1983. Because the brown coal is a relatively recent deposit from the Pleistocene and Holocene, archaeological materials from many periods have been unearthed by the mining. Thieme and his colleagues have surveyed approximately 6 km² (2.3 mi²) within the area of the mine. Materials from the Paleolithic to the Iron Age have been uncovered.

The Lower Paleolithic sites were first discovered in 1992 in the southern part of the mine at a depth of 8–15 m (25–50 ft) below the present surface. In the deposits of brown coal lie a series of mud and peat layers that mark erosion channels and former lakes in an ancient, buried landscape. The archaeological sites were found along these former lake and stream shores, buried in the organic materials that have preserved them so well. The remains of many species of animals have been found at Schöningen, among them mammoth, bison, wild cattle, horse, and red deer. The early humans came here during an interglacial period, between the colder episodes of the Pleistocene, in northern Europe. The climate at the time was cool and temperate; the vegetation in the region was a mix of meadow and forest steppe.

Fig. 2.14.
The skull of a Pleistocene horse from Schöningen.

There are several concentrations of archaeological materials from the Lower Paleolithic. Three sites are discussed here, designated as Schöningen 12, 13:1, and 13:4. Schöningen 13:1 is the oldest and deepest of the three, along a former lakeshore. This site contained stone tools, some of which had been

burned, and the bones of mammoth, wild cattle, horse (Fig. 2.14), and red deer. Just above the layer with the archaeological materials were found the complete skull of a bison and the footprints of large mammals in the hardened mud.

Schöningen 12 also lies along a former lakeshore and holds more than a thousand bones from the straight-tusked elephant, a common prey animal in the Lower Paleolithic, along with ten other mammal species, and the remains of birds, fish, and reptiles. Of particular interest were several wooden objects, branches broken from a silver fir tree and split diagonally across the knobby end, in all likelihood to serve as a haft for an inserted stone tool. If this supposition is correct, these would be the earliest known composite artifacts, tools made of more than one material.

The spear site (13:4) was found about 10 m (33 ft) below the present ground surface, originally along the shore of a small lake. The scatter of artifacts and other materials extends for about 50 m (164 ft) and is roughly 10 m (33 ft) wide. This is a remarkable place because of the quality of preservation and the age of the site, ca. 400,000 years. More than 25,000 animal bones and fragments have been found; 90 percent are from at least twenty horses and the remainder are largely deer and wild cattle. Many of the horse bones have cut marks and fractures typically produced by butchering. Several of the bones with cut marks also have impressions from carnivore teeth superimposed on the earlier cut marks (Fig. 2.15), indicating that the humans got the prey before other predators did. Breakage patterns in the horse bones show the hunters were after marrow as well as meat. The stone tools are made of flint and include a variety of scraping and pointed pieces and many sharp edges.

Fig. 2.15.
A horse rib with cut marks from filleting with a stone tool found beneath tooth marks from a carnivore, indicating that the early human ancestors at Schöningen had first choice of the meat on the animal.

Diverse wooden artifacts have been found. One of the first was a spruce throwing stick, sharpened at both ends, about 80 cm long (2.6 ft) and 3 cm (1.2 in) thick. This weapon could have been used to hunt waterfowl such as the geese identified among the bones at the site.

The spears at Schöningen were used to hunt fast, mobile Pleistocene horses—testimony to the skills of these hunters. At least eight spears have been found at the site, lying among the skeletons of horses. The spears were made from small, straight spruce trees approximately thirty years old and averaging 2 m (6.6 ft) in length (Fig. 2.16). These were designed for throwing, carefully worked and weighted weapons with a balance point. The spears resemble the modern javelins used in athletic competition. The sharp end was fashioned at the base of the tree, where the hardest wood is found. A modern copy has been thrown accurately a distance of 60 m (almost 200 ft). For whatever reasons, and fortunately for archaeology, the hunters left their spears behind when they left this place.

At least four hearths have been found, each about one meter in diameter with burned and discolored earth clearly marking the location of the fire. Fire

Boxgrove supplies good evidence that early humans in Europe were predators, eating meat as the first feeders. But how were the animals killed? How did our early ancestors obtain their meat?

This question is at the center of a controversy in archaeology concerning scavenging versus hunting. Some scholars believe that our early human ancestors were primarily scavengers, visiting the kills of predatory animals, taking the morsels that remained, competing with other scavengers. These individuals argue that the actual hunting of large animals is a relatively recent development in human prehistory. Others contend that early human ancestors were successful hunters—stalking, killing, butchering, and eating the creatures of Pleistocene Europe. The previous evidence was scanty and open to debate. The discoveries at Schöningen, however, have ended that debate.

The remarkable Paleolithic finds at Schöningen come from a modern strip mine for brown coal, located about 100 km (62 mi) east of Hannover, Germany (Fig. 2.13). Brown coal, or lignite, is an organic deposit of ancient

Fig. 2.13.
Aerial view of the excavations at Schöningen in 1995. The structure on the terrace covers some of the Paleolithic excavations. The huge excavations are part of an open pit coal mine.

must have been a major factor in the increasing success of human adaptation and the move into new, colder habitats. The oldest known evidence for the use of fire comes from Israel and dates to 800,000 years ago. Cooking with fire offers a number of advantages, in addition to making food more tender and palatable. It improves the digestibility of many foods and destroys harmful bacteria. For *Homo antecessor,* cooking probably made it possible to add new foods to the diet. The hearth as a source of warmth and cooked food was probably responsible for changing human subsistence activities from a feed-as-you-go-and-eat-raw-food strategy to the sharing of cooked foods. The hearth became an attractive location for increased social interaction between individuals.

This is clearly a hunting-and-butchering site from the Lower Paleolithic. Thieme, the excavator, believes the site was used in the late summer or fall when the water level in the lake was lower. He also suggests that the materials at Schöningen 13:4 are the result of a single hunting episode in which a group of hunters killed a number of horses along the shore of this lake. Twenty or more horses would have yielded a huge amount of meat. There are some indications that it may have been cut into strips and smoked or dried for later use. This was elaborate and thoughtful behavior on the part of *Homo heidelbergensis* 400,000 years ago.

Fig. 2.16.
One of the wooden spears from Schöningen in its original position of discovery.

NEANDERTHALS

As noted earlier, Neanderthals evolved from *Homo heidelbergensis* in Europe around 250,000 years ago as a rather isolated branch of the genus *Homo*. Fossil skeletons of Neanderthals are recognized by several characteristic features in the skull and teeth. The cranium is relatively low, and the face is long. Prominent brow ridges—bony protrusions above the eyes—and generally heavy bone structure give the skull a distinctive look. The face is large, the forehead slopes sharply backward, and the nose and the teeth sit farther forward than in any other hominin, giving the entire face an elongated appearance. The front teeth are often heavily worn, even the deciduous teeth of young children, suggesting they were used constantly for grasping or heavy chewing.

The skeleton of the Neanderthals differs somewhat from anatomically modern forms, although they had the same posture, dexterity, and mobility (Fig. 2.17). Neanderthals were generally short and stocky, averaging about 1.5 m (4.9 ft) in height, with bowed limbs and large joints supporting a powerful physique. Neanderthal bones are generally described as robust; they had heavier limb bones than anatomically modern humans, suggesting greater muscular strength and a more powerful grip. This strength is also evident in the shoulder blades and neck, and on the back of the skull, where heavy muscle attachments are noticeable. The average brain size of the Neanderthals is slightly larger than that of modern humans, perhaps a consequence of their heavier bone structure.

The heavy limbed appearance of the Neanderthals may be related to the strength and endurance required for travel over irregular terrain or to cold climate, similar to that of the Eskimo. Or perhaps Neanderthals had to be stronger to accomplish physically what anatomically modern humans accomplished with sophisticated tools. Neanderthal skeletons exhibit more traumatic damage, especially fractures to the head and neck, from accident or violence than many modern populations, perhaps from close encounters with large game. The Neanderthals often lived to their late thirties or midforties, a rather long life span in deep antiquity.

Neanderthals are generally found with flake tools, shaped into a variety of forms for more specialized uses (Fig. 2.18). The term Middle Paleolithic is used

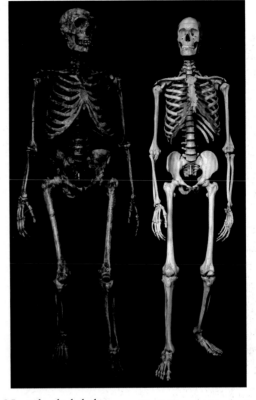

Fig. 2.17.
Neanderthal (left) and
Homo sapiens skeletons
(right).

Fig. 2.18.
Flake tools from the
Neanderthal deposits
at Gorham's Cave,
Gibraltar.

to describe these kinds of artifacts, which date from approximately 250,000 to 30,000 years ago in Europe. Handaxes continued to be made, but large retouched flakes are hallmarks of the period.

The Neanderthals were large-game hunters. Isotopic studies of their bones document a heavily carnivorous diet. Their prey varied across Europe; reindeer were hunted primarily in the west and mammoths were more commonly hunted in eastern regions. Cultural innovations during this period include the first intentional burial of the dead, sometimes accompanied by what appears to be food or gifts. The presence of these materials in graves may imply concepts of death as sleep, or of life after death. It also possible that Neanderthals decorated themselves with beads, pendants, and body paint. Perforated shells and animal teeth were made to be strung and worn. "Pencils" of manganese dioxide have been found in several Neanderthal living spaces and were likely used to draw lines on animal and human skin. This evidence for self-decoration, however, is speculative.

Neanderthal fossils and Middle Paleolithic artifacts are found primarily in Europe. An extremely cold period around 75,000 years ago may have pushed some Neanderthal groups southeast into Southwest Asia and eastward into western Asia. Five sites related to Neanderthals are visited in these pages. At Krapina in Croatia, skeletal remains from Neanderthals and a variety of animal species paint a rather grisly picture of life in the Middle Paleolithic. The bones of at least thirteen Neanderthal individuals were found, burned, split to extract marrow, and treated like the other animals that yielded meals for the occupants of this site. Cannibalism, it seems, was not uncommon in the Paleolithic. Salzgitter-Lebenstedt in northern Germany offers convincing evidence that Neanderthals were well adapted as big-game hunters to the cold conditions of Pleistocene Europe 55,000 years ago.

El Sidrón in northern Spain contains a large number of Neanderthal fossils of great interest in genetic studies because of the good conditions of preservation. At Arcy-sur-Cure in central France, Neanderthals occupied a series of caves along a lovely, meandering river and left substantial remains for archaeologists to puzzle over. The Neanderthal sites here are among the last in Europe and a good place to seek an answer to the question of why the Neanderthals disappeared. Finally, at Vindija, Croatia, not far from Krapina, bones and stones also from the time of transition between Neanderthals and anatomically modern humans lend further insight as to the changes that were taking place.

By 30,000 years ago, almost all the Neanderthals were gone from Europe, extinct, end of the line. A few refuge populations appear to have hung on in southern Iberia until perhaps 25,000, when they too were replaced by *Homo sapiens*, individuals like ourselves. The question of how that replacement happened remains an intriguing puzzle in prehistory, not yet fully solved. The mystery is discussed in more detail later in this chapter.

KRAPINA, SERBIA, 130,000 YEARS AGO

There are two very important sites in northwestern Croatia for our understanding of the Neanderthals. Krapina is a famous place because of the large number of skeletal remains found there and the convincing evidence for cannibalism. Vindija Cave contained some of the youngest Neanderthal remains in Europe and is particularly significant because of the layers dating from the transition from Neanderthals to anatomically modern humans. Here I discuss the discoveries from Krapina and some information on Neanderthal diet. Toward the end of this chapter, we return to Vindija and what the remains from that Croatian cave tell us about ourselves and our ancestry.

In 1856, three years before Charles Darwin published his groundbreaking book *On the Origin of Species,* proposing natural selection as a mechanism for evolution, pieces of a strange skeleton were unearthed in a limestone cave in the valley of the Neander River, near Düsseldorf, Germany. At this time, the existence of human forms earlier than *Homo sapiens* was not accepted, and there was only limited awareness of a concept such as human evolution. Leading authorities first described the bones from the Neander Valley as those of a deceased Prussian soldier, a victim of Noah's flood, or a congenital idiot—but definitely not an early human ancestor. Gradually, however, more examples of these individuals came to light. In 1886, at the cave of Spy in Belgium, two similar skeletons were discovered in association with early stone tools and the bones of extinct animals, clearly demonstrating the antiquity of humans in Europe.

Shortly thereafter, at the turn of the century in 1899, a Croatian paleontologist with the wonderful name of Dragutin Gorjanovic-Kramberger visited a large rockshelter near the top of a limestone hill called Hušnjak, near the town of Krapina in northern Croatia. Archaeological materials on the surface deposits of the shelter convinced him to start digging. Between 1899 and 1905 almost 900 human fossil remains (Fig. 2.19), including 200 loose teeth, were unearthed, along with numerous Middle Paleolithic artifacts and animal bones. The animal bones came from a variety of species such as cave bear, woolly rhinoceros, and aurochs (wild cattle). The age of the deposit—including Neanderthal remains—is estimated to be around 130,000 years.

Fig. 2.19.
Eye orbits and partial cranium of one of the Neanderthals from Krapina.

Gorjanovic-Kramberger's careful excavations had a lasting legacy. He was one of the first in Europe to preserve a stratigraphic section from a prehistoric site as a record of the layers. He saved virtually every Neanderthal bone from the excavations and recorded the levels in which they were found. He also saved most of the stone tools and animal bones. He published his results quickly and invited foreign scholars to study the remains. His efforts meant that Krapina has been included in virtually every discussion of Neanderthals in the last hundred years. Gorjanovic-Kramberger was also the first to publish photographs of the hominin fossils and to point out the evidence for cannibalism, based on fragmentation and dispersal of the bones, burning, cut marks, and other damage.

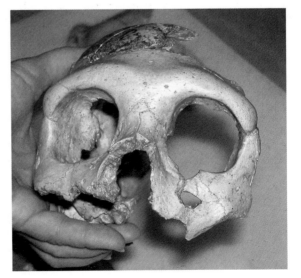

There is a very long and detailed series of investigations of the skeletal remains from Krapina, which may be the most studied set of prehistoric fossils in existence. The anatomical analysis of the Neanderthal bone material suggests that at least seventy-five individuals are represented, the largest collection of Neanderthals anywhere. The majority of the individuals died between the ages of sixteen and twenty-four. The material was fragmentary, and although there were pieces of most of the parts of the skeleton, there was no complete skeleton for any single individual.

Many of the bones from Krapina were X-rayed in the 1990s. The results indicated a generally healthy population with few indications of trauma or disease, other than normal wear and tear due to age and activity. Several individuals exhibited symptoms of osteoarthritis, and one person showed evidence that a hand may have been amputated.

The case for cannibalism among the Neanderthals seems clear-cut, with several sites across Europe recording similar kinds of evidence. El Sidrón, discussed later in this chapter, holds convincing evidence of such a practice. Several recent studies, however, have questioned this information and the nature of the cannibalism taking place at Krapina. Erik Trinkhaus has argued that none of the damage present in the Krapina Neanderthal skeletal sample can be explained solely as a result of cannibalism. Moreover, he points out, the frequencies of skeletal part preservation—particularly the survival of fragile pieces of the skeleton—indicate that the Krapina Neanderthals were buried, by either natural or human processes, soon after death. Trinkhaus argues against cannibalism among the Neanderthals.

Two other studies have suggested that Neanderthal cannibalism may have been important as a ritual activity, rather than for a meal. The first was done by Jill Cook, David Frayer, and Jakov Radovcic. They believe that the flesh was removed from the bones of these skeletons, but that it was done quite systematically, perhaps as part of a mortuary ritual. Corpses were mutilated by slicing off the ears, removing the tongue, detaching the lower jaw, and skinning the head. Muscle and fat was removed from the limbs, and from the torso by cutting, scraping, and scrubbing. The location and direction of the cut marks suggest that the bodies were lying face-down during this process.

The second study, by Jörg Orscheid, has raised serious questions about the evidence itself, specifically the breakage patterns and cut marks. Orscheid reports that certain elements such as the facial skeleton, base of the skull, and hand and foot bones as well as vertebrae are underrepresented or missing at Krapina. It seems unlikely that the bodies were buried in an undisturbed, articulated manner. He further argues that the breakage patterns were not caused by human activity, but rather by rock fall in the shelter as well as by carnivore activity. The reported cut marks were generally not visible in his study, and ones that were present appear to have been inflicted during the excavations at the site! There is no consensus yet in this debate, but similar evidence at several other Neanderthal sites in Europe strengthens the argument for cannibalism.

SALZGITTER-LEBENSTEDT, GERMANY, 55,000 YEARS AGO

Salzgitter-Lebenstedt is located in Germany, some 50 km (30 mi) southeast of the city of Hannover. The site lies along the slope of a small river valley, at a point where the valley changes from narrow and steep to wide and flat. This may have been a strategic spot along the migration route of reindeer herds. A total area of 150 m² (1,600 ft²) was first excavated in 1952; the site was reopened in 1977 and another 220 m² (2,400 ft²) were exposed. The site has garnered quite a bit of attention because of the well-preserved organic remains from waterlogged deposits and the Middle Paleolithic age of the materials. The evidence from Salzgitter-Lebenstedt has helped to resolve several important questions about the behavior and abilities of the Neanderthals.

The age of the site has been determined from several lines of information. The more than 800 flint artifacts that were found include small handaxes, scrapers, and distinctive Levallois flakes that clearly belong to the Middle Paleolithic and the Neanderthals. The Levallois technique involves some planning for production of flakes of a specific size, through careful preparation of a core before the flake is removed. The bones of several arctic and subarctic species have been found at the site. The vast majority of the faunal remains come from reindeer, mammoth, and horse, with 75 percent from reindeer alone. There are a few bones and teeth from wolf, woolly rhinoceros, and bison. In addition, there are five bones from *Homo neanderthalensis*, cranial fragments from at least two individuals.

The evidence from pollen and other environmental indicators preserved at the site suggests that the vegetation was a shrub tundra, with many cold-adapted species of plants. Trees were rare and dwarfed in the cold conditions. Dwarf birch and willow were present as shrub and bush vegetation. The faunal remains confirm this picture of a cold, open landscape with stunted vegetation and subarctic conditions. Pollen and other geological evidence indicate that the sediments at the site belong to the last glacial period. The best estimate for the age of the site is ca. 55,000 years ago, during a slightly warmer phase of the later Pleistocene.

In addition to the stone tools found at the site, there were thirty-some artifacts made from bone and ivory that document use of these materials by Neanderthals. Most of these tools are pointed ribs and fibulae, along with a distinctively carved bone point. The tools were shaped by whittling, which can be seen in microscopic study of the worked points. Neanderthals were definitely able to produce simple bone tools such as points and sharpened ribs. The excavator interpreted the pointed ribs and fibulae as long bone daggers, perhaps used to finish off wounded reindeer. Flaked bone artifacts are known from other Neanderthal sites, including even flaked bone handaxes.

These materials were deeply buried at 4.5–5.5 m (ca. 16 ft) below the surface in water-lain deposits (Fig. 2.20). Sandy sediments from moving water and peaty mud from lakeshore deposition were most common. The archaeological finds from the site were found in a band about 1 m (3.3 ft) thick

Fig. 2.20.
Excavations in progress at Salzgitter-Lebenstedt in the late 1970s. The floor of this excavation shows some of the animal bones *in situ*. The seated human figure at ground level provides some scale.

within the water-lain deposits. Fragmented bones and stones from this band could be fit back together, and their distribution covered large vertical and horizontal distances in the deposits, suggesting that all of the archaeological materials may have resulted from a single depositional event. In essence, even though the materials are found in a thick band, they were probably deposited as part of the same set of activities and then moved around somewhat by nature.

One of the major problems in investigating the oldest archaeological sites is the question of context. Did the materials found together come from the same set of activities? Are the stones and bones and other materials at Salzgitter-Lebenstedt the result of human hunting, butchering, and consumption of the animals? Or are these various materials from numerous sources simply found together fortuitously, washed into eddies and bays by moving water, deposited together by an accident of nature?

This is a difficult question to answer. Some archaeologists have argued for years that there is no irrefutable evidence of large-game hunting in the European Paleolithic until the arrival of *Homo sapiens*. The assumption has been that Neanderthals were not capable of the abstract thought, planning, and cooperation that such hunting required.

Careful analysis of the animal remains can also suggest answers to many questions, including whether the bones found at the site were associated with the tools and other artifacts, if the animals were food for the site inhabitants, what parts were eaten, if animals of a specific age or sex were more commonly hunted, what time of year the animals were hunted, and if there was specialization on a particular species or hunting was instead more opportunistic and any animal encountered was considered as prey. Answers to these questions help to define Neanderthal hunting capabilities and strategies and assess their differences from and similarities to more recent humans.

Archaeozoologists are trained to identify the genus and species of an animal from small fragments of bone, as well as to determine the age and sex of the animal, how bone was fragmented, and how many individual animals are represented in the bone assemblage. The results of this work at Salzgitter-Lebenstedt were particularly informative.

The predominance of reindeer bones helped confirm that specialized hunting was indeed an important aspect of Neanderthal behavior. The fact that almost all the bones of the reindeer skeleton are present in the archaeological deposit argues that these materials are *in situ* and largely undisturbed. The age and sex of the animals was determined by bone size, tooth wear, and other distinctive features. The majority of the animals were males. Age was estimated primarily from tooth size, eruption, and wear on seventy-four mandibles. The age of the animals ranged from calves to thirteen years. Almost half of the slain animals were eight or nine years of age, indicating a selection for these individuals in their prime, and there were only three animals over ten years of age.

The reindeer remains at Salzgitter-Lebenstedt were different from the bones of the other species in several ways, in addition to being far more numerous. Bone preservation of the reindeer was very good, the same skeletal parts were present from all the animals, and there was very little indication of gnawing by other animals on the bones. It appears that Neanderthal hunters at Salzgitter-Lebenstedt likely killed many or all of these animals in one hunt or only a few.

There was a high incidence of cut marks and breakage made by humans cutting and fracturing the bone. Almost 40 percent of the bones have cut marks and about 25 percent show marrow fracture impacts. The cutting marks from sharp stone tools document dismemberment of the animal carcasses. These marks are located at the normal places used for butchering an animal such as a reindeer (Fig. 2.21). Although reindeer of all ages were killed in the hunt, the focus in butchering the animals and extracting marrow was on the prime adult males. Much less attention was given to females and young animals.

Season of death was determined from several lines of evidence. Three young animals among the Salzgitter-Lebenstedt reindeer were between three and six months old. Likely born in May or June, these calves would have died between August and October. Antlers also provide some information. Measurements of the diameter of the base of the antlers showed a bimodal distribution, reflecting a larger group of adult males and a smaller group of subadult males, females, and young animals. The archaeozoologist estimates that the adult male animals died in a short period during the autumn, from September to early October. This is also the time when all members of the herd—males, females, and young—are together and on the move.

The predominance of animal bones from a single species, strongly suggestive of intentional human hunting, is seen often at Paleolithic sites after ca. 125,000 years ago. The evidence from Salzgitter-Lebenstedt suggests that Neanderthals organized the ambush and mass kill of migrating reindeer

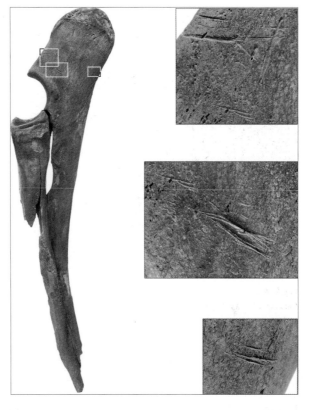

Fig. 2.21.
Cut marks made by stone tools at three locations on a reindeer ulna.

herds in the autumn of the year. The carcasses of the animals were butchered intensively and marrow taken from the long bones and jaws. Prime adult males were the focus of the hunt. Salzgitter-Lebenstedt and other Middle Paleolithic sites in Europe clearly document that Neanderthals were successful hunters who sometimes concentrated on a single species and selected prime-age prey. The evidence from Salzgitter-Lebenstedt also confirms that Neanderthals were capable of living and surviving in cold environments such as northern Europe more than 50,000 years ago.

Archaeologists are also concerned with the social and ideological implications of past activity and the issues that make us human. Cooperative large-game hunting, as documented at Salzgitter-Lebenstedt, must have required complex, probably verbal, communication and social interaction between individuals from different groups. The amount of meat available in such communal hunts was substantial, and even if the hunters took only the best portions there was a great deal to go around. Perhaps these occasions were moments of shared excitement and pleasure. A brief gathering of neighbors and relatives meant partaking in the bounty of the hunt, and the opportunity to eat, laugh, dance, flirt, argue, and become more human.

EL SIDRÓN, SPAIN, 43,000 YEARS AGO

Spain has become the hot spot in Europe for Paleolithic studies. In the last twenty years there have been many new sites, old human ancestors, and older artifacts and animal bones discovered. El Sidrón can be added to the list.

El Sidrón has gained a great deal of attention for the Middle Paleolithic materials found there, especially the bones of Neanderthals, discovered by a group of spelunkers in 1994 who were exploring a small cave in the north of Spain. Archaeologists then went to the cave and began careful excavations. Since the year 2000, more than 1,600 bones and 350 stone tools have been uncovered, dated to ca. 43,000 years ago.

An underground river here many thousands of years ago carved a long, winding channel through the sandstone, creating many small side chambers and diversions. The name Galeria del Osario (gallery of bones) was given to the chamber with the Neanderthal remains. The bones come from an estimated twelve individuals: three adult men, three adult women, three teenagers, and three children including an infant. The discovery of so many individuals who died at the same time suggests they may have been members of the same group or family.

The bones were broken and deeply scratched in such a way that there was no question they had been part of a meal, fractured to remove the fatty marrow, butchered to remove the meat from the bone. The researchers at the site believe these individuals were killed and butchered outside the cave on the ground above. Soon after, part of the roof of the cave collapsed, carrying the human remains along with rock and sediments into the Galeria del Osario, where they were protected for millennia by the undisturbed burial conditions.

The stone tools were typical Neanderthal artifacts made of locally available lithic materials—side scrapers, points, denticulated pieces, and a small handaxe.

These tools may have been used in butchering the El Sidrón hominins or were perhaps just in the area affected by the collapse of the roof.

Study of the bones and stone tools produced information on the nature of the deposition of the materials. All of the human remains were found in a single deep layer in the deposits. By fitting some of the broken stone artifacts and bones back together, it was possible to plot the location of the pieces that fit together. This information is available because the archaeologists recorded the exact location of discovery for many of the finds. A plan showing the vertical distribution of these refitted pieces indicated they were fairly regularly spread over about one vertical meter (3'3"), no doubt a consequence of the catastrophic collapse of the roof and the subsequent washing of these materials into the cave. The study of the refits shows conclusively that this deposit was the result of a single event and did not accumulate over a longer period of time.

The physical anthropology of the human remains is fascinating. Although the materials are fragmentary, all parts of the skeleton are represented in the collection. In fact these remains were used in the forensic reconstruction of a Neanderthal female (Fig. 2.22). The more than 1,600 bones found clearly fall within the Neanderthal range of variation, and there are no anatomically modern human features present. There is extensive evidence for cannibalism

Fig. 2.22.
A forensic reconstruction of a Neanderthal female.

on the bones recovered from El Sidrón; some of the skulls were skinned, their leg joints dismembered, and other long bones broken.

There is a high incidence of enamel hypoplasia seen in the teeth of all the individuals in the deposit. These small, horizontal lines in the teeth represent stress-related interruptions in development of the tooth enamel and likely reflect nutritional shortages for the members of this group. The presence of these stress markers is not uncommon among Neanderthals and probably confirms the difficulty of the food quest in the rigors of Pleistocene Europe.

Some of the Neanderthal teeth from El Sidrón were examined recently using the giant synchrotron near Geneva, Switzerland. This instrument is powerful enough to make highly magnified and detailed photographs of the growth layers in human tooth enamel. This information from the synchrotron reveals a pattern of growth and development with daily growth lines, interrupted by heavier stress lines from events such as birth, disease, injury, or hunger. This study makes it possible to establish a more precise age for the children from El Sidrón. The data also suggest that Neanderthal youngsters were reaching puberty and adulthood several years before their anatomically modern equivalents.

The major finds at El Sidrón were, of course, the treasury of Neanderthal bones. The physical, anatomical evidence from the skeletal remains is enormously important—even more so because of the molecular evidence they have yielded. Because of the extraordinary quality of preservation, the El Sidrón bones have been very useful for the study of ancient DNA.

Mitochondrial DNA furnishes additional evidence that this may have been a related group of family members. The three males appear to have been genetically related and the three women were different, suggesting that females may have moved in with the groups of their male partners at this time. Studies have also demonstrated that the so-called FOXP2 locus found in modern humans was also present in two of the Neanderthal individuals. This gene is responsible for some aspects of speech and language ability in the brain and the nerves that control the vocal apparatus. Presumably Neanderthals were capable of speech. But of course, speech is not necessarily language.

As we have discussed, there is considerable debate over the humanness of Neanderthals: whether they purposefully interred their dead, if they had complex thoughts, whether they spoke a language, if they created art and decorated their world and themselves. In addition, there is the continuing question about the demise of the Neanderthals—were they killed off by the incoming anatomically modern humans, or absorbed genetically into the larger population of *Homo sapiens*? Certainly the evidence from El Sidrón speaks volumes in regard to the question of speech and language. Moreover, the ancient DNA evidence also suggests that there was some interbreeding between Neanderthals and early *Homo sapiens* in Europe, implying their relationship was not always hostile.

GROTTE DU RENNE, FRANCE, 40,000 YEARS AGO

Some of the northernmost caves in France are found near the village of Arcy-sur-Cure, 100 km (60 mi) southeast of Paris. Although known for a very long time—and under investigation by prehistorians for more than two centuries—the discoveries continue, and continue to amaze. The caves lie in south-facing limestone cliffs along the Cure River (Fig. 2.23). It's a lovely spot on the river, with some extraordinary archaeology.

The series of small caves at Arcy have been occupied intermittently, at least since the time of Neanderthal. Many of their charming names are taken from the animal species found among the archaeological bones: Abri du Lagopède (grouse), Grotte du Cheval (horse), Grotte de l'Hyène (hyena), Grotte du Trilobite, Grotte des Ours (wild cattle), Grotte du Renne (reindeer), Grotte du Bison, Grotte du Loup (wolf), Grotte du Lion, Grotte des Fées (fairies), Grotte des Deux Cours, Grande Grotte, Petit Abri, Grand Abri. Archaeological materials have been found in all the caves and from a wide range of time periods.

These caves are important for a number of reasons. They contain substantial deposits from the Middle Paleolithic, the time of Neanderthal. This includes a complete small chamber with an unburied living area that was found when excavations exposed the entrance. The caves also hold significant deposits from the transition between the Middle and Upper Paleolithic and have the potential to help resolve questions about when and how the replacement of Neanderthals by *Homo sapiens* took place. In addition, there are some very early paintings, discovered recently at the site, that document the northernmost (and some of the oldest) cave art in France. This art at the Grande Grotte is discussed in the next chapter.

One of the most unusual and fascinating discoveries at Arcy-sur-Cure came some years after work got under way in Grotte du Renne. As the excavations removed layer after layer, going deeper and deeper, the opening

Fig. 2.23.
Arcy-sur-Cure. The caves are in the limestone bluffs in the upper center of the photograph.

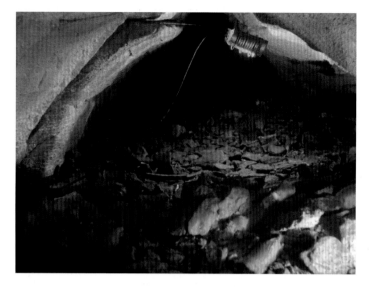

Fig. 2.24.
The Galerie Schoepflin
at the Grotte du Renne,
a Neanderthal den
preserved for tens of
thousands of years.

of a new chamber was slowly exposed, buried beneath the deep deposits. This new chamber had never filled with sediments and was basically in the same condition as the Neanderthals left it, more than 40,000 years ago (Fig. 2.24). It was given the name the Galerie Schoepflin. This small, low chamber is more than 30 m (100 ft) from the entrance to the cave, in an area of total darkness. Neanderthals must have sheltered in this interior chamber for some period of time; the floor of the chamber was littered with thousands of animal bones and many stone tools, and it resembles the den of animals. There was no fireplace and little pattern to the scatter of bones and stones on the floor of the chamber.

The other very important evidence from the Grotte du Renne comes from layers dating from the time of the transition from Neanderthals to *Homo sapiens*. These archaeological layers are known as the Châtelperronian, dating to about 35,000 years BP and were followed by Aurignacian deposits, ca. 29,000 years ago. The Châtelperronian was the earliest Upper Paleolithic in France and Northern Spain. The Aurignacian is another early phase of the Upper Paleolithic and widely considered a product of *Homo sapiens*. The earliest evidence for Upper Paleolithic technology comes from East Africa more than 50,000 years ago and includes bone tools, shell beads, and pendants, along with a distinct set of artifacts.

The question is whether Neanderthals or *Homo sapiens* produced the Châtelperronian because these materials include a number of items thought to be associated only with anatomically modern humans, such as blades, objects of personal adornment, and art. Figure 2.25 shows the remains of jewelry made of animal teeth, bone, and shell, found in the Châtelperronian layer at Grotte du Renne, If the Neanderthals did produce all these artifacts, then the differences between these two species may not have been so great. Such a possibility confounds the view of modern humans arriving with better brains, better technology, and art and quickly replacing the Neanderthals.

The issue really is how different Neanderthals and anatomically modern humans were. Much of the debate surrounding Grotte du Renne centers on the portable art and ornaments that were found in the Aurignacian layer, which closely resemble similar objects in the underlying Châtelperronian horizon. The same layer contained a large number of Neanderthal teeth and a skull fragment. That materials from the two layers were mixed together in the past suddenly appears more likely now, with publication in 2010 of a series of new radiocarbon dates documenting a wide range of dates from

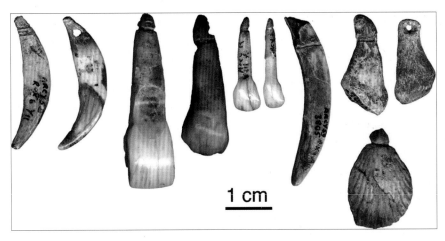

Fig. 2.25.
Animal teeth and bone perforated or notched for use as jewelry, from the Châtelperronian layer at Grotte du Renne.

the Châtelperronian layer. Now the association of Neanderthals with objects of art and decoration seems dubious. An even more recent article, however, reasserts the original context of these items in the Châtelperronian layer and argues for their association with Neanderthals. The debate continues.

Similar information comes from the southwest of France. The archaeological site of Saint-Césaire contains a number of layers from the Middle and Upper Paleolithic periods, including the Châtelperronian. The dramatic evidence from Saint-Césaire is the presence of a nearly complete Neanderthal skeleton dated to 36,000 years ago in the Châtelperronian layer. When it was discovered in 1979, the skeleton created an instant sensation; at that time, Neanderthals were not considered capable of producing complex stone tools. Today, it is clear that Neanderthals hafted flint points on wooden spear shafts and may well have produced more complex artifacts such as the ones seen at Saint-Césaire. The site is often regarded as evidence of the co-existence of Neanderthals and *Homo sapiens*, depending on whom you ask!

VINDIJA CAVE, CROATIA, 34,000 YEARS AGO

In most excavated Paleolithic sites in Europe, where there are layers from both the Middle and Upper Paleolithic, there is a clear-cut difference between older layers with Neanderthal–Middle Paleolithic bones and artifacts and younger layers with Upper Paleolithic artifacts and the remains of anatomically modern humans. But not always. The Grotte du Renne and Saint-Césaire have been mentioned.

Vindija is also an exception because of the layers with a mixture of Middle and Upper Paleolithic artifacts and both Neanderthal and *sapiens* individuals. Many of the finds date from the period between 40,000 and 25,000 years ago, the time of the transition from Neanderthal to anatomically modern humans in Europe. In conventional archaeological wisdom, the Middle Paleolithic is associated with Neanderthals and the Upper Paleolithic is found with *Homo sapiens*. This is not the case at Vindija.

The most important layers in the cave for this discussion are labeled G, F, and D. Layer G is subdivided into several phases. G3 dates from 45,000 to 38,000 years ago and contains Neanderthal remains in association with Middle Paleolithic artifacts, as expected. G1 (34,000–32,000 years ago) contains some of the youngest Neanderthals in Europe in a layer with both Middle and Upper Paleolithic stone tools and early Upper Paleolithic bone points. Layer F dates to 31,000–28,000 years ago, with the remains of individuals who seem to have had a mix of *sapiens* and *neanderthalensis* features, in a layer among artifacts thought to belong to the Upper Paleolithic, from a phase called the Aurignacian. Level D is younger than 18,500 years and contains only anatomically modern humans and distinctly Upper Paleolithic artifacts associated with a younger Upper Paleolithic culture known as the Gravettian.

The anatomical and archaeological evidence from Vindija appears to show a transition between Middle and Upper Paleolithic in which Neanderthals are present in the early Upper Paleolithic levels. Such evidence would suggest that there was interaction between these two human species between 40,000 and 30,000 years ago in Europe. At the same time, there are always doubts and questions about the context and validity of such evidence because of the possibility of disturbance and mixture of the archaeological layers. The genetic investigations add another dimension to the argument and foster some further resolution. These are discussed in more detail below.

ANCIENT DNA

In 2004 a group of ancient-DNA scientists at the Max Planck Institute for Evolutionary Anthropology in Leipzig, Germany, issued a categorical statement to the effect that there was no genetic evidence that Neanderthals and modern humans ever interbred. In 2009, when the group first announced that they had begun to decode the Neanderthal genome—a huge step for comparing genetic composition with our earlier relatives—they again reported no significant evidence of interbreeding.

Then in 2010 the same scientists reversed themselves. By this time the Leipzig group had reconstructed more than 60 percent of the Neanderthal genome. The collagen preserved in the Vindija bones has been of great use to geneticists in this investigation. Ancient DNA (aDNA) was extracted from these bones and used to reconstruct the genetic code of the Neanderthals. They used samples of bone from several sites, including Vindija, because of the more recent date and the overlap with AMH individuals in time.

Now the scientists say they have found several indicators that there was gene flow between the two species. By comparing the Neanderthal genome with that of present-day humans, the research team concluded that Neanderthals contributed 1–4 percent of the genome of Eurasians. The lead scientist, Svante Pääbo, went so far as to say about the Neanderthals: "I would see them as a form of humans that are bit more different than humans are today, but not much." In actual fact, it is difficult to know what to think given the amount of contradictory genetic information regarding Neanderthals and modern humans.

The Leipzig group suggested that the flow of Neanderthal DNA into early human DNA went in only one direction: from Neanderthals to *sapiens*. The study found no early modern human DNA in the Neanderthal genome. Another surprising aspect of this announcement was the argument that the mixing between AMH and Neanderthal took place much earlier in time, perhaps 60,000 to 100,000 years ago, not in Europe but in the Near East. These results have not been readily accepted by other specialists, and the question of the relationship between Neanderthals and sapiens remains unresolved.

NEANDERTHAL DIET

Organic proteins in human tissue are generally fragile, and after death these molecules disappear quickly under most conditions of burial. Fortunately there are exceptions to this process, and under extraordinary conditions protein can persist for thousands of years. This is the case for some of the human remains from Vindija. The protein portion of bone, called collagen, is generally intact in the Vindija human remains and can be used for dietary and genetic studies rarely possible with materials this old.

Dietary studies of bone collagen focus on the isotopes of carbon and nitrogen in the protein. Human tissue is ultimately constructed from the nutrients in our food; the old maxim "you are what you eat" definitely applies in this case. Carbon isotopes in bone collagen contain information about the importance of seafood or certain kinds of plants in the diet. Nitrogen isotopes reveal information about the position of the individual in the food chain, or trophic level. Nitrogen isotopes in the bones at Vindija were the key to understanding Neanderthal diet and pointed to a very carnivorous diet, comparable to contemporary predators such as cave lions. These groups appear to have been almost 100 percent meat eaters.

It is also possible to learn a bit about how they ate—and even more—from their teeth. Microscopic examination of seven front teeth, incisors and canines, of individuals from Vindija Cave revealed a series of scratches (Fig. 2.26). The most parsimonious explanation for these marks has to do with the table manners of Neanderthals. Observed among many groups around the world, meat eaters often hold a large portion in their teeth and use a knife to cut a bite-size piece off at their lips, the so-called stuff-and-cut method. Those knives, stone or steel, sometimes rubbed against the teeth and left scratches.

That's interesting, but what is more interesting is the pattern of the scratches. The majority of these scratches, or striations, are oblique and run from upper right to lower left. The direction of the marks means that the person wielding the knife was right-handed. Studies of teeth from Vindija and other Neanderthal sites show a ratio of 15:2 for right-handedness, similar to the proportions today. This pattern has also been observed in the teeth from Sima de los Huesos at Atapuerca, some 600,000 years ago, suggesting a long antiquity for handedness in our human ancestors.

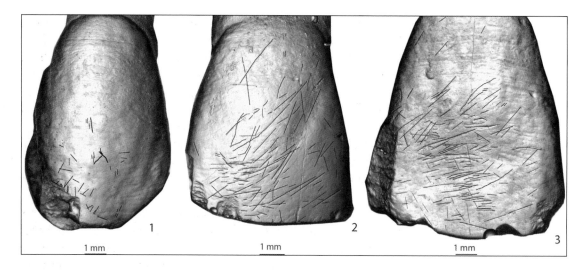

Fig. 2.26.
Microscopic scratches on the front teeth of Neanderthals from Vindija Cave.

That's also interesting, but more interesting again is what handedness means. We are right- or left-handed because of the way our brains are organized, to function in two parts, the right and left halves. Although such generalization is much too simplistic, linear reasoning and language components of grammar and vocabulary are usually found on the left side of the brain. Other activities such as the processing of sight and sound input, spatial manipulation, facial perception, and artistic ability are usually functions of the right hemisphere. Thus handedness is at least in some way related to the complexity of human brains, and perhaps also to the emergence of language abilities.

The importance of meat in human diet may be related to the increasing size of our brain during human evolution. The brains of our earliest ancestors were around 500 cc, the size of an orange; modern human brain capacity is around 1300 cc, the size of a large grapefruit. Clearly our brains—and presumably our intelligence—have increased during human evolution.

Neanderthals lived in the cold Pleistocene of Europe and most of their food came from animals. Vegetation was sparse and plant foods were likely not available for large parts of the year. Meat was food. Hunting provided most of the diet. Steven Churchill, a paleoanthropologist at Duke University, has calculated that a typical Neanderthal male would have needed up to 5,000 calories a day to support his body mass in the cold climate, almost the same as what a bicycle racer burns every day in the Tour de France.

Another aspect of this intriguing argument about the importance of meat in our diet has been put forward by Leslie Aiello, a biological anthropologist, who argues that brains are "expensive" tissue and need lots of energy to operate; larger brains need more energy. The brain uses twenty times as much energy as the same amount of muscle tissue. Aiello believes the transition to a high-fat and high-calorie meat diet allowed the body to invest more energy in brain growth. She believes this shift toward more meat in the diet began with the emergence of the genus *Homo*, ca. 2.5 mya. As part of the evidence for her argument, Aiello points to human tapeworms, whose closest genetic relative lives inside African hyenas and wild dogs. Aiello suggests that deep in our human past our ancestors were eating meat, feeding on the same carcasses as these other scavengers, and came into contact with these parasites.

Another aspect of past human diet involves cooking. Richard Wrangham, an anthropologist, argues that cooking is really what has shaped our human body. He points to research showing that people on a diet of raw foods, including oil and meat, lost weight. They reported feeling better but also experienced chronic energy deficiency. Raw food is nutritious, but it requires more energy to process and metabolize in the body. The use of fire probably improved taste, but cooking certainly made some foods easier to digest. As Wrangham notes, barbequed meat is altered by the heat that breaks up long protein chains, softens cartilage and makes tougher tissues more palatable. All of this makes meat more digestible for stomach enzymes. Cooking also kills bacteria and can prolong shelf life. Smoking meat helps to preserve it. We don't know precisely when early humans began cooking their food, but they probably started shortly after they began regularly making fires.

SOME REFLECTIONS

The early prehistory of Europe lies in the deep past, and little information survives to the present. The stones and bones from Atapuerca present the most detailed picture of what those ancestors looked like and what they were doing in Iberia more than a million years ago. The skeletons of *Homo antecessor* are mixed with the remains of various animals in the oldest sites. There is little information on group size, season, or duration of visit that survives. Many years ago, Martin Wobst pointed out the difficulties of understanding human behavior in deep time. The bones of one hundred animals in a cavern at Atapuerca, for example, could be the result of one visit by a small group, or one hundred visits each by a single individual over a thousand years, or anything in between. It is usually impossible to separate individual episodes of behavior in deposits from so long ago.

These individuals were small-brained compared to their later descendants. They made simple stone cutting tools, but we know little of their abilities as foragers. The bones of larger animals exhibit cut marks from stone tools and breakage patterns that indicate marrow extraction, suggesting that these first Europeans were taking meat and marrow. But whether they hunted or scavenged is not clear. There is convincing evidence of cannibalism from these deposits, which might suggest that social conventions are not in place, that social relationships—as we know them—are not well established.

The body of evidence then, although limited, intimates that human society as a set of recognizable relationships, roles, and obligations was not yet established. A closer behavioral analogy might be to groups of apes, moving together in small troops through the landscape, stopping for short periods, sleeping, eating, and leaving behind some lasting indication of their visit. As well as occasionally eating other members of their own species.

Atapuerca also offers some information for early human ancestors in Europe between 1 million to 500,000 years ago. In this interval, several changes are clear. The brain grows slowly in size and probably capacity. Stone tools evolve and the handaxe becomes the common tool for these individuals, now known as *Homo heidelbergensis*. Sites such as Gran Dolina remain a mix of human and animal bones and stone tools, with little context beyond meat eating. The evidence for cannibalism is reiterated.

One of the most enigmatic discoveries in the entire Paleolithic comes from Sima de los Huesos: the remains of the thirty-two individuals found in the dark depths of the big cave at Atapuerca, some 600,000 years ago. The questions of how and why these individuals ended up in that hole may never be answered. It may be that we witness in this deposit the beginnings of concepts about death and ancestors in an unexpected context. Whatever the case, the mix of young and old, male and female, suggests membership in a complete social unit of all ages and sexes.

Many more archaeological sites began to appear in Europe after half a million years ago, and more changes are evident in human behavior. Boxgrove is one of the first of these sites in northern Europe. The concentrations of artifacts here appear to be the remains of hunting and butchering activities. Cut marks on bones always underlie scavenger tooth marks, suggesting the early humans were the primary predators. Big game hunting is dramatically documented at the site of Schöningen, where long wooden throwing spears were found among the bones of wild horses.

Most of the earliest archaeological sites are found in the southern parts of Europe. Archaeological remains that do occur in the north are almost certainly from the warmer intervals during the Pleistocene. It is unlikely that early humans could have survived in the extremely harsh winters of Ice Age cold. The Pleistocene was a frozen forge that shaped and molded these early human ancestors, demanding adaptation or death. Early humans had to hunt successfully for winter food in the absence of edible vegetation. Early humans had to stay warm and avoid frostbite and hypothermia. Fire and shelter and perhaps some form of clothing were essentials in that hostile climate. Until these capabilities were available, the Pleistocene cold had to be avoided.

The earliest controlled use of fire in Europe dates to ca. 400,000 years ago, when constructed fireplaces began to appear at a number of sites, such as Schöningen in Germany. Fire brought substantial changes to human life. It illuminated the night and prolonged the day, extended summer into winter, permitted access to dark caverns, improved the nutrition and taste of many foods, and may have constituted the focal point for the emergence of truly human societies. The hearth became the center of action and interaction for human groups. The distribution of artifacts, food remains, and other archaeological materials around hearths reflects essential aspects of social behavior and communication. The hearth ultimately defines social space. The appearance of hearths may be an expression of the emergence of concepts of home and camp.

Natural shelters in the form of caves and overhangs were used for refuge in the rockier areas of Europe, but indications of camps or settlements have yet to be observed in the earlier part of the Paleolithic. In spite of the optimism of a few archaeologists, it seems unlikely that actual structures or camps are present until later in time. Much of what has been observed archaeologically in the early Paleolithic appears to be accumulations of materials, without significant patterning or systematic distribution. Chu suggests some of these early dwelling places may have been windbreaks to buffer the extreme cold of winters in these regions, rather than true huts or shelters. Even the often-reported mammoth bone "houses" from the Middle Paleolithic site of Molodova in the Ukraine may well be natural features of some kind. Stringer and Gamble have described some of these purported dwelling structures from the earlier Paleolithic as more like nests than houses. Certainly the preserved Neanderthal den in the Galerie Schoepflin at Grotte du Renne fits that description. Kolen has reviewed a number of purported dwelling structures from the sites of *Homo heidelbergensis* and *neanderthalensis* and finds no convincing evidence for built structures. He argues that the earliest built dwellings date to the Upper Paleolithic, associated with *Homo sapiens*.

Indications for clothing are difficult to find at archaeological sites because of the decay of fragile organic materials, but a completely new line of evidence comes from a surprising source, the genetic code of lice. There are two kinds of lice in this story: head lice live in the hair on the head and have been around for millions of years, while body lice live in clothing, not on the body, and are a relatively recent species. Using mutation rates in modern lice genes, Ralf Kittler and his associates estimated that the body louse first appeared between 42,000 and 72,000 years ago. Humans must have been wearing some form of clothing or wrap at that time to furnish a habitat for this creature. More convincing evidence for actual textiles comes from the Upper Paleolithic, where both impressions of cloth in fired clay and dyed fibers of wild flax have been found in excavations.

Between 300,000 and 200,000 years ago, *Homo heidelbergensis* became Neanderthal across Europe. The human brain reached its present-day size. New tools and ideas prevailed against the harsh environment. Life became something more than eating, sleeping, and reproducing. Burial of the dead and care of the handicapped and injured illustrate concern for fellow hominins. The remains of an elderly man buried at La-Chappelle-aux-Saints in France indicated that he had suffered from severe paralysis and arthritis, including a broken jaw and missing teeth. Given those limitations, he must have been cared for in the last years of his life.

Two big, related questions about Neanderthals stand out. The nature of the Neanderthals is one; were they like us? Current thinking seems to favor more alike than different. This question is in fact closely related to the second, concerned with their fate: What happened to the Neanderthals, who became extinct after 30,000 years ago? If *Homo sapiens* eradicated Neanderthals in Europe, it implies major differences between the species and a certain superiority of the anatomically modern humans. If Neanderthals and moderns shared technological achievements and were romantically inclined, it becomes much easier to accept them as close relatives of the human race.

Current anatomical evidence from Southwest Asia suggests that the first *sapiens* individuals moved into this area around 90,000 years. The bones of *Homo sapiens* from this time are found in layers with Middle Paleolithic tools. Neanderthal skeletons have been found nearby, dating between 75,000 and 45,000 years ago. It is entirely possible that the Neanderthals in Southwest Asia were forced there from Europe during a period of intense cold. It appears that anatomically modern humans coexisted with Neanderthals in Southwest Asia until around 45,000 years ago when the Neanderthals disappeared. In Europe, the transition is less clear, and evidence for the first anatomically modern humans is much later. Neanderthals are first known in Europe by approximately 250,000 years ago, yet the earliest bones of anatomically modern humans do not appear until after 40,000 years ago.

There were significant differences between *neanderthalensis* and *sapiens*. Neanderthals hunted a limited range of species and used tools that changed little over time compared to anatomically modern humans. Neanderthals invested little in constructing shelter or organizing camps, perhaps a reflection of shorter-duration stays and more mobility. In general the archaeological record for Neanderthals is much more basic and limited than for *Homo sapiens*.

Several lines of evidence for the relationship between Neanderthals and anatomically modern humans are available. Ancient DNA sends a mixed message. The early studies of genetic relationships between Neanderthals and sapiens suggested no contact; more recent investigations point to some gene flow between the two species. The archaeological evidence is also ambiguous, but it appears that both populations were involved in making the creative artifacts that are thought to define the modern mind. Physical anthropologists argue that the anatomy of several burials from Europe reflects a mix of Neanderthal and *sapiens* characteristics.

Erik Trinkhaus, one of the proponents of acculturation between Neanderthals and *sapiens*, has summarized the current evidence regarding the question, a sort of things-we-know list. Trinkhaus, a biological anthropologist, focuses on the anatomical evidence.

1. The earliest *Homo sapiens* appear in East Africa around 200,000 years ago, with a mix of ancient and modern human features.
2. These anatomically modern humans expanded into southwestern Asia around 90,000 years ago. AMH remains are found with Middle Paleolithic stone artifacts at that time. These sapiens groups may have coexisted with Neanderthals there between 75,000 and 45,000 years ago, one of the colder parts of the Pleistocene. After 45,000 years ago, Neanderthals disappeared in Southwest Asia and *Homo sapiens* began to expand into the rest of Asia and Europe.
3. Prior to 25,000 years ago, early *Homo sapiens* had a mix of ancient and modern anatomical features.

Trinkhaus argues that biological data from the skeletal remains support the assimilation, or mixture, model for the Neanderthal and AMH relationship—expanding *sapiens* populations absorbed local Neanderthal groups. Although we know little about population in the Paleolithic, some scholars have suggested that the number of Neanderthals never exceeded 15,000 in western Europe. If such relatively small numbers are reasonably accurate estimates, then acculturation of these groups does seem feasible.

The jury is still out in this scientific trial. Certainly, there is a growing body of cases in the archaeological record that appear to show late Neanderthal remains found in early Upper Paleolithic cultural layers in sites in France, Croatia, and elsewhere. At the same time, there are important questions regarding the disturbance of archaeological sites and possible mixture of layers, and issues about interpreting small, fragmentary remains of human skeletal material.

In spite of a vigorous and ongoing debate, the evidence is growing to suggest that the assimilation model fits at least some of the data. The aDNA evidence, in spite of earlier statements to the contrary, now appears to support some genetic mixture between Neanderthals and AMH. In sum, there is accumulating information to support a peaceful, even romantic, encounter between these two species. At the same time, there must have been violent encounters as well. In all likelihood, both models of the transition to anatomically modern humans in Europe are correct, and interaction between these species took place in a variety of ways.

The fact is that the accumulating evidence for assimilation between Neanderthals and moderns, including the presence of AMH in Middle Paleolithic layers in southwest Asia and possible Neanderthals in Upper Paleolithic levels in Europe, suggests that the differences between *Homo neanderthalensis* and *sapiens* may not have been as substantial as was imagined and that perhaps our long-lost cousins should be admitted back into the family. The debate will continue, and the reputation of the Neanderthals will no doubt waver until more convincing evidence finally resolves this dispute. More on this issue in the next chapter and the site of Pestera cu Oase in Romania.

The question is also whether we can project our modern perspectives and analogous behaviors back into the deep past of our human ancestors. Hunter-gatherers are an anthropological construct, a model to describe pre-farming human groups and their behavior. The model covers many aspects of such societies, assumed to live in small groups of families and move around a lot, with more or less egalitarian social relationships, and reciprocal economies. But when does this form of social and subsistence behavior become the norm in our Paleolithic past? Have we always been hunter-gatherers? Likely not.

Clive Gamble questions the existence of human society in the early and middle part of the Paleolithic, where society implies several family units cooperating together in the hunt and other aspects of survival. Rather, Gamble views our early ancestors as small gatherings of individuals surviving by hunting. In this sense, our ancestry as hunter-gatherers seems less remote.

Perhaps a generic term other than hunter-gatherers is needed for human groups prior to the arrival of *Homo sapiens*.

There is so much we don't know about our early human ancestors—in Europe and elsewhere. As noted, there is little evidence and what exists is fragmentary and often altered, moved or modified over the very many years to the present. Research into human origins and evolution can be thought of as a kind of identity quest. We want to know how "they" became "us," which raises all kinds of existential questions about what it means to be human. The conventional qualifications for a human ancestor include bipedalism, larger brains, and tool use. These criteria are met by *Homo habilis* in Africa some 2.5 mya. In this sense, early hominins were humans when they moved out of Africa and into Asia and Europe sometime after 2 mya.

But there is more to being human than walking, thinking, and making tools. The persistent ecological dominance of humans across the planet is unprecedented among other species. Humans have unique capabilities, notably cooperation among nonkin, language, advanced cognitive functions, and technological virtuosity. Humans can walk, make tools, and have larger brains; human *beings* can be altruistic, have free will, fear death, use complex languages, plan for the future, enjoy art, and fall in love.

The origin of human speech and language is one of the more fascinating aspects of humanness, but perhaps the most difficult to explain. The question of when language appeared in human evolution is probably moot. Human language evolved from the utterances and cries of communication found among most primates to the complex grammar and vocabulary that characterizes modern speech. Most animals make sounds. Chimpanzees have a repertoire of twenty or more vocalizations and gestures for expressing their needs. Although these apes can manipulate symbols, they are unable to connect more than two or three concepts in a single phrase. To understand the changes in language from gestures and cries to its complex form today, we must consider the path of its evolution. The question is not when language appeared, but rather when language became an important part of human survival.

Aiello and Dunbar argue that a close correlation between the neocortex in the brain and size of human groups offers a means to predict the point in human evolution when language would have been necessary to integrate larger social groups and maintain cohesion. The neocortex is the outer layer of the cerebral hemisphere associated with higher functions such as sensory perception, motor commands, spatial reasoning, conscious thought, and language. The appearance of larger group size, they believe, resulted in use of language as a bonding mechanism.

Language poses a nonphysical form of social contact in larger groups where such physical contact is not feasible. According to this hypothesis, language came into existence as a kind of social glue. The members of larger groups shared information on the location of other members and learned about the availability of food resources. This information was shared with the larger "cognitive" group. Language made such exchange of information about resources and coordination of foraging activities possible. Their study concludes that language was a gradual development in human evolution, and by the time of Neanderthals such enhanced vocal communication was in place. Others such as Richard Klein have argued that a substantive change in language and communication, perhaps initiated by important changes in the organization of the brain, led to the creative explosion witnessed only 50,000 years ago, culminating in the Upper Paleolithic, the subject of the next chapter.

CHAPTER THREE

The Creative Explosion

ORIGIN AND SPREAD OF MODERN HUMANS

Two related phenomena characterize the last 30,000 years or so of the Pleistocene and the Old Stone Age in Europe, a period known as the Upper Paleolithic. The first of these is the arrival of a version of ourselves, *Homo sapiens,* around 40,000 years ago. The second is the creative explosion in technology, equipment, raw materials, art, and decoration that took place in this period. There appears to have been a substantial upgrade in human abilities and the variety of activities taking place. The first part of this chapter examines some of the sites and places that tell this story.

At the end of the Pleistocene and the Paleolithic, 10,000 years ago, hunter-gatherers continued to thrive in a warmer, "postglacial" Europe, but their time

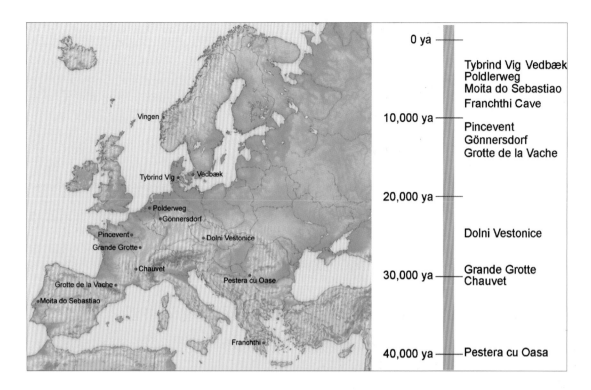

Fig. 3.1.
The location and time scale for sites mentioned in this chapter.

was coming to an end. Agriculture had been invented in the Near East and was spreading toward the continent, arriving in the southeast by 7000 BC and reaching the northeast by 4000 BC. This period of post-Pleistocene hunter-gatherers in Europe is known as the Mesolithic and is the focus of the second part of this chapter.

By the end of the Pleistocene, *Homo sapiens* had created art, invented many new tools, made tailored clothing, started counting, and spread to almost all parts of the world. As noted earlier, the oldest known representatives of anatomically modern humans have been found in East Africa, from almost 200,000 years ago. Further evidence of the activities of these individuals comes from caves around Pinnacle Point on the Cape of Good Hope in South Africa and dates to 165,000 years ago. This evidence is not in the form of fossil skeletons, but artifacts. Several finds—small stone blades, pieces of red ochre (an iron mineral used as a pigment), the earliest known collection and consumption of shellfish—point to new kinds of food, new tools that probably required hafting, and the use of powdered mineral as a pigment or preservative. These are firsts in the archaeological record and likely document the beginnings of the creative explosion witnessed more fully after 50,000 years ago.

The earliest skeletal remains of *Homo sapiens* found in western Europe date to almost 40,000 years ago, following the appearance of blade tools and other distinctively Upper Paleolithic artifacts. These anatomically modern individuals were originally called Cro-Magnon, after the place in France where they were first discovered. In spite of this distinctive name, they were indistinguishable from anatomically modern humans. Lacking the robust frame, heavy brow ridges, and protruding jaw of the Neanderthals, the *H. sapiens* face sits almost directly under a bulging forehead. A chin reinforces the smaller, weaker jaw and its smaller teeth. Cranial capacity is anatomically modern, and there is no obvious reason to assume that Cro-Magnons were intellectually different from ourselves.

THE UPPER PALEOLITHIC

The Upper Paleolithic is characterized by a variety of changes and innovations that developed over the last 30,000 years or so of the Pleistocene. These include the arrival of anatomically modern humans in Europe; extensive use of stone blades; widespread manufacture of objects of bone, antler, ivory, and wood; invention of new hunting equipment, such as the spearthrower and the bow and arrow; creation of art and use of decoration; and domestication of the dog. The earliest evidence for dog domestication dates to 33,000 years ago and comes from southern Siberia.

The Upper Paleolithic also represents an important phase in the geographic expansion of the human species. There were more sites in more places than ever before. Virtually all the earth's diverse environments, from tropical rain forest to arctic tundra, were inhabited during this period. Africa, Europe, and Asia were filled with groups of hunter-gatherers, and Australia and North and South America were colonized for the first time.

The archaeological materials of this period are best known from Europe, and especially from southwestern France, which was an important hub of archaeological activities during the twentieth century. Excavations over the last hundred years in the deep deposits of caves and rockshelters in this area have exposed layer upon layer of materials from the last part of the Pleistocene. These excavations and studies of the contents of the layers resulted in recognition of a sequence of Upper Paleolithic subperiods, known as the Châtelperronian, Aurignacian, Gravettian, Solutrean, and Magdalenian (Fig. 3.2). The term Gravettian has largely replaced Perigordian in its use in European archaeology. These terms come from famous French sites where these subperiods were first recognized.

Fig. 3.2.
Upper Paleolithic chronology, archaeological cultures, and temperature.

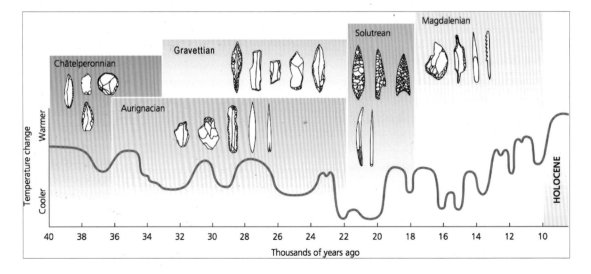

The material remains left by these Upper Paleolithic societies reinforce the idea that by this time our species had indeed arrived as creative creatures. Blade manufacturing techniques and blade tools characterize the Upper Paleolithic. Stone blades are a special form of elongated flake, with a length at least twice its width and sharp, parallel cutting edges on both sides. Blades can be mass-produced in large quantities from a single nodule of flint, removed from a core in a fashion akin to peeling a carrot. Blades also provide a form, or blank, that could be shaped (retouched) into a number of tools. Projectile points, burins (cutting and engraving tools made from flint), knives, drills, and scraping tools can all be made from a basic blade form.

Many new kinds of tools—made of materials such as bone, wood, ivory, and antler—also distinguish the Upper Paleolithic. Spearthrowers, bows and arrows, harpoons, ropes, nets, oil lamps, torches, and many other things have been found. Hafting and composite tools, incorporating various materials, were also introduced during the Upper Paleolithic. Resin and other adhesives were used to hold stone tools in bone, antler, or wood handles.

Fine bone needles with small eyes document the manufacture of clothing and other equipment sewn from animal skins. Several categories of carved artifacts—buttons, gaming pieces, pendants, necklaces, and the like—marked a new concern with personal appearance, expression of self, and aesthetic embellishment of everyday objects. This development was closely related to the appearance of decorative art (see Chapter 1, Fig. 1.3). Figurines, cave paintings, engravings, and varied decorations of other objects reflect the creative explosion that characterized Upper Paleolithic achievement. There is also compelling evidence for celebration of the seasons and awareness of time in the archaeological remains from the Upper Paleolithic. Finally, counting systems and the beginning of a calendar of sorts—at least a recording of the phases of the moon—may have begun in this time (Fig. 3.3).

In this chapter our story moves from the arrival of modern humans in Europe until the appearance of Neolithic farmers, about 35,000 years between the beginning of the Upper Paleolithic and the end of the Mesolithic. The Upper Paleolithic (40,000–11,000 bp) is the last phase of the Paleolithic and witnesses major changes in human life. The Mesolithic is the time of the last hunters in Europe, between the end of the Paleolithic and the arrival of Neolithic farmers (11,000–6000 BP).

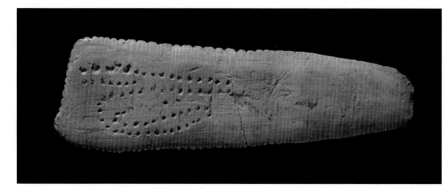

Fig. 3.3.
The decorated bone plaque from Abri Blanchard, France. The outer edge of the object is serrated, and the pattern of small holes made by different stone tools has been interpreted as a recording of the phases of the moon; ca. 14 cm in length.

We begin in a deep, dark cave in Romania, Pestera cu Oase, where the oldest anatomical evidence for the first *Homo sapiens* in Europe has been found. One of the hallmarks of this period is the appearance of art, dated to more than 30,000 years ago. There are so many marvelous Upper Paleolithic sites in southern France and northern Spain that it is difficult to select a few examples. There are literally hundreds of painted caves and dozens of important excavations that have pursued the denizens of the late Pleistocene. So I have chosen three. The Grande Grotte at Arcy-sur-Cure documents some of the archaeological evidence for the start of the Upper Paleolithic. The journey continues with the site of Chauvet, a recently discovered cave along a tributary of the Rhone River in the south of France. Another cave, Grotte de la Vache, is fascinating in its own right in terms of portable art pieces and other contents, but the site was also the focus of an innovative archaeological investigation that has provided new information on the lives of the inhabitants, in addition to its connection to the painted art in the nearby cave of Niaux.

Upper Paleolithic hunters in the cold steppe and tundra of late Pleistocene Europe concentrated on two species of animals. In western Europe reindeer was the prey of choice, while mammoth were more commonly hunted in the cold steppes of eastern Europe. The site of Dolní Věstonice in the Czech Republic contains remarkable evidence of the settlement of mammoth hunters in this region. Pincevent, in the environs of Paris, exhibits the remains of reindeer hunters' camps in northern France, Gonnersdörf and Doggerland.

PESTERA CU OASE, ROMANIA, 40,000 YEARS AGO

The Danube River carves a deep gorge through the Carpathian Mountains along the border between Serbia and Romania in eastern Europe. This river valley would have been a major route of east-west movement for human groups. The area is rich in archaeological sites. (The site of Lepenski Vir, discussed in the Neolithic chapter, yields some additional information about the region.)

The limestone mountains of the gorge are riddled with caves. In the winter of 2002, a group of local spelunkers explored a large cave in southwestern Romania. This was not an easy job. The cavers had to walk from the entrance of the cave, more than 200 m (650 ft) through an underground river to a point where they had to dive underwater and swim 25 m (80 ft) or so to reach the interior caverns (Fig. 3.4). The dive was slow and difficult because of the equipment and clothing they carried in and the archaeological materials they carried out; usually two trips were required in each direction to move all the gear, supplies, and samples. Then they climbed up from the bottom of a 30 m (100 ft) deep pit, the equivalent of a ten-story building, to a higher level in the cave to gain access to an unexplored series of chambers.

At the end of the last of these galleries was a small "mouse" hole in the cave wall. A draft of air through the hole suggested it might open on another chamber. The cavers removed enough rocks and earth so that one person could clamber through the hole. On the other side were more galleries. These new chambers had been sealed off for thousands of years and were littered with the skeletons of cave bears, wolves, wild goats, and other animals (Fig. 3.5). They named the place Pestera cu Oase, the Cave of the Bones.

After looking around for sometime, one of the spelunkers spied a lower jaw of human form. The jaw was taken to the local museum, and experts were involved in a study to determine how old this mandible might be and to whom it belonged. Erik Trinkaus, a specialist in early human remains at Washington University in St. Louis, Missouri, noticed the presence of a bony chin and other features on the specimen, characteristic of modern humans. Radiocarbon

Fig. 3.4.
Spelunkers at the entrance to Pestera cu Oase, Romania. They follow the stream in the cave until it goes underground. The spelunkers dive through this passage into the interior chambers of the cave. Passage to the place with the human remains requires about an hour.

dates from the jaw indicated an age of almost 40,000 years ago, making this the oldest known *Homo sapiens* in Europe. The next year, during continuing investigations at the site, an almost complete human face and many of the fragments of the skull of that individual were recovered (Fig. 3.6).

Together, over the course of three years of investigation, the international research team excavated more than 5,000 bones from the gallery, mapped the cave bear hibernation nests, and collected samples for dating and geology. The discovery of the human remains in Pestera cu Oase rekindled debate about the relationship between modern humans and Neanderthals. The issue here again is what happened to the Neanderthals. Trinkaus argues that the specimens from Pestera cu Oase document the mixture of Neanderthal and AMH features that might be expected at this critical date in the transition from Neanderthals to *Homo sapiens*.

Fig. 3.5.
A portion of the floor of the Cave of the Bones, Pestera cu Oase, covered with the remains of cave bear and other species.

Fig. 3.6.
Stefan Milota, one of the Romanian spelunkers at Pestera cu Oase, and the face of the anatomically modern individual found in 2003.

GROTTE CHAUVET, FRANCE, 32,000 YEARS AGO

The magnificent art of the Upper Paleolithic represents an awakening of the creative spirit, an explosion of our aesthetic senses. Such a transformation may also signify major changes in the minds of Upper Paleolithic people and/or in the way they viewed the world and organized their lives and their society. More than 200 painted caves from the Paleolithic have been discovered in France over the past hundred years, and new caves continue to be found.

Discoveries from the Grotte Chauvet have pushed back the date for the earliest cave paintings by almost 10,000 years. The Ardeche River in the south of France is a tributary of the Rhône and a popular outdoor destination for kayakers and canoers. The river winds for more than 30 km (20 mi) through a limestone gorge with high white cliffs and a natural arch over the water (Fig. 3.7). This area is crowded with visitors in the summer, and there are walking paths, picnic spots, and people everywhere. The region is also a spelunker's paradise; the limestone landscape is riddled with caves and caverns. In December 1994, an archaeologist/caver named Jean-Marie Chauvet and two of his friends entered a small cave not far from one of the spectacular bends in the river. On an earlier visit he had noticed a slight draft of air at the back of the cave. Digging out the rocks and earth, the group found a small passage to a deep shaft. Down this 9 m (30 ft) shaft they came upon a huge

Fig. 3.7.
The gorge of the Ardeche River in southern France, the location of Grotte Chauvet.

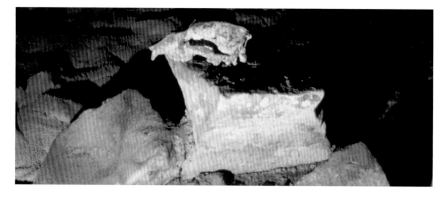

Fig. 3.8.
Skull of a cave bear perched on a stone block on the cave floor at Chauvet.

new cave with two major chambers and many side passages and galleries. The entire cave was almost 2 km (1.2 mi) in length.

After the three had explored most of the cave, one of them noticed a painting of a small mammoth on the wall, an animal extinct in Europe for thousands of years. The cave had been hidden for more than 20,000 years by the collapse of the entrance. Over the course of their subsequent exploration, the explorers found hundreds of paintings and engravings. The bones and skulls of extinct animals were scattered on the floor, and there were human footprints preserved in some out-of-the-way places. Nothing had been touched. The soft, claylike floor of the cave also retained the tracks of cave bears and large, rounded, depressions the bears made as hibernation "nests." Animal bones were abundant and included the skulls of cave bears and the horned skull of an ibex (wild goat). One of the cave bear

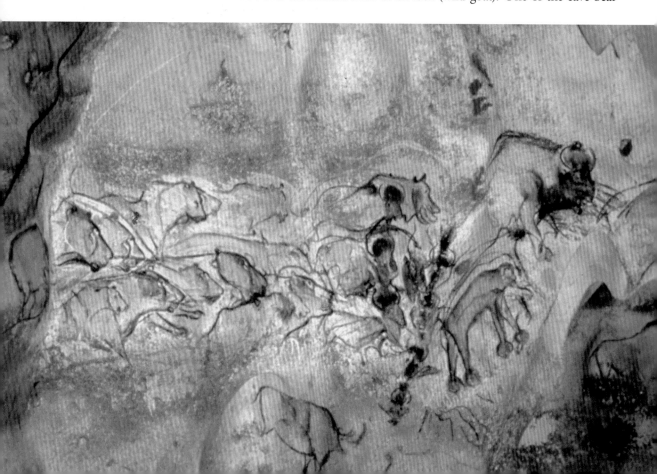

skulls was found perched on the edge of a stone block (Fig. 3.8), no doubt placed there by one of the Upper Paleolithic visitors.

More than 300 paintings have now been recorded in the Grotte de Chauvet, depictions of some thirteen species of animals. Perhaps because of the age of the paintings, their style and appearance is distinct from later Upper Paleolithic caves in the southern France and northern Spain (Fig. 3.9). Moreover, there are several species in Chauvet that are rare in other painted caves. The walls of the Chauvet Cave are often covered with predators: lions, panthers, bears, owls, and hyenas. Jean Clottes, a leading French specialist on cave art, believes that by painting these species that "symbolized danger, strength and power," the artists may have been attempting "to capture the essence of the animals." Other species include mammoth, aurochs, giant red deer, woolly rhinoceros, horse, reindeer, and bison.

The techniques used to make the paintings at Chauvet were unusual. Many of the animals were painted on a surface after debris and concretions on the wall had been scraped away, leaving a smoother, lighter canvas. In addition, the outline of some of the animals forms were carved into the cave wall, perhaps to guide the artist, but these lines also have the effect of lending depth to the painting, and in the light of a torch they create shadows around the edge.

There are no full human figures on the cave walls, but there are several depictions of female genitalia, one perhaps with the upper body of a bison. There are panels of red palm prints and others of hand stencils made by spitting red pigment over hands pressed against the cave surface (Fig. 3.10). Abstract markings—lines and dots—are found throughout the cave. There are also engravings and finger drawings, depictions of animals made by dragging a finger through the soft muddy walls found in parts of the cave.

Today we are aware that Chauvet contains some of the earliest known cave paintings from the Upper Paleolithic. Radiocarbon dates from the paintings themselves, from charcoal in torch soot on the walls, and from fireplaces on the cave floor indicate that there were two periods of use, between 32,000 and 30,000 years ago (the Aurignacian period of the Upper Paleolithic) and between 27,000 and 25,000 BP (the Gravettian). Some archaeologists have suggested that the black paintings of animals in the caves may date from the earlier period, while the red scatters of palm and hand prints belong to the younger, Gravettian period.

As was the case with most of the painted caves of the Upper Paleolithic, the interiors were not living areas. They were visited only briefly by the artists and other members of society. People chose to use the shelter at the mouths of caves as living areas, rather than reside in the dark, damp, cool recesses.

Although Upper Paleolithic art was also likely painted at cave entrances and along cliff faces and rock outcroppings as well, it survived the erosive forces

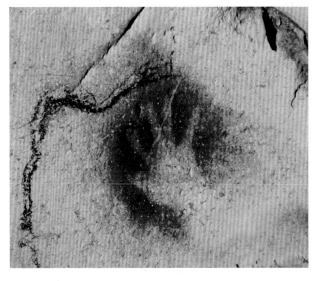

Fig. 3.10.
Panel of the Hand Stencil. The design was created by blowing paint over a hand held against the wall (length about 10 cm). The black outline is part of a mammoth, drawn before the hand.

Fig. 3.9. (opposite)
Chauvet, the Lion Panel (ca. 4.5 m in length). Above, to the right, a bison has been drawn as if coming out of a hollow in the wall. Below it is a young mammoth with huge feet. Immediately to its left, four bison heads are seen from the front. To their left several bison and rhinos are followed by a group of lions (perhaps the lions are hunting bison). Under the panel there is an isolated rhino and a horse.

of nature only inside caves. Cave art is, by and large, skillfully planned and executed, capturing both the movement and the power of the animals that are rendered (Fig. 3.11). For the most part it is not graffiti; nor is it hastily sketched. The quality of the paintings is such that we must assume there were recognized artists in the Upper Paleolithic.

Researchers at Chauvet believe that groups of people came repeatedly into the cave to participate in ceremony or ritual activities. Footprints preserved in the muddy floors of various painted caves in Europe indicate that people of all sizes walked in the caves. Margaret Conkey, of the University of California, Berkeley, argues that these places may have served as a focus of social activity for larger groups of people. She suggests that the caves may have been a permanent symbol on the landscape and a place for the ceremonies and rituals associated with the assembly of several groups of hunters.

Werner Herzog, the famous German director, released a 3D documentary film on the discoveries at Chauvet in 2011: *Cave of Forgotten Dreams*. The art of the Paleolithic fascinates and confounds us modern humans because of its remarkable location on dark cave walls, the emphasis on animals many of which are now extinct, and the mysterious minds that produced this art. What were our ancestors thinking? Why is this spectacular art an important part of Upper Paleolithic life? What did it mean? The fascination and mystery continues.

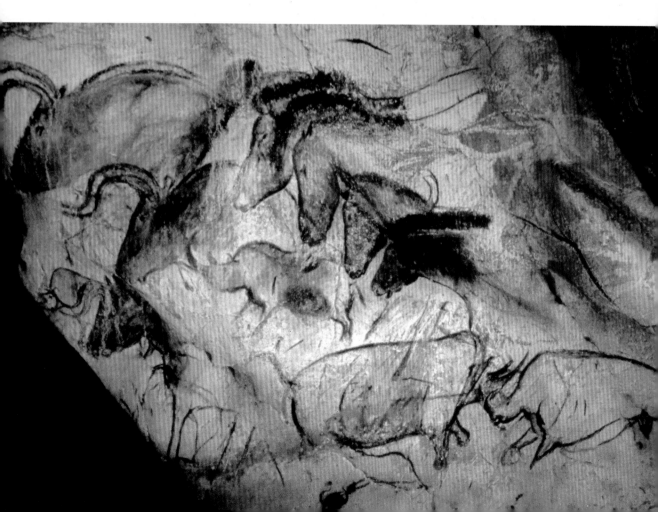

The magnificent art of the Upper Paleolithic represents an awakening of the creative human spirit, an expression of our aesthetic senses. Such a transformation may also signify major changes in the minds of Paleolithic people and in how they viewed the world. The discoveries at the site of Dolní Věstonice in the Czech Republic, one of the next stops on our tour, certainly support that statement.

GRANDE GROTTE, ARCY-SUR-CURE, FRANCE, 32,000 YEARS AGO

Now for the rest of the story from the Upper Paleolithic at Arcy-sur-Cure. The largest of the caverns at Arcy, called Grande Grotte, was a show cave for many years that was open to paying tourists to see speleological formations and underground lakes but lacked the marvelous Paleolithic art that captivates the visitor in other French caves. After a fortuitous discovery, the Grande Grotte now features some of the world's oldest and most unusual cave paintings. It was in 1990, as a French TV crew was filming a program on the geology of the cave; bright klieg lights brought a new perspective to the walls and ceiling. One of the crew suddenly noticed a painting of an ibex, and soon more paintings were recognized through a thin coating. These images had been hidden by a cloudy layer of calcite, several millimeters thick in places, that accumulated on the walls of the cave over time.

Some twenty years later, researchers have since discovered more than seventy depictions of various animals and as many abstract symbols and handprints on the walls and ceiling of the cave (Fig. 3.12). Early cave artists seem to have focused on predators and perilous animals, while later in the Upper Paleolithic the theme changed to large herbivores, the hunters' prey. Most of the animals painted at Grand Grotte were dangerous: rhinoceroses, bears, lions, mammoths. Mammoths make up about 50 percent of the animals depicted in the cave. In addition there are numerous negative handprints and abstract signs—dots, wavy lines, and trapezoidal forms. Artifacts found in the cave lay beneath 30 cm (1 foot) of deposits and were usually related to the artwork, pigments, palettes, pestles for grinding, and hearths and lamps for light.

Arcy's images have been radiocarbon-dated between 28,000 and 33,000 years ago. They are contemporary with the paintings from Grotte Chauvet and represent some of the oldest examples of rock art in the world. These painted caves convey fascinating images of various types to those who view them today. Why did people paint in these caves in the first place? They could just as easily painted on the cliff faces and rock overhangs found throughout the region. Why were the animals painted so frequently, and humans and plants so rarely? The extinct animals that are depicted tell of a very different time in this region, with arctic species and many dangerous predators. What was it about the caves that attracted these Paleolithic peoples? And why did ancient peoples paint these pictures?

There are several schools of thought on the meaning of the cave paintings from the Upper Paleolithic. An apparent emphasis on pregnant animals has

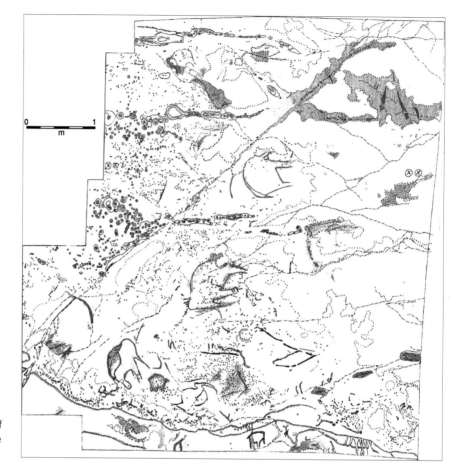

Fig. 3.12.
A schematic reproduction of some of the painting on the ceiling from Grande Grotte, France. Most of the representations are of elephants.

often been interpreted to represent concern with fertility and the bounty of nature, reflecting awareness of the importance of reproduction and the replenishment of the herds on which these people depended for food. Other scholars, pointing to the exaggerated hips and haunches of the animals and spears in flight, argue for a concern with hunting animals for meat. Ceremonial hunting rites and imaginary slaying of animals before a hunt might have magically helped ensure success in the quest for food.

A few prehistorians suggest that the cave paintings were simply "art for art's sake," a means for artists to express themselves and to change how their fellow humans saw the world. Still others suggest that the painted caves were primitive temples, sanctuaries for ceremony and ritual, such as initiation of the young into society. Huge animals flickering in the light of torches and lamps deep within the bowels of the earth would have been a breath-taking experience for the uninitiated. David Lewis-William in *The Mind in the Cave* writes about the role of the paintings in the activities of religious specialists in Upper Paleolithic societies in terms of trance and magic, reflecting the power of the spirit. It may also be the case that all of these factors were reasons for the art.

DOLNÍ VĚSTONICE, CZECH REPUBLIC, 27,500 YEARS AGO

The remains of a series of camps from Paleolithic mammoth hunters lie in the southern Czech Republic, not far from the Danube River Valley. The landscape is dominated by a local river and steep, limestone hills with elevations up to 550 m (1,800 ft). The limestone adds a more calcareous chemistry to the soils and creates conducive conditions for preservation. Excavations have been ongoing here at several localities for almost ninety years (Fig. 3.13).

The archaeological materials, which date from between roughly 24,500 and 27,500 BP, are deeply buried in loess. This loess is a Pleistocene aeolian silt, probably picked up by the winds across the freshly denuded and ice-free landscape of northwest Europe and spread across Central and Eastern Europe in deposits tens of meters (25–50 ft) thick. Many prehistoric sites were slowly covered by this airborne dust; bone, ivory, and other materials have been preserved in it.

The major problem with such sites is simply finding them, because they are hidden under very deep deposits (Fig.3.14). Fortunately loess is useful and often quarried for brick making. In several parts of Central and Eastern Europe, these quarries have uncovered deeply buried archaeological materials, permitting access to these remains.

Near the town of Dolní Věstonice, the enormous bones of extinct mammoths were uncovered in the course of digging up loess for brick making. The first mention of prehistoric finds was in the seventeenth century, when a doctor

Fig. 3.13.
The location of Upper Paleolithic sites of Pavlov and Dolní Věstonice in the Czech Republic.

Fig. 3.14.
The deep loess deposits on top of the Gravettian layer (dark layer) at Dolní Věstonice, some 6 m below the modern ground surface.

reported several huge bones found in the vicinity of the village. Archaeological excavations were initiated in 1924 and have continued intermittently until the present. Large horizontal excavations removed the deep loess deposit over the archaeological layer and exposed an area containing dwelling structures and many intriguing artifacts. The remains of 800 to 900 mammoths have been found, along with several examples of horse and reindeer.

The woolly mammoth of Pleistocene Europe was a magnificent creature. As seen in cave paintings and frozen examples from Siberia, this animal had a huge domed head atop a massive body covered with long fur. The mammoth was roughly one and a half times the size of a modern African elephant and must have been formidable prey for the later Pleistocene hunters of Europe. In addition to mammoths, herds of wild reindeer, horses, woolly rhinoceros, and other species roamed the cold steppe. At another site near Dolní Věstonice from the same time period, smaller mammals such as wolf, fox, glutton, and hare were found. The mammoth, however, was the primary game and probably provided the bulk of the diet for the inhabitants.

During the late Pleistocene, the area around Dolní Věstonice was one of forest-steppe, not far from the limits of forest growth (the tree line) in northern Europe. Some wood was available; pockets of spruce and pine and even some deciduous trees such as oak, lime, and beech grew in sheltered valleys. Broad expanses of grass, moss, and lichen were food for the animal herds. The plant evidence suggests a continental climate, relatively cool, but lacking extremely cold temperatures, permafrost, or the tundra vegetation that dominated during the colder episodes of the Pleistocene. The occupation of the site probably took place during one of the warmer oscillations of the last glacial cycle.

Permafrost sometime after the occupation at Dolní Věstonice was responsible for large-scale movement of the surface, a phenomenon known as solifluction. This alternate freezing and thawing of the ground resulted in the disturbance of many of the remains. For this reason, interpretation of the evidence and its context at the site can be difficult and controversial.

There are two separate concentrations of excavated archaeological materials from the Upper Paleolithic period known as the Gravettian, marked by heavy concentrations of mammoth bones and a series of structures. These huts were built on deliberately leveled floors, 4–5 m (ca. 15 ft) in diameter, dug down into the loess with a superstructure of mammoth bone and perhaps wood to support a roof. Postholes and large mammoth bones on the floor of the structures may represent the roof-bearing components of the houses. These structures had permanence, and there are indications of repeated use of the same pits and hearths over time. These sites may have been occupied for months at a time, either through the calendar months or via repeated visits over the years.

Our focus is on the site found at Dolní Věstonice I because of the abundance of new and unusual features and artifacts that have been found there, including semisubterranean structures, fireplaces and ovens, and flint and bone tools, along with thousands of fragments of clay figurines, carved and decorated objects of known and unknown function, and several human burials.

The highest layers in the deposits, which appear to contain a campsite, are still reasonably well preserved (Fig. 3.15). This camp lay on a projecting tongue of land, along a local stream that became a bog just at the eastern edge of the site. Part of the site sits on a low ridge, affording a good view of the valley of a nearby river. The effectiveness of the mammoth hunters is dramatically portrayed in the scatters of mammoth bones marking the boundaries of the settlement. The bones of at least a hundred mammoths were piled up in an area 12 by 45 m (45 by 150 ft). Stone tools and broken bones suggest

Fig. 3.15.
Hypothetical plan of the site of Dolní Věstonice with piles of mammoth bones, huts and hearths, and fencing. The scale and north arrow are approximate.

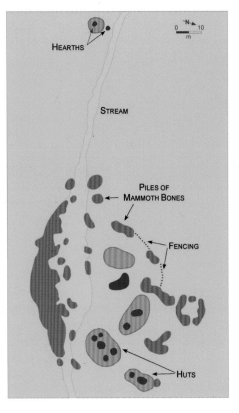

that this was a zone where animals, or parts of animals, were butchered and where skins may have been cleaned and prepared. Other piles of bones were found throughout the settlement, often sorted according to kind of bone, presumably for use as fuel and raw material for construction. Fires were lit on some of these bone piles, as evidenced by ash, perhaps as a defense against predatory animals.

Stones, earth, wooden posts, and mammoth bones were used for the construction at the site. There were several kinds of structures, among them roofed huts, windbreaks, fencing, and an unusual lean-to. Lines of wooden or bone posts were set as fencing around the northern margin of the site.

The first building found was a large, oval structure, 9 by 15 m (30 by 50 ft) in size, with five regularly spaced fireplaces inside the walls. The size of the structure, about half a tennis court, and its contents suggested to the excavators that this was an open windbreak, without a ceiling, rather than a roofed structure, and probably used during the summer. The wall posts were supported with limestone blocks and were likely covered with animal hides. At least three other roofed huts have been found in this area. These structures are partially dug into the loess; they contain one or two hearths and have numerous large mammoth bones on top of the floor. These bones are probably the remains of the framework for the walls and roof, which would have collapsed onto the floor of the structure after the site was abandoned.

Another structure, uncovered in 1951, was found some 80 m (260 ft) along the stream to the west of the main concentration. This structure was smaller, 6 m (20 ft) in diameter, and very unusual. The floor of the hut had been dug into the loess slope to level it and to provide more protection against the elements. Limestone blocks were placed against the excavated slope to buttress the wall. Posts were also supported by these blocks at the front of the hut. Hollow bird bones were found inside; they were cut at the ends and may have functioned as musical instruments.

In the center of the hut was an ovenlike fireplace with a domed clay structure raised around it. The oven was made of fire-hardened earth and ground limestone. In the deep pile of ashes and waste on the floor of the hut were found more than 2,300 small clay figurines that must have been fired in the oven. These fired clay figures document the first known examples of ceramic objects in prehistory, some 10,000 years before the invention of pottery in the Far East. The figurines consisted of heads, feet, and other parts of animal effigies and fired lumps of clay. Even the fingerprints of the maker were preserved in some of the pieces. Not only that, but careful study of other impressions in the clay figurines and balls revealed the oldest known fiber technology and evidence for production of nets, basketry, and perhaps textiles.

Fireplaces are common at Dolní Věstonice and take two forms: hearths of various sizes and kilns. The concentrations of artifacts, construction materials, and foodstuffs are associated with the hearths, which must have been a focus of human activity. Two kilns were found, the domed clay structure in the isolated lean-to hut, and another horseshoe-shaped kiln with clay walls that also contained fired clay figurines.

Most of the huts had one or more fireplaces for heat, light, and cooking. In addition, there was a large hearth, almost 1 m (3'3") deep and several meters across, in an open area near the center of the compound, which may have served as a common, central fire for the community. In the ashes of this fire, a clay carving of a female figure, called the Venus of Vestonice, was found. In addition to the Venus figurine, many figures of animals—bear, lion, mammoth (Fig. 3.16), horse, fox, rhino, and owl—and more than 2,000 balls of burnt clay have been found.

The Venus of Vestonice is a small, ceramic statue of a nude female, 11.1 cm (4.5") tall (Fig. 1.3). The breasts and hips are shown in some detail. The limbs and head are largely stylized; the eyes are two simple, enigmatic slashes across the face. There are at least two other Venus figurines found at the site. Such figurines in bone, stone, and ivory are known from Upper Paleolithic sites across most of Europe. Their ubiquity must reflect their significance as icons or symbols of some shared beliefs and behaviors.

There is an extraordinarily rich assemblage of tools, equipment, objects, and jewelry. More than 35,000 pieces of flint were found in the habitation area. About 30 percent of the flaked stone tools were made of local flint and hornstone, and about 70 percent were made from an exotic material, from more than 100 km (60 mi) away in southern Poland. Stone tools in the form of points, knives, and burins are made from narrow blades, typical of the Gravettian tradition. There are also many items made from mammoth bone and ivory: awls, needles, knives, spear points, lances, and digging equipment.

Ornaments for use as pendants, necklaces, on headbands, and the like are made of carved bone, ivory, and shell. Some of the shells were from the Mediterranean, several hundred kilometers to the south, evidence of either

Fig. 3.16.
A fired clay mammoth figurine from Dolní Věstonice, ca. 6 cm in length.

travel or trade. Other objects carved of antler or ivory, or made of baked clay, have no clear practical purpose and may have served as ritual objects in the ceremonies that took place at the site.

Perhaps the most remarkable finds involve two representations of what is probably the same individual. Excavations in 1936 uncovered a small ivory plaque about 4 cm (1.6 in) high, with a crudely incised human face portrayed on it. The face is asymmetrical, with the left eye and the left half of the lip somewhat lower than the right. A second carved ivory head was found in 1948 in the open summer hut. This three-dimensional head also portrays an individual, and the left side of the face is somewhat distorted and asymmetrical. Finally, a burial was excavated in 1949, discovered beneath two huge shoulder blades from a mammoth. The skeleton belonged to a woman and was covered with red ochre, a red mineral pigment. A study of the facial bones of this individual showed that she suffered from partial paralysis of the left side of her face. It seems plausible that the two faces carved in ivory are representations of this person in the grave.

Other burials have been uncovered as well. A child buried at Dolní Věstonice III had a necklace of twenty-seven pierced fox teeth; the skull was covered with red ochre, and the burial lay beneath the shoulder blades of a mammoth. In 1986, the bodies of three teenagers were discovered in a common grave (Fig. 3.17). Two of the skeletons were strongly built young males. The third individual was determined to be female, seventeen to twenty years of age. A

Fig. 3.17.
The triple grave at Dolní Věstonice.

marked curvature of the spine, along with several other skeletal abnormalities, suggested that she had been painfully disabled in life. The two males had died healthy, in the prime of their lives. The evidence of a thick wooden shaft or spear thrust through the hip of one of the males indicates his death at least was violent. The simultaneous burial of all three individuals certainly suggests a traumatic end to their lives.

The bodies had been buried with special care. The skeletons leaned into one other, like nestled question marks. Both young men had been laid to rest with their heads encircled with necklaces of pierced canine teeth and ivory; the one with the pole thrust up to his coccyx may also have been wearing some kind of painted mask. All three skulls were covered in red ocher. The woman was placed between her two companions. The man on her left lay on his stomach, facing away from her but with his left arm linked with hers. The other male lay on his back, his head turned toward her. Both of his arms were reaching out, so that his hand rested on her pubis. The ground surrounding this intimate connection was splashed with red ocher.

The mammoth were clearly the major source of food at Dolní Věstonice, but the remains of other animals—reindeer, horse, wolf, fox, glutton, and hare—have been found as well. Plant remains have also been recovered from the site, a rarity in Paleolithic archaeology. Among the bits of charcoal at the site were pieces of burned bulbs and tubers from plants with edible roots.

One of the more fascinating aspects of life in the Upper Paleolithic is the explosion that takes place in ornamentation and self-expression. In some ways it seems that for the first time individualism has a place, and ego is visible, perhaps permitted. This individuality is expressed in jewelry and decorated equipment, perhaps in body paint, tattoos, clothing, hairstyles. For the first time in the past we see the individual, the personality, of the members of the group. There is an identity in death as well, with distinctive grave goods and equipment, gifts and souvenirs for the afterlife.

New roles and identities in the group may also appear, e.g., shamans/curers. Shamans in human societies are believed to be intermediaries or messengers between the human world and the spirit world, often through the medium of trance. Shamans function as healers, mediators, and seers in small-scale societies. The presence of shamans in the archaeological record is vague, but burials like the elderly woman beneath the mammoth shoulder blades point in that direction. Accompanying her in the grave were the bones of an arctic fox.

At the same time there is a group or regional identity emerging, expressed in local styles, designs and motifs. Artifact types are no longer continental in distribution; smaller regional patterns appear that must denote networks of interaction and shared norms. Group identity likely was fostered by shared belief, ceremony, and ritual. The large communal fireplace in the center of the site at Dolní Věstonice would seem to be one of the shared spaces where individuals were forged into a larger amalgam of the group or band.

The archaeologist who originally excavated the site, Bohuslav Klima, believes that Dolní Věstonice was a mammoth hunters' village, with 20 to 25 people per hut. Given an estimate of five or six huts at the site, there may have been as many as 100–120 occupants. Some have argued that the substantial size and nature of the site, along with the burials, argues for a permanent or semipermanent arrangement. The depth and extent of deposits at Dolní Věstonice suggest that this site may have been occupied throughout the year. The substantial house structures and burials reiterate this impression. Others point to the difficulties involved in determining if the structures were used simultaneously and the complexity of the deposits given disturbances and solifluction. Interpretation of site population and duration of occupation is not an easy undertaking.

Whatever the case, Dolní Věstonice is very different from everything we have discussed up to this point. A large campsite for a substantial group of people with purposefully built residences, perhaps living for long periods or even permanently in one spot, as mammoth hunters of the Upper Paleolithic. The camp is organized and structured, and a wide range of activities took place: house construction; hearth maintenance; birth, death, and burial; manufacture of tools; import of exotic raw materials such as shell and certain types of stone for tools; production of art; butchering of animals; and collecting of plant foods. The remarkable ceramic artifacts and other materials found at the site confirm the sense that this is a special place indeed. Previously unknown from the earlier human past, locales now become places of social occasion, in addition to basic survival and routine domestic activities. There are clearly new ideas, new motifs, and no doubt new beliefs that are structuring human thought and behavior, and human society.

GROTTE DE LA VACHE, FRANCE, 14,000 YEARS AGO

The province of Ariège in southwestern France, near the Spanish border, has more prehistoric painted caves than any other in the country. Toward the end of 1952, a French archaeologist named Romain Robert was exploring a cave known as the Grotte de la Vache (Cave of the Cow) on the steep slope of a deep valley in the foothills of the Pyrenees (Fig. 3.18). The site was occupied toward the end of the Pleistocene, when a warming trend and a retreat of the glaciers had begun.

There, in a chamber known as the Salle Monique (Fig. 3.19), sealed beneath more recent deposits, he discovered a rich archaeological deposit on the floor of the chamber. In this room near the entrance to the cave, a small group of Magdalenian hunter-gatherers camped repeatedly between 12,000 and 15,000 years ago and left behind the evidence of their visits. Today the cave maintains a steady temperature of 13°C (55 °F) throughout the year. The Salle Monique receives some light from the entrance of the cave and is not completely dark.

Twelve years of excavation on the chamber floor by Robert, from 1953 to 1964, uncovered more than 200 m² (2,150 ft²) of an extremely rich archaeological level, sealed beneath layers of clay and calcium carbonate. The

archaeological deposit is a black sandy layer, rich in charcoal, between 10 cm (4 in) and nearly 1 m (3'3") thick. Because of the clay and carbonate cap, preservation in the cultural layer was quite good. Charcoal from the cultural layer has yielded a radiocarbon date for the site of approximately 13,600 years before the present.

Fig. 3.18.
The location of Grotte de la Vache and Grotte de Niaux in the French Pyrenees.

Fireplaces on the floor of the cave, ringed with stone, marked the living areas of these people (Fig. 3.20). Although the original excavator argued that a hut had been built near the entrance of the cave, there is no definitive evidence. The quantity of archeological material, particularly the number of carved bone objects, is staggering. The deposit contained more than 143,000 animal bones, 36,000 stone artifacts, 2,000 harpoons and points made of reindeer antler, 300 bone needles, 200 animal teeth and shells perforated as ornaments, and 220 pieces of portable art decorated with carved and engraved designs.

Paleolithic art is generally divided into two kinds, the mural art of the cave wall paintings (such as at Chauvet), and portable art on objects that can be moved. The mural art is largely confined to southwestern France and northern Spain. Portable art is found throughout Europe in the Upper Paleolithic and includes decorated objects and figurines made of stone, bone, or antler, sometimes clay or ivory. Small, three-dimensional objects such as the widely known Venus figurines and carved animal bone tools, and two-dimensional relief carvings are all varieties of portable art.

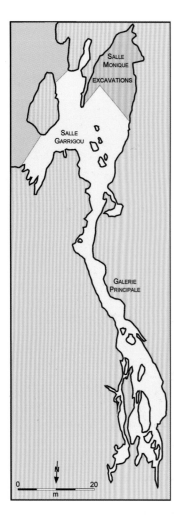

Decoration was applied to diverse objects, both practical tools and purely aesthetic forms. Designs were made by carving, cutting, grinding, and engraving. A wide range of motifs are depicted, usually animals, sometimes plants, and even human figures. In addition to the representational designs there are also geometric patterns, lines of dots, rows of tally marks, and other kinds of graffiti or notation.

The artists at Grotte de la Vache masterfully decorated small stone pebbles and polished pieces of bone and antler with remarkable depictions of cave lion, bear, antelope, salmon, and wolves (Fig. 3.21). Horses, bison, reindeer, ibex, and deer are also common. Human figures, though rarely portrayed in this time period, appear on several pieces.

The animal remains are essentially the product of the hunt and food preparation. A range of species were represented. The hunters typically pursued mountain game. A major part of the diet was ibex and ptarmigan (grouse). Ptarmigan, a large bird, was the single most abundant animal in the bone remains; more than 4,500 individual birds were represented in the kitchen refuse in the cave. The ibex was also important in the diet, and a minimum of 1,800 animals were counted among the many bones. There were also reindeer and chamois (another wild goat). The local wildlife was exceptionally rich and diverse, including hare, rabbit, red deer, wolf, fox, wild horse, wild boar, and a variety of other birds, among them ducks, geese, hawks, and eagles.

Raw materials from the animals were also important. Fur came from trapping animals such as arctic foxes, red foxes, hare, and several species of wild cats. Most of the worked harpoons and some of the decorated pieces were made on antlers shed by male reindeer in the autumn and collected by the Magdalenian hunters. Bone used for the decorations and designs came from the larger mammals. Long bones were often used; the surface of the bone was scraped and polished before the design was applied. Some of the carved pieces found at the Grotte de la Vache were also stained with both red and black pigments. The color would have made the carved designs stand out against the white bone. There were thirty-nine mortars and forty-four pestles used for grinding color pigments.

Fig. 3.19.
Plan of the cave of Grotte de la Vache, France.

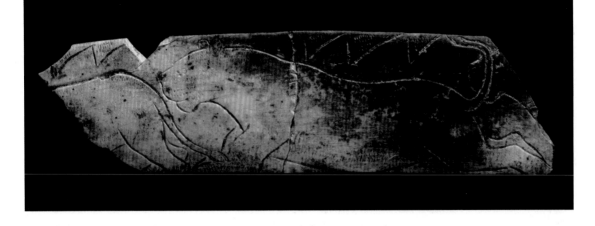

It is interesting to compare the proportions of animals depicted in the carved bone objects to the bones of the animals that were hunted and eaten. For the most part there is an inverse relationship. Animals that appear in the artwork are rarely eaten, and vice versa. The ibex is clearly an exception.

The sex of the animals could be determined by measuring the size of certain bones, since males were significantly larger than females. Males made up about 40 percent of the total number of ibex. About 30 percent of the ibex bones came from juveniles, animals younger than twenty-eight months. These age and sex proportions are very similar in populations of wild ibex today, suggesting that the Magdalenian hunters took male or female animals, young or old, as they encountered them. Since they also seem to have hunted a variety of other animals, it would appear that hunting was often opportunistic, attacking whatever prey was available, rather than planned and directed toward specific species or selective in terms of the age or sex of the prey.

It was also possible to determine when the prey had been killed. The individual animal jaws were examined for information on tooth wear, the presence of deciduous teeth, and the state of eruption of permanent teeth to estimate the age of death of the animal. Since these species have a known calving season (usually a few months in the spring), the season of death can be determined by counting forward from the calving season. Ibex and chamois are more easily estimated than reindeer, which have a longer calving season.

On the basis of the age of the animals, it appears that the wild goats (ibex and chamois) were hunted from autumn to spring, most heavily during the winter months. In November, at the start of the rut, large herds of animals of both sexes and all ages would have gathered in the vicinity of Grotte de la Vache, leaving the higher mountains for the winter. Reindeer, on the other hand, appear to have been hunted as they migrated biannually through the valley during the same periods each year, between mid-August and mid-October, or in May and June.

Most of the evidence suggests that the dwellers of the Hall of Monique lived there during the colder months of the year. It is easy to imagine that during the spring and summer such groups would have moved into more open, lighter, and warmer places to live. They may not have moved far.

Fig. 3.21.
A happy lion engraved with two others on a piece of bone from Grotte de la Vache; length ca. 20 cm.

Fig. 3.20. (opposite)
The living area at Grotte de la Vache, with in situ fireplaces in the floor. The signs mark two of the fireplaces.

There is one more intriguing aspect to the archaeology of Grotte de la Vache. Directly across the valley, within sight of la Vache, is the cave of Niaux, one of the more famous painted caves in the Pyrenees (or in Europe for that matter). Niaux has an enormous entrance today, 55 m high by 50 m wide. There are more than two kilometers of galleries running deep within the mountain, displaying a hundred or more superb paintings from the later part of the Upper Paleolithic, many of which are almost one kilometer (1,100 yards) inside the cave. Many of the paintings are done in the classic style of the Magdalenian, animals outlined in black or red pigment. Niaux is contemporary with Grotte de la Vache and almost the opposite in terms of its contents and characteristics. Niaux is huge; la Vache is relatively small. There is very little cultural refuse in Niaux, many wall paintings, and no portable art; la Vache itself has only a few small engravings on the walls of the cave.

Yet in all probability the inhabitants of la Vache visited Niaux and may have even been responsible for the paintings. The styles of the portable art of la Vache and the wall paintings of Niaux are very similar. Perhaps here we are seeing the secular and the sacred in Upper Paleolithic life. Clearly the caves were used in very different ways. In this case, it may be the warmth and light of the south-facing mouth of la Vache that drew its residents, in contrast to the darker and colder, north-facing Niaux. As real estate agents say, location is everything.

GÖNNERSDORF, GERMANY, 11,500 YEARS AGO

Many archaeological discoveries are accidental. This was certainly the case for the site of Gönnersdorf. In 1968, a resident of the town of Feldkirchen-Gönnersdorf along the Rhine in western Germany, about 15 km (10 mi) northwest of Koblenz, was digging a basement for a new house. Lots of strange things began to turn up, bone, slabs of slate, various stone tools; the archaeologists were called in. Gerhard Bosinski of the University of Köln spent his summers over the next eight years excavating one of the most fascinating Upper Paleolithic sites in Europe.

Some of the finds at Gönnersdorf were typical of the Upper Paleolithic Magdalenian culture: flint artifacts, fireplaces, even the animal bones. But many of the finds were highly unusual, especially the remains of living structures and associated pits and other features, scatters of red ochre, small figurines of ivory and antler, beads made from jet (a black mineral), perforated animal teeth, a pavement of stone slabs, and hundreds of engraved slate tablets. There was something special about the site.

Gönnersdorf was a large, open-air settlement on a terrace above the Rhine River with a spectacular view over a broad region. Today, this is one of the great wine-producing regions of Germany. The landscape is dominated by high hills and water. The Rhine is a major, navigable river until it reaches the Swiss border in southern Germany. It would have carried even more water in the late Pleistocene as Alpine glaciers quickly melted and the water drained out the Rhine to the Atlantic. In fact, the area around Gönnersdorf is cut by several rivers, making the location a rather central place for hunters of large migratory animal herds that would have moved through this crossroads. On the western side of the site a small stream has cut a steep, narrow valley that marks the boundary of the settlement. This small ravine was the source of the slate materials that were found in abundance on the site.

This region of Germany has seen volcanic activity in the last 20,000 years, both before and after the Gönnersdorf occupation. The Laacher See Volcano is only 11 km (7 mi) to the west; the last large eruption, around 10,900 BC, buried the site in pumice, protecting and preserving the remains. The Magdalenian layer at Gönnersdorf sits on top of an earlier layer of pumice from an eruption around 20,000 years ago. Radiocarbon dates on animal bones from the site itself indicate an age of approximately 13,400 BC, during the late Magdalenian.

This period near the end of the Pleistocene was characterized by several fairly rapid oscillations between cold and relatively warm climate, along with associated changes in vegetation. The colder episodes were very dry, with mild summers and very cold winters. Vegetation was treeless arctic tundra with a ground cover of grasses and herbs. The warmer episodes witnessed a longer growing season, milder winters, and more precipitation. The vegetation has been described as grass-covered steppe with scattered bushes and small trees of willow and birch, especially in sheltered areas along the stream valleys.

Gönnersdorf was excavated with great care, recording the exact location of many of the finds in both horizontal and vertical dimensions. A number of experts in geology, pollen studies, and archaeozoology were involved in the project. A total of almost 700 m² (7,500 ft²) was excavated. Sediments were sieved through fine screens, and many small finds were recovered in this way. At least four separate concentrations of materials were distinguished in the excavation area.

The most visible material at the site and the most widespread was also the biggest. Pavements of stone slabs, or plaquettes, covered large parts of the excavation area and were particularly concentrated in certain areas (Fig. 3.22).

Fig. 3.22.
Part of the pavement, bone, and stone artifacts found in Concentration IIa at Gönnersdorf.

These stone slabs were primarily of slate, collected in the sides of the deep valley next to the site. Other types of stone were also brought to the site for pavement slabs, including quartz, quartzite, and basalt. The stone slabs varied in size from less than 10 cm (4 in) in diameter to larger pieces more than 50 cm (20 in) in diameter. Many of these slabs appear to have been broken at the site. A layer of powdered red ochre (hematite), 1–5 cm (½–2 in) thick, was deposited among the stone slabs, densest in highest concentrations of slabs. There is an enormous number of these slabs present, representing a great deal of effort on the part of the Magdalenian inhabitants. The slabs from one concentration alone weighed more than 1,000 kg (2,200 lb). These pavements reflect a significant investment in the construction of the settlement.

The larger structures would have been substantial, built to last for some time and made from materials that were not easily portable. These houses were 6 to 8 m in diameter, and the floors were paved with slate slabs. The floor of each house was prepared by digging into the hill slope to create a level platform. The house itself is marked by a circle of small pits to support posts; higher densities of slabs, artifacts, and debris; and the red ocher layer. A larger post was placed in the center of the structure to support the roof. Many of the slabs on the floors were engraved with profiles of animals and other figures.

These are substantial structures, and the excavator believes they were used repeatedly for long periods, over some years. At least three episodes of occupation can be recognized from the artifacts and pits. Bosinski has also suggested that the wooden frames of the houses were covered with animal hides, perhaps from horses (Fig. 3.23). About forty horse hides would have been needed to cover one of the frames.

The four concentrations of materials seen at Gönnersdorf are suggested to represent remnants of dwelling constructions. Concentrations I, II, and III would have been large, sturdy structures. Concentration IV appears to be the remains of a lighter tent framework. The tent was approximately 5 m in diameter, marked by a circle of large stones. There is a fireplace inside the tent and another just outside. There are no pits or postholes in the tent circle, no red ochre on the floor, and relatively few finished artifacts associated with the tent. The similarity among the artifacts and the refitting of lithic material, however, demonstrates that the tent and Concentration III (and probably Concentration I) were in use at the same time.

This discussion focuses on Concentration III. The red ochre and the pits also have a distinctive distribution in this structure. The red ochre is found outside the structure; elsewhere it is confined to the interior areas. No outer ring of supporting posts was observed in Concentration III. Most of the remains appear related to activities taking place in this area. One pit with a number of unusual finds and finished tools may have been a cache of materials for making clothes. Two pits were used for cooking, and another with lots of backed bladelets may have been used for storing hunting equipment.

In addition to the structural features of the houses and the pavements, there are large quantities of various artifacts at Gönnersdorf: stone, bone, antler, and

Fig. 3.23.
An artist's reconstruction of the structures at Gönnersdorf with both large huts and smaller tents.

ivory objects, jewelry and items of personal adornment, and a huge number of engravings. There is also a large quantity of animal bones, food waste from the hunt that can tell us about the diet and some of the habits of these people. A brief description of these materials may provide some sense of the richness of the materials at Gönnersdorf and the rather special nature of the settlement.

Stone tools and their manufacturing waste are the most common type of artifact at Gönnersdorf. More than 50,000 pieces, 1 cm (½ in) in diameter or larger, were excavated. About 1 percent of these were finished tools and the remainder were largely unretouched blades, waste flakes, and cores. The finished tools are typical for the late Magdalenian: many blade tools, end scrapers on blades, blacked blades and bladelets, burins, and small borers. Burins for cutting and engraving were the most common formal tool type present at the site.

The raw material for the stone tools came from several sources. Some of the raw material used at Gönnersdorf was available locally. Quartzite and siliceous shist could be obtained within a few kilometers of the site. Other raw materials came from quite some distance; there was a Baltic flint whose closest source was near Duisburg, 100 km (60 mi) to the north in the Lower Rhine River, and west European flint from the Meuse River area at least 100 km to the northwest.

Lamps were another interesting category of stone artifact. Other examples are known almost exclusively from cave sites where torches were also used as a light source. These lamps likely burned animal fat using a small wick and were best suited to producing light, rather than heat for warmth or cooking.

Although it is difficult to accurately establish the season of occupation, there is evidence from Gönnersdorf to indicate a human presence during both the warmer and colder parts of the year. The more intensive use of the site, however, appears to have taken place during the winter. Several lines of evidence found in Concentration I support this contention. Fetal bones from horses show that mares, pregnant over the winter, were hunted from Gönnersdorf. Bones from migrant geese that likely overwintered in the Rhineland were also found in Concentration I. Arctic fox is common here as well, and this animal was probably trapped in the winter when its fur is in prime condition. Finally, the tooth eruption pattern in the reindeer mandibles indicates that some of the animals were killed in the colder months.

Concentration II shows another pattern in terms of seasonality. The fetal bones from horses are from a later stage in pregnancy, and the bone development in young horses shows they were killed during their second summer. The flint raw material in Concentration II comes from the Meuse river area to the north, while the material used in Concentration I was local quartzite. The sum of the evidence suggests that these two concentrations were used at contrasting times of the year, perhaps by different groups of people.

Animal products such as bone, antler, and ivory were also used as raw material for tools. Shed reindeer antler and mammoth tusks were probably collected and brought to the settlement. The standard technique for working these materials is described as groove-and-splinter. Two parallel grooves are cut with a sharp stone tool along the length of the bone or antler raw material; a splinter of the material can then be removed and shaped into numerous kinds of artifacts, including antler and ivory points, harpoons, decorated bone rods, and even a few fish hooks. Eyed bone needles are the most common type of nonstone tool.

Personal jewelry and adornment becomes the style in the Upper Paleolithic, and Gönnersdorf is no exception. Several kinds of material were used to make such items. Small pendants or beads of jet, perforated animal teeth, fossil shell, and sea shells are found at the site. The sea shells must have been traded or exchanged over the long distance from the Mediterranean. Black jet, a kind of fossil wood, comes from a valley ca. 50 km to the west. "Rondelles" are another intriguing object: small perforated slate disks, 3–4 cm (1–3 in) in diameter, some of which are engraved with fine lines and designs. Almost 400 were found at Gönnersdorf. These may have been used as buttons or pendants.

There are two other major categories of artifacts at Gönnersdorf that require some discussion: carved figurines and engraved slate plaquettes or small tablets. The figurines are small statuettes made of ivory, antler, or slate. The slate tablets often have similar figures engraved on them. These figurines schematically depict the female figure with large buttocks, some with breasts and usually without head or limbs.

The engraved slate plaquettes are the most common art at the site. About 10 percent of the slates in the pavement at the site have been engraved with various motifs, particularly female figures (Fig. 3.24), animals, and abstract symbols. A flint burin was probably used to etch the fine lines in the slate.

Fig. 3.24.
Several female figurines engraved on a stone plaque in a very abstract style. The plaque is 11.8 by 10.8 cm.

There are approximately 300 female figures in the slate engravings, similar to the figurines but shown only in outline. In a few cases, several figures are depicted together in what might be a dance scene.

Although the female figures are quite abstract, the animal engravings show significant detail and are very naturalistic. The animals depicted in the engravings are the same ones identified in the bones at the site, but there are some intriguing differences. The mammoth, for example, is one of the most common animals shown on the plaquettes (sixty-one engravings), but only a few pieces of bone and tusk are known from the site. The most common engraving is of the wild horse (seventy-four examples), often just the head of the animal, and this species was also most common in the food remains. Reindeer and fox, which are common in the bone assemblage, are not depicted in the engravings. The cave lion and the seal, which are not found in the kitchen refuse, do appear among the engravings. The seal is of particular interest since this is a marine animal and the sea was at least 250 km to the north and west. Perhaps seals were observed swimming up the Rhine, or perhaps these horse hunters at Gönnersdorf sometimes traveled to the coast.

Engraved stone plaquettes (Fig. 3.25) are well known in the Upper Paleolithic, and examples are found at many sites across Europe, although usually not in such quantity. There are perhaps 500 examples at Gönnersdorf, 6,000 at Parpalló near Valencia on the east coast of Spain, and 1,500 at La Marche in west-central France.

In sum, Gönnersdorf is a remarkable archaeological site in many ways. The large outdoor structures, repeated use of the location, and the enormous quantities of artifacts and art are witness to the intensity of human use. The extraordinary variety of materials is testimony to the skills and technology of the Magdalenian people who lived at the site. The fact that the sources

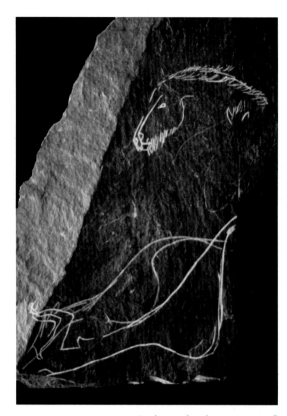

Fig. 3.25.
Two engraved female silhouettes and a horse head on slate plaque from Gönnersdorf. The engraved lines have been highlighted to make them more visible. The larger female is almost 12 cm long.

for materials such as shell and flint are hundreds of kilometers distant is a comment on either the exchange networks in operation or the mobility of these groups, or both. The importance of personal decoration and ornamentation is strongly manifest at Gönnersdorf in the variety of beads and pendants. Self-awareness is human nature in the Upper Paleolithic, and individuals likely sought to distinguish themselves in terms of dress, appearance, and behavior.

The artwork, figurines and plaquettes may require a different understanding of the past. We cannot know the significance of these objects to the people who made and used them. Sacred or profane, do such materials reflect belief systems or just artistic expression? Do we witness art, or religion, or a combination of the two? The disparity between the animals eaten and the animals that appear engraved on the slates is intriguing. Mammoths are common in the art, but almost invisible on the site. This powerful animal must have been one of the most impressive sights on the steppes of late Pleistocene Germany. Perhaps the depictions reflect the things that were strongest in the minds of the hunters, rather than the mundane. Many of the animals are drawn in striking detail, reflecting the deep knowledge these people had of the environment in which they had to survive.

Gönnersdorf also tells us a great deal about the human condition and the nature of human society at this time in our prehistory. The term *hunter-gatherer* describes a human way of life before farming that was dependent on the bounty of nature. Wild animals were hunted and wild plants were gathered for food. Such societies were generally smaller, less sedentary, and more egalitarian than farming groups. Because wild resources vary in quantity and location throughout the year, such small groups often moved frequently to take advantage of available foods. This pattern is clearly operating in the Upper Paleolithic, in which many archaeological sites appear to be temporary or short-term places of residence where animals were hunted.

These groups often have a regular and repetitive annual cycle of activity, returning to the same areas every year when foods become available. At the same time, it is essential for small human groups to be part of a larger network to find mates, share information, and exchange materials and ideas. To solve this need, hunter-gatherers usually come together in larger groups at what have been called aggregation camps for some part of the year, normally when resources are particularly abundant.

In the Upper Paleolithic, it may be the case that the fall hunt provided sufficient stores in the form of dried or smoked meat and fat that larger groups could aggregate over the winter months. This may be what we see at Gönnersdorf, and perhaps at Dolní Věstonice as well. Patterns of behavior that characterize hunter-gatherers described in recent times such as many groups of North American Indians, the Inuit of Alaska and Canada, and others seem to be in place during the Upper Paleolithic. It remains difficult to envision such behaviors prior to 40,000 years ago. It may be the case that being hunter-gatherers (as we understand the term) requires many of the attributes that make us human, that come along with the arrival of *Homo sapiens*. I return to this issue at the end of the chapter.

PINCEVENT, FRANCE, 12,000 YEARS AGO

Geologists like acronyms. One favorite is LGM, or Last Glacial Maximum. This term describes the last time continental ice sheets reached their maximum extent during the Pleistocene. This happened during a period of extreme cold, between 26,000 and 19,000 years ago. Average winter temperatures were at least 5–10° C (8–15° F) colder than today.

Northern Europe was covered with a continental ice sheet during the LGM, across Britain and the North Sea, all of Scandinavia into the northern Netherlands, Germany, and Poland. Enormous mountain glaciers buried the Alps and Pyrenees. Permafrost covered the ground south of the ice sheet into present-day France, Hungary, and points east. Sea level was approximately 120 m (almost 400 ft) lower than today. Much of the northern half of Europe was simply uninhabitable, and there is a distinct absence of human evidence there from this time.

Beginning around 19,000 years ago, a gradual warming trend resulted in the retreat of the ice, rising sea level, and changes in the environment. The melting ice sheet left a thick layer of gravel, sand, and clay, remnants of the former land surface bulldozed up and pushed along by expansion of the ice. At first this was completely barren ground (Fig. 3.26), but a sequence of plant species colonized the area, beginning with low ground cover of dwarf shrubs, grasses, mosses, and lichens, and eventually by birch and willow groves, pine woods, and finally a mixed oak forest. Animals followed the vegetation. Initially there were herds of large, migratory animals: reindeer, horses, mammoth, shifting in time to forest species such as red deer, roe deer, wild boar, and brown bear.

It was in this context of dramatically changing environment and a newly formed landscape that the early human inhabitants of northern Europe began to enter the region. Initial human settlement

Fig. 3.26.
After the Ice. The fresh land surface after the retreat of glacial ice in modern-day Greenland.

of this area began after 14,000 years ago. Radiocarbon dates suggest that the first human occupants were seasonal visitors, arriving several thousand years after the initial spread of vegetation and animals. These pioneer hunting groups were followed a few hundred years later by more permanent residents. The colonizing groups came from refugia in the south, where Magdalenian groups had sheltered from the extreme cold of the Last Glacial Maximum.

A fascinating question pertains to this expansion: Why did human groups move into new, unknown, and often inhospitable regions? There is no clear answer, but it is the case that the human species has constantly been moving to new frontiers since *Homo ergaster* left Africa some 2 million years ago. The Upper Paleolithic represents an important phase in the geographic expansion of the human species. There were more sites in more places than ever before. Perhaps the only answer to the question of why is that human nature entails a curiosity, a need to explore.

It's difficult to imagine Paris as a cold, windswept plain with few trees, herds of reindeer, wild horses, and the occasional mammoth. Yet 12,000 years ago at the end of the Pleistocene, northern France was a generally barren, subarctic landscape, cold and dry, with open woodlands (Fig. 3.27). One of the coldest periods of the Pleistocene had ended, and the climate was gradually ameliorating. Permafrost had disappeared and low ground cover and shrubs expanded across the region. Large migratory herds of reindeer, wild horses, and several other species moved across the landscape. The Magdalenian reindeer hunters preyed on these herds.

In the vicinity of Paris, the Seine River and its tributaries in northern France were likely a significant barrier on a major route of reindeer migration, with large herds moving north every spring and back to the south in the autumn. There are a number of shallows and fords along the river that must have been important crossing points for these herds. The sandy banks and bars of the Seine at these fords and shallow crossings were the location of camps of Magdalenian reindeer hunters approximately 12,000 years ago.

More than ten such sites have been excavated in the last seventy years in the area around Paris. Deeply buried scatters of stone, bone, antler, hearthstones, and charcoal mark these ephemeral autumn encampments of reindeer hunters. Preservation is generally good because these sites were quickly covered by the annual flood of the river and deposition of a fresh layer of silt. The river floods must have sometimes been gentle, because in a few cases there is little disturbance of the materials. Some artifacts have been found standing upright, and crushed eggshells have been uncovered at some sites.

Fig. 3.27.
European vegetation 12,000–11,000 BP. Warming conditions—though with some cooling—allowed open woodland cover (green) to spread back over much of southern, central, and eastern Europe during this interval. Coniferous woodland predominated in eastern Europe (blue-green). Some closed forest vegetation formed in central Italy. In the northwest of Europe, tree cover (mainly birch and pine) remained relatively sparse, and steppe forest (pink) predominated. In parts of southern Europe, steppe vegetation (yellow) remained predominant.

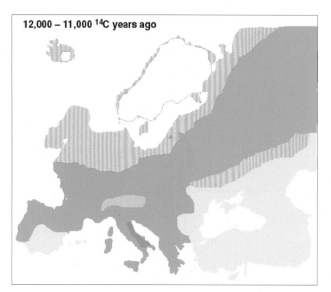

12,000 – 11,000 ¹⁴C years ago

The focus here is on a site called Pincevent. The archaeological layers at Pincevent are deeply buried, up to 1 m (3'3") below the modern ground surface. These layers are a mix of sand and silt that accumulated over the last 15,000 years or so along the Seine. The sandy layers built up during drier periods and were often wind-deposited. The silty layers were deposited by the spring flood waters of the river, which rose almost every year into historical times. At Pincevent, at least four thin layers with archaeological remains have been identified, extending over an area of 2 hectares (5 acres), more than a soccer field.

The project, originally under the direction of André Leroi-Gourhan and Michael Brezillon, began in 1964 as a rescue excavation. During the first twenty-five years, twenty large hearths and approximately a hundred tents or habitation structures were uncovered. The excavators intentionally exposed broad horizontal areas of the site, leaving features, artifacts, and bones in place. In this way, entire "living floors" could be seen and the pattern of discarded materials studied to determine where people slept, cooked, made tools, and so on. The excavators also made latex rubber casts of many areas, which were then painted to reconstruct and permanently preserve the distribution of the archaeological materials. They are remarkably realistic.

By clearing broad horizontal areas, the excavators were able to identify distinct concentrations or clusters of archaeological remains. Pieces of concentration contained 20,000–30,000 flint artifacts, animal bones and antler, and some blocks of stone, ochre, and charcoal (Fig. 3.28). Concentrations average 60–70 m² in size, about a quarter of a tennis court. These concentrations probably represent single tents or structures as the residence and focus of activity of a few hunters. The concentrations were very similar. The tent or structure has an oval outline, ca. 3 m (10 ft) in diameter, with a small, circular hearth, 50 cm (1½ ft) in diameter, at the entrance. The inside of the tent was usually stained with red ochre and covered with many small artifacts. The back part of the structure typically had a very low density of finds, suggesting this may have

Fig. 3.28. Concentration of flint, stones, bones, antler, red ochre and charcoal at Pincevent. This surface is a painted latex copy of the original excavated area at the site that now sits in a nearby museum. See Fig. 3.29 for a drawing of this concentration.

Fig. 3.29.
A tent circle and hearth at Pincevent with stone, splintered bone, and stone tools adjacent, larger bone fragments to the right, between the hearth and a dump of ash, fire-cracked rock and bones. The black hearth is approximately 75 cm in diameter.

Fig. 3.30.
Distribution of conjoined metacarpals in one zone of concentrations at Pincevent. The lighter and darker contours indicate density of artifacts. Red ovals are hearths. Connected dots are pieces of the same bone that have been fit back together.

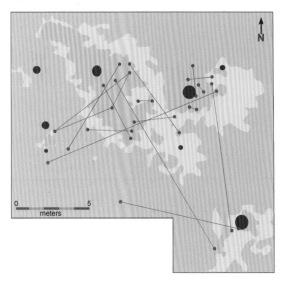

been the sleeping area. Stone and bones were scattered outside the front of the tent up to 7 m (almost 25 ft) from the entrance. It looks as if flint tools were prepared in the tent and the waste material was thrown outside.

At Pincevent, one of the most important excavated areas is in Layer IV. This area contains 9,400 kg (almost 10 tons) of flint artifacts, the skeletal remains of at least forty-three reindeer, fire-cracked rock, ochre, and several shallow pits and fireplaces. Red ochre stains are concentrated around three large fireplaces. The excavators suggest that activities were centered on three contemporary huts, each with an associated fireplace. The hut contained a central zone of actual living space and surrounding zones of domestic activities and refuse disposal. The intensity of activity decreased with distance from the hearths. Small piles of waste materials from stone tool manufacture lie on one side of the hearths, finished tools and red ochre on the other (Fig. 3.29).

Near one of the hearths is a large stone that was likely the seat of a flint worker. Most of the flint was available in the immediate area of the site. A few pieces, however, came from some distance, confirming the mobility of the hunters who had camped here. Reconstruction or refitting of the pieces removed from the flint nodules is a good indication of how tools were made. Moreover, pieces that are missing and not found at the site provide evidence of which tools were carried elsewhere. Finally, the scattered locations of pieces that fit together reveal how the tools and waste materials were moved about at the site.

The distribution of bones on the living floor is similar to that of the flint debris (Fig. 3.30). Larger bones were at the periphery; smaller pieces and fragments were found near the fireplaces. The bones from a meal were apparently tossed away from the hearth. Small fragments of antler were found near the hearths, but larger pieces were discarded at the edge of the activity zone. Making antler into tools was apparently done at this periphery. The lack of sweeping or cleaning of the living area suggests that the occupation at Pincevent was brief.

Analysis of the faunal remains was highly informative. Virtually all of the animal remains come from reindeer, with a very few horse, hare, and mammoth bones scattered in the deposits. The presence of specific bones and teeth from the reindeer skulls near the hearths suggests that the heads were cooked and eaten in the tents. The number of rib and sternum pieces was quite low compared to the number of reindeer identified at the site. These parts of the animal are known to have been smoked or dried for later use by historic Eskimo groups and perhaps the Magdalenians were doing the same thing.

Most of the reindeer at the site were killed and butchered during the late summer and fall. Several methods were used to determine the season of settlement. There were no fetal bones from pregnant reindeer among the animal remains, as would be expected if these animals were killed in the winter. There were no newborn calves among the bone evidence, so spring occupation is unlikely. Differences in the size of the reindeer at the site indicate that both males and females were present. The reindeer sexes do not spend the year together, except during the fall migration. Both male and female antlers at the site were attached to the skulls, not shed, thus delimiting a period between the end of May and October when both sexes are carrying their antlers. Finally, the sequence of tooth eruption in young animals at Pincevent demonstrates that these animals were most likely killed between September and the end of November. In sum, the evidence from the reindeer bones, antler, and teeth strongly argues for Magdalenian hunters at Pincevent between the end of summer and the beginning of winter.

One of the hallmarks of most hunter-gatherers is egalitarian behavior and food sharing among the members of the group. James Enloe argues that food sharing can be observed in the distribution of bones at Pincevent. He focuses on the hearths as the center of all families or units at the site. He then examines how an individual reindeer was cut up and distributed among the hearths by refitting the broken and split pieces of bone. The bone waste from the initial butchery of the animals following the slaughter is absent at Pincevent, so Enloe reasonably argues that the animals were killed and butchered into large pieces elsewhere, off the site.

Eskimo reindeer hunters in Alaska butcher a caribou (the North American version of the reindeer) into eight parts. The limbs are the favored parts because of the quantity and quality of meat. The distribution of limbs at Pincevent suggests that the best cuts of meat were shared between the hearths. Refitting pieces of the limb bones at Pincevent (including the metacarpals, part of the foreleg; Fig. 3.11) indicates that there were three donor hearths that shared meat with three receiver hearths. These receiver hearths may have belonged to less successful hunters, elderly individuals, or others who had less food. Food sharing is a very human behavior.

DOGGERLAND, NORTH SEA, 11,000 BC

Doggerland is the only place in this book without a country. It is the name given to a large portion of the floor of the North Sea that was dry land during the

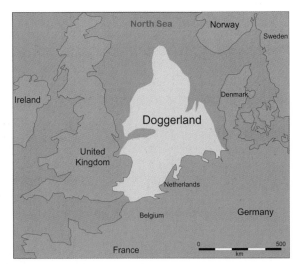

Fig. 3.31.
The outline of
northwestern Europe
during the Last Glacial
Maximum. Doggerland
is the area of the North
Sea floor that was dry
land during that period.

colder periods of the Pleistocene. The Dogger Banks, a shallow water area in the middle of the North Sea that today is a hazard point for fisherman, lent their name to Doggerland. During the LGM, with sea levels as much as 120 m (almost 400 ft) below present, this area would have been part of the European continent, connecting Britain to Belgium, the Netherlands, northern Germany, and Denmark (Fig. 3.31). The total area submerged by rising sea waters, as the temperatures warmed and the Pleistocene came to an end, was about the size of the state of California.

This area would simply have been an extension of the continent, a landmass with features similar to the rest of northwest Europe. Initially this would have been a zone of permafrost and tundra as the ice sheet retreated, but during the warming at the end of the Pleistocene forests of pine and birch, and eventually mixed oak forest, likely dominated this landscape.

It is important to remember that the ice sheets kept melting and sea level kept rising through the early Holocene, gradually drowning Doggerland. Britain was cut off from the continent around 6500 BC. The Dogger Banks, an upland region of Doggerland, would have been an island during this period, and it was eventually submerged after 5000 BC.

A major undersea event during this period may have had a substantial impact on Doggerland and its human and animal populations. Around 6200 BC there was a huge underwater landslide off the coast of Norway that triggered a massive tsunami or tidal wave. This tsunami, with waves estimated to have been 3–10 m (10–35 ft) high, would have had a powerful impact on coastlines throughout the North Sea region. This tsunami is even recorded in deposits along the east coast of Greenland, some 1,500 km (930 mi) to the west.

Doggerland, then, is a region that was home to human groups in the late Paleolithic and early Mesolithic of northwestern Europe. The human presence on Doggerland was dramatically documented in the 1930s when a fishing vessel dredged up a late Paleolithic barbed point made of antler from deep water in the North Sea. Heavy nets from these fishing boats drag along the sea floor and bring up a variety of items in addition to fish and shellfish. Since the 1930s a number of artifacts and animal remains (including mammoth and reindeer) from the Pleistocene and Holocene have been found (Fig. 3.32). Recently fragments of a Neanderthal skull were dredged up off the coast near Rotterdam in the Netherlands.

Doggerland was a place of human occupation and activity for some time. Late Paleolithic groups likely pursued reindeer herds in this large region. Mesolithic hunter-gatherers would have feasted from the forest and the sea in the rich habitat that this mix of forest, wetlands, and seacoasts would have supplied. At the same time, Doggerland is a lesson in global warming and

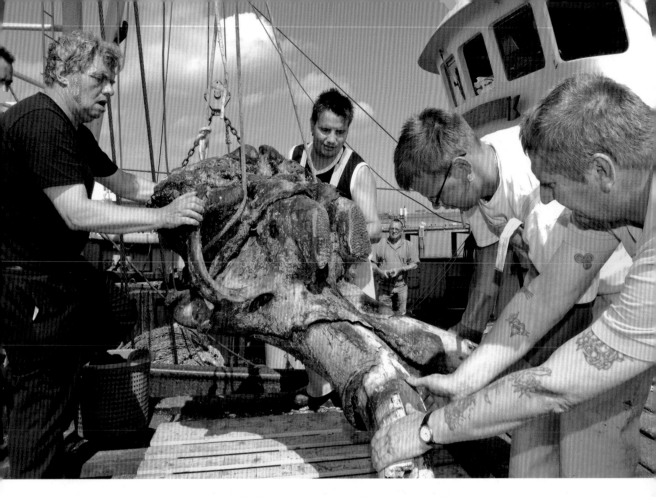

catastrophe. Warming at the end of the Pleistocene gradually inundated a huge part of the North Sea floor as sea levels rose, displacing a substantial Mesolithic population. In the middle of this process a major tsunami struck, probably catastrophically flooding large parts of the generally low, flat landscape and no doubt eradicating portions of those same populations before their abandonment of the area. Similar events take place today. The past repeats itself.

Fig. 3.32.
Part of a mammoth skull from the North Sea floor being moved ashore for analysis and curation in the Netherlands.

THE LAST HUNTERS

The last ten millennia in Europe witnessed enormous changes in the human condition, many times over what took place in the preceding million years. Europe 10,000 years ago was occupied by hunters who had survived the cold and ice of the Pleistocene and were adjusting to new conditions on a warmer, forested continent as the period came to an end. Europe entered the Holocene, our current geological epoch, and the warmer temperatures of an interglacial cycle in the Earth's oscillating climate. Temperatures for the last 10,000 years measured in the Greenland ice layers provide evidence of warmer temperatures with a gradual cooling trend toward the present (Fig. 3.33).

Changes were also taking place in the Near East, where experiments at controlling nature—domesticating plants and animals—would lead to a revolutionary new way of life. This village farming culture expanded quickly and reached the southeastern shores of Europe by 7000 BC, bringing crops and

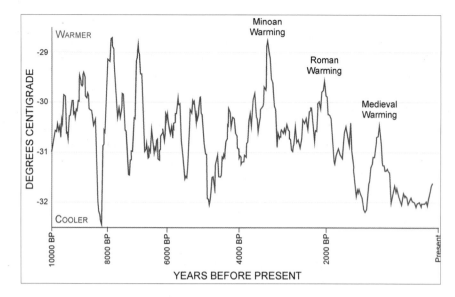

WARMER

Minoan
Warming

Roman
Warming

Medieval
Warming

COOLER

Fig. 3.33.
A plot of temperature recorded in oxygen isotopes in the Greenland ice core for the last 10,000 years.

herds, and new ideas and technologies. The Neolithic agricultural adaptation moved inexorably across the continent, reaching the northwestern corners of Europe by 4000 BC. Everything changed.

The term *Mesolithic* is used for the period between the end of the Pleistocene and the beginnings of agriculture. The end of the Pleistocene is conventionally set at 9000 BC. The end of the Mesolithic is marked by the introduction of agriculture, earlier in southeast Europe (7000 BC) and later in northwest Europe ca. 4000 BC. The Mesolithic was a time of innovation, interaction, and successful adaptations among these early postglacial foragers. Europe's last hunters thrived in rich new environments along the coasts and rivers of the continent.

Among the distinctive characteristics of this period are a broad diet of plants and animals and highly specialized technologies. Sophisticated equipment included the bow and arrow, domesticated dogs for hunting, water transport in the form of canoes and seagoing craft, a variety of fishing gear such as nets, hook and line, weirs, traps, and ground stone tools for woodworking and grinding. Pottery is used in later Mesolithic northern Europe. In addition, this area was the home of spectacular Mesolithic art in a variety of forms and media: carved amber figurines, engraved wooden objects, and numerous decorated bone, stone, and antler pieces.

Subsistence activities appear to have greatly intensified in the Mesolithic. Humans became more omnivorous; the number of species incorporated into the diet is significantly greater than in the Upper Paleolithic. New additions to the diet in the Holocene generally come from lower trophic levels in the food chain and require more complex procurement and processing techniques. Certain resources—particularly nuts, shellfish, and marine species—become more visible in the archaeological record. Of perhaps greatest importance is the increasing use of the resources of the sea.

Several sites document this Mesolithic period of the past. Franchthi Cave in the south of Greece contains a deep sequence of archaeological materials from the late Paleolithic through the Neolithic. The Mesolithic remains document a range of exceptional activities related to the use of the Mediterranean. In Portugal the site of Moita do Sebastião, an enormous shell midden, was filled with the refuse of a Mesolithic hunters' camp and many graves of their dead. From the Netherlands, the site of Polderweg is a sterling model of how archaeology should be done. The site was excavated in front of railroad construction and published within a few years of the end of the fieldwork. The investigations at Hardinxveld have completely rewritten the early prehistory of the Netherlands. Finally we turn to Denmark and the remarkable place known as Tybrind Vig, the Mesolithic under the sea.

FRANCHTHI CAVE, GREECE, 9000 BC

Franchthi Cave, in southern Greece, is remarkable for the very long sequence of human occupation that has been left in the cave over the last 20,000 years or more (Fig. 3.34). The stratigraphy in the lower layers belongs to the Upper Paleolithic, and the more recent levels contain deep layers from the Mesolithic and Neolithic periods. The cave has also been used in recent times by shepherds.

Franchthi is an exceptionally important archaeological site for a number of reasons. It contains evidence of very early seafaring, of deep sea fishing, of dietary changes over time, and some of the earliest evidence for the arrival of agriculture in Europe. Our focus here is on the Mesolithic levels at Franchthi, but at the same time it is possible to observe changes from the preceding Upper Paleolithic and to foreshadow the arrival of the Neolithic in Europe.

Fig. 3.34.
Franchthi Cave in the Peloponnese, Greece.

Thomas Jacobsen of the University of Indiana directed excavations at Franchthi Cave over eight field seasons between 1967 and 1979. An international team of scholars worked, and continues working, on publication of the vast and complex materials and data recovered from the site. The cave is huge, a horizontal cavern 150 m long, with good shelter from the elements. Massive rock falls sometime in the past opened two chimneys through the ceiling of the cave (Fig. 3.35).

The archaeologists dug several deep trenches in the cave, and a huge amount of earth was removed. The deepest trench went 11 m (36 ft) down through deposits dating from 20,000 to 8300 BC. Today, the cave lies along the Aegean coast. In the late Pleistocene and early Holocene, however, when sea levels were lower, a fairly level plain and several kilometers separated Franchthi from the sea.

The body of evidence from the Upper Paleolithic deposits generally falls within the range of what is known about other parts of the western Mediterranean at this time. What is astounding at Franchthi in this period is the presence of pieces of obsidian in the late Upper Paleolithic levels around 11,000 BC. Obsidian is a translucent, hard, black or dark green glass, produced during volcanic eruptions. Molten silica can flow out of a volcanic core and harden into this glassy, black rock which was highly sought by prehistoric makers of stone tools. Obsidian, like glass and flint, fractures easily and regularly, creating very sharp edges (Fig. 3.36). It is available from only a few sources, limited by proximity to volcanic terrain and chance formation of a silica flow.

Fig. 3.35.
A view from the chimney in the roof of Franchthi Cave, toward the excavated areas.

Most volcanic sources for obsidian are known because they are rare and the material is unusual. Moreover, the sources can be distinguished chemically by their elemental composition. It is possible to fingerprint specific flows of obsidian through minor differences in the chemistry of the material. In this way one can accurately determine where obsidian found in an archeological site has come from.

There are very few sources of obsidian in continental Europe. The Carpathian mountains have a few minor deposits, and more sources are known from several volcanic islands

Fig. 3.36.
Obsidian, a black volcanic glass used to produce extremely sharp stone tools. The flake is ca. 5 cm in diameter.

in the central Mediterranean and Aegean. The obsidian in the later Upper Paleolithic levels at Franchthi comes from the Aegean island of Melos. Melos lies in the Cycladic Islands; at the closest point it is 100 km (60 mi) from the Greek mainland to the north and 135 km (85 mi) from Franchthi to the west.

The presence of Melos obsidian at Franchthi proves beyond the shadow of a doubt that late Upper Paleolithic people were navigating the Mediterranean in watercraft. Either people from Franchthi went to Melos to get this stone or they were involved in an exchange network that moved the material to mainland communities around the end of the Pleistocene. We know nothing of the type of boat or raft in use at this time, but there is no question that people were crossing the waters between Melos and the mainland. The amount of obsidian from Melos increases in the Mesolithic and again in the Neolithic period at Franchthi.

The Upper Paleolithic occupation ended ca. 9000 BC, and the cave was apparently unoccupied for roughly 500 years until the arrival of early Mesolithic hunter-gatherers. The Mesolithic period at Franchthi was relatively brief, just 1,500 years, and has been divided into two phases on the basis of stratigraphy, radiocarbon dating, and changes in the artifacts and fauna. The Lower Mesolithic runs from 8500 to 8000 BC and the Upper Mesolithic from 8000 to 7000 BC.

The area around Franchthi at this time was covered with an open oak woodland, mixed with other trees and shrubs such as juniper, pistachio, wild pear, and almond. Franchthi was 2 km (1.2 mi) away from the sea during the Mesolithic, overlooking a grassy coastal plain. A river ran through the coastal plain; marshes, salt flats, and mud shoals at the river mouth probably created a rich habitat for marine resources.

The Lower Mesolithic inhabitants of Franchthi exploited a range of terrestrial and marine resources at the beginning of the Holocene. The animal bones document about 65–70 percent red deer, 25–30 percent wild boar; wild horse and wild goats have disappeared, and wild cattle were rare. In addition there are substantial numbers of hare and birds, as well as fox, probably taken for fur. A great increase in the amount of seeds and plant remains was observed. There were roughly 700 seeds from nineteen species of plants in the Upper Paleolithic, compared to almost 28,000 seeds from twenty-seven species in the Lower Mesolithic.

The plants identified in the Mesolithic sample were collected in the spring, summer, and autumn. Many of the edible species of seeds and nuts could have been stored through the winter, so the absence of identifiable winter plants does not rule out winter occupation of the cave. Further evidence came from the marine shellfish. Analysis of the season of death of these mollusks showed they were being collected year-round. In addition, oxygen-isotope analyses of shells from marine mollusks from the Lower Mesolithic suggest that two species, sea snails and lagoon cockles, were collected in all four seasons of the year.

The Lower Mesolithic level at Franchthi also contained the only burials at the site. Initially a single burial was encountered, a twenty-five-year-old male buried in a contracted position in a shallow pit near the mouth of the cave. The man had died from blows to the forehead, but he seems to have already been suffering severely from malaria. The first male burial lay on top of five inhumations and two cremations, plus the fragmentary remains of another two to five individuals. These bones represent persons of all age groups.

The Upper Mesolithic levels at the site indicate even greater reliance on the sea. The remains of tuna and the increased import of obsidian from Melos document use of the sea on the part of the residents of Franchthi. Bones from large tuna constitute about 30 percent of the animal remains in these layers. Measuring up to 2.5 m (8 ft) long and weighing up to 200 kg (450 lb), tuna can be caught only in the deeper waters of the Aegean and Mediterranean. Obsidian continued to be brought across the sea to Franchthi in the Upper Mesolithic, and grinding stones of the mineral andesite were imported from the Saronic Gulf to the north.

There appears to be a break of about 500 years in occupation of the cave between the latest Mesolithic and the earliest Neolithic. The Neolithic period, beginning around 7000 BC, saw substantial changes in subsistence practices at Franchthi Cave with the introduction of domesticated sheep and goats as well as wheat and domestic forms of barley and lentils. The first appearance of domesticates occurs in levels with few or no ceramics. The domesticated plants and animals appeared rather suddenly at Franchthi and must have come from Southwest Asia via the Aegean. Some 3,000 years after their first appearance in Greece, farming societies had replaced hunter-gatherers across most of the European continent. The introduction of agriculture and the spread of the Neolithic is the subject of the next chapter. Next we move to westernmost Europe, a distance of some 3,000 km (almost 2,000 mi), and the Mesolithic of Ireland.

MOUNT SANDEL, IRELAND, 7000 BC

Ireland is a remote and distinctive outpost of Western Europe, a landscape of rocky uplands and steeply cut valleys, mantled with dense vegetation that grows almost year-round in a climate tempered by the Gulf Stream. At the western margin of the continent, the island has long been isolated from Britain. This insularity has resulted in the absence of many common European mammals, such as wild cattle, red deer, and roe deer. Species present after the end of the

Pleistocene included wild boar, Irish hare, Irish stoat, pine marten, beaver, otter, and brown bear. Ireland has no Paleolithic and apparently was not inhabited until about 9,000 years ago, one of the last places in Europe to be colonized.

This insular character also lent a distinctive cast to the Irish Mesolithic that became more pronounced over time. Artifacts at the earliest sites already exhibit features that are distinct from those in neighboring Scotland, only a few kilometers across the straits of the North Channel. By the end of the Mesolithic, many stone tools are uniquely Irish in design, indicating an absence of contact with the rest of Britain and the continent. For example, there were no flint arrowheads in the later Mesolithic of Ireland, although these objects were common in England and on the continent during that period.

Radiocarbon dating for the earliest humans in Ireland yields an age of 7000 BC for the site of Mount Sandel in Northern Ireland, the oldest evidence for a human presence in Ireland. This name was originally given to an Iron Age hillfort atop a 30 m (100 ft) high bluff above the River Bann. Today, the small Mesolithic site east of the fort is of much greater importance in the prehistory of Western Europe.

The River Bann runs into the sea some 5 km (3 mi) north of the site. Today the tidal ebb and flow of the sea reaches this far inland and creates an estuary below Mount Sandel. This would not have been the case earlier in prehistory, when sea level was lower. The Bann would likely have been a series of rapids below Mount Sandel during the Mesolithic occupation, and the mouth of the estuary would have been a few kilometers further to the north.

The area was excavated in advance of housing construction in the 1970s by Peter Woodman from University College, Cork, to determine what, if any, remains from the Mesolithic period could be recovered. What started as a minor rescue operation quickly grew, however, into a major project, as the excavations required some forty weeks of work over five years of field seasons, opening an area of more than 1,000 m² (1200 yd²; Fig. 3.37).

Fig. 3.37.
Excavations at Mount Sandel, Ireland, revealed a large hut.

Fig. 3.38.
An artist's reconstruction of the huts at Mount Sandel.

The excavations exposed a series of large, circular structures, roughly 6 m (20 ft) in diameter (the size of a large room), each with a central fireplace and interior pits, rebuilt repeatedly on the same spot. The huts were marked by peripheral rows of postholes, many more than 20 cm (8 in) deep, set at an angle in the ground. A circle of saplings or branches had been shoved into the ground and then brought together in the center to form these structures (Fig. 3.38). The ground was cleared to the subsoil in the interior of the hut, and the sod may have been used to cover part of the outside of the hut. Estimates by Woodman suggest that eight to twelve people may have inhabited such a structure.

Stone artifacts in the huts included worn or broken and discarded arrow tips and drills, along with a substantial amount of waste material from making stone tools. Axes and scraping tools were discarded around the edges of the hut. A number of flint blades with traces of red ochre were also found here; their use is unknown. Evidence for tool manufacture was also found to the west outside the huts.

Fireplaces in the huts were used for cooking and heating. Their contents included stone artifacts, burned animal bones, and large quantities of hazelnut shells. Seeds of water lily and wild apple were also recovered in the excavations. Most of the identifiable bones from the site were those of wild boar, predominantly young animals; hare was present, but rare. Bird and fish bones were common. Duck, pigeon, dove, goshawk, and grouse were taken by the Mesolithic hunters of Mount Sandel. Sea bass, eel, and especially salmon were well represented in the bones that were preserved. Salmon bones, which usually do not survive, were found at the site because they had been charred in the hearths. Freshwater fish remains were not found.

The substantial nature of the residential structures, the numerous pits and rebuilding episodes, along with evidence from the diverse plant remains and animal bones all suggest that Mount Sandel may have been occupied

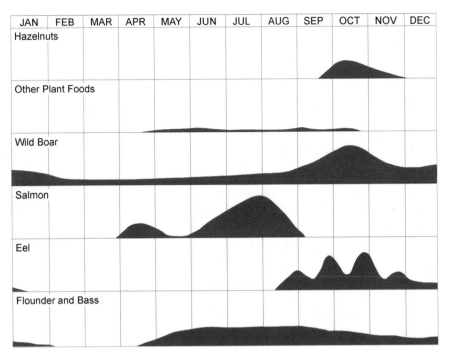

Fig. 3.39.
The time of year of residence at Mount Sandel. The season and relative abundance of various resources is shown by the graphs. This evidence indicated that the site was probably inhabited year-round.

year-round. Various foods would have been available throughout much of the year, enabling the occupants to remain at the site for most seasons (Fig. 3.39). Salmon were present in the streams and rivers during summer; eels ran downstream in autumn, when hazelnuts were ripe. Water lily seeds were collected in September. Most of the pig bones came from young animals killed during winter.

The evidence of year-round occupation at Mount Sandel, Franchthi, and other places highlights an important phenomenon in the Mesolithic: hunter-gatherers living on or near the coast were largely sedentary. This shift toward a less mobile way of life may be one of the characteristics of the early Postglacial period.

MOITA DO SEBASTIÃO, PORTUGAL, 6000 BC

The term *shell midden* is used in archaeology to describe heaps of shell, usually found near the sea coast, that represent accumulations of the remains of tens or hundreds of thousands of marine mollusks such as oyster, mussels, and other species. The term *midden* itself refers to a dump or deposit of trash. Shell middens often contain archaeological materials in the form of fireplaces, artifacts, bones, and occasionally human burials. They may have been residential or simply short-term campsites or feasting places for the consumption of shellfish and marine foods. These middens can be enormous, hundreds of meters long and several meters high. There was a famous series of prehistoric shell middens in San Francisco Bay more than two stories high. There are also examples of freshwater shell middens in some parts of the world. Shell middens are found on every continent except Antarctica, dating from a wide range of time periods.

Fig. 3.40.

The edge of the valley terrace seen from the Muge River area in Portugal. The site of Moita do Sebastião lies beneath the agricultural buildings on the terrace.

In Portugal, the term for such shell middens is *concheiro*. Massive prehistoric shell heaps were first reported in Portugal in 1863; the Portuguese middens date largely from the Mesolithic period. There are several groups of shell middens in the country; the best known, referred to as the Muge middens, are in the lower valley of the Tagus River (Fig. 3.40). The Muge is a small branch of the Tagus, which empties into the Atlantic at Lisbon, some 45 km (30 mi) to the southwest. During the Holocene there was an enormous tidal effect in the Tagus, reaching the Muge and creating a rich estuarine zone at the limits of the tidal flow with extensive brackish water mollusk beds. In addition, the waters of the river and the upland areas of the valley margin and nearby hills would have provided access to waterfowl, fish, and large game such as aurochs, red deer, and wild boar.

There are at least 13 separate middens in this area (Fig. 3.41). These sites lie within a few kilometers (1–2 mi) of one another, and early excavations uncovered large numbers of human skeletons buried in the middens. Carlos Ribeiro, digging at two of the sites in the 1880s, reported more than 170 burials. Radiocarbon dating of four human skeletons from the site of Moita do Sebastião has indicated an age of 6100–5900 BC, well within the Mesolithic period.

In 1952–1954 excavations were conducted at Moita do Sebastião to salvage the remaining parts of the midden that had been damaged in preparation for construction of farm buildings. The original shell midden, at least 2.5 m (8 ft) high and covering an area of some 300 m² (3,200 ft²), had been largely removed by the farm owner, leaving only about 20 cm (8 in) of the lowest levels of the midden. A number of pits and postholes were observed beneath this level. Excavations focused on these features, including an arrangement of postholes that suggested the presence of a structure almost 40 m² (430 ft²) in size.

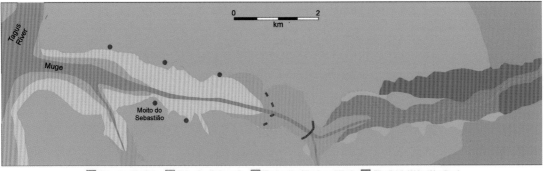

Estuarine Mudflats   Estuarine Saltmarsh   Freshwater Marsh and Pools   Floodplain/Alder Woodland
Terrace (> 7m)   Upland (<95 m)   Alluvial Fan   Active Alluvial Fan

Fig. 3.41.

The location of Moita do Sebastião and other shell middens (red dots) at the confluence of the Tagus and Muge rivers. The dotted red line is the limit of saltwater and the solid red line is the limit of tidal influence.

Subsistence information comes primarily from animal remains at the shell middens. A large range of animal species were present: red deer, aurochs, roe deer, wild boar, and an occasional horse. Smaller mammals included rabbit and hare, birds (both waterfowl and pigeon and partridge). The shell middens are made up of a range of marine invertebrates and lots of crab and shellfish, with a predominance of cockles in the Muge valley. Estuarine and open-sea fish and sea mammals such as otters were also found in the deposits. Plant remains at some of the sites include unidentified seeds and pine and pistachio nuts. Stable isotopes of carbon and nitrogen in Portuguese skeletal material indicate a mixed diet of marine and terrestrial components.

The burials at the site are one of the more interesting features at Moita do Sebastião. There are at least one hundred human burials reported from this midden, and probably more disappeared or were destroyed during the bulldozing of the mound.

Mary Jackes and Pedro Alvim have suggested that the burials were placed in a distinctive arrangement. The skeletons were found on the same surface and so are roughly contemporary, and in several pits over which small mounds may have been erected. They argue that the pits and graves were arranged in a horseshoe or U-shape, just beneath the high point of the shell midden that stood over the burials. There is also a possible U-shaped alignment of postholes inside the horseshoe of burial pits. If this scenario is correct, one of the original functions of the shell midden at Moita do Sebastião may have been for interring and commemorating the dead. Jackes and Alvim suggest that some of the animal remains may have come from feasting activities during funerary ceremonies.

The health of the buried individuals as seen in the skeletal remains was generally good. Evidence of injury in the skeletal remains from Moita do Sebastião includes a broken flint point in the heel of one male, and three examples of forearm fractures in two females and one individual of unknown sex. It is difficult to determine if these injuries are the result of accident, domestic violence, or intergroup conflict. The rather low incidence of traumatic injury observed in the skeletal remains as a whole suggests that violence was not a major aspect of life or death. One of the adult males apparently underwent cranial surgery, or trephination. A small hole was drilled in the top of his skull, some 10 mm (less than ½ in) deep, perhaps as a medical procedure.

POLDERWEG, NETHERLANDS, 5500 BC

The explosive growth of infrastructure in the last twenty-five years—related both to the success of the European Union and the expansion of the global economy—has meant a multitude of new archaeological excavations. Most of the countries in Europe have legislation requiring developer-funded archaeological investigations in advance of construction. A good guess would be that in the last twenty-five years these activities have at least doubled the amount of material and information we have about the prehistory of Europe. Hundreds of new sites have been discovered and excavated. Thousands of human remains have been recovered. Hundreds of thousands of artifacts and other archaeological materials have been removed from the ground.

Massive construction projects and the rise of developer-funded rescue archeology in Europe have completely changed how archaeology is being done. No longer a shoestring enterprise, large rescue projects spend millions of euros. The funds provide not only for excavations but also salaries, analyses, and publication. The scale of these projects has also undergone a revolution. Small areas of a few tens of square meters were the norm for Mesolithic fieldwork until the advent of developer-funded investigations. Now large-scale, horizontal excavations can expose complete areas of settlement and allow archaeologists to see the complexity of human occupations in a single view.

Fig. 3.42.
The Rhine delta region in the southern Netherlands with the new rail line to the German border. The location of Polderweg is shown.

The Netherlands is one of the countries where development has been fast-paced and construction of new roads, railroads, sewage treatment facilities, industry, and housing has boomed. In the late 1980s a new freight railroad was planned, running east from the enormous Europort harbor near Rotterdam to the German border. This rail corridor went through the middle of the Rhine River valley in this part of the Netherlands, an area rich in archaeological sites (Fig. 3.42). Enormous amounts of money were provided by the railroad

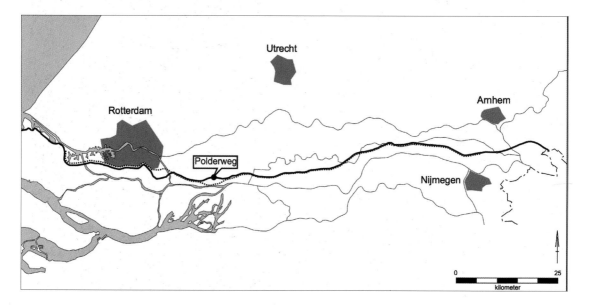

to investigate these sites. Projects on a scale unimaginable twenty years earlier were scattered across the landscape in advance of construction.

In this case, the commercial archaeological unit at the University of Leiden won the contract to conduct studies of two late Mesolithic and early Neolithic sites that would be destroyed by the rail line. The project was directed by Leendert Louwe Kooijmans. One of the sites was at a place called Hardinxveld-Giessendam Polderweg (Polderweg for short). Radiocarbon dates place the site between 5500 and 5000 BC, firmly in the late Mesolithic period in the Netherlands. Farming arrives in the southeastern Netherlands ca. 5250 BC.

The site is in one of the many reclaimed areas in the Netherlands where the Dutch have built dikes and pumped out the sea to create new land. The Polderweg site is situated on an old river dune, 5 m below modern sea level. The top surface of the dune measured ca. 80 m (260 ft) by 50 m (165 ft), or 4000 m² (43,000 ft²), half a soccer field. During the late Mesolithic the water level in the extensive swamps of the Rhine was several meters below the dune tops. At that time, the dune tops would have been virtually the only dry land in a large region of river, streams and reed marsh. Today the site is buried beneath several meters of more recent sediments.

These sites were discovered in 1994 by archaeologists boring deep holes into the earth in a systematic grid along the planned route for the railway. Excavation of part of the southern slope of the dune at Polderweg took place in 1997–98. A 20 m (65 ft) deep cofferdam was put in place and water was pumped out from an area of 30 m (100 ft) by 18.5 m (60 ft) for the excavations. The entire

Fig. 3.43.
Excavations inside the coffer dam at Polderweg. The horizontal steel pipes are support beams for the coffer dam. Excavations inside the coffer dam took place under a temporary shelter for protection against the wind and weather.

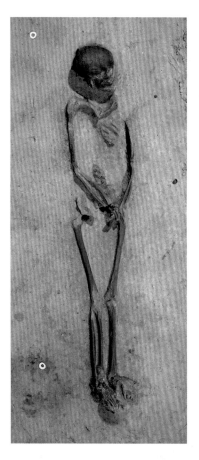

Fig. 3.44.
Burial of a young
female on the dune top
at Polderweg.

area was roofed and furnished with pumps for keeping the water out, and a gantry for lifting heavy materials (Fig. 3.43). All the sediments from the cultural layers were washed through screens with water to increase the recovery rate and reveal small objects. The excavation was placed on the side of the river dune in order to be able to excavate both the top surface and the lower slopes of the dune. The maximum depth of the excavations was 7 m (23 ft) below ground level.

Four stratigraphic phases were distinguished in the deposits. The most important is Phase 1, dated between 5430 and 5350 BC. Most of the discussion that follows involves the discoveries, analyses, and interpretation from this period, perhaps four to six generations of human life.

There were two major areas of archaeological remains, a residential area on top of the dune and refuse deposits in the reeds and water at the base of the dune. The sandy top of the dune retained the traces of a number of structures and other features. Pieces of charcoal from fires were scattered across the dune, perhaps more concentrated in the oval pits. For the most part, artifacts made of stone were small and few in number. The excavation exposed large oval pits—possible house structures, round pits interpreted as hearths, and postholes. The four large, circular or oval pits exposed on the top of the dune in Phase 1 at Polderweg ranged in size from 3 by 3 m to 4 by 6 m (10 by 10 ft to 13 by 20 ft). They are interpreted to be the remains of sunken floor huts or shelters.

Two burials were uncovered in the excavation, one intact and one badly disturbed (Fig. 3.44). In addition, there were eighty fragments of scattered human bone in the deposits at the site, representing at least ten individuals. An isolated human collar bone was found with repeated identical cut marks, caused by a sharp stone tool. These cutmarks were identified as perimortem, inflicted at or around the time of death. Carbon and nitrogen isotopes from the human bones point to a predominance of terrestrial and freshwater foods in the diet. There were also three dog burials.

The wetland deposits surrounding the dune contained abundant, well-preserved ecological, economic, and artifactual information, as the occupants had used this zone as a rubbish dump. Here larger objects, waste bone, wood, broken equipment, and paddles and possible pieces of dugout canoes were found.

Analysis of the various materials recovered in the excavations has generated a wealth of detail about the activities at the site, the season of occupation, the diet of the inhabitants, and other information. Major categories of finds include stone tools, animal bones, and wooden artifacts. In addition, during the last phase of settlement at Polderweg fragments of simple, coiled pottery vessels with a pointed base began to appear in small numbers. This ceramic tradition is Mesolithic and arrived before domesticated plants and animals and other Neolithic artifacts.

The stone artifacts are of particular interest because there is no natural stone in this part of the Rhine River delta. All stone material had to be carried into the site. Most of the flint used at the site came from the gravels of the Meuse River, 75 km to the east. There are also a few pieces of quartzite from central Belgium, perhaps 100 km (60 mi) to the south. A large block of distinctive flint came from the Limburg region of the southern Netherlands, also 100 km distant. Finally, there are two lumps of pyrite (an iron mineral) almost certainly available only in the Ardennes region of Belgium, 200 km (120 mi) to the southeast, and at Boulogne-sur-Mer on the Channel coast equally far to the southwest. Clearly the movement of raw materials, and human interaction, covered long distances in this period.

The primary subsistence activities in all phases involved hunting wild boar and red deer, trapping beaver and otter, fishing, and fowling. The animal remains include bone, antler, and teeth from a variety of species. There seems to have been a special focus on trapping fur-bearing animals such as beaver and otter, and fishing for pike. The excavator estimated that there must have been around 10 million fish bones from Polderweg Phase 1, reflecting the importance of fish in the diet. Pike accounted for 50 percent of the fish remains, with the remainder largely from members of the Cyprinidae family (roach, bream, and tench). Pike spawn in shallow water in the winter and are more easily taken at that time of year.

Almost 650 bird bones were identified from Phase 1 at Polderweg. The presence of these species provides information on the ecological context of the site at the time of occupation. Some 90 percent of the identified bones come from wetland dwellers, mainly ducks, geese, and swans—red-throated diver, cormorant, little grebe, grey heron, rail, and reed bunting. Their normal habitat is open, moving water bordered by a lush vegetation of reeds. Ducks seem to have been the primary target of the hunters. The other 10 percent are characteristic of a wooded environment: sparrowhawk, buzzard, eagle, owl, woodpecker, and woodcock.

Almost all of the wetland species either are winter visitors or are present in much higher numbers during the colder months. The bird remains document occupation from November to March, with an emphasis from December to February. Summer species are notably absent. This has led to the unexpected conclusion that the Late Mesolithic occupants of the site chose to locate their winter residence in the wetlands, perhaps to take advantage of the migratory waterfowl present at that time.

The animal bones and other products are not just sources of food; these are also raw materials for production of tools, weapons, jewelry, and other items. Boars' tusks were made into chisels. Heavy red deer antler was used for axes and adzes (Fig. 3.45). Bone was used for many types of artifacts, among them heavy adzes and finer awls and gouges.

There were important plant foods in evidence at Polderweg: hazel nuts, water chestnut, tubers, and crab apple. The first two can be collected in the autumn, while tubers are best collected from fall to early spring. Crab apple likely did not grow at the site and was probably transported to the settlement, perhaps in a dried state. The charcoal evidence likely reflects wood collected for fuel and is dominated by alder, oak, ash, and wild apple (not crab apple).

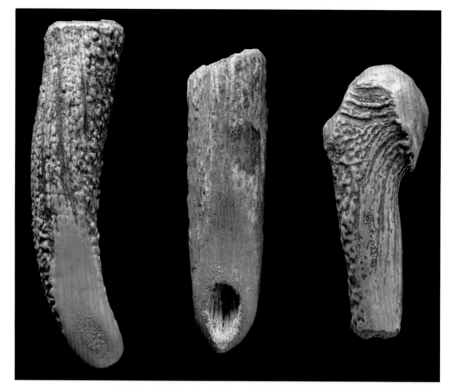

Fig. 3.45.
Antler tools from
Polderweg: chisel, awl,
and hammer. The chisel
is ca. 15 cm in length.

The wood preservation at Polderweg is exceptional and offers some of the first examples of such artifacts and equipment from the Mesolithic in the Netherlands: posts, fragments of a bow, an axe haft, paddles, digging sticks, skewers, planks, possible spear points, fragments of canoes, and unidentified "round" wood. "Round" wood refers to pointed pieces other than posts. Intentional selection of different species for specific kinds of wooden artifacts indicates a thorough awareness of the properties of these various trees.

The river dunes of the Rhine delta would have been small wooded islands in the midst of a large marshland during the Mesolithic in the Netherlands. The site of Polderweg is probably typical for human settlement in this area. The excavator suggests that the population of the dune in Phase 1 might have been twenty-five to fifty people in ten households. The burials of dogs and people, including women and children, the size of the site, and the large amount and wide variety of flint, bone, and antler artifacts indicate this was a substantial residential settlement for at least part of the year.

Several lines of evidence—migratory waterfowl, the emphasis on pike—indicate that this place was largely for winter residence. Trapping beaver and otter for fur may have been one of the primary activities taking place from this location. Subsistence seems to have focused on wild boar and fish. Other animals are represented, but only in smaller numbers. The artifacts of stone, bone, antler, and wood are also typical of the Mesolithic; introduction of pottery during the last phase of occupation at Polderweg is not. Ceramics presage the arrival of the Neolithic, bringing dramatic change across all of Europe. More about Mesolithic pottery at the next site of Tybrind Vig.

TYBRIND VIG, DENMARK, 5000 BC

One of the most important Stone Age sites in Europe lies beneath 3 m (10 ft) of water between the peninsula of Jutland and the island of Funen in Denmark. Sports divers have been finding and recording submerged archaeological sites and historical wrecks off the coasts of Denmark for decades. Archaeological sites from the Mesolithic period and even fossil landscapes with standing tree trunks from that period remain largely intact in places on the Danish sea floor.

Tybrind Vig was discovered by divers in 1972. Because of the large amount of material that was found, they contacted Søren H. Andersen, a professional archaeologist to assist them. Excavations were begun in 1978. The group of divers raised the funding to cover costs and spent a month of their vacation time, for ten years every summer, diving and digging at Tybrind Vig.

Denmark sits on a geological tilt line; the northeastern half of the country is rising up and the southwestern half is sinking. Two processes operate; to the north the rebound of the earth's crust in response to the disappearance of the weight of continental ice at the end of the last glaciation continues, and to the south a large salt dome centered under the Netherlands is gradually lowering the land surface. Sites from the later Mesolithic period in southwestern Denmark are drowned beneath the waves.

Excavations beneath the sea were not easy (Fig. 3.46). New techniques had to be developed to replicate dry-land methods of careful recording. The divers worked in one-meter units and eventually excavated about 180 m² (almost 2,000 ft²). They recorded the precise location of important finds, and all the

Fig. 3.46.
A diver brings a humanly worked antler from a red deer (North American elk) from a submerged Mesolithic site in Denmark.

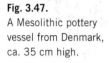
Fig. 3.47.
A Mesolithic pottery
vessel from Denmark,
ca. 35 cm high.

sediments were sieved to look for small pieces that could be easily missed.

Tybrind Vig is a wonderfully informative place to learn about the Mesolithic of Northern Europe. The finds are remarkable because of both the quantity and the extraordinary conditions of preservation. It seems there is a little bit more of everything from Tybrind Vig.

The settlement was used between 5000 and 4000 BC. The archaeological deposits represent only a part of the former human settlement; the actual dry land occupation with fireplaces and activity areas was destroyed by wave erosion millennia ago. However, because the settlement was directly at the seashore, artifacts and waste material were also dumped or lost in the water in what are called refuse deposits. These remains today are found in waterlogged, oxygen-free, organic sediments that accumulated to a meter or more in depth during the period of human occupation. Tybrind Vig has some of the best conditions for preservation of organic materials such as wood, bark, fibers, and bast anywhere in the world.

It is important to remember that almost everything found at the site was originally lost, tossed, or intentionally deposited in the water. And it has remained there ever since. Most of the remains are connected in one way or another with getting food: equipment for hunting and fishing, travel and transportation, the animals that were prey, and the plants that provided nourishment and raw materials.

The artifacts from the site document a simple, functional technology designed for efficiency. A complete wooden bow and several fragments were found, made of elm. The complete bow is 3 cm in diameter at its midpoint and tapers to a narrow rounded tip at each end. The total length is 1.66 m (5'6"), the average height of a man in Mesolithic Denmark. Stone tools flaked from flint are abundant and include large numbers of arrow points, two kinds of axes, and some specialized scraping and cutting tools. Small groundstone axes were also made by these people.

Pottery was used in the northern areas of Europe during the late Mesolithic (Fig. 3.47) and was noted also at the site of Polderweg. Pottery is normally thought to be a product of Neolithic peoples, characteristic of a village way of life. Although the inhabitants of Tybrind Vig were typical hunter-gatherers, they made distinctive pointed-base pottery vessels in several sizes for cooking and storage. This ceramic technology probably came from the east, spreading from points of origin in China and Mongolia, and arriving in Scandinavia shortly after 5000 BC. In addition to the containers, they also made small, shallow oval bowls of fired clay that served as lamps, burning fat or oil with a wick.

Numerous worked wooden stakes were uncovered in the excavations. These pieces, of varying length and diameter, were found both standing vertically and lying horizontally in the deposits. The stakes were usually part of the fishing fences and weirs in the sea in front of the site—barricades that guided fish and eels into large wicker traps. These stakes were made of hazel wood and had been worked, some just cut away from the tree and others sharpened to a point. The wooden stakes varied in age from five to twelve years at the time of cutting. Many of them were long and straight (more than 2 m, ca. 7 ft, in length), typical of coppiced trees.

Coppicing is an ancient form of woodland management that involves pruning the branches of trees so they can regrow from shoots. Hazel does not naturally grow in long, straight sections unless coppiced. The coppiced shoots of the hazel tree will grow straight as long as there is adequate space and light.

Other plant materials were carefully selected for specific properties. Bows were made of elm, the dugout canoes were lime, the wooden paddles were ash. Part of a fish trap woven of alder and willow twigs was also found. Spear fishing is documented by a number of finely worked leister prongs of the wood of the thorn tree attached to a shaft of hazel with strands of fiber, probably from the nettle plant. The arrangement of these pieces was made clear by the find of an intact leister head (Fig. 3.48).

Water transport is well documented by three dugout canoes from Tybrind Vig, one complete and two partial examples. The complete canoe was carved from the trunk of a lime tree and is 9.5 m (31 ft) in length. The cavity in the canoe is 50–65 cm (1.6–2.1 ft) wide and about 30 cm (12 in) in depth. The boat has a stern board fitted into place to close off the end. There was a place near the stern, covered by a thin layer of clay, 65 by 30 cm (25 by 12 in) in size—a large placemat, on the floor of the canoe. The clay had been heated to hardness, and part of the area beneath the clay layer was charred. This was likely an area for carrying coals or embers for warmth, or perhaps for quickly starting a fire at a new location. This boat could have carried six to eight individuals and their equipment. The canoe had been deliberately submerged and weighted down with a large stone, perhaps to keep the wood from drying out and decaying.

In addition to the dugouts, at least fourteen wooden paddles were found, most with a shaft of more than 1 m (3'3") and a heart-shaped blade around 30 cm (12") in diameter. After excavation, these paddles were normally cleaned by brushing, but one day a very careful washing of the blade of one of the paddles revealed a distinct design on the surface (Fig. 3.49). A new form of Mesolithic decoration was revealed. Eventually four decorated blades were identified.

Other plants with other purposes included a kind of mushroom or fungus that when dried is excellent tinder for starting fires. Bark was also used, perhaps for flooring or construction. Bast fibers from lime bark and nettles, and other plants and trees, were used for string and rope. The line preserved on one of

Fig. 3.48.
A reconstructed fishing leister from Tybrind Vig, complete except for the shaft, ca. 40 cm in length.

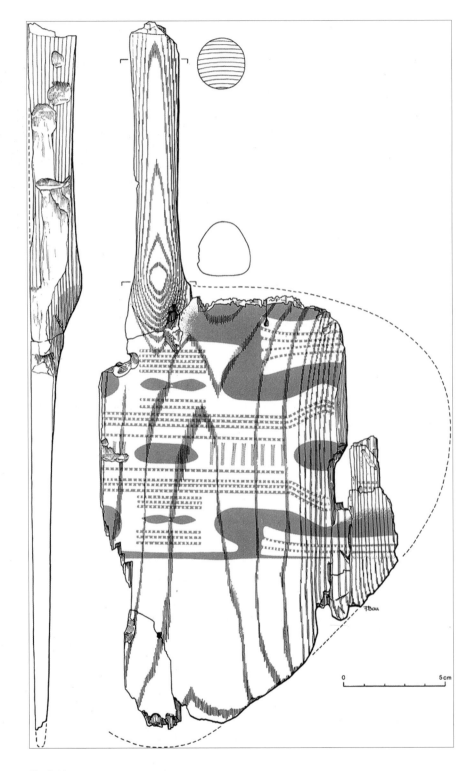

Fig. 3.49.
Decorated paddle blade from Tybrind Vig.

the bone fishhooks from Tybrind is made of plant fibers (Fig. 3.50). Spun plant fibers also used to make nets or textiles, with a technique known as needle netting. Several pieces were found that are among the oldest examples of textiles known anywhere in the world.

Plant remains were plentiful at the site. There is very little evidence for consumption of vegetables and other plant foods in the Paleolithic period. The evidence from Tybrind Vig suggests that there were at least five categories in the local diet: roots, nuts, grains, wild berries and other fruits, and green vegetables. Direct evidence for starchy tubers comes from the sea beet and the common reed. Hazel nutshells were abundant in the deposits at Tybrind, and charred acorn husks suggest this nut was consumed as well. Nuts could be stored for long periods (acorns have to be leached to remove tannic acids before eating). Seeds were found from plants such as nettle and goosefoot, and from a variety of fruits, including raspberries, wild strawberries, dewberries, rowan berries, and rosehips. Rosehips are rich in vitamins. Pips from crabapples and seeds from berries of dogwood and hawthorn were also found in the layers.

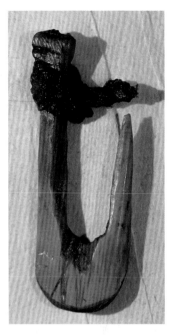

Fig. 3.50.
A bone fishhook from Tybrind Vig with part of the line still attached; height 3 cm.

The animal bones at the site revealed a mixed diet of seafood and forest animals. The primary game animals were red deer, roe deer, and wild boar. Evidence from tooth eruption and wear from the deer jaws indicates that these animals were hunted year-round from the site. Other species included a few examples of aurochs (wild cattle) and a wild horse. Dogs were common, and their bones were found among the refuse.

A variety of marine foods were consumed, ranging from oysters to seals, dolphins, and small whales, but it is fish—particularly cod, spurdog, and eel—that were of primary importance in the diet. Sixteen species of fish were found at the site; twelve species of birds including ducks and geese were counted among the animal remains.

Studies of the isotopic composition of human skeletons from Mesolithic burials indicate that seafood played a predominant role in the diet. More evidence of consumption of fish came from the pottery. Because of the quality of preservation at this underwater site, traces and residues from heating and cooking have been preserved on some of the pots. Soot or burn marks on the outside of a vessel are one indication of use for cooking. Other residues, known as food crusts, are the result of the burning and charring of food in and on the vessel. On several of the pots from Tybrind there were heavy charred remains with visible traces of fish scales and small bones of cod. Under a microscope thin, grasslike stalks of plants can also be seen.

Animal bones were also used to make certain equipment. Small fishhooks were made from the rib bone of red deer and sharp fishing spear tips of bone were made of deer bone. Antlers were used for a variety of artifacts, including heavy axes; two of these antler axes had been polished and decorated with a pattern of fine geometric lines. Tooth pendants were worn as jewelry and ornaments on clothing in the Mesolithic. Canine teeth from a variety of species were perforated near the end of the root and worn as pendants or sewn onto clothing.

Some animals were apparently hunted for fur rather than food. There were a large number of intact marten skeletons with skinning marks from a stone knife. Other fur-bearing species included wild cat, fox, otter, badger, and polecat. Fatal fractures on the rear of the skull represent blows from either the trapper or the traps that captured these animals. Clearly the furs of these animals were of importance, perhaps for exchange as well as domestic use.

The use of the site appears to have been almost continuous during the fifth millennium BC. Several graves were present at Tybrind Vig. Scattered human bones and fragments from at least four persons were found in the excavations. One largely complete grave was uncovered containing the skeletons of a young girl, twelve or thirteen years of age, along with a young baby, and a second grave that probably held two adults.

VEDBÆK, DENMARK, 5000 BC

Two hundred kilometers to the east of Tybrind Vig and just north of the city of Copenhagen, more Mesolithic graves were found near the town of Vedbæk, dated to around 5000 BC. In 1975, a graveyard was discovered here during construction of a new school (Fig. 3.51). Of the twenty-two individuals who

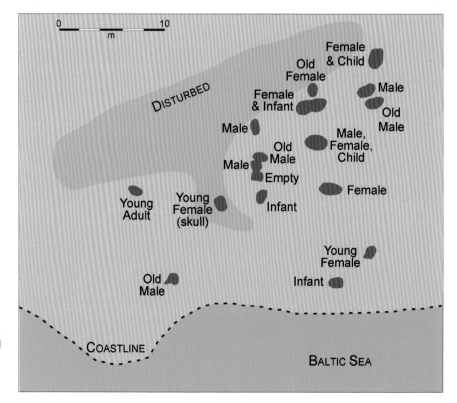

Fig. 3.51.
The cemetery at Vedbæk, Denmark. The gray area was disturbed by construction activities before the archaeologists arrived.

were buried in the cemetery, four were newborns, and eight more died before reaching the age of twenty. There were nine men, five of whom were over fifty; of the eight women, two died before age twenty, and three lived to be over forty. Two women died in childbirth and were buried with their newborns beside them.

Powdered red ochre was found in many of the graves. Ochre was also used in the Upper Paleolithic for cave paintings and in some burials; it occurs naturally in a yellow or light brown form in many parts of the world and turns darker red when heated. Red-deer antlers were placed with elderly individuals. Males were buried with flint knives, and females were often interred with jewelry made of shell or animal teeth. In one grave, a newborn infant was found buried with a flint knife on the wing of a swan next to his mother (Fig. 3.52). The mother's head had been placed on a cushion of material, perhaps an animal skin, that was elaborately decorated with ornaments of snail shells and deer teeth. Similar materials were found around her waist, suggesting a skirt or clothing of some kind.

Fig. 3.52.
The grave of a mother and newborn child from the cemetery at Vedbæk. The baby was buried on the wing of a swan.

The cemetery also contained rather dramatic evidence for conflict among the people of northern Europe at that time. Almost half of the individuals in the cemetery show some signs of traumatic injury. Simultaneous burial of three individuals in a single grave—an adult male with a lethal bone point in his throat, an adult female, and a child—suggests both the violent death of all three and the existence of the nuclear family. The incidence of trauma and injury recorded in human bones from the Mesolithic is remarkably high.

Intentional burial of the dead has been practiced by humans since the time of the Neanderthal. What seems new in the Mesolithic is the presence of cemeteries, groups of graves, which must reflect both longer-term residence and growing group identity. In small groups of fifty people or so, only one or two deaths per year would be expected. Cemeteries with tens of individuals imply either much larger group size or more likely the extended use of place to bury relatives in familiar ground.

ROCK ART: VINGEN, NORWAY, 5000 BC

Rock art is the oldest surviving form of human expression, probably dating as far back as 40,000 years ago. Rock art is known from every continent except Antarctica and from most of the periods of prehistory. It is almost ubiquitous in human societies where rock is part of the landscape. This art falls into two major categories, depending on how it is made: petroglyphs are carved into rock, and pictographs are painted on the rock.

Both types have a long history. There are cave paintings and engravings from the late Paleolithic, as we have seen at Chauvet and Grande Grotte at Arcy-Sur-Cury. There are also large concentrations of Upper Paleolithic petroglyphs, in the Coa Valley in Portugal for example. There are Mesolithic petroglyphs in various parts of Europe, perhaps best documented in Norway. There are a multitude of localities from the Neolithic, Bronze Age, and into the Iron Age. In this volume I discuss three groups of rock art from the Mesolithic in Norway, the Neolithic in Spain, and the Bronze Age in Sweden at the end of each of these chapters. We begin with Mesolithic Norway.

One of the problems with studying rock art is the difficulty of dating the depictions. In Norway, dating is based on a process called shoreline displacement. The method is possible because the landmass of Norway is gradually getting higher as the land rises from the sea. The land is rising, or rebounding as geologists say, from removal of the enormous weight of glacial ice that sat on it. Norway was at the center of continental glaciation during the Pleistocene period, and the ice sheet there was several kilometers thick. Now the land that was pressed down by such weight is slowly returning to its former elevation. The rate of rebound over time has been determined for various parts of Norway, and old coastlines high in the mountains today can be dated.

The second aspect of dating by shoreline displacement concerns human settlement and placement of rock art. Most of the human activity in prehistoric Norway was along the coast: settlement, fishing, placing petroglyphs. Because the rebound of the land, and the rise of the coast, goes on at a relatively constant rate, and because the coast from the end of the Pleistocene is now several hundred meters above modern sea level in Norway, archaeological sites at different elevations can be dated within a few hundred years. In the city of Oslo, for example, Mesolithic rock art dating to ca. 5000 BC can be found almost 60 m above sea level. At the site of Alta in northern Norway, a detailed chronology of the changes in rock art over time can be constructed because of well-documented shoreline displacement (Fig. 3.53).

Rock art is found in many areas of the Norwegian coast. One of the richest and most spectacular sites is a place called Vingen, north of Bergen, along the west coast. Vingen lies in a fabulous fjord setting, with cliffs rising from the sea, high peaks everywhere, white water falling down the mountainsides, the deep blue sea, and the bright blue sky. Yet the rock art itself is the highlight.

There are petroglyphs on virtually every flat rock surface at the site (Fig. 3.54). The number of images on a single surface varies from one to 200. Geometrically carved animals cavort on large rocks scattered across a level terrace along the shore of the fjord. The dominant motif is the red deer, with a few moose and reindeer. There are also wolves or dogs, whales and porpoises, birds, and a few snakes. Human figures constitute about 3 percent of the depictions. The rock art at Vingen cannot be dated by shoreline displacement, but radiocarbon dates from small huts around the rocks point to a time between 5000 and 4000 BC for creation of this art. The people of Vingen were hunter-gatherers of the Mesolithic.

Fig. 3.53.
Rock art from the site of Alta in northern Norway, dated by shoreline displacement. The depiction of various motifs changes over time.

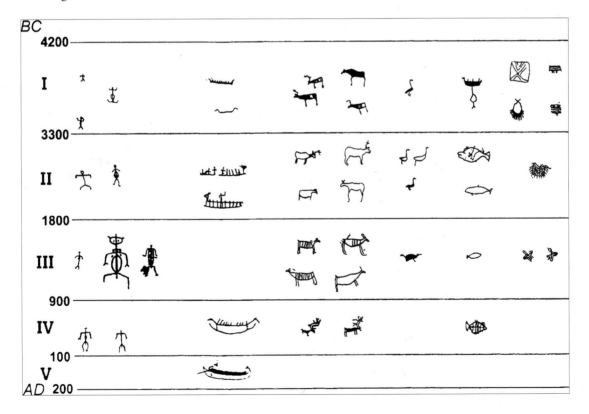

Fig. 3.54.
Vingen, Norway, a treasury of Stone Age rock carvings. In this photo there are several petroglyphs on the large rock to the right. The petroglyphs have been filled with red pigment in recent years to make them more visible. There are hundreds of petroglyphs at Vingen.

SOME REFLECTIONS

The arrival of *Homo sapiens* in Europe is a fascinating period for many, many reasons. So much happens, so much changes, it is hard to know where to begin a discussion. Groups of anatomically modern humans expanded from an origin in East Africa ca. 200,000 years ago and eventually crafted an essentially new human culture. The Upper Paleolithic in Europe is characterized by a variety of innovations that developed over the last 30,000 years or so of the Pleistocene, following the arrival of this new human species.

The Upper Paleolithic was the culmination of many long trends—in biology and culture, in language and communication, in ritual and ideology, in social organization, in art and design, in settlement and technology—that had begun several million years earlier. Evolution brought humanity to our modern form, *Homo sapiens.* New continents were explored; Australia, North America, and South America were colonized.

More kinds of implements were made from a wider variety of materials than ever before. Bows, boats, buttons, fish hooks, lamps, nets, spearthrowers, and many other items were produced for the first time during this period. Fine bone needles with small eyes document the manufacture of sewn clothing and other equipment from animal skins. The dog was domesticated, probably as a faithful hunting companion and occasional source of food.

Sites from the Upper Paleolithic were larger and more common than those from previous periods. From almost any perspective, this period of the Upper Paleolithic represents a dramatic change in human behavior, almost certainly associated with changes in the organization of the brain or the use of language, or both. Essentially modern behavior appeared following this transformation; a rapid change from archaic to modern, from the past to the present, had begun.

Several categories of artifacts—buttons, gaming pieces, pendants, necklaces, and the like—marked a new concern with personal appearance, an expression of self. It seems that a number of very human traits (identity, ego, perhaps even vanity) are emerging at this time. Figurines, cave paintings, and engravings reflect the creative explosion that characterized Upper Paleolithic achievement, as awareness of art and design erupted in the human consciousness. More generally, there is an aesthetic embellishment of portable, everyday objects. There is awareness of time in the archaeological remains from the Upper Paleolithic. Finally, the beginnings of counting systems and a calendar of sorts, or at least a recording of the phases of the moon, appeared at this time, as seen for example in the bone plaque from the site of Abri Blanchard.

A really intriguing question concerns when society, not just individuals, became human—the transformation from social animals to human society. The term *gatherings*, coined by Clive Gamble, might perhaps provide a semantic concept for the concentrations of remains—the archaeological sites—left behind by groups of early humans in this murky period.

When did we change from roving, foraging troops of apelike humans to integrated bands of hunter-gatherers molded into humanlike societies? The term *hunter-gatherer* is used in archaeology and anthropology to designate small-scale societies in which food is obtained from the wild. Wild animals are hunted and wild plants are gathered for food. Such groups would move camp frequently, in search of new resources. An annual round often characterized the repeating yearly cycle of the food quest. In addition to the distinctive pattern of subsistence and settlement, hunter-gatherer societies were generally smaller, less sedentary, and more egalitarian than farming groups.

It is aspects of organization that truly separate these groups from their earlier relatives. Kinship structured social relationships. Food, property, and information were shared. Status was earned through achievement, and it was ephemeral, held only by the individual who gained it and not passed on to offspring. Nonkin relationships were maintained by exchange of mates, goods or foodstuffs. At some point, early foraging groups became hunter-gatherers. Kuhn and Stiner have argued this transition took place during the Upper Paleolithic, citing evidence such as exchange of exotic materials and technological solutions to seasonal or regional variation.

Human society has a structure that is rare in the animal world. Humans live in groups to satisfy their basic needs for reproduction, defense, food, and other resources; but a range of group sizes, organization, and activity could fulfill these same needs. The best structural and organizational arrangements to achieve these goals in terms of co-residence group size and affiliated social units seem to involve family units. Families are reproductive groups and often live as an extended unit with three generations. Subsistence groups are often larger. Security groups could be the largest units, with both local and areal networks. A single co-resident individual will defend his or herself, but may also belong to an alliance that can assemble larger units for protection.

Paul Roscoe argues that living in larger groups creates problems, among them optimality and conflicts of interest. Optimality refers to the need for efficient operation. Conflicts of interest arise as group members and groups seek differing goals, such as mates, or food resources, or alliances. The optimality problem is solved by nesting segments, organizing units of various sizes (and different sets of individuals) to carry out activities. Conflicts of interest are normally resolved by a mechanism called social signaling through which individuals and social groups communicate their desires, capabilities, and situation. Displays of social and martial power substitute for actual conflict. The combination of nested segments and social signaling constitutes an effective structure for human societies of increasing size to fulfill their needs.

The Pleistocene and the Paleolithic came to an end some 10,000 years ago. The ice sheets retreated as warmer temperatures prevailed, and our present epoch—the Holocene—began. Archaeological time in the Holocene begins with the Mesolithic, the period of the last hunters prior to the arrival of farming and the Neolithic.

The Mesolithic witnessed continuing intensification in the variety of human activities and organization. These hunter-gatherer societies consumed a wide range of wild plant and animal species, using highly specialized technology. An incredible range of fishing gear, including nets, weirs, hooks, and harpoons, was developed during this period. Evidence of water transport in the form of dugout canoes and paddle is found in various parts of Europe. Ground stone artifacts appear as axes, celts, grinding stones for plant materials, and other tools. Projectile weapons were equipped with a variety of tips made of bone, wood, antler, and stone. In those areas of Europe where bone and other organic materials have been preserved, artifacts are often decorated with fine, geometric designs.

Evidence from several areas suggest less mobility among some of these groups as the duration of site occupation extends and the same places are repeatedly used over a period of years. Cemeteries, found in some parts of Europe in the Mesolithic, also suggest more sedentary occupations and return to the same dwelling places.

It seems reasonable to conclude that hunter-gatherer behavior and organization, as we know it from more recent contexts such as North American Indians in the early contact period, was achieved in the late Paleolithic and Mesolithic. The archaeological remains and the activities that we can infer reflect patterns observed historically. Some years ago Binford suggested a useful model for the study of hunter-gatherer behavior that is based on ethnographically known, or more recent, hunter-gatherers. Binford distinguished foraging versus collecting patterns according to residential mobility. Foragers move to food, while collectors have more permanent

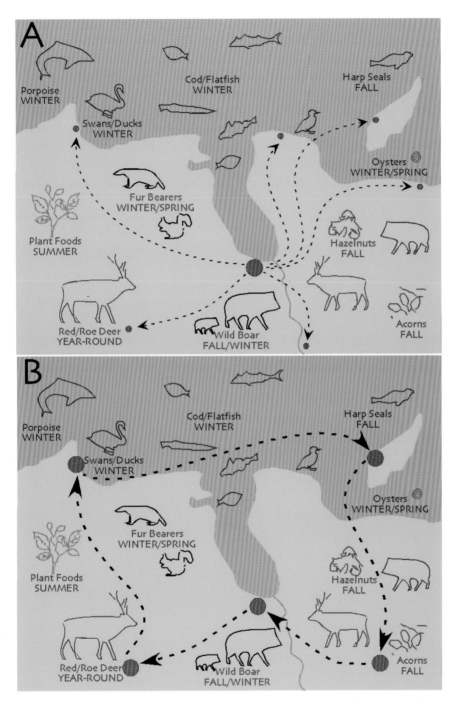

Fig. 3.55.
A schematic representation of foraging and collecting patterns of subsistence and settlement among hunter-gatherers. A. Collectors occupy a fixed base camp; a number of smaller, temporary, specialized hunting and gathering sites are used to extract resources from the environment and return them to the base. B. Foragers move residential camps regularly during the year to take advantage of seasonally abundant food resources.

residences and bring foods back to their base. In essence, this is a continuum between more and less mobile strategies for survival.

An example from southern Scandinavia illustrates the more intense use of the landscape that is reflected in sedentary settlement (Fig. 3.55). The coastal environment in this area was rich with a variety of wild game and nuts and other plant foods on land, and abundant marine mammals, fish, and shellfish in the sea. Migratory waterfowl enhanced the larder at certain times of the year. Two options were available to human groups in such environments: foraging and collecting. Because of the abundance of foods available year-round in this region, the archaeological evidence suggests that Mesolithic hunter-gatherers were collectors and following patterns of behavior known in more recent times.

In this context of successful hunting and gathering societies, agriculture and the Neolithic arrives and changes human ways forever. This is, of course, the subject of the next chapter.

CHAPTER FOUR

The First Farmers

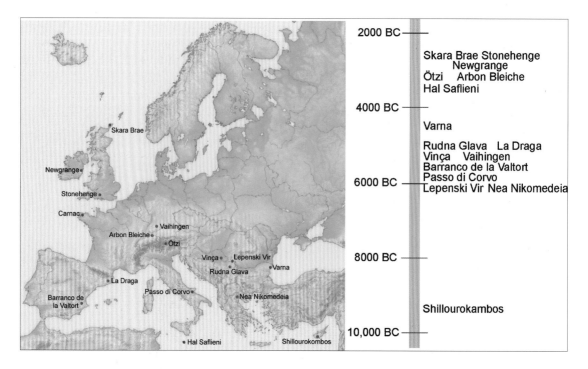

2000 BC

Skara Brae Stonehenge
Newgrange
Ötzi   Arbon Bleiche
Hal Saflieni

4000 BC

Varna

Rudna Glava   La Draga
Vinča   Vaihingen
Barranco de la Valtort
Passo di Corvo
Lepenski Vir Nea Nikomedeia

6000 BC

8000 BC

Shillourokambos

10,000 BC

Skara Brae
Newgrange
Stonehenge
Carnac
Vaihingen
Arbon Bleiche
Ötzi
Vinča   Lepenski Vir
Rudna Glava   Varna
La Draga
Passo di Corvo
Barranco de
la Valtort
Nea Nikomedeia
Hal Saflieni   Shillourokombos

Fig. 4.1.
The location and
time scale for sites
mentioned in this
chapter.

THE ORIGINS AND SPREAD OF AGRICULTURE

The origins and spread of agriculture and a Neolithic way of life marked a major turning point in the evolution of human society. Farming changed everything. Our heritage as food collectors, consuming the wild products of the earth, extends back millions of years. Nevertheless, at the end of the Pleistocene some human groups began to produce their own food rather than collect it, to domesticate and control wild plants and animals, achieving what is perhaps the most remarkable transformation in our entire human past.

Agriculture is a way of obtaining food that involves domesticated plants and animals. But the transition to farming is much more than simple herding or cultivation. It also entails major, long-term changes in the structure and organization of the societies that adopt this new way of life, as well as a totally new relationship with the environment. Hunters and gatherers largely live off the land in an *extensive* fashion, generally exploiting diverse resources over a broad area; farmers *intensively* use a smaller portion of the landscape and create a milieu that suits their needs. With the transition to agriculture, humans began to truly change their environment.

Cultivation of plants and herding of animals, village society, and pottery did not originate in Europe. Domestication arrived from the ancient Near East. The Neolithic began in southwest Asia some 11,000 years ago and eventually spread into the European continent, carried by expanding populations of farmers. The mountains of western Iran and southern Turkey and the uplands of the Levant (the coastal region of the far eastern part of the Mediterranean, from the northeastern Sinai Peninsula through modern Israel, Lebanon, and Syria, and west along the modern Turkish coast) form an elevated zone somewhat cooler and wetter than much of the Near East. The area has been described as the Fertile Crescent. A variety of wild plants grow in abundance. This region was the natural habitat of many of the wild ancestors of the first species of plants and animals to be domesticated at the end of the Pleistocene: the wild wheats and barleys, the wild legumes, and the wild sheep, goats, pigs, and cattle that began to be exploited in large numbers at the origins of agriculture.

In the period just preceding domestication, there was intense utilization of wild plant foods. The focus at that time was in the northern Levant (northern Syria and southern Turkey), where changes appear early and quickly. Particularly noticeable is the range of equipment for using plant foods: sickle blades and grinding stones, along with storage pits and roasting areas for preparing wild wheat.

Between 9000 and 8000 BC, changes in the size, shape, and structure of several cereals indicate that they were domesticated. The Neolithic, defined by the appearance of domesticated plants, began at that time. Eight species of plants were domesticated during the period 9000–7000 BC, including three cereals—emmer wheat, einkorn wheat, and barley—and at least four pulses—lentils, peas, bitter vetch, and chickpeas. (Pulses are the edible seeds of leguminous plants, such as peas and beans.) Flax also was domesticated during this period and probably used for both oil and fiber; linen cloth is made from the fibers of the flax plant. In this same time period, animals were domesticated and herding became part of human activity. Goats may have been the first domesticates, soon joined by sheep, pigs, and cattle.

The first towns appeared. Major changes in human diet, and in the organization of society as well, began to take place. The number and the size of prehistoric communities expanded greatly during the early Neolithic, as populations apparently concentrated in settlements. By 7500 BC, new forms of residential architecture (rectangular houses) appeared and the earliest public constructions are seen. Pottery came into use around 7500 BC to serve as easily produced, waterproof containers for holding liquids, cooking, and storage. Shrines and ritual paraphernalia appear frequently, suggesting formalization of religious activity. The complete Neolithic package of domesticates, village architecture, and pottery was thus in place shortly before 7000 BC, as the Neolithic began to spread to Europe, Africa, and western Asia.

Think about the arrival of farming in Europe in terms of millennia, or thousand-year blocks of time. Plants and animals were domesticated in Southwest Asia sometime after 11,000 years ago, in the tenth millennium BC. The Neolithic village complex of square houses, pottery, and agriculture first moved to Europe in the seventh millennium BC. This spread took place both by land, across the Bosporus from Turkey to the Balkan Peninsula, and by sea from Cyprus and Anatolia, through the Aegean, to the Greek mainland.

The sixth millennium BC witnessed a move out of the Balkans along two routes (Fig. 4.2). One was along the north coast of the Mediterranean, probably by ship with intermittent stops that left behind communities of farmers and pastoralists. A second arm of the spread went inland, crossing Central Europe

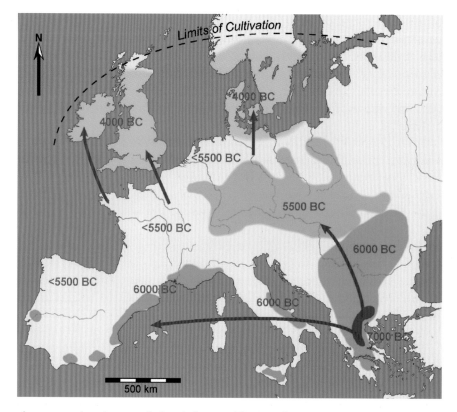

Fig. 4.2.
The spread of
agriculture across the
European continent.

almost to the shores of the Atlantic. The Mediterranean group is usually described from its pottery as the Cardial Culture; the inland group also has a distinctive pottery that provides its name, the Linearbandkeramik culture. The final stage, expansion into the British Isles and Northern Europe to the limits of cultivation, took place during the fourth millennium.

The entire journey from the plains of Thessaly in Greece to Scandinavia (ca. 2,000 km, 1,200 mi) and Britain (2,300 km, 1,430 mi) took about 3,000 years. These movements from Asia to Europe, from southeast Europe to Central Europe and the Mediterranean, and to the northern limits, took place quickly as rapid leaps or spreads, followed by long periods of stability and adjustment. One of the lasting questions about the spread of agriculture across Europe is how it occurred. Was farming carried by new colonists across the continent, or did it spread among local peoples adopting a new way of life?

One of the more pronounced trends in the European Neolithic was regionalization, the development of distinctly local traditions. Initial farming cultures expanded over broad regions. Settlements were generally located in open and unprotected spaces, and pottery styles were similar across very large areas. Quickly, however, population growth and development of permanent field systems resulted in competition and conflict between groups. By 3000 BC, the continent was occupied by well-entrenched farming populations making stone tools and pottery, cultivating, trading, and fighting.

In southeastern Europe developments in the Neolithic were dramatic, witnessing the rise of large towns, often on top of tells, which are huge mounds of human refuse and building material, accumulated in the same place over generations. This was a time of major cultural fluorescence among a series of cultures in Serbia, Romania, Bulgaria, and eastern Hungary; population numbers increased, large villages and towns appeared as tells, technological innovations including the first copper production flourished, long-distance trade expanded, and social inequality became pronounced.

Later Neolithic settlements across Europe were often located in defensible positions and heavily fortified. Pottery-making traditions became more limited in their distribution. At the same time, trade and exchange expanded in scope. A variety of materials and finished goods were moved long distances across Europe. Obtaining raw materials, manufacturing trade items, and transporting finished goods were an important part of Neolithic economic systems. Flint, for example, was mined in Denmark, Belgium, England, and elsewhere and polished into fine axes for trade.

Our consideration of the arrival, spread, and intensification of the first farmers in Europe follows their expansion across the continent. Examples of important sites in each region document the nature of these societies and their adaptations.

NEOLITHIC CYPRUS

We begin this chapter outside of Europe. The island of Cyprus holds critical information on the spread of agriculture, as a stepping stone between the Near East and the European continent. Cyprus lies more than 60 km (almost 40 mi) off the coasts of Turkey and Syria in the northeastern corner of the Mediterranean. In spite of the distances involved, early Neolithic farmers sailed there from the mainland more than 10,000 years ago. Even more remarkably, they brought domesticated plants and both wild and domestic animals with them. It is an extraordinary story.

At the time of colonization, Cyprus was a rather barren place, devoid of most species of animals, populated largely by pygmy hippos, pygmy elephants, mice, and genets (a small relative of the wild cat family). Although there is evidence of a pre-farming human presence on Cyprus, it was intermittent. The site of Akrotiri-Aetokremnos on the south coast of Cyprus, dating to ca. 9500 BC, has provided the earliest indications of human occupation on the eastern Mediterranean islands. Here the remains of more than 500 pygmy hippos have been found, in association with human artifacts and hearths.

The arrival of farmers 700 years later brought cattle, sheep, and goats, along with a number of crop plants originally domesticated in the Near East. Some of these animals were not yet completely tame. They appear to have brought their pets: dogs and cats. Cats may have been domesticated to control the mice that were attracted to the stored grain and wastes of early farming villages. The mice probably came as stowaways in the cargo of the farmers' boats. Red deer were not present on the island prior to this time, strongly suggesting that the farmers crossing the sea brought these wild animals as well. In essence, these very early Neolithic farmers carried a new ecosystem with them to Cyprus and changed the nature of life on the island forever.

Early Neolithic sites have been found on the south coast of the island, a long distance from the closest landing points to the mainland in the northeast. Ancient water wells offered the first evidence. These wells, uncovered during construction of tourist accommodations, were almost 10,000 years old, 8 m (more than 25 ft) deep or more. The contents, things fallen or dropped in, very much resembled the PPN (Pre-Pottery Neolithic; discussed just below) culture of the original farmers of Southwest Asia—on Cyprus. It was absolutely astounding. Remarkably, these wells were dug by Neolithic people at the same time domestication was just beginning on the mainland in the Near East. Following discovery of the wells, the French-Cypriot excavations at Shillourokambos, and more recently the international archaeological project at Asprokremnos, have further documented a very early Neolithic presence on Cyprus.

To understand the chronology and relationships of these sites, it is important to know a bit more about the origins of agriculture in the Near East, where the farmers who colonized Cyprus came from. There is a pre-Neolithic period known as the Natufian, which witnessed the beginnings of sedentism as hunter-gatherers first moved into small villages and subsisted on various animals, especially gazelle, and collected the abundant wild wheats, barleys, and other species that grew around them. Site variability and long-distance exchange of exotic materials increased, cemeteries appeared, and material culture reflected more symbolic or ritual behavior.

The first 3,000 years or so of the Neolithic in the Near East are without fired clay pottery, and so the period is known as the Pre-Pottery Neolithic. The PPN is divided into two periods, an earlier PPNA, 9500 to 8500 BC, and later PPNB, 8500–6400 BC. Everything changed with the onset of the Neolithic. During the PPNA some communities grew in size and became nodes in economic exchange networks. Communal architecture makes an appearance in the form of large-scale stone structures at cult sites. Cultivation of wild cereals likely began during this period, but there is no reliable evidence for morphological changes in the plants due to domestication. A similar picture pertains to animals. Several wild species were likely managed, or even herded, during this period, but there is no evidence of domestic animals other than the dog and cat.

During PPNB growth and change continued. Major sites were now two to three times larger, and new ritual and burial practices are witnessed in dramatic artifacts and cemeteries. The earliest clearly domesticated plants (wheats, barley, lentils, chickpeas, flax, and others) are found in archaeological sites from this period. The first definitively domesticated animals are also known from PPNB sites. Goats and sheep were probably the first domestic species. Cattle and pigs took a slower path to domestication and are not observably present until ca. 7500 BC in the later PPNB. These animals were likely managed, perhaps herded, for many years, however, before the anatomical changes that result from domestication became apparent.

SHILLOUROKAMBOS, CYPRUS, 8200 BC

It is in this context that the first farmers from the Near East traveled to Cyprus, carrying Neolithic culture, plants, and animals with them. Shillourokambos is a very early PPNB site in southern Cyprus, closely related to farming cultures in the Levant and southern Turkey, where agriculture originated. Excavations at the site began in 1992 and continued until 2004 under the direction of Jean Guilaine. More than 5,000 m² were excavated, exposing many structures, various pits, and narrow ditches in the subsoil (Fig. 4.3). The first two phases of the settlement, from 8200 to 7500 BC, are characterized by circular dwellings with wattle and daub walls. Holes were cut into the subsurface to support the wooden posts for these structures. Some deep pits probably served as wells (Fig. 4.4). The site also has evidence for construction of circular cattle enclosures.

Connections with the mainland, the homeland of these farmers, are clearly evident in the form of obsidian from Turkey and other materials. There are a number of similarities in the architecture and artifacts at the site shared between Cyprus and the Levant. Round houses, typical for the early prehistory of Cyprus, are known even earlier in the Levant. Stone blades for sickles are made in multiple segments, and arrowheads are made on a distinctive type of stone blade. Both forms have precursors on the mainland.

Fig. 4.3.
The excavation area at Shillourokambos, Cyprus, with various pits and other features.

Fig. 4.4.
A bottom-up view of one of the Early Neolithic wells at Shillourokambos. Note the footholds in the side wall.

The plants under cultivation in the early phase of settlement at the site were not demonstrably domesticated in terms of changes in the size and shape of the cereal grains. Wild barley and wild emmer wheat were the two main cereal crops. These species were brought to Cyprus by the farmers. Domesticated forms appear in the second phase of occupation at the site, after 8000 BC. A variety of other wild plants appear in the deposits and were likely collected for various uses—food, medicine, and raw materials for construction and crafts. Some of these included great cane, wild asparagus, wild oats, capers, hawthorn, broom, wild olive, wild lentils, pistachios, and wild peas.

The animal remains were well preserved, numerous, and tell us a great deal about the nature of farming villages in the early part of the Neolithic. These materials were studied by Jean-Denis Vigne. Pigs were the most common species in the early phase of settlement; sheep and goats were also present among the faunal remains. All of these animals were eaten, and very likely controlled by the farmers of Shillourokambos. However, only dog bones show the kind of size reduction that archaeozoologists use to identify domesticated animals (as a general rule of thumb, domesticated animals are smaller in size than their wild ancestors).

Cattle were introduced to Cyprus ca. 8300 BC or shortly before, at a time when domestic cattle had begun to appear on the mainland. Cattle bones are rare in the earliest phase at Shillourokambos and do not provide information on their morphology and domestication status. Sheep, goats, and cattle are in the size range of their wild ancestors. The culling pattern of goats suggests hunting of feral populations, while cattle and sheep were probably tamed and controlled. Fallow deer were present as well but seem to have been hunted as wild animals. Fish and bird bones were also found among the animal remains. The earliest known domestic cat has been found buried next to a human grave dating to 7300 BC (Fig. 4.5). A cat was also portrayed in a figurine found at the site (Fig. 4.6).

ASPROKREMNOS, CYPRUS, 8800 BC

The discovery of Shillourokambos and other PPNB sites on Cyprus was a huge surprise. Now, even earlier Neolithic evidence has been found on the island. PPNA farmers settled at the site of Asprokremnos in central Cyprus, as well as other locations on the island. Excavations here are recent, and the full report of the finds is not yet complete. Nevertheless, it is clear that an Early Neolithic farming community was established between 8800 and 8600 BC, dating from

ST283

Fig. 4.5.
Two burials, a human
and a domestic cat, at
Shillourokambos.

the PPNA. The abundant lithic remains and nearby sources of raw materials—
flint, rock for grinding stones, and red ochre—suggest that exploitation of
these lithic resources may explain the inland location of the site.

The excavations exposed several structures, one of which is very intriguing
because of its size and special context. The structure was dug into the

Fig. 4.6.
Cat head from a clay figurine found at Shillourokambos. Height 3 cm.

subsoil to create a semisubterranean packed earth floor for a structure more than 5 m (16 ft) long. The superstructure of the building was destroyed by fire and the contents on the floor remained in place: stone vessels, a variety of querns and grinding equipment, and a human figurine. Among other finds at the site, shell beads were common. Faunal remains document an emphasis on wild boar; these animals were previously absent on the island. It seems incontrovertible that wild boar were brought to Cyprus by humans from mainland Southwest Asia. A few bird bones and freshwater crab remains were also present.

The Early Neolithic of Cyprus affords dramatic evidence of the mobility of early farmers. This expansive, colonizing behavior characterized early farmers and was responsible for the rapid spread of agriculture to the limits of cultivation across Europe. Crossing the sea to the Mediterranean islands, these groups initiated the passage of agriculture to the continent of Europe. The farming groups expanded, leaving the core area of the northern Levant, even before the process of animal domestication was finished, before pottery arrived, and before the adoption of rectangular house forms. These groups hopped across the islands of the Aegean moving toward mainland Greece. At the same time, or perhaps slightly later, land-bound farmers spread from Anatolia across the Bosporus to Europe. The next question, of course, is what these groups looked like when they arrived in mainland Europe. For information on the first European farmers, we turn to such sites as Nea Nikomedeia in Greece and Lepenski Vir in Serbia.

NEA NIKOMEDEIA, GREECE, 6200 BC

The Early Neolithic sites in Greece and the Balkan Peninsula are often found as tells. Early Neolithic farmers in this region built their houses with mud walls. After the houses were abandoned and collapsed, sediments accumulated in the mound, creating excellent conditions for preservation. New houses were erected on the old ones, and gradually mounds of earth and refuse accumulated, with a few growing many meters high. Because there is so much material on top of the early layers, it is usually difficult to excavate deeply and expose the foundation of the mound.

The alluvial plains of southern Macedonia and Thessaly in Central Greece have an unusually high concentration of early Neolithic tells (Fig. 4.7). The environment and topography of these areas, with fertile soils and sufficient rainfall, were particularly hospitable for settlement by early farming groups.

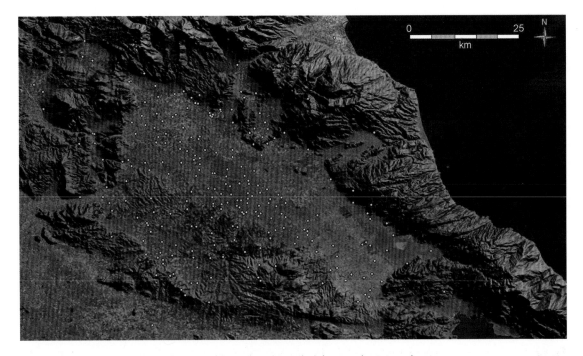

The early Neolithic site of Nea Nikomedeia (Fig. 4.8) lies in the Macedonian Plain of northern Greece. Nea Nikomedeia does not contain the earliest evidence of farming in continental Europe, but the site is among the best known for this period. The background to its fame rests in the fact that most of the upper layers were removed by local road builders for highway fill before archaeologists recognized the importance of the place. The absence of the upper layers of the original mound meant that a large area of Early Neolithic deposits was open and accessible.

A series of radiocarbon dates from Nea Nikomedeia indicate foundation of the settlement around 6200 BC. At this time there were a number of Neolithic tells across the landscape to the south in Thessaly. The Neolithic in Greece was well under way. The original tell at Nea Nikomedeia must have been substantial, probably on the order of 2.4 ha (6 acres) in size and several meters high before the earth was removed for road construction.

The site was excavated in the 1960s by a joint Harvard-Cambridge project under the direction of Robert Rodden. When Rodden first visited the site, Early Neolithic pottery fragments and other artifacts were scattered over the surface of the leveled mound. Most of the site had been disturbed by the road builders and later plowing, such that there was only half a meter (20 in) of archaeological deposits remaining. But this was the earliest and most important layer. In the end, removal of the upper part of the mound made it possible to study the earliest levels.

The excavations revealed a series of houses, individual structures 2–5 m (6–16 ft) apart on a slight rise at the edge of a marsh. There were at least three phases of building at the site, separated by periods of abandonment or disuse (Fig. 4.9). The earlier settlement was somewhat smaller than the later one, with seven structures in

Fig. 4.7.
Distribution of Neolithic sites in the Plains of Thessaly, east central Greece.

Fig. 4.8.

Aerial photo of the excavations at Nea Nikomedeia showing the square excavation units and the outlines of structures.

the excavated area. Houses were oriented more or less east-west, but there seemed to be no indication of planning in the layout of the community.

The houses were built using oak posts, 8–20 cm (3–8 in) in diameter, for the heavy uprights. Between the oak posts, the mud walls were constructed by placing cut saplings vertically 1–1.5 m (3–5 ft) apart in a shallow ditch, and filling in the spaces between them with bundles of reeds, laced among the posts. This framework was then plastered with mud mixed with chaff on the inside of the structure and with white clay on the outside. To protect the mud walls from the rain, it is assumed the roofs were peaked with thatch to carry off the water (Fig. 4.10). All the houses are roughly square, about 8 m (25 ft) on a side, with similar layouts.

Several of the houses were partitioned into two connected rooms, which may have had different functions. A room in one of the houses had a plastered platform with hearth and storage bin, suggesting it was used for food preparation and storage. House floors were carefully constructed with hard-packed clay. Some of the houses opened onto fenced patios or porches; these areas seem to be an integral part of the domestic space with hearths and ovens. Clay ovens were found outside of several houses, apparently half-domed structures of clay, on top of a small pit in the ground. Whether these were enclosed ovens or more simply windbreaks for an outdoor hearth is difficult to say.

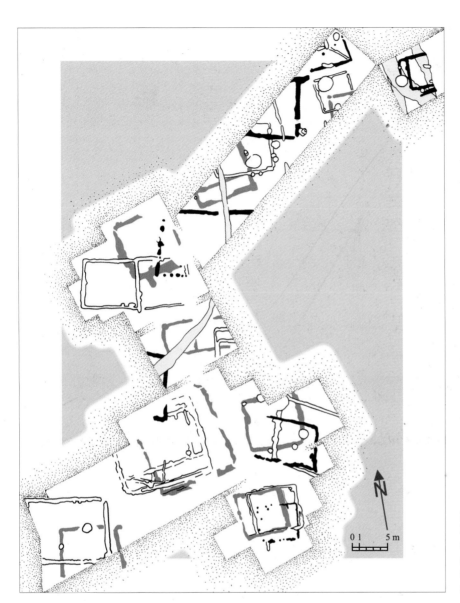

Fig. 4.9.
Plan of the excavations at Nea Nikomedeia, showing three phases of house construction (white, gray, black).

There was one larger and very unusual structure near the center of the tell, 12 by 14 m (40 by 46 ft) in size, divided into three interior sections by parallel rows of timber post. The contents of the house were also highly unusual and included a number of female figurines and fragments, large greenstone axes, hundreds of unused large flint blades, "shoe-shaped" pottery vessels, and several hundred clay disks found in one corner. There was little evidence of normal domestic activity in this house; it was described as a possible shrine by the original excavators. It is certainly unusual, but the specific function is uncertain.

Various kinds of pits were found around the houses at the site. Some may have been dug originally for construction mud, and later used for refuse disposal. Rubbish pits could be distinguished by dark fill of animal bones, ash, charcoal, and broken artifacts. Storage pits were clay-lined and often relatively clean. Carbonized plant

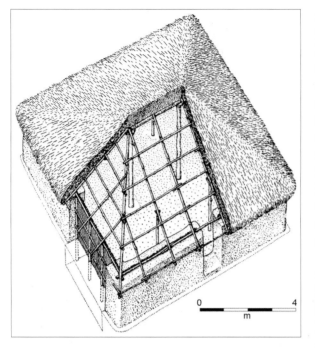

0   4
m

Fig. 4.10.
Artist's reconstruction
of a house at Nea
Nikomedeia with wood,
reed, and mud walls
and a peaked, thatch
roof.

remains were abundant at the site and revealed the crops in cultivation; the farmers at Nea Nikomedeia grew wheat, barley, peas, lentils, and bitter vetch. The faunal remains indicate that sheep and goats were the primary herd animals. Cattle and pigs were present, but in much lower numbers. The people of the village also relied on wild foods from the surrounding region and spent a good bit of time hunting, fowling, and fishing. Deer, hare, and wild pig bones were found in the deposits along with the remains of fish, freshwater mussels, and saltwater cockles—two kinds of shellfish from two contrasting environments.

The tools and artifacts at the site are typical of the Neolithic. Stone tools, made largely from locally available material, included both polished and flaked forms. Flaked stone tools were not abundant and consisted largely of simple blades and flakes with a few stone scrapers, arrowheads, and sickles. More than 400 ground and polished stone tools were found, made from serpentine (a fine-grained green stone) and marble, including adzes, chisels, pestles, pounders, querns, grinders, and lightly worked pebbles. Unusual artifacts of marble and serpentine took the form of large nails or studs. The excavator suggests that the nails may have been decorations for the hair and that the studs were used as earrings. I will get back to these items again.

Bone was used for needles, awls, and fishhooks. Basketry must have been an important technology at the site, but the baskets themselves are not preserved. There are, however, examples of the technology visible on the bottom of ceramic vessels pressed into woven mats when the pottery was still soft clay, permanently preserved when the pot was fired.

Tens of thousands of pottery sherds were found in the excavations, representing more than 1,000 vessels. Pottery found at the site exhibits a range of shapes and decoration. Shapes included open bowls, large narrow-mouth storage jars, small ladles, and several others. Decorated pottery was only a small proportion of the total, painted or ornamented with finger-impressed designs on the exterior, similar to what is found at the site of Vinča to the north. Painted designs in red on a cream background appear as blocks, triangles, and wavy lines. Some of the pots have a human face portrayed on the upper, outer surface.

Ceramic objects also include spindle whorls, spools, loom weights for making cloth, and clay disks. Evidence for the sling as a weapon was in the form of hundreds of fired clay pellets, but these items might also have been used as cooking or heating stones. Fired clay was used to make figurines, found in large numbers in the excavations, including a quantity of female human forms (Fig. 4.11). These female figurines have a distinctive style: a cylindrical

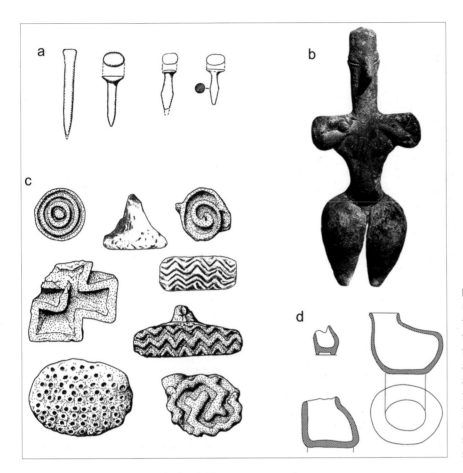

Fig. 4.11.
Unusual artifacts from Nea Nikomedeia that may be related to contracts and accounting: a. stone and clay nails, b. a female figurine, c. fired clay stamp seals, and d. askoid, or shoe-shaped vessels. Not to scale.

head with narrow eyes and a beaklike nose atop a disproportionate torso with a T-shaped upper body, small breasts held in the hands, and large, globular legs with little indication of the feet. A few male figurines were also found. Animal figurines were common, represented by crude depictions of sheep and goats.

One of the most intriguing artifact types is the fired clay stamp seal. Some twenty-one were found. These objects have a small knob or handle on the opposite side of a decorated area a few centimeters squared (about a half-inch) in size, ranging from circular to rectangular in shape, usually covered with a geometric pattern of some kind. Originally these seals were thought to have been dipped in coloring or dye and used to reproduce their pattern in textiles and animal skins, or perhaps to decorate human skin.

A recent study, however, suggests more complex use of these objects, related to an early form of accounting. They are more or less standardized in shape and size and appear throughout much of the Aegean and Balkan region in the Early Neolithic. The author of the study, Miha Budja, speculates that these unusual objects—nails, studs, seals, and figurines—may have been involved in a system of exchange involving reciprocity and obligation—contracted partner exchange between individuals or small groups. The items may have been signs of agreement or contract (the human figurines); markers of ownership, content, or destination (stamp seals); signs of identification (animal figurines);

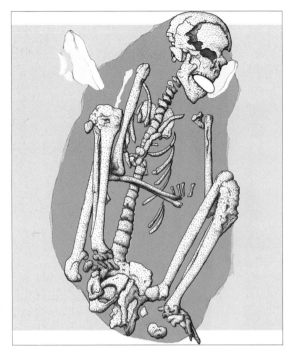

Fig. 4.12.
Burial of an adult male with a large stone in his mouth.

and counting tokens (disks, nails, and studs). The first systems of writing arose in the ancient Near East from a similar system of tokens and containers used in accounting for trade and exchange.

The total population of Nea Nikomedeia in the Early Neolithic was probably on the order of 200–300 individuals, an estimate based on the size of the site and the apparent number of houses. If we assume that there were fifty to a hundred houses at the site in any one period, not all of them in use, and five to ten individuals per house, this number appears reasonable.

A total of twenty-one burials were found within the excavated area of the site, individuals of all ages and both sexes, their bodies oriented largely north-south with the head to the south. All of the burials were inside the settlement. The dead were buried outside the houses and sometimes in the debris of abandoned homes. The deceased were usually placed in a small pit with few or no grave goods. One striking grave contained an individual interred with a large stone in his mouth (Fig. 4.12). Children are more common in the graves than adults. There is one case of a mass grave with the skeletons of three children and another of an adult woman with two children. Cause of death is unknown, but disease is a reasonable possibility; one of the consequences of sedentism and larger communities is the rise of communicable diseases.

LEPENSKI VIR, SERBIA, 6200 BC

Some 60 km (40 mi) east of the modern city of Beograd, Serbia, the slow waters of the Danube River funnel into a narrow torrent as they cut a gorge, known as the Iron Gates, through the Carpathian Mountains (Fig. 4.13). The combination of the steep-sided mountains and the fast-paced river foster an extraordinarily rich and diverse environment along this 100 km (60 mi) stretch. The area was home to hunter-gatherers from the Paleolithic and Mesolithic and contains some of the earliest evidence for the arrival of farming in Eastern Europe.

The Iron Gates is a spectacular place, with green woods clinging to the steep walls of the gorge and bare rock exposed where the trees cannot cling. The area is isolated and difficult to enter. Nevertheless, two millennia ago the Romans recognized the importance of this passage connecting the upper and lower stretches of the Danube. In typical Roman fashion, they carved a road along the base of the cliffs on the south side of the river. It cost many lives and a number of years of effort. Today, however, the

modern road follows that ancient Roman track, past the monument the Romans raised to the original builder, permitting access into and through the Iron Gates.

High mountain ridges shelter the gorge from the extremes of summer heat and chilly winter winds. The river mists, warm soils, and moderate seasons protect an unusual vegetation and animal life that have changed only a little since the Pleistocene epoch. Temperate species of trees—birch and spruce—survive alongside more Mediterranean varieties such as hackberry and beech.

The forests in the hills above the river were rich with game, particularly red deer, and the river was full of fish. Where the waters of the Danube rushed into the narrower channels of the gorge, whirlpools appeared and constantly stirred up the bottom sediments, providing rich nourishment for the inhabitants of the river. Danubian carp and catfish were enormous in this area; sturgeon migrating upstream from the Black Sea may have reached a weight of 200 kg (450 lb).

In the 1960s, the Yugoslavian and Romanian governments began a joint project to build a hydroelectric plant to tap the enormous power of the river. The dam for this project would raise the water level in the gorge by 35 m (115 ft). Archaeologists working ahead of the construction searched the shores of the Danube to document prehistoric sites that would be submerged by the river rising behind the dam. A large number of early archaeological sites, especially from the Mesolithic, were encountered in this process.

Here and there along the steep sides of the gorge are a few relatively level places. Lepenski Vir is the name given to one of the great whirlpools in the

Fig. 4.13.
The Iron Gates, gorge of the Danube River through the Carpathian Mountains, between Romania and Serbia.

middle of the gorge. On the sunny right bank just opposite this whirlpool is a broad, level, arc-shaped shelf of sand that lies beneath the steep, forested sides of the gorge. On this shelf the archaeologists discovered one of the most remarkable and unusual archaeological sites in all of Europe (Fig. 4.14)—and one about which there has been much debate over its precise age and function. The site was named after the whirlpool.

Most of the settlement at Lepenski Vir (ca. 2,400 m², 25,000 ft²) was excavated between 1965 and 1970 by the Serbian archaeologist Dragoslav Srejovic. The excavations revealed more than 3 m (10 ft) of deposits in several layers. There was evidence for elaborate constructions, plastered floors, stone-lined fireplaces, human skeletons, and art—Europe's oldest stone sculptures. Srejovic believed that most of the houses and other artifacts from Lepenski Vir belonged to the Mesolithic period. Deer, pig, and abundant fish bones document a large part of the diet of the inhabitants. Some pottery and other artifacts indicated a Neolithic presence in the upper levels, but he assigned the major features of the settlement to pre-Neolithic times. The Mesolithic date for Lepenski Vir was controversial because of the very unusual structures and sculpture at the site. These features were unknown elsewhere in Europe during the Mesolithic.

The age of the site has finally been settled by new radiocarbon dates obtained in the last decade. It has become clear that most of the deposits date between 6200 and 5900 BC and belong to the early Neolithic culture of southeastern Europe. In addition to the radiocarbon dates, Early Neolithic pottery has been found on the floor of at least two of the houses at the site.

Fig. 4.14.
The excavated site of Lepenski Vir on a sandy shelf in the Danube Gorge, Serbia.

There are at least two phases of house construction at Lepenski Vir. In the lowest level, approximately twenty structures were found in irregular rows on a series of terraces, a total area of some 60 by 30 m (200 by 100 ft;

Fig. 4.15). A central plaza sits amid the houses, adjacent to the shoreline. There was also one larger building located in the upper middle of the village. In the later levels at the site there are some changes in domestic architecture: houses had indoor ovens, perhaps for baking bread, domestic sheep were present, and obsidian and *Spondylus* (thorny oyster) shell was imported from the Adriatic or Aegean seas. The basic plan of the community and houses, however, remained the same.

The settlement contained a total of more than one hundred structures, called "houses" or "shrines," ranging in size from 5 to 30 m² (50 to 320 ft²) in floor area, or the equivalent of small to very large rooms today. The trapezoidal huts often included an elaborate stone-lined hearth and red plastered floor (Fig. 4.16). The plaster floor was surrounded by large postholes, indicating

Fig. 4.15.
Plan of the trapezoidal houses at Lepenski Vir. Note the larger structure, top center.

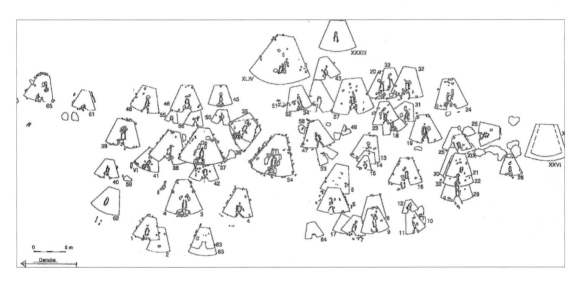

Fig. 4.16.
An artist's reconstruction of one of the trapezoidal structures at Lepenski Vir.

a substantial timber superstructure. The broader end of the houses faced the river, while the narrow end often contained an area of stone paving, sometimes with hollowed stones or more elaborately sculptured boulders with fish-human features (Fig. 4.17). Some of these large stones may have served as altars.

There were a large number of graves at Lepenski Vir, leading some to suggest that this site, at least in its latest phase, may have been a cemetery. Human skeletal remains were uncovered in and around the houses. There are 134 graves reported, containing the remains of approximately 190 individuals. In addition there were partial skeletons from adults (thirty-four), subadults (five), and newborns (three) in unidentified contexts. Skulls and parts of heads were recovered in areas between houses, while the remainder of the skeleton was often found beneath the house floor. In one example, the body of an old man was laid out with the head of an older woman (minus her lower jaw), an aurochs skull at his shoulder, and a deer skull near his hand.

Lepenski Vir is unique in almost every way: the red plastered trapezoidal structures, the stone sculptures, the elaborate stone-lined fireplaces, the large number of structures, the relative absence of domestic equipment. And the place itself is very unusual. The largest area of level land along the entire gorge, across from a spectacular red sandstone, trapezoidal-shaped mountain, is in front of one of the largest whirlpools in the Danube. Before the dam was built the river flooded every year, often more than once. This meant the inhabitants

Fig. 4.17.
One of the stone sculptures from Lepenski Vir. The face of the sculpture is ca. 25 cm in diameter.

of Lepenski Vir would have been forced to move elsewhere for at least part of the year. A reasonable question arises: Was this a permanent residential settlement for Early Neolithic farmers, or something else? One possibility to consider is that this special place was a large ritual center for certain ceremonial and funeral practices of the first farmers in this area.

The evidence from Lepenski Vir is particularly important for understanding the transition to agriculture in southeastern Europe because of the presence of Mesolithic hunter-gatherers prior to the onset of the Neolithic. The Iron Gates region was the focus of Mesolithic settlement during the period after 10,000 years ago. A number of rich Mesolithic sites have been found along the banks of the gorge. Less than 1,000 years after the arrival of agriculture in the Aegean, the first farmers appear in the interior of southeastern Europe, notably the Iron Gates region. The radiocarbon dates for the Early Neolithic in the Balkan Peninsula are 6600–5200 BC. Lepenski Vir was a special sort settlement in this time period, on top of an earlier Mesolithic site.

Today the original Lepenski Vir lies under the waters of the Danube, but the site can still be visited as a national monument of Serbia. In 1969, as the waters rose slowly behind the hydroelectric dam, many of the structures and other remains at Lepenski Vir were raised more than 30 m (100 ft) up the side of the gorge to the plateau above. A small museum stands adjacent to the new location; an elaborate roof protects the reconstructed archaeological remains. It was remarkable that the original place of dwellings along the river could be moved and restored higher up the hillside so that visitors could appreciate these extraordinary Early Neolithic creations.

VINČA, SERBIA, 5500 BC

The Vinča culture of the middle Neolithic flourished from 5500 to 4000 BC in the territories of what is now Bosnia, Serbia, Romania, and the former Yugoslav Republic of Macedonia (Fig. 4.18). The Vinča culture was named after a major settlement, located just 15 km (10 mi) from the modern Serbian capital of Beograd. The massive mound, or tell, of Vinča sits on a rise called Belo Brdo (white hill) along the riverbank near the confluence of three large rivers, a place of strategic and economic significance. This crossroads permitted ready access to most of southeastern Europe.

The tell of Vinča is 10.5 m (35 ft) high, the equivalent of a three-story building, and covers an area of 10 ha (25 acres), or about two city blocks (Fig. 4.19). Excavations began at the site in 1908 and have continued with interruptions since. Vinča is the only known tell within a 100 km (60 mi) radius and one of the more important Neolithic sites in Europe.

Fig. 4.18.
The distribution of Vinča culture in the Balkan Peninsula and the location of several sites mentioned in the text.

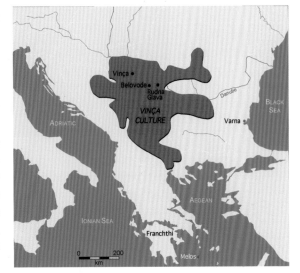

Fig. 4.19.
The huge tell of Vinča during earlier excavations. The maximum height of the tell is 10.5 m.

The primary period of Neolithic residence at Vinča was between 5500 and 4500 BC. The site was fortified with a palisade enclosing the settlement, with straight lanes between the houses. These houses were generally large square buildings with 40–60 m² (430—650 ft²) of floor space and several rooms and built-in earthen furniture—benches, braziers, tables, and sleeping areas. Floors and walls were plastered. The size of the settlement and the range of activities taking place increased over time. In the deep layers of the tell there are a number of distinct building phases from the Middle Neolithic, or Vinča, period. Rectangular houses were common, frequently with evidence of what is most likely accidental burning. Houses were separate (the areas between them served as yards), with stamped earthen floors, open fireplaces, clay ovens, and a number of pits. There is a later early Bronze Age occupation, a medieval cemetery, and even a Celtic settlement on top of the Neolithic layers that make up the bulk of the tell.

Vinča must have been a very special place. Not only was the tell the one high, permanent mound in the region, three types of finds occur earlier and in much higher concentrations at Vinča than elsewhere: ritual objects, personal ornaments, and exotic lithic material.

Ritual objects often take the form of figurines. These fired clay figures are anthropomorphic, small, usually broken, and normally found outside of the houses. Clay figurines are one of the spectacular hallmarks of the Vinča culture, found by the thousands across southeastern Europe. A figurine may have been placed beneath the floor of a house as a foundation deposit, an amulet for good fortune. As Douglass Bailey suggests, many of these figurines were everyday objects, seen, handled, worshipped, or cursed. What is important is how the figurines functioned to reiterate the shared identity of individuals and the community.

These stylized figurines depict nude or elaborately costumed figurines of women (and the occasional male), standing, kneeling, or sitting, wearing distinctive beaked masks (Fig. 4.20). Perforations in the ear region must have

Fig. 4.20.
The head of a Neolithic figurine (foreground) and an anthropomorphic pot cover from Vinča. The head of the figurine is ca. 3 cm high.

held rings or other attached decoration. The masks are usually three- or five-sided and highly stylized, generally similar from one to the next. Every depiction of costume, however, is different, likely individualized. The significance of these figurines is unknown, but they probably involved individual participants in ceremonial or religious practices, judging from the combination of masked figures and distinctive costumes.

Svend Hansen of the German Archaeological Institute has studied Neolithic figurines in great detail and estimates that the total number in Southeast Europe is around 50,000, emphasizing their important symbolic role in Neolithic societies. The tradition of Neolithic figurines originated in the Near East and spread from east to west with other aspects of the Neolithic. The human figurines are characterized by symmetry and frontality, and they depict both male and female individuals. More than half are of indeterminate sex. One particular pose, females holding their hands or arms under the breasts, is a common motif from the earliest Neolithic in the Near East, perhaps 9,000 years old. The figurines at Nea Nikomedeia followed this form as well. A distinctive stylistic change can be seen in the female figures in Southeast Europe. Many of the figurines of the Early Neolithic have rounded, voluptuous bodies; but by 5500 BC the shape is more abstract and schematic. The masked figures with differentiated costumes become the more typical forms of figurines.

Other kinds of ritual artifacts include vessel lids with faces, *bucrania*, and incised signs. Elaborate lids for ceramic vessels document a special-purpose vessel, likely used in ritual activities. These covers take the form of humans or eared animals with eyes and nose clearly depicted (Fig. 4.20). The surface of the lid is often inscribed with a series of abstract geometric lines. *Bucrania* is the term used for bulls' heads displayed in a ritual context. The skulls of cattle were heavily covered with plaster, sometimes painted, and mounted in prominent locations on house gables or interiors.

Incised signs are another fascinating aspect of the Balkan Neolithic—and a revealing aspect of archaeological bias. These signs and symbols appear on a variety of artifacts: pottery, figurines, loom weights, spindle whorls, tablets, and plaques. The most famous and controversial of these inscriptions come from Tărtăria, a Neolithic site in Romania roughly contemporary with Vinča. The tablets were found in a ritual pit, along with burned human bones and other objects. The so-called Tărtăria tablets are three small, fired clay objects, no more than 6 cm (2.5 in) in maximum dimension and 1–2 cm (approximately half an inch) in thickness and displaying a series of unusual inscriptions on one side only (Fig. 4.21). One of the pieces is circular and two are rectangular; the circular piece and one rectangle are perforated.

The inscriptions are the focal point of these objects. The rectangular tablet without a hole depicts a horned animal, another figure, and a branch or tree. The two other pieces have a variety of mainly abstract symbols. These abstract symbols appear to be pictographs—signs resembling a physical object. The meaning and significance of the tablets, however, is uncertain and hotly debated.

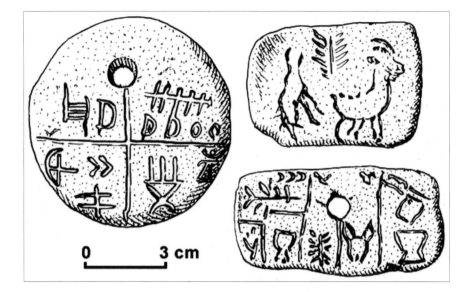

Fig. 4.21.
The Tărtăria tablets.
The circular object is
6 cm in diameter.

The original discoverer and several colleagues argued the tablets dated to ca. 2800 BC and resembled Sumerian scripts from Mesopotamia. A recent radiocarbon date of ca. 5300 BC for the tablets means these inscriptions pre-date the earliest writing in Mesopotamia by almost 2,000 years. Similar signs and symbols have been found in a variety of contexts in Neolithic Eastern Europe, and the early date is no doubt correct. The question becomes, What do these symbols mean? Is this the world's first writing system? The earliest clear writing system in Europe is found on Crete and mainland Greece in the Linear A and B scripts, dating to the second millennium BC.

The signs and symbols from Neolithic Eastern Europe were studied in detail by Shan Winn. He found a total of 210 signs, most composed of straight lines and rectilinear in shape. He concluded that all the Vinča signs were composed of five key elements: a straight line, two lines intersecting at the center, two lines intersecting at one end, a dot, and a curved line.

A number of interpretations are possible in situations of strange objects of unknown meaning. Usually archaeologists invoke some kind of ritual behavior to explain such items. These inscriptions could be some form of prayer or entreaty to spirits or deities. Some examples appear to be amulets, intended to be worn. The question of whether these symbols constitute a written language is difficult to answer. The symbols have not been deciphered; no message can be interpreted. Until further information becomes available, it is probably best to think of these as a series of signs and symbols, rather than a form of written language.

Personal ornaments and jewelry are another distinctive group of artifacts at Vinča found in larger numbers than at other sites. These objects are often made of semiprecious stone (marble, alabaster, and rock crystal) and are carefully shaped by grinding, faceting, and polishing into several distinctive forms, including various animal heads and an abstract "mushroom" shape. These pieces are small, a maximum of 9 cm (3½ in) in diameter, and were probably used as pendants or worn in other ways. In terms of exotic lithic material, more than 60 percent of the flaked stone tools at Vinča are made from obsidian, that black volcanic glass so popular for its sharpness and ease of manufacture. This obsidian comes from the only significant source in southeast Europe outside the Aegean, the mountains along the border of Slovakia and northeast Hungary, at least 350 km (220 mi) to the north.

RUDNA GLAVA, SERBIA, 5000 BC

The latter part of the Neolithic occupation at Vinča is more appropriately termed the Chalcolithic, or copper age. Metal production, smelting and casting of copper and gold, began in the Balkans ca. 5000 BC, among these Neolithic cultures. In all probability, this was the earliest known smelting of copper anywhere in the world. These metals constituted an important base for the economic wealth of the site of Vinča and similar large centers.

Copper sources are scattered around the Balkan Peninsula. One of the earliest and best known was found at Rudna Glava in eastern Serbia. The site is located about 150 km (90 mi) east of Vinča on the Romanian border. Modern mining in the area exposed the older shafts from the copper mines of the Neolithic period. Archaeological excavations by Borislav Jovanović in the 1970s revealed more than twenty prehistoric mine shafts that followed veins of copper ore in the mountain (Fig. 4.22).

Fig. 4.22.
Some of the excavated shafts of the Neolithic copper mines at Rudna Glava.

The Neolithic miners used techniques similar to those employed in mining flint and other stone. Stone mauls and antler picks were used to follow vertical veins of copper ore into the hillside. A method of alternate heating and cooling helped to break up the ore and facilitate quarrying. Fires were lit along the face of the vein, and then water was thrown on the hot rock to cause fissures and fractures. Pottery from the Vinča culture was found in the mineshafts. Some of the veins were followed 15 to 20 m (50 to 65 ft) into the hill, with small horizontal access chambers extending off the main shaft. In those cases where the shaft appeared to be in danger of collapsing, stone supporting walls were built from the mining wastes.

Copper ores give up their metal at around 800 °C (1,472 °F). The copper pellets produced at that temperature can be cold-hammered and shaped into a limited number of forms.

Casting requires higher temperatures, 1,083 °C (2,000 °F), in order to remove impurities and air in the molten copper. Cast copper axes and other artifacts began to appear quite early in this region, in part because kilns with bellows to reach this temperature were already in use to make sophisticated pottery.

Vinča and Rudna Glava are part of the spectacular development that took place in southeastern Europe in the Neolithic, what archaeologist Marija Gimbutas called Old Europe, the oldest "civilization" on the continent. This period goes by different names across the Balkans. It is Vinča in Serbia and Montenegro, Gumelniţa in Romania, and Karanovo in Bulgaria. Though the names change, the phenomenon is similar. The Neolithic in this part of Europe witnesses dramatic increases in the size and number of sites; in construction of substantial permanent houses, sometimes of two stories; in nucleated villages and a few proto-cities with populations in the thousands; in production and exchange of exotic materials, sophisticated pottery with graphite and gold finishes; in long-distance trade; and in uneven distribution of wealth and the rise of social inequality, characteristics that reflect more complex organizations than the smaller, tribal societies that originally carried agriculture into this region. Change is happening quickly following the introduction of farming and a Neolithic way of life.

VARNA, BULGARIA, 4500 BC

Fig. 4.23.
Gold, shell, stone, and bone treasures from Varna.

In 1972 construction workers digging near the city of Varna on the Black Sea coast of Bulgaria uncovered several graves containing unusual metal objects. Thinking the metal was copper, they called in the local archaeologist, Ivan Ivanov, who then excavated the cemetery from 1973 to 1991, often employing prisoners from the local penitentiary. By the end of excavations, they had uncovered 7,500 m², 310 graves, 3,000 gold artifacts weighing more than 6 kg (13 lb), 160 copper artifacts, and 1,100 *Spondylus* and 12,200 *Dentalium* shell pieces.

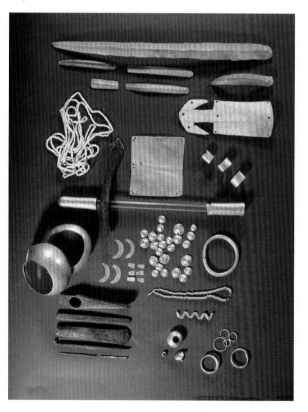

The discoveries at Varna have dramatically altered our impressions of early farmers in southeastern Europe because of the rare and valuable materials that accompanied the burials (Fig. 4.23). The gold found at Varna is the earliest worked gold in graves anywhere in the world. Radiocarbon methods date the site from approximately 4560 to 4450 BC, contemporary with the Vinča culture in Yugoslavia.

The discovery and use of metals in the Old World was a relatively slow process. A few small pieces of copper, in the form of jewelry, appeared in the Near East by 7000 BC. at early Neolithic sites. This was native copper, simply hammered from its original shape into a new form. The melting and casting of copper probably began in both southeastern Europe and the Near East shortly after 5000 BC. Copper mines were opened in Yugoslavia, and various copper artifacts, primarily axes and jewelry, found their way throughout much of Europe. Gold objects also began to be produced during the fifth millennium BC.

The graves at Varna are simple rectangular pits with rounded corners, dug into the earth to varying depths up to 3 m (10 ft). Red ochre was spread over most of the burials. A wide range of other materials were also found in the graves, including flint, obsidian, bone, clay, ochre, shell, graphite, marble, and copper. Impressions of decayed textiles could be seen on the walls of the graves and were preserved with some of the copper artifacts.

The graveyard at Varna covers a large area, the size of a soccer field. The dead were buried with the head toward the Black Sea. Seventy-five percent of extended graves were male; females were more often buried in a flexed position on their right side. Sex has been determined for sixty-two of the burials, thirty-nine males and twenty-three females. There were few graves with children; the youngest individual in the cemetery was about fourteen years old. More than 80 percent of the graves contained exotic materials: gold from stream deposits to the south in Bulgaria, copper probably from mines also to the south, various stones, and *Spondylus* and *Dentalium* shell from the Aegean. Most male burials included a copper axe or pottery and flint tools; female graves usually held a few ceramic pots.

Almost 20 percent of the graves did not contain a body, a pattern seen elsewhere in the Neolithic of southeastern Europe. Such graves are known as cenotaphs. Most of these empty graves contained only a few offerings, usually gold rings and copper axes, and sometimes a life-sized clay mask of a human face. Certain features, such as the teeth and decorations on the ear, chin, or forehead, were made from gold plaques. In three of the "mask" graves, thousands of gold pins and beads of *Spondylus* and *Dentalium* shell, copper needles, marble drinking cups, figurines, and graphite-and-gold-painted pottery were found. The graphite and gold ceramics are exceptional examples of the technological sophistication of the potters of this period. Graphite is applied as a powder to the burnished clay surface of the pottery and must be fired at a temperature of at least 1,000 °C to fix the graphite. Gold powder may have been applied to pottery in a similar fashion, but the exact technique is unknown.

Other empty graves contained even more wealth. The offerings and grave goods were arranged in these tombs as though a body were present. Grave 1 contained 1,225 gold objects weighing 2,093 g (4.6 lb), in fifteen groups. (At the price of gold today, the value would be roughly $1.2 million.) These items included two gold tubes and parts of the shaft of axes. Golden masks were found in two of the graves. Grave 36 included a solid gold axe and shaft, two gold bull effigies, thirty miniature golden horns, and various gold adornments and jewelry, a marble dish, four pottery vessels, and miscellaneous bone and flint tools.

Grave 4 contained 320 gold objects, weighing 1,500 g (3.3 lb; Fig. 4.24). The list of items in the grave is remarkable. There were several ceramic vessels near the head of the individual in the grave, and at his right shoulder was a stone axe on the end of a gold-covered wooden shaft; also found were several copper axes and chisels, another stone axe, an enormous flint blade more than 40 cm long, two breastplates of gold and a massive convex gold disk, arm rings, earrings, beads and necklaces all of gold, a gold cup, and perhaps a penis sheath. More than forty small gold disks were found around the grave, which may have been sewn into a shroud or clothing. Finally a mass of beads of shell and semiprecious stone were scattered throughout the grave.

The graves at Varna provide spectacular evidence for status differentiation in the Neolithic of southeastern Europe. Only a few graves contained most of the wealth; 5 of the 6 kg of gold came from just four graves. Categories of people in this society were distinguished by the wealth that accompanied the burials. Variation in grave contents is clear evidence of social inequality in the Late Copper Age in the Balkans, related to production of valuable raw materials (metal ores) and increased long-distance trade.

Fig. 4.24.
Grave 4 at Varna, one of the richest burials in the cemetery.

The rich graves may have been those of religious or political leaders or merchants. Certainly, the location of this important cemetery points to the role of trade and exchange. Varna is located at the shore of a former inlet from the Black Sea, perhaps a natural harbor; trade routes for gold, copper, obsidian, marble, shell, pottery, and many other items must have run through or very near this area. Such a strategic location may well have led to the rise of an elite at Varna and accumulation of extraordinary amounts of wealth. The fact that the wealth of the living was buried with the dead is both a remarkable testimony to the complexity of Neolithic society in the Balkan peninsula and a boon for archaeology.

PASSO DI CORVO, ITALY, 6000 BC

Peninsular Italy is a bridge between the eastern and western Mediterranean. Southern Italy appears to have received the Neolithic very early, probably as a result of movement from the Balkan peninsula across the Adriatic Sea when the early European farmers began to spread from Greece. The arrival of these early farmers in the south of Italy took place between 6150 and 5950 BC. The transition to agriculture in the western Mediterranean witnessed the appearance of sheep and goats, domesticated wheat and barley, obsidian artifacts, and distinctive ceramic containers known as Impressa or Cardial Ware. Impressa pottery is found in Italy, and the related Cardial pottery is found from Provence in France to central Portugal.

Tavoliere means tableland in Italian and is the name of a special part of the east coast of southern Italy. This area, known as the granary of Italy, is the largest plain in the southern half of the country. The Tavoliere is only 70 by 50 km (45 by 30 mi) in size, but the remains of more than 500 Early Neolithic sites have been found in the region. The Early Neolithic in this area has been identified by the discovery of ditched enclosures observed in crop marks and air photos of the landscape (Fig. 4.25).

A British Royal Air Force officer, John Bradford, was stationed at a nearby air base during World War II and for some years after. Bradford discovered

Fig. 4.25.
Aerial photo of one of the Neolithic enclosures in the Tavoliere, Italy.

many of these sites from the air and recorded their presence on the landscape through aerial photography.

Aerial photographs can supply information on the location, size, and shape of certain kinds of archaeological sites. When prehistoric structures were originally abandoned and collapsed, the depressions that remained often filled with rich topsoil. This means better growth condition for vegetation. During dry years when the crop is ripe, these differences can be seen from above. Buried walls result in less moisture and shorter, drier vegetation. Buried pits, depressions, and ditches contain more moisture and produce greener, richer vegetation compared to the rest of the field (Fig. 4.26). In fields of wheat, for example, such changing soil conditions might result in a distinctive pattern showing the outlines of houses, or whole villages. Old foundations or prehistoric agricultural fields, overgrown with vegetation and almost hidden on the surface, may appear in photographs taken from the air. Another example of the use of aerial observation for finding sites in this book is discussed in Chapter 6, from the site of Gournay-sur-Aronde.

These ditched sites vary in size from small, less than 1 ha (2½ acres) with just a few structures, to the more common medium size that are 1–4 ha (2½–10 acres) in area, and a few very large sites such as Passo di Corvo, which covers 28 ha (70 acres) and has multiple ditches and outer enclosures (Fig. 4.27). The outer ditches are up to 4 m (13 ft) deep and 1–2 m (3–6 ft) wide. The amount of labor involved in digging such trenches around the site is estimated to be on the order of 100,000 man-hours. These ditches do not appear to be defensive in nature since no palisade or weapons have been discovered. In all likelihood, the ditches were intended to keep animal herds inside the enclosure. Many ditched enclosures contained a number of smaller C-shaped ditched areas, which may have been the boundary of individual domestic compounds of huts, pens, and storage facilities. These compounds vary from 15 to 45 m (50 to 150 ft) in diameter.

Passo di Corvo is marked by an inner enclosure with up to three surrounding ditches. An even larger, single-ditch enclosure of 40 ha (100

Fig. 4.26.
Differences in vegetation due to buried archaeological remains visible from the air. The diagram shows a ditch with more moisture (A) and a wall with drier, thinner soil above it (B) below a cultivated field. Ditches are more visible when the crop is ripe; walls are more visible when the crop is green.

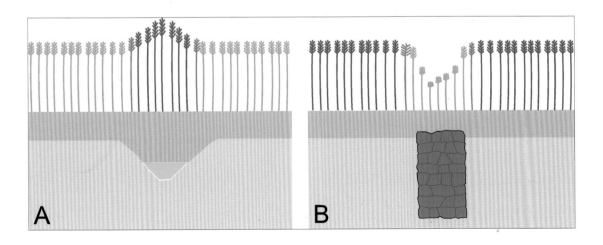

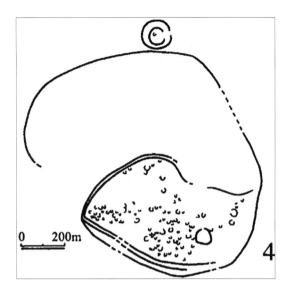

Fig. 4.27.
Plan of the site of
Passo di Corvo on
the Tavoliere. The
lines indicate ditches
marking houses and
boundaries of the site.

acres) is attached to the inner enclosure (Fig. 4.28). A small, older enclosure with a single C-shaped compound lies to the north on the outer ditch. Passo di Corvo contains a total of ninety of the C-shaped compounds. Excavation of one such compound revealed roughly rectangular structures with stone footings and postholes. Population estimates for the site assume these compounds are households and suggest numbers between 150 and 300 people for the entire settlement.

The excavations unearthed large quantities of stone tools, pottery, and animal bones in the ditches and pits at Passo di Corvo. Burned wheat was also found in the deposits. Stone tools were largely blades made of a locally available flint and obsidian from the Lipari Islands off the northeast coast of Sicily. Several ground or flaked axes of flint or heavy stone were also recorded along with a quern made of volcanic lava. The animal bones came primarily from domesticates—sheep and goat, with a few specimens of pig and dog—and wild hare.

Fig. 4.28.
A cross-section through
the enclosure ditch at
Passo di Corvo. Note
the workman in the
ditch for scale.

Because this region is one of the "granaries" of Italy, plow agriculture has been going on for thousands of years, and many of the Early Neolithic archaeological sites have largely been destroyed. Even where the deep parts of the ditches remain, the actual living area of the sites has often been chewed up by the plow and little information remains regarding various activities at the site.

Passo di Corvo and the other early Neolithic sites from the Tavoliere are remarkable in many ways. These are large, visible settlements from the very first Neolithic people in Italy, part of the spread of agriculturalists across the northern Mediterranean coast. Clearly these groups were successful farmers and herders from their first arrival. The huge size of some of these settlements, and the enormous investment of labor in the ditches and construction, is truly striking. Farmers change the landscape in ways that hunters never imagined.

LINEARBANDKERAMIK

The site of Vaihingen, discussed in the next section, belongs to a famous Neolithic period in Central Europe known as the LinearBandKeramik (LBK), dating from approximately 5700 to 5000 BC. The name for the Linearbandkeramik is German, taken from the style of pottery decoration that characterizes their fine ceramics. These farmers introduced cultivation and stock rearing; large, permanent houses; and a distinctive pottery to much of Central Europe. Linearbandkeramik villages are found along the middle Danube and its tributaries and spread from eastern Hungary to Holland and Belgium in the west, to the edge of the North European Plain to the north, and the Ukraine to east (Fig. 4.29).

The LBK has for many years been regarded as a classic example of migration by farmers, expanding into new territory. The earliest radiocarbon dates for the LBK are almost identical from Germany to Hungary, suggesting very rapid spread across hundreds of kilometers. On average, the LBK appears to have moved across Central Europe at a rate of 3.5–5 km (2–3 mi) per year.

Many of the characteristics of this archeological culture support such a view. The remarkable uniformity of LBK material culture, as seen in settlement plans, house construction, pottery, lithic artifacts, burials, and exotic materials such as *Spondylus* shell, is often interpreted as a marker of its rapid dispersal. As an example, LBK pottery in the Ukraine looks very much like LBK pottery in southern Germany.

The distribution of LBK settlement across Central Europe, however, is not continuous but patchy, clustered in areas of well-watered, loess soils. Loess is a windblown sediment that was deposited across much of Central Europe in the late Pleistocene. It has been argued that Neolithic farmers were attracted to loess basins by the natural fertility of the soil and an absence of indigenous Mesolithic population. Prior to the arrival of the LBK farmers, the loess areas were probably covered by dense mixed forest of elm, oak, and linden/lime. Not a very good environment for hunter-gatherers, but apparently just right for early farmers.

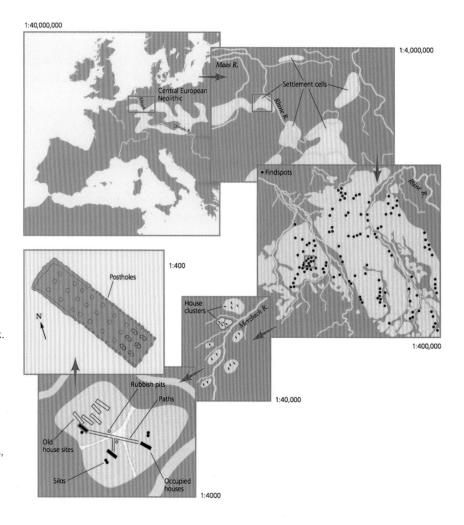

Fig. 4.29.
Powers of 10 view of the Linearbandkeramik. The first map shows the distribution of LBK materials across central Europe. Each subsequent map zooms by a power of ten, showing the local pockets of homesteads, and finally the basic residential longhouse from this period.

Settlements were usually small, dispersed farmsteads and hamlets, consisting of a few massive timber longhouses, separated by some distance. Settlements typically occur in clusters of as many as forty farmsteads and hamlets, often within a single stream valley. There are also a number of larger, more permanent settlements with dozens of longhouses, lanes for movement, water wells, and other types of features. Some of these sites were enclosed or fortified with ditches or palisades, normally circular in shape. An example at Vaihingen is discussed in the next section.

The most distinctive feature of LBK settlement is the longhouse, varying in length from around 10 m to 30 m (33 to 100 ft) or more long and about 7 m (23 ft) wide—perhaps the largest free-standing timber buildings in the world at the time. Because LBK sites were usually located on good agricultural soils, cultivation has continued for millennia in these places. Consequently the former ground surface of the LBK community has been plowed away. The traces of the early farming settlement remain only as deep post holes, pits, and burials beneath the modern plow zone.

The longhouses usually have two to four rows of outer posts for walls and three rows of inner posts to support the roof. The walls between the widely spaced timber posts were made of a wickerlike structure of branches covered with mud plaster or daub. Sediment for the mud daub was dug from pits next to the house, which were later used for trash.

Another feature of Linearbandkeramik settlements are the graves of the dead. LBK burials usually contain a single individual, found in a slightly flexed position and often in cemeteries of several dozen or more graves (up to several hundred) in or near the settlement. Grave goods are limited and often include a pottery vessel or two, a stone axe, or shell bracelets. Not everyone is carefully interred in a grave, and there are examples of bodies tossed into ditches and mass graves with dozens of individuals buried together. These latter cases are usually interpreted as the result of conflict.

LBK pottery comes in two major categories: a decorated fine ware (Fig. 4.30) and a plain, coarse ware. Coarse ware was used primarily for everyday storage and cooking. The function of the fine vessels with bands of decoration is uncertain. Bands or zones are defined by incised lines, cut in the clay paste before firing, creating linear bands. The bands are not particularly straight, but they do delimit the zones of design. Repeated motifs on these vessels include spirals, rectangles, triangles, and chevrons, usually placed outside the linear bands. The range of fine ware ceramics included open and closed bowls and flasks decorated with incised bands. The hallmark of LBK pottery is a decorated fine ware in the form of a hemispherical bowl.

Stone tools in the Linearbandkeramik took several forms. There were heavy ground-stone adzes for woodworking; flaked stone tools for various cutting, scraping, drilling, and incising activities; and grinding stones for processing cereal grain and other materials. LBK stone tools also included adzes for wood

Fig. 4.30.
Linearbandkeramik hemispherical bowl with linear bands, ca. 20 cm high.

working (a blade-based stone tool industry) and grindstones and pounders. Saddle querns for grinding were ubiquitous at LBK sites. Raw materials for stone tools sometimes were exchanged over hundreds of kilometers. *Spondylus* shell from the Adriatic or Aegean Sea was another material in demand for bracelets and jewelry, and also traded long distances into Germany and further west. *Spondylus* has a strong and colorful shell that was very popular in prehistory.

The food of the Linearbandkeramik people came from both wild and domestic sources. In the early part of the LBK, wild foods made up about 20 percent of the diet; this proportion declined as farming and herding become more productive. Animal domesticates included cattle, sheep and goats, pigs, and dogs. Cattle were the most important species among the domesticates for meat, milk, and other products such as horn, bone, and skin. Wild animals hunted included red deer, roe deer, and wild boar, along with some fur-bearing species. Crops included emmer, einkorn, and spelt wheat, and legumes (peas and vetch). Small amounts of barley and rye were present. These farmers also grew flex, hemp, and poppies. Flax provides fodder and fiber, along with oily seeds. Hemp produces a strong fiber for rope and cloth. Poppies were likely used as a narcotic, perhaps the hemp as well. LBK farmers probably cleared small fields within about a kilometer of their village for both farming and pasture. It has been estimated that approximately 0.4 ha of field and pasture per person is needed to fulfill annual food requirements. Wild plant resources were also exploited, especially fruits (apples and pears) and berries (blackberries and raspberries).

A study using strontium isotopes in the tooth enamel of Linearbandkeramik burials documented a high degree of mobility. Tooth enamel forms shortly after birth and retains the isotopic signature of the place of birth. Strontium isotopes vary geologically among different rocks and sediments. If an individual moved from one isotopically distinct geology to another, the signature in his or her enamel would differ from that of the place of burial. Analysis of enamel from early LBK burials from Germany revealed that about 60 percent of the individuals were nonlocal, having moved to the place of death from elsewhere, a very high degree of mobility.

In spite of the strong evidence that Linearbandkeramik peoples colonized much of central Europe, questions remain about the relationship between LBK farmers and the Mesolithic people of Central Europe who preceded them. A recent study of ancient DNA (aDNA) throws some light on this question. The study compared mitochondrial DNA (mtDNA) sequences from late European hunter-gatherer skeletons with those from early farmers and from modern Europeans. There were large genetic differences among all three groups that cannot be explained by population continuity. The ancient hunter-gatherers share mtDNA types that are relatively rare in central Europeans today. These analyses give some confirmation that the first farmers were not the descendants of local hunter-gatherers but immigrated into central Europe at the onset of the Neolithic.

Not all was peace and harmony among the Early Neolithic farmers, however. There are several sites that reveal evidence of violent conflict. Talheim

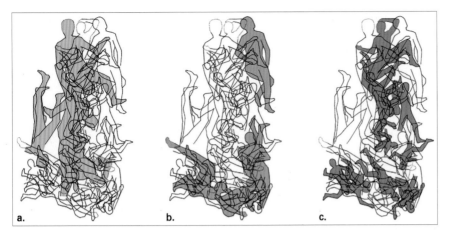

Fig. 4.31.
The mass grave at Talheim, Germany, shown in three views: a. adult males, b. adult females, and c. subadults.

in southern Germany is a mass grave dating to approximately 5100 BC. and belonging to the Early Neolithic period. Figure 4.31 shows part of this mass grave and the jumble of human remains that were found. The thirty-four individuals were buried in a square pit 3 m on a side; there were nine men, seven women, two adults of unknown sex, and sixteen children.

All of these individuals bear evidence of a violent death. The remains are of a single massacre, possibly the residents of a single village. Twenty of the victims were killed by a massive blow to the left back of the head, as if they had been bound, placed on their knees, and struck from behind. The shapes of the wounds match closely the cross-sections of two types of heavy stone axes. These axes were the typical tools and weapons of the Linearbandkeramik, evidence that this conflict was among groups of the farmers themselves.

Herxheim is another German Linearbandkeramik site with evidence of violence preserved among the human remains, dating to ca. 5000 BC. Herxheim has a double-walled enclosure with long, overlapping large pits between the walls. Sometime later, broken and mutilated human remains were placed in these pits and buried (Fig. 4.32). Here the skeletal remains of more than 450 individuals bore evidence of butchering and cooking. Cannibalism appears to have been rampant at this site, whether for ritual or other purposes is not clear, but the number of deceased and mutilated individuals—men, women, and children—is enormous. The evidence from strontium isotope analysis indicates that these broken-up skeletons belonged to individuals whose place of birth was nonlocal and some distance from Herxheim.

VAIHINGEN, GERMANY, 5300 BC

The Linearbandkeramik site of Vaihingen was excavated from 1994 to 2003 and is an excellent example of typical settlements from this period. The modern town of Vaihingen, in the Neckar Valley near Stuttgart, was planning to open a new industrial zone, and an important archaeological site was located in the area. German law requires that archaeological remains be either preserved

Fig. 4.32.
One of the enclosure ditches at Herxheim, Germany, filled with the remains of cannibalized individuals.

or salvaged prior to construction. The excavations were directed by Rüdiger Krause and recovered enormous quantities of material and data. The particular soil conditions and topography of the site afforded very good conditions for preservation of features and other archaeological materials (Fig. 4.33).

Vaihingen sits in an area of rolling hills and valleys. Much of the landscape is covered with a thick layer of loess, and this rich soil has been farmed for millennia. The site is located between two small streams in an area with

Fig. 4.33.
Aerial photo of excavations in progress at Vaihingen near Stuttgart, Germany. There are two areas of fieldwork separated by a field of maize. Excavation of a long house proceeds to the left. Several longhouses are exposed as stains in the ground to the right along with the circular enclosure.

immediate access to good agricultural soils. The 6 ha (15 acre) site contains more than one hundred LBK longhouses, from several phases of settlement, some up to 32 m (100 ft) in length, generally oriented NNW-SSE. It appears that the village was planned because the longhouses are very evenly spaced, 10 m (33 ft) apart. Some of the longhouses are oriented slightly differently, N-S, and probably represent a later phase of construction. Vaihingen was first occupied at the beginning of the LBK period in this region, when a small nucleus of three or four houses was built. Parts of the settlement continued in use until the end of the LBK, ca. 4900 BC.

Some time after the early houses were built, a large flat-bottom ditch 2–2.5 m (ca. 8 ft) wide and 1.3 m (5 ft) deep was dug around most of the settlement (Fig. 4.34). Associated with the ditch were several smaller trenches that marked the line of a palisade. The ditch was 630 m long and enclosed an area of 2.7 ha (almost 7 acres). It does not seem to have been defensive in function and had at least five openings or entrances to the settlement. This palisade and ditch construction may have functioned to keep animals inside the settlement area at night or during certain times of the year; other reasons for its construction are also possible. The ditch was never finished, and there is a 100 m (330 ft) gap on the south side of the settlement. This ditch was in use for only two or three generations, about fifty years.

There were 138 human skeletons found at Vaihingen, in the ditch itself, in pits adjacent to it, or in graves around the houses. Most of the burials are found in the northern half of the site. Fragmentary human remains were found scattered throughout the site. Skeletons in the ditch were usually found with little more than several potsherds alongside. A few burials in the ditch area seem to have been simply thrown in unceremoniously. The skeletons were well preserved because the loess at Vaihingen has a high calcareous content. In all, about eighty-five human burials were found in the ditch fill. The ditch seems to have become a burial ground after it was no longer in use. Most of the burials

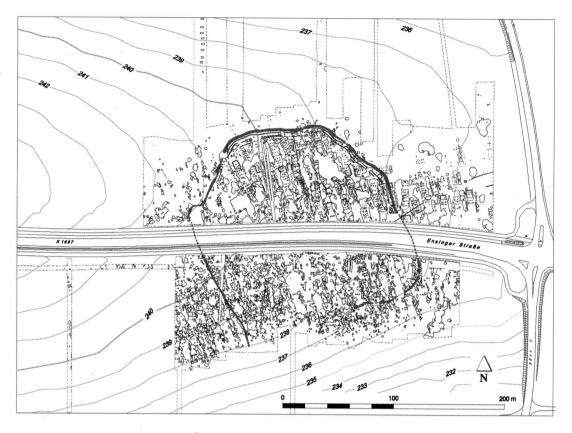

Fig. 4.34.

Plan of the site of Vaihingen. There is a circular ditch around most of the site and a number of long houses and graves both inside and outside the enclosure. The numbered lines are elevation contours.

were in a flexed or crouched position; they were placed in spatially separated groups. These groups include all age and gender categories, suggesting that kin-based or family groups may be represented.

Forty-some graves were found outside of the ditch, mainly in pits or around the houses, usually with more grave goods. Grave 130 (Fig. 4.35) is a typical example of a burial adjacent to a house, found within a large borrow pit next to a longhouse. The grave contains a child, crouched on the left side with tightly flexed limbs. Two undecorated ceramic bowls were placed in front of the child's head as grave gifts.

Many of these individuals exhibit evidence of traumatic injury. Measurements of the bones reveals that the remains scattered in the ditch were more robust than the typical flexed LBK burials in the graves and pits. These individuals may well have been indigenous hunter-gatherers who were killed during conflict with incoming farmers. Analysis of strontium isotopes in the tooth enamel of these burials furnishes evidence that the flexed burials were local and that the scattered remains tended to be nonlocal.

The density of artifacts varies across the site. A relatively high proportion of the ceramic, stone, and worked bone finds come from the southern half of the site. An abundance of animal remains included the antlers of red and roe deer. Antler was an important raw material. Most antler pieces exhibit signs of working, either heating in order to divide up the beams or cut marks or polishing on the points of the tines. Curiously, there is little comparable evidence for the manufacture of flint tools at the site.

POLISHED FLINT AXES

Polished flint axes were one of the most important commodities in Neolithic Europe. Dense forest enveloped much of the continent in the postglacial warmth that characterized much of the Holocene. The beginnings of farming in this area required open areas for fields and pasture. Forest clearance must have been one of the major activities of Neolithic agriculturalists. To fell large trees, the simple flaked stone tools of the preceding Mesolithic period were too light and fragile. Heavy, durable stone axes that could be resharpened were essential equipment for forest clearance. The polished flint axe presented the solution to this problem (Fig. 4.36). There are hundreds of thousands of these tools scattered across the landscape of Neolithic Europe.

The axes were usually made of the best flint available, and they were normally beautifully finished and polished. Other types of stone were also used to make axes, but these are much less common. The axes were hafted in a wooden shaft, usually of ash, and were very functional tools (Fig. 4.37). Experimental studies conducted by various archaeologists indicate that stone axes are three to five times less efficient than steel axes, but fully effective in cutting down large trees.

Size was an important attribute of these axes. Because flint found on the surface of the ground is subject to natural forces that reduce the original nodules in size, the best flint for making axes had to be obtained from the original geological deposits. Flint mining became an important activity in those parts of Europe where there was high-quality flint relatively near the surface of the ground. An example of such mining is discussed in the next section, about the site of Spiennes in Belgium.

The amount of time and labor to produce a polished flint axe was considerable. The people involved in mining and producing axes must have been craft specialists at least part-time. Manufacturing a four-sided axe requires a great deal of experience and practice. There are five stages in the production sequence (Fig. 4.38): (1) selecting raw material, (2) shaping a rough square

Fig. 4.35.
Grave 130 at Vaihingen with two Linearbandkeramik pots near the head of the burial.

Fig. 4.36.
A cache of polished flint axes found together in Denmark. The axes are unused and may represent an offering of some kind.

form by flaking with a hammerstone, (3) finer shaping by flaking with antler tools, (4) shaping the blade and edges with indirect flaking, and (5) polishing, which includes grinding, polishing, and sharpening. Time requirements vary substantially in each stage. Mining for the raw material may take many hours, depending on the availability of the flint. Initial shaping of the raw flint nodule into a square form takes only 5–10 minutes. Three hours are required, however, for flaking the stone into the final rough-out form (stages 3 and 4).

Polishing was done against another stone, using sand and water; almost 30 hours are needed to finish and sharpen an axe; it is actually moved almost 50 km in the process, back and forth against the grinding stone. Total production time once the raw material is obtained is in excess of 32 hours.

In southern Scandinavia, the first such axes were polished on all four sides, on both surfaces of the blade and on the narrower sides. After some centuries, the polish on the sides was no longer added and was likely unnecessary. The original four-sided polish may have been intended to enhance the appearance and value of the axes. Collections of these axes were sometimes ritually sacrificed and deposited in the bogs.

The utility and perhaps status of these tools gave them value. Polished flint axes were traded in large numbers across long distances. The sources of large flint nodules were limited, so there must have been substantial trade in flint axes across much of Europe north of the Alps. For example, there is no high-quality flint in Norway, yet polished flint axes from Denmark or southern Sweden are found in substantial numbers around the Oslo fjord. Neolithic farmers on the island of Bornholm in the middle of the Baltic, 40 km (25 mi) from the nearest mainland, imported tens of thousands of polished flint axes from southern Sweden or Denmark. Similar patterns of long distance trade are seen in other areas.

Fig. 4.37.
An example of a hafted polished flint axe in a shaft of ash from Denmark.

SPIENNES, BELGIUM, 4400 BC

Chalk deposits are the prime source for flint; flint forms as nodules in thin layers or bands within beds of chalk and limestone. Large chalk deposits are found primarily in the northern and western and parts of Europe. Flint mines from the Neolithic period have been found in England, Belgium, France, the Netherlands, Germany, Denmark, Sweden, Iberia, Hungary, Poland, and elsewhere. In fact, flint is available in many parts of Europe, though it is not ubiquitous (Fig. 4.39).

A variety of methods were used to extract the flint, depending on the conditions and depth of deposit. Surface exposures of flint nodules were exploited with small open pits (Fig. 4.40). Actual mining techniques were

Fig. 4.38.
Five stages of polished flint axe manufacture, from raw nodule to rough-out to finished, polished form. The nodule is approximately 35 cm long.

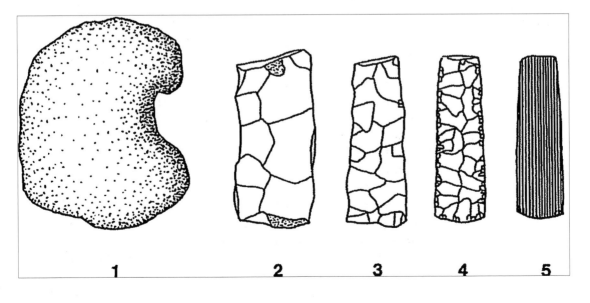

1   2   3   4   5

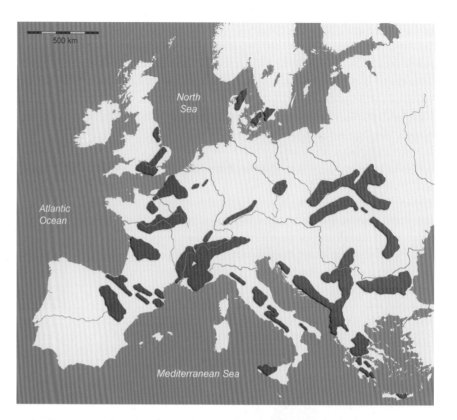

Fig. 4.39.
The distribution of major flint deposits in Europe.

Fig. 4.40.
Grimes Graves in the chalklands of eastern England; the depressions in the ground surface mark the entrances to ancient flint mining shafts.

used where geological conditions required. In the upper levels, where the risk of collapse was high, they dug wide pits with sloping walls. Flint mining was risky business. Skeletons of miners have been found in collapsed shafts at Spiennes. At deeper levels, the chalk bedrock became more stable, and proper shafts could be dug (Fig. 4.41). The shafts were continued until the veins of quality flint were encountered, often at a depth of 5–6 m (15–20 ft) or more. From there horizontal passages were carved out to the sides to collect as much flint as possible. In some cases these lateral shafts extend up to 60 m (200 ft).

Fig. 4.41.
An artist's drawing of a shaft mine with side chambers.

The Neolithic flint mines at Spiennes, covering more than 100 ha (250 acres) of chalk land, are the earliest and largest concentration of ancient flint mines in Europe. They were actively used from 4400 to 2000 years B C. The extraction was carried out in both open quarries and in pits (Fig. 4.42). Digging was done with heavy stone mauls, flint picks, and deer antler picks; the nodules were extracted with the antler picks. There are also bone shovels made from the shoulder blade of red deer. Some of the tabular flint nodules removed from the mine were 2 m (6'6") in length. Axes were roughed out by flaking to their final shape. There are millions of flint flakes and broken rough-outs scattered about the shafts and pits at Spiennes. Polishing was done elsewhere. The level of extraction of flint and the production of axes was enormous, far beyond the needs of the local population. This specialized

Fig. 4.42.
Schematic drawing of the open pits and shaft mines at Spiennes.

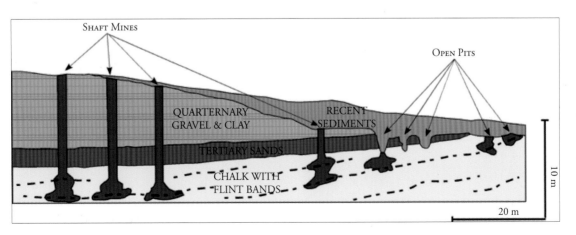

SHAFT MINES

OPEN PITS

QUARTERNARY GRAVEL & CLAY

RECENT SEDIMENTS

TERTIARY SANDS

CHALK WITH FLINT BANDS

10 m

20 m

community activity was a commercial enterprise, trading their product, the polished flint axe, over long distances throughout Belgium and beyond.

There are an estimated 20,000–30,000 pits and shafts in the Spiennes area. Each pit comprises a single shaft and side chambers; there is no horizontal network that connects the shafts below ground. When a new pit was dug out, the older pit was used as a dump for the rubble. The quarry sites often exhibit piles of waste flakes, as well as rejected rough-outs, indicating that initial axe production was done at the mines.

A nearby, fortified Neolithic village was home to the miners and craft persons who dug out the flint and turned it into finished products. In addition to polished flint axes, long blades of flint were also manufactured. A substantial quantity of pottery as well as animal remains have been found in the mines, likely the meals of the miners. Ancient humans are also present, some the remains of those who died in mining accidents.

LA DRAGA, SPAIN, 5000 BC

The rowing events for the 1992 Olympics were held at Estany de Banyoles, a small lake about an hour northwest of Barcelona, Spain. That doesn't seem particularly significant for the Neolithic prehistory of Europe, but in fact it was. Preparations for the Olympic facilities at the lake in 1990 uncovered a previously unknown type of site from the time of the earliest farmers in Iberia.

La Draga is the name given to this early Neolithic village from the end of the sixth millennium BC. The basic materials at the site are similar to those from other Cardial sites with similar shell-decorated pottery, found in caves and rockshelters along the north Mediterranean coast of France, Spain, and Portugal. The general picture of Cardial has been of small groups of herders, spreading by sea along the north shore of the Mediterranean, stopping sporadically to camp or colonize. But La Draga is different because of the preservation of organic materials. The site is one of the very few Early Neolithic settlements in Mediterranean Europe with well-preserved organic remains. Excavations took place in both the shallow waters of the lake and on the wetlands inshore. Some of the wooden objects that were recovered looked almost freshly made. Previously Cardial sites were known only from pottery, stone tools, and animal bones. Now a complete, well-preserved settlement has been uncovered.

La Draga completely rewrites our understanding of the Cardial Culture. The site is inland, it is open-air, and it is on a lake, and with excellent preservation. La Draga contains the remains of large rectangular huts built with oak posts, many objects of wood and basketry and huge amounts of animal bones and cereal grains. La Draga is basically a lake dwelling settlement from the earliest Neolithic in Iberia.

The site lies along the eastern side of the lake on a small peninsula that was almost an island around 5000 BC when the settlement stood there. The shore of the lake during the Neolithic was approximately the same as today, and the actual settlement lay on dry land adjacent to the shore, though likely subject to flooding. There are two major zones at the site, the lakeshore and the higher, more inland settlement area (Fig. 4.43). The two zones are about 20 m (65 ft) apart and connected with a kind of causeway. More than 800 m² (8,500 ft²) have been excavated to date; work still continues at the site. Preservation is excellent on the lakeshore and not as good in the settlement zone, which is slightly higher and drier. The lakeshore zone contains lots of wood, basketry, posts and beams, and other organic materials.

Determining the size and number of houses built at La Draga was difficult because of the huge number of posts driven into the ground. There were 345 posts in one area of 284 m²

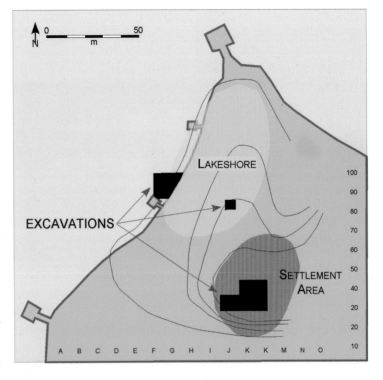

Fig. 4.43.
Plan of the site and excavations along the lake shore. The excavation areas are shown in black. The two zones of the site, lakeshore and settlement, are demarcated. Contour lines indicate elevation; the settlement area is a few meters higher than the lakeshore.

(3,000 ft²), or 1.2 posts per m². Tree ring studies allowed dating of the posts and made it possible to determine that the individual structures were rectangular. There was probably a row of eight to ten houses in each of the two zones. The huts were about 10–12 m (30–40 ft) long by 3–4 m (10–14 ft) wide, and their floors were raised approximately 1 m above the lake level to reduce the impact of flooding. Floors of the huts were made of split planks, and every hut had a hearth inside. Population for the village has been estimated to be about one hundred people.

In addition to the rectangular houses, there were a series of small, oval huts with stone slab floors and one or two interior posts to support a roof. The abundance of charred grains (wheat and barley) and legumes (peas and broad beans) inside these huts suggests they were used as granaries.

Because of the good organic preservation and the wooden posts, the site can be dated by both radiocarbon and tree ring methods. A number of radiocarbon dates from the hearths, cereal grains, animal bones, posts from huts, and wooden tools point to the time span of 5300 to 5150 BC as the most likely period of occupation. It is not possible to determine exact calendar years from the tree rings at La Draga, but a duration of site occupation of approximately one hundred years is a reasonable estimate, based on dates for when the trees were felled. This fits generally well with the radiocarbon dates.

As seen at other sites from the Mesolithic and Neolithic, different species of trees were used for different purposes. Oak was preferred for building. Firewood came from oak, laurel, or boxwood. Wooden tools were made from a variety of species. Boxwood was used for handles (Fig. 4.44) and yew for bows;

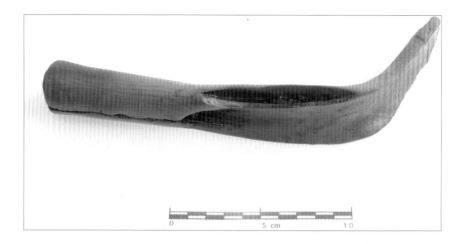

Fig. 4.44.
Boxwood sickle handle from La Draga. A stone blade for cutting would have been inserted in the long depression.

arrow shafts and tips were mostly made from willow or dogwood. Sharpened tips of boxwood shafts between 12–52 cm (5–18 in) long and 1.2–2.7 cm (½–1 in) in diameter were probably parts of javelins or spears. Other items were made from oak, pine, maple, laurel, elder, hazel, juniper, or apple wood. Cord was made from *Clematis* (a fibrous vine) plants and bast—the interior bark of the linden tree—was used for rope. Many fragments of baskets were found, made of reeds or other aquatic plants and probably used as containers for storage or transport.

Most of the domestic equipment was made of local materials, wood, bone and horn, clay, and stone. Bone and horn were used for a variety of implements, including spatulas, long pins, curved, eyed needles, spoons, and toothed spatulas for decorating pottery. Small, hollow tubes were made from bird bones. Querns, made from nearby basalt or coarse-grained rocks such as granite or sandstone, were small and slightly concave.

Fig. 4.45.
A typical Cardial pot with a lug on either side and shell impressed designs around the neck of the vessel. The pot is approximately 25 cm high.

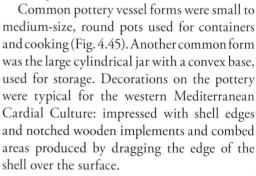

Common pottery vessel forms were small to medium-size, round pots used for containers and cooking (Fig. 4.45). Another common form was the large cylindrical jar with a convex base, used for storage. Decorations on the pottery were typical for the western Mediterranean Cardial Culture: impressed with shell edges and notched wooden implements and combed areas produced by dragging the edge of the shell over the surface.

Some specialized materials were imported: schist and hornfels rock was used for polished stone adzes, shells for beads and pendants, and flint for flaked stone tools. Tools included blades with a retouched edge, which were inserted into the wooden handles of sickles or used as knives, microlithic arrowheads, and borers and scrapers set in deer antler handles.

A few items came from great distance; a small container, a brooch, and a few bracelets were made of marble from Sardinia, almost 600 km (400 mi) across the western Mediterranean.

Cultivation and herding met most of the subsistence needs of the population. The inhabitants grew naked wheat, emmer wheat, and naked and husked barley. Naked wheat was found in huge quantities; amounts of other crops were limited. Broad beans and peas were also grown, perhaps in gardens in the village itself. Fruits, nuts, and berries were gathered in the nearby woods: hazelnuts, walnuts, acorns, pine nuts, blackberries, sloe, crab apples, wild pears, cherries, and grapes are found in large numbers.

The 22,000 pieces of animal skeletons document the importance of herding at La Draga. Cattle and pigs were most abundant; sheep and goats were kept in some number. Few cattle and pigs are known from the cave sites of the Cardial culture. The age of death of the cattle indicates that they were herded for both meat and dairy products. Wild plants and animals were also important in the diet, and they included species from the sea, the forests, and the mountains. Surprisingly, the lake yielded relatively little food beyond migratory waterfowl and a few small fish. The presence of marine mussels around the hearths at La Draga is unexpected and indicates that the inhabitants were getting shellfish from the coast, 50 km (30 mi) to the east. That is a long way to carry mussels.

The diet of the Neolithic inhabitants of La Draga also depended to a considerable extent on plant gathering and hunting wild animals. Hunting produced meat and furs and included animals such as aurochs, wild boar, red deer, roe deer, ibex, fox, weasels, rabbits, and birds. These activities ensured a wide variety of foods, which were obtained from the sea, the lake, the nearby forests, and the mountains.

Today the area is a park and the site is preserved for future excavations. Several Early Neolithic houses have been reconstructed in the park to try to understand and recreate the construction techniques that were used in the past.

ARBON-BLEICHE 3, SWITZERLAND, 3384 BC

The famous Swiss Lake Dwellings of European prehistory are dwellings, but they are not just Swiss and they are not built in the lakes, but along the shore. There are in fact hundreds of these lakeshore settlements known from the circum-Alpine region in Central Europe. In addition to the La Draga site in northeastern Spain, Neolithic lake dwellings have been found in Switzerland, southern Germany, northeastern France, northern Italy, western Austria, Slovenia, Croatia, Albania, and Greece. Quite a number of these have been carefully excavated. In 2011, more than one hundred such sites were added to the UNESCO world heritage list.

The earliest report of these sites goes back to the fifteenth century in Switzerland. During periods of low water, the ancient pilings could be observed along the edges of Alpine lakes (Fig. 4.46). In 1854 Ferdinand Keller,

Fig. 4.46.
Preserved wooden posts on a dry lake floor at a lake dwelling site in France. The posts were exposed during a period of lower lake levels in 1906, revealing the ancient site.

president of the Antiquary Society in Zurich, published a newspaper article on the contents of these sites and described them as lake settlements. His reports were very popular and contributed greatly to the impression that these settlements had been built out over the water, much like similar structures known at the time from Southeast Asia.

Most of the lake dwellings were built between 4300 and 2450 BC, during the Neolithic period. There were some villages with six to ten houses and others with as many as one hundred houses. If six to eight persons occupied each house, populations may have ranged from 50 to 800 people.

Because these houses were built along the wet foreshore of Alpine lakes, much of the debris and waste material generated by the settlement has been buried in fine wet deposits. Preservation is superb. Because wood was the common building material and is so well preserved, there are thousands and thousands of timbers available for inspection that were used as posts and planks in these sites. Tree ring dating has been extremely productive, and many timbers can be precisely dated to the year of cutting. In fact, the tree ring sequence for oak in Central Europe now goes back 12,000 years from the present. The build date for individual houses in the community can sometimes be determined, and even the season of the year when the tree was felled can be established.

Many of these sites have been excavated with great care in the last twenty-five years (Fig. 4.47). The excellent preservation in mud, in the absence of oxygen, also means that organic materials remain in the deposits around the dwellings. Items such as fruits, seeds, leaves, wood, and even fragments of textiles, bread, and dried apples are recovered. In addition other more common archaeological materials—animal bones, stone tools, and ceramics—are present and in fine condition.

Fig. 4.47.
Excavation of a lake dwelling site in downtown Zurich. The black archaeological layer is easily visible beneath the white clay of the natural lake sediments.

Another extraordinary aspect of the lake dwellings is the stratigraphy created by the deposit of settlement waste and debris along the lake shore (Fig. 4.48). Many of these Alpine lakes are calcareous and the natural sediment in the lakes is marl, a white chalky deposit. The settlement deposits are dark brown to black and appear very distinct in the natural white sediments of the lake. The settlement layers were buried under more marl during periods of high water in the lakes. There are often several settlement layers present.

Because the ground was soft and damp, floors had to be rebuilt every four to five years and the wall posts renewed. It is also the case that the levels in the lakes changed considerably, and higher levels meant abandonment of such settlements, either temporarily or for some years.

To illustrate the lake dwelling settlements in more detail, focus turns to the site of Arbon-Bleiche 3 (AB3). This site is both typical and atypical of the lake dwellings. It is typical in most ways, in terms of location, size, construction, layout, and daily life. It is atypical because it was in use for only a very short period. The settlement was founded in 3384 BC and grew quickly in five years to a community of fifty houses and perhaps 300 people or more. Fifteen years later, in a disaster during June 3369 BC, the village of Arbon-Bleiche 3 burned, following a catastrophic flood, and was abandoned forever. Thus, buried in the mud on the Swiss side of Lake Constance is a very brief moment in the life of a Neolithic lake shore community. For archaeologists, the short life of AB3

Fig. 4.48.
Excavation of village deposits along the shore of Lake Zurich, Switzerland. The white layers are natural lake marl deposits. The black layers are anthropogenic, the result of human occupation and deposits of charcoal and waste from settlement. A series of settlement layers are visible between the lake marls, and the remains of posts from the pile dwellings are clearly visible in and beneath the archaeological layers.

means less-complicated deposits and easier reconstruction of the community plan and activities.

The Swiss excavated about one-half of the site, 1,100 m² (12,000 ft²), between 1993 and 1995 (Fig. 4.49). This project produced one of the most detailed records of lake dwellings available anywhere. The excavations at AB3 were published in three superb volumes between 2000 and 2004 that represent a benchmark for such studies.

This settlement today lies a few hundred meters (500 ft) from the lake, but during the Neolithic the village was situated on the shore of a small bay. Some twenty-five houses were excavated, 6 to 12 m (20 to 40 ft) long and 3 to 6 m (10 to 20 ft) wide. The houses were built according to a plan, along separate rows with their long side facing the lake. There was a broad alley through the middle of the houses connecting to the lake. Different kinds of posts and wood were used in various parts of the settlement construction. The houses were begun using vertical posts of white fir. Smaller posts and planks between the posts were used for walls. Large roof shingles were made from white fir and other wood.

Some evidence suggests that the house floors were raised slightly above ground level. Attic space may have been used for sleeping and storage. Clay ovens and fireplaces were inside the houses. Some houses were divided into two rooms, one large room with a fireplace and a smaller one. The house was the probably home for a large family of several generations. Cooking was carried out at the fireplace, where pots of cereals, herbs, meat, or fish stewed for several hours. These cooking pots were large, up to 40 cm

(15 in) high and 20–25 cm (ca. 10 in) in diameter.

Thousands of animal bones were preserved at the site along with lots of plant parts and seeds. These materials make it possible to reconstruct subsistence activities and diet at the settlement. Agriculture and much of the diet was focused on cereals, primarily wheats and barley. Winnowing baskets were found about the site, and there was at least one quern stone for grinding in every house. Cereals were cooked in pots as part of a stew and also eaten as bread. Large quantities of flax and poppies were also grown. The flax may have been used for fodder, and for its oily seeds and fiber, the source of linen cloth. The poppies may have been used for narcotics, although the oil-rich seeds could also have been eaten.

Collecting wild plants was important. In total, more than one hundred species of wild plants were found in the deposits. Gathering produced animal fodder, wood for firewood, construction timber, and tools, and food. About 50 percent of the plant calories for the villagers came from wild resources. Hazelnuts made up a large proportion of caloric intake. Fruits rich in vitamins, such as rose hips, raspberries, wild strawberries, blackberries, sloe, and crab apple, were collected in large numbers (Fig. 4.50). Apple remains and gooseberry were also found inside pots. Wastes from the houses were dumped between the structures. This material included lots of chaff from cereal threshing, and human feces. The feces contained large amounts of berry seeds and bran, among other things.

Meat came from both wild and domesticated animals in almost equal proportions. Cows and pigs yielded beef and pork; cows constituted about two-thirds of the domestic animal bones and were also used for draft and milk. Sheep furnished only about 6 percent of the meat and were likely kept primarily for wool, and perhaps milk. Herd sizes for the domestic animals have been estimated around 28–55 cattle, 20–40 sheep or goats, and 75–145 pigs. Analysis of the feces of domesticated animals indicated these animals spent most of the year away from the village. In the winter, however, they were kept close by and were fed from various wild plants and leaves.

There are two lines of evidence for dairying, often difficult to document archaeologically. Chemical analysis of trace residues in potsherds from AB3 documented a fatty acid and the stable carbon isotopic signature from fat residues of animal origin, most likely cow, sheep, or goat. Second, and

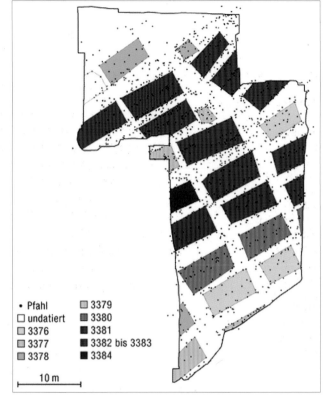

• Pfahl   ▨ 3379
☐ undatiert ▦ 3380
▨ 3376   ■ 3381
▨ 3377   ■ 3382 bis 3383
▨ 3378   ■ 3384

|— 10 m —|

Fig. 4.49.
Plan of Arbon-Bleiche 3, Switzerland, excavated houses and two smaller structures. Year of construction for each house is indicated by color and provided in the key. The black dots mark vertical posts (pfahl) at the site.

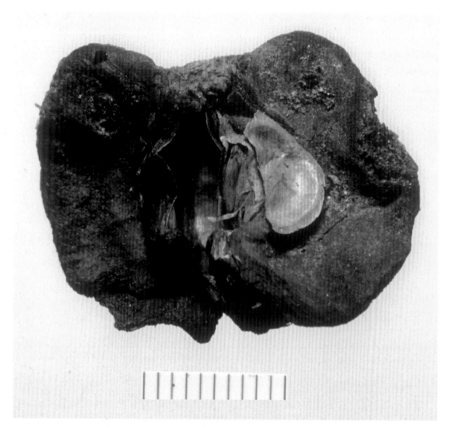

Fig. 4.50.
Half of a crab apple
from Arbon-Bleiche 3.
Scale in mm.

beyond question, there were actual milk residues preserved in several vessels from the site.

Dogs were common as work animals for hunting, and they were also eaten. Red deer provided most of the wild game, but aurochs, wild boar, and bear were also hunted. The great level of detail made available by tree rings allowed excavators to estimate that six red deer and three wild boar were killed by the villagers every year. The smaller bones from fish and amphibians document the importance of frogs and fish in the diet as well. Whitefish was most common, although there were also many bones from large pike.

Stone tools took several forms. Arrowheads, sickles, knife blades, and even a dagger (Fig. 4.51) were made from flint. Heavy, wood-cutting axes were made from either ground greenstone or red deer antler and were found everywhere in the village. These axes were fixed directly into ash-wood handles. Bone and antler were used for a variety of tools. Bone awls were employed to work leather and to weave textiles or basketry. Bone chisels could work wood, bark, or even softened antler. Other bone or antler points were used as arrowheads or for fishing. Fine bone combs served to separate linen fibers for the production of cloth. Antler, bone, and especially animal teeth went into ornaments; wild boar tusks were made into pendants. The canines and metapodial bones of dogs, wolves, and bears were perforated and used for beads and pendants.

Finds of linen, spindle whorls, and loom weights show that textiles were woven in these villages. Wool production for fiber was also important at some settlements during this period. Copper was produced and used locally in eastern Switzerland after 3900 BC. Special crucibles and copper celts and jewelry began to appear.

Experimental archaeology is one way to learn more about the past by trying to recreate aspects of it. The scientists involved in the excavations at AB3 wanted to know more about the structures they had uncovered. There is a Lake Dwelling Museum on the north (German) side of Lake Constance, with a series of reconstructed houses. House 23 from Arbon-Bleiche 3 was recreated in full size there in the summer of 1998 (Fig. 4.52). The reconstruction was as accurate as possible, with the same (original) species of wood used for the different parts of the house. The pilings were the same size and placed at the same angle in the ground as the original. The walls and roof of the house did not survive at the archaeological site, of course, so these constructions involved some conjecture based on the construction material that had been excavated, such as collapsed timbers, rope, and burnt daub from the walls.

Because of the uneven ground beneath the house, the floor had to be raised almost one meter. That elevation was also useful in years with higher lake levels. The walls were made of vertical boards and wattle; cracks between the boards were sealed with moss that was also found at the archaeological site. The roof shingles were tied to the beams and weighed down with long poles. The roof has already survived a number of heavy storms. The reconstructed lake dwellings at the museum are of great interest; in the five years after its construction, the Arbon-Bleiche 3 house and the museum welcomed 1.5 million visitors.

The detailed history of AB3, and other lakeshore sites around the Alps, is almost unparalleled in archaeology. The extraordinary conditions of preservation in the cold lake mud means that a wide range of artifacts and other materials survive to the present. The large number of wooden posts that survive mean that dating these sites to specific calendar years is both possible and extraordinary. To know that the site was in use for only fifteen years before it was destroyed and abandoned; to be able to estimate the number of animals killed every year; and to have visible remains of milk, bread, dried apples, along with intact hafted tools, baskets, and the like is simply remarkable and very, very rare. At such places it seems you can almost see the past.

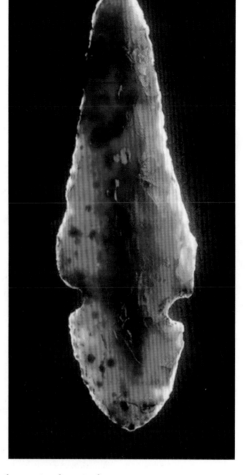

Fig. 4.51.
Flint dagger from Arbon-Bleiche 3, 10 cm long.

Fig. 4.52.
The reconstructed house from Arbon-Bleiche 3 (right) at the Pfahlbaumuseum Unteruhldingen, Lake Constance.

ÖTZI, ITALY, 3300 BC

One of the most important finds of the twentieth century in Europe, was made in 1991 in the high Alps, on the border between Italy and Austria. Two German hikers noticed a human body, half-frozen, face-down, in the snow and ice along the trail (Fig. 4.53). The hikers contacted the local authorities, who assumed it was the body of an unfortunate mountaineer. A number of people die in the Alps each year. The remains were somewhat carelessly removed from the ice and taken to a morgue. After inspection of the body and particularly the items found with the corpse, however, it became clear that this was not the result of a climbing accident; it was the frozen body of a man from the Stone Age.

The body was taken to the University of Innsbruck for study. A wide range of scientists have been involved in the ongoing research. At 3,200 m (10,500 ft),

Ötzi the Iceman, as he has come to be known, is the *highest* archaeological find in Europe. Sometime fairly soon after his death, snow covered his body; there are no traces of scavenging by birds or other animals. He was mummified, dried by the sun, wind, and ice of the mountaintops. Over time, a small glacier on the mountaintop expanded to cover the depression in which the Iceman lay. Amazingly, this thick, heavy layer of ice did not crush the body, but sealed it into a small depression for 6,000 years, as if in a huge freezer. The glacier retreated during the warm summer of 1991 and exposed the corpse.

Ötzi was about 1.60 m tall (5'3")—about the average height of a Neolithic male—and slim, probably weighing about 50 kg (110 lb). The extent of preservation is remarkable; most of the internal organs, as well as the eyeballs, are intact. His eye color was blue. The Iceman was approximately forty-five years old at the time of his death. Although the body was hairless from the effects of freezing and thawing, hair was found around the body. Tattoos were clearly visible on his back and right leg. X-rays revealed several broken ribs and indicate that the Iceman suffered from arthritis in his neck, lower back, and right hip. An absence of stomach contents and the presence of material in the large intestine indicate that he had not eaten for eight hours. His last meal included unleavened bread, some greens, and meat. DNA analysis had identified the meat as coming from red deer. Analysis of pollen in the stomach contents indicates he died

Fig. 4.53.
The body of the Iceman as he appeared to the hikers who found his remains.

Fig. 4.54.
A recent forensic reconstruction of the Iceman by Kennis and Kennis.

between March and June. Radiocarbon dates from the body and the equipment the Iceman carried provided a date of around 3300 BC, clearly in the Neolithic period. A forensic reconstruction reveals the face of this 5,300-year-old man (Fig. 4.54).

Until recently there were several theories about how the Iceman died in the high Alps, involving either an accident or some kind of escape. Some suggested he may have been a shepherd in the mountains, caught by an early fall blizzard. Autopsy of the body, however, has revealed several wounds. Deep cuts to his hand and wrist suggest he was in an armed struggle. An arrowhead lodged in his back may well have been the cause of death if it cut an artery. In addition, recent CAT scans of the crania suggest that the Iceman suffered severe trauma to his head at the time of death, either from a fall or a blow. It now seems that the Iceman died as a result of violent conflict. It also appears that after death, his body floated around in a pool of water during an earlier thaw of the ice. That floating would also explain the dispersal of his clothing and equipment away from the body.

The Iceman was carrying a substantial amount of gear with him—seven articles of clothing and twenty items of equipment. The items included a bow and quiver of arrows, bow strings, bone points, a needle, a hafted copper axe, a wooden rucksack frame, two birch bark containers, a hafted knife of flint and its sheath, several flint tools (including a scraper, an awl, a flake, and a tool for pressure flaking flint), a net (perhaps for catching birds), a piece of ibex horn, a marble pendant, and birch fungus (possibly used as medicine). Most of the arrows were unfinished; he carried several items that were incomplete or in need of repair.

His clothing included a large belt with a pouch, holding up a leather loincloth and skin leggings, a coat of deerskin, a cape of woven grass, a conical leather cap with fur on the inside and a chin strap, and shoes with bearskin soles filled with grass for warmth (Fig. 4.55). No obvious food was found among his possessions, but a few small bone fragments and a few small pieces of fruit were found nearby. The bones come from ibex, a mountain goat. The fruits are sloe, a small, bitter, plumlike fruit.

More than 150 specialists have been studying all aspects of the Iceman and his equipment. More than 300 scientific articles and books had been published as of 2008. One of the more interesting investigations involves his almost pure copper axe (Fig. 4.56). When first discovered, the axe was assumed to be made of bronze, dating the iceman to the Bronze Age (early copper axes were almost unknown in this part of Europe). The Iceman's axe is perhaps the earliest known in western Europe and almost certainly came from the Vinça culture of Serbia. This new metal documents the use of copper during the latter half of the Neolithic period. Copper was being mined and smelted in several areas of eastern Europe by this time and was eventually traded as far as Scandinavia.

One of the more difficult questions about the Iceman involves where he came from. The high Alps are uninhabitable in winter; the Iceman's home must have been at lower altitude, either north or south of the Alps. He probably came from valleys to the south in Italy, less than a day's walk away. The grains of wheat attached to his clothing and his last meal suggest connections with farming villages. His lungs were black with the hearth smoke that filled early Neolithic houses. He carried a small ember of charcoal, for use in starting fires, from the wood of trees that grow south of the Alps. Pollen found in his intestines came from the hornbeam tree, which grew only to the south.

New scientific methods have been employed to resolve this question about Ötzi's place of origin. Wolfgang Müller and his colleagues undertook an isotopic study of the Iceman's tooth enamel, bone, and stomach contents. Tooth enamel forms shortly after birth and retains the isotopic signature of the place of birth. Their study focused on strontium, lead, and oxygen isotopes to determine his movements. They identified four major rock units

Fig. 4.55.
A museum reconstruction of the Iceman's clothing.

in the potential homelands of the Iceman on the basis of strontium and lead isotope ratios. Strontium isotope ratios in the enamel of the Iceman averaged 0.721, and values in his bone were approximately 0.718. These values are most congruent with the volcanic and phyllite/gneiss rocks largely to the south of the find spot in Italy, and they suggested to the researchers that the Iceman spent most of his life in this area, no more than 60 km from where he was found.

The Iceman has now been returned to the cold. His body today is displayed through a small window in a large freezer in a $1.9 million exhibit in the South

Fig. 4.56.
Some of the Iceman's equipment: the copper axe, quiver, flint knife with sheath.

Tyrol Museum of Archaeology in northern Italy. The study of the Iceman's frozen corpse, clothing, and the artifacts that were found with his body reveals an extraordinary picture of his life and death. The autopsy and archaeological chemistry that were done tell us that this forty-five-year-old man died in the spring of the year from a violent encounter that included an arrow in his back. The technological sophistication of his equipment is remarkable. The very early copper axe reveals long-distance exchange networks across Europe more than 6,000 years ago. Several lines of evidence point to the valleys south of the Alps as his place of birth. Mysteries of course remain—part of the allure of the past. For example, what was Ötzi doing high in the Alps at the time of his death? Some of these questions may never be answered.

The Iceman is one of those rare finds in archaeology that attract enormous public attention because of the unusual conditions of preservation. The mysteries of the Iceman—how the body was preserved for so long, and how and why he died—add to the aura of intrigue surrounding the discovery. Equally important, however, is how much we are learning from the Iceman about the artifacts, clothing, and equipment of the Neolithic—and especially how those people were not so very different from ourselves.

THE MEGALITHS OF WESTERN EUROPE

Agriculture spread to western and northern Europe at the beginning of the fourth millennium BC. The early farmers there built tens of thousands of massive stone structures, some still visible today, along the western fringe of Europe in Portugal, Spain, France, Belgium, Ireland, Britain, the Netherlands, Germany, Denmark, and Sweden (Fig. 4.57). These megaliths (monuments of large stones) are distributed geographically in a curious, patchy pattern that defies explanation. Different traditions of pottery and house construction were associated with these monuments; apparently different groups of people built the same kinds of monumental tombs.

Radiocarbon dates indicate an age for these structures generally between 4000 and 2000 BC. Most of the megalithic structures were built early in this period and sometimes within a very short period of a few hundred years or less. Varying greatly in size and in the number of stones used for construction, they were all built to withstand the test of time—to last for many generations.

The megaliths fall into three major categories: menhirs, henges, and tombs. Menhirs are large standing stones, erected either singly or collectively in linear or circular arrangements. Standing stones have various heights, usually in the range of 1–5 m (3–16 ft). The largest known menhir comes from Brittany in northwestern France. It now lies on the ground, broken into five huge pieces. Originally this stone was 23 m (75 ft) long, the height of a six-story building, and weighed at least 350 tons.

Perhaps the most impressive linear arrangement of stones is found at Carnac, also in Brittany, where in one instance approximately 3,000 large stones were arranged in thirteen parallel lines, stretching almost 6 km (4 mi) across the

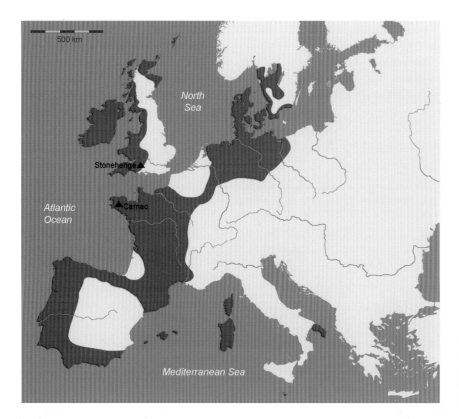

Fig. 4.57.
Distribution of megalithic tombs in Neolithic Western Europe.

landscape (Fig. 4.58). The stones are shorter to the east, around 1 m (3 ft), and reach up to 4 m (13 ft) high to the west. The purpose of these linear arrangements is unclear. What is intriguing is that an arrangement of wooden poles could easily have been used as markers in place of such massive stone sentinels.

Henge monuments, or circles, are defined by an enclosure, usually a circular earthen ditch and bank system. Not all henges contain stones; some appear to have been large timber structures. Stone circles, found primarily in the British Isles, are a special form of alignment with definite astronomical significance. Although the best known of these is Stonehenge, hundreds of other stone circles dot the landscape of northern England and Scotland. The size of these monument varies from tens to hundreds of meters in diameter. Such henges are also known on the continent.

A megalithic tomb is a roofed stone chamber. Large stones and piles of earth were used to create these chambers. These tombs usually had a burial area in or on the ground, surrounded by a chamber made of great vertical stones capped by huge horizontal stones (Figs. 4.59). No mortar was used in these constructions. The entire stone tomb was usually covered with a mound of earth to create an artificial cave. Sometimes a covered passage at the edge of the mound provided an entrance for reuse of the tomb.

Megalithic tombs range from small, single chamber structures to enormous hills of rock and soil that may hide a number of rooms and crawlways. There are three categories of these megalithic tombs. A dolmen is a small megalithic tomb or chamber with a large stone for a roof (Figs. 4.59a and 4.60). Passage

Fig. 4.58.
One of several areas at Carnac, France, with multiple lines of standing stones known as menhirs.

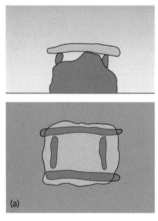

(a)

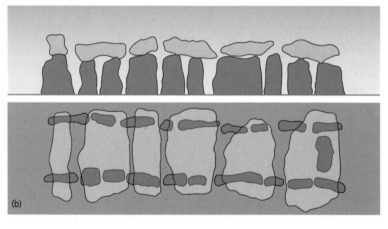

(b)

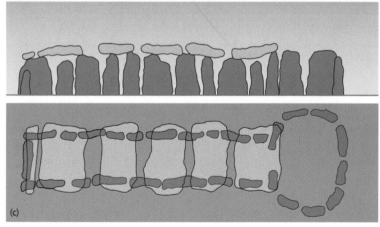

(c)

Fig. 4.59.
Three common types of megalithic tombs in western Europe:
a. dolmen, b. gallery grave, c. passage grave.

Fig. 4.60.
A megalithic dolmen in
Sweden. The tomb lies
on an earthen platform,
surrounded by a ring of
large stones.

and gallery graves are two types of larger tombs (Figs. 4.59b and 4.59c). A passage grave is entered via a long, low, narrow tunnel that opens into a wider room, generally near the center of the structure. A gallery grave, or long tomb, lacks an entrance passage, and the burial room or rooms form the entire internal structure. These tombs may have been intended for all the members of a related group of farmsteads or hamlets; the tomb may have symbolized the collective and cooperative nature of the group.

Megalithic structures give us dramatic and enduring evidence of the Neolithic in western Europe. The stones and mounds of these monuments serve today as a powerful reminder of ancestors and what was. It is difficult to grow up in areas of standing prehistoric monuments without some appreciation of the past. The next stop on our tour is on the Orkney Islands on the northwest coast of Scotland, where megalithic and Neolithic are almost synonymous.

SKARA BRAE, ORKNEY ISLANDS, 3200 BC

The Orkneys Islands lie at the margins of habitability, 16 km (10 mi) off the northeastern tip of Scotland. Along with the Shetlands, further north and east, they are known as the Northern Isles of Britain. Most of the seventy Orkney Islands are made up of a series of long rounded hills with high cliffs at some edges, lovely sand beaches in small hidden niches, and always the sea. The topography is very visible; there are almost no trees. Views are uninterrupted, except by cloud or mist; long vistas across land and sea are the norm. Light and wind define the place. The vegetation is largely grass, with heather on higher ground. Small fields hold hay or pasture, and only a few carry other crops— barley, potatoes, turnips. Beef cattle and sheep are the animals of pasture. The sea holds rich resources of fish and shellfish (crab, lobster, scallop, shrimp) along with seals, whales, and other marine species.

The Gulf Stream warms the waters of Orkney. The mean air temperature varies less than 10 °C (20 °F) over the course of the year. Temperatures are cool, not cold, year round; a warm summer temperature is around 20 °C (68 °F). Frost and snow are uncommon, yet the islands lie near the limits of cultivation because of a short growing season. Although tempered by the Gulf Stream, the wind and rain don't stop. Measurable precipitation reaches almost 1 m and falls 188 days a year, basically every other day. Rainfall is less in summer, more in the fall. The wind is always; in the absence of trees, there is little to interrupt its passage.

Fewer than twenty islands are inhabited today, by approximately 20,000 people. The smaller islands have lovely names—Rousay, Westray, Hoy, Sanday. The largest is prosaically known as Mainland. They are covered with archaeology: Iron Age brochs (fortified settlements), Bronze Age funerary barrows and burnt mounds, and Neolithic sites in all sizes, shapes, and forms.

Nearing the western shore of Mainland, one sees rising in the distance the House of Skaill, the home of the local laird, William Watt, who in AD 1850 discovered an extraordinary Neolithic community outside his house. A massive winter storm had blasted the coast of the island and carried away the tops of the dunes below the castle. Hidden beneath the sands was a warren of finely built, circular stone structures (Fig. 4.61). These buildings were the homes and ceremonial places of early Neolithic farmers. By 1924, when the site was taken into state guardianship, five of the houses had been cleaned out and many artifacts removed.

Skara Brae became familiar to the archaeological world following excavations there by V. Gordon Childe, professor of archaeology in

Fig. 4.61.
Aerial view of Skara Brae, Orkney Islands.

Edinburgh. Childe was a well-known prehistorian even before the investigations at Skara Brae. His activities there certainly raised awareness of the site and of the prehistoric importance of the Orkneys. Childe spent three seasons at Skara Brae, from 1928 to 1930, uncovering a number of the structures. Another series of excavations took place in 1972–73 under the direction of David V. Clarke. These two projects have established the basic information for the site.

Skara Brae was occupied from approximately 3180 to 2500 BC. It is often described as Europe's most complete Neolithic village (Fig. 4.62). Ten houses have been uncovered, and more of the site extends unexcavated into a nearby field. Additional structures may have been destroyed in earlier storms, prior to the site's discovery and construction of a protective seawall.

The houses are remarkably well-built stone structures, constructed with dry wall by stacking thin sandstone slabs that peel away from bedrock in the area. The structures still stand today more than 2 m (6 ft) high in some places. A central underground passage ran between the houses, connecting the lot. Each dwelling was entered from a tunnel to the passage through a low doorway with a stone slab that could be closed and sealed. A drainage system was part of the village plan, with a simple form of toilet in each structure. Seven of the houses have almost identical furnishings, also of stone, with bed frames and shelving in the same place in each house (Fig. 4.63). An eighth house lacks such boxes, shelves, and central hearth. This structure has been divided into small cubicles. Fragments of stone, bone, and antler tools found here suggested

Fig. 4.62.
The buried houses at Skara Brae.

Fig. 4.63.
House interior, Skara Brae.

to the excavators that the building was used for making tools such as bone needles or flint axes.

A population of fifty to one hundred people seems a reasonable number for Skara Brae. The houses measure 40 m² (450 ft²) in size on average, a large square room with a central hearth used for light, heating, and cooking. The fuel was probably wood, either driftwood or local trees, but this is often debated because of the absence of wood on the island today. There is some evidence that dried seaweed may also have been used for fires. A glassy, slaglike material has been found at several sites that may be the remains of burned seaweed.

The people who built Skara Brae were primarily pastoralists who raised cattle and sheep, but they also grew some crops. Fish bones and shells are common in the refuse heaps, indicating that inhabitants supplemented their diet with seafood. Seals and perhaps whales likely added to the larder. The 1972–73 excavations uncovered deeper, waterlogged layers in the site with preserved organic materials, items that otherwise would have disappeared. They included cereal grains from cultivated barley, a twisted skein of heather stalks (one of a very few examples of Neolithic rope), and a wooden handle for a tool.

Many other interesting artifacts have been recovered in addition to the ubiquitous flint tools and broken pieces of pottery. A number of enigmatic "carved stone balls" have been found (Fig. 4.64). These are elaborately worked and were time-costly to produce. Their function is unknown, but they may have been mace heads or more deliberately shaped religious objects of some kind. Lumps of red ochre found at Skara Brae are suggested to have been used for body painting. Nodules of another reddish iron mineral pigment, hematite, with highly polished surfaces have been found, implying that these nodules were used to work leather. Other artifacts were made from animal bone, whale and walrus ivory, and killer whale teeth, among them awls, needles, knives, beads, adzes, shovels, small bowls, and lovely ivory pins up to 25 cm (10 in) in length.

A low, narrow Neolithic road ran east from Skara Brae toward the center of the island to an area known as the Ness of Brodgar, 9 km distant. Here has been found a remarkable complex of contemporary Neolithic monuments and structures that are unsurpassed anywhere in Britain or continental Europe.

The Ness is a narrow spit of land between two lakes in the interior of Mainland. This peninsula and the surrounding area contains one of the densest concentrations of Neolithic monuments known anywhere. Maeshowe is a carefully corbeled stone structure, a type of passage grave (or cairn, in the lingua of Scotland and the Orkneys), buried beneath an immense mound of earth. The Stones of Stenness (Fig. E.1) and the Ring of Brodgar are henge monuments of extraordinary appearance, with sharp-cut pillars 4–5 m (12–16 ft) in height striking up at the sky. The Ring of Brodgar still counts twenty-seven of the original sixty sentinel stones that stood in a true circle more than 100 m (330 ft) in diameter. The Ring sits inside a circular, rock-cut ditch 3 m (10 ft) deep on a rise above the Ness, overlooking the lakes, the Ness itself, the Stones of Stenness, and Maeshowe.

Fig. 4.64. Carved stone balls from Skara Brae. The round stone ball is ca. 8 cm in diameter.

The entire area is no more than 3 km (almost 2 mi) in diameter. These spectacular monuments were sufficient to bring recognition as a World Heritage Site in 1999, but ongoing discoveries on the Ness since then are going to completely rewrite the prehistory of this remarkable place.

The southern end of the Ness is a humpback ridge of land, previously assumed to be a natural feature of the landscape (Fig. 4.65). This is the new area of archaeological investigation, and several clues came early. Two standing stones rise near the tip of the peninsula. A decorated stone slab was discovered on the Ness in 1925. More materials began to show up in recent years, as plowing at the site reached deeper into the soil. Archaeologists from the Orkney Research Center decided to go to work.

The first step involved a geophysical survey of a large part of the Ness, peering into the earth with magnetometry. These instruments measure the magnetic field of the sediments and subsurface features as they move along the surface of the ground. Eventually a map is produced that shows magnetic irregularities and anomalies from the normal background of the area. The magnetometer map of the Ness showed some astounding features: huge earthen and stone walls and chambers.

Excavations in the last few years have revealed that the humpback ridge is not natural at all, but the accumulation of a series of massive stone structures,

Fig. 4.65.
Aerial view of the excavations at the Ness of Brodgar.

collapsed walls, and refuse heaps that mark one of the most fascinating complexes of ruins from the Neolithic anywhere in Europe.

To date, four large structures have been exposed, and more are known from the geophysical survey. The first excavations revealed a spectacular Neolithic wall, part of a large rectangular structure, with sharp internal angles, fine coursed stonework, and beautiful corner buttresses. Designated as Structure 1, a building 15 by 10 m (50 by 33 ft) in size with walls still standing to a height of 1 m (3 ft), was eventually revealed in the excavations. Further excavations have uncovered two more huge buildings next to Structure 1, both more than 9 m wide and at least 15 m (50 ft) long. The side walls of these structures (8 and 12) have regular compartments, or stalls, separated by fine stone coursed piers. In Structure 8 not only has evidence for a regular roofing system of stone slates been uncovered, but the first evidence in northern Europe for Neolithic painted walls has also come to light. All of these free-standing buildings had apparently been razed at some point, perhaps for the construction of what was found next.

The most recent excavations have surpassed all expectations. The new building, Structure 10, is massive, 20 m by 25 m (65 by 80 ft) in size, with external walls of exceptionally fine stone coursework 5 m (16 ft) thick (Fig. 4.66). These walls enclosed a central, cross-shaped chamber about 6.5 m (21 ft) in diameter. The stone work on the interior walls of this chamber is a

combination of red and yellow sandstones that must have been brought some distance to the site.

The entire complex of buildings at the Ness appears to be enclosed by a huge wall, up to 6 m wide. The wall encloses the main structures of the Ness, an area of 125 m by 75 m (400 by 250 ft) in extent, forming what is perhaps a Neolithic temple precinct. In its final phase Structure 10 would have dominated the Ness, sitting on the top of the ridge, visible for many kilometers across the landscape. Whatever the function of these structures, they are among the most remarkable in all of Neolithic Europe.

Fig. 4.66.
Excavation of the large Neolithic stone structures on the Ness of Brogdar.

STONEHENGE, ENGLAND, 3100 BC

About 150 km (90 mi) west of London lies the Salisbury Plain, an extraordinary part of the British Isles, at least in terms of archaeology. This is the home of Stonehenge, the most impressive prehistoric monument in England, perhaps in all of Europe. It is not the largest or the richest, but Stonehenge holds an enormous fascination, as much for the mysterious aura that surrounds it as for the impressive feat of its construction. Some of the stones have been taken away over the centuries; many have fallen and lie half-buried in the earth. Other stark, brooding, gray stones still stand, arranged in the circles and arches that outline this "temple to the sun" and ceremonial center of late Neolithic Britain. Stonehenge is indeed a place of mystery and wonder.

What many don't know is that Stonehenge is only one of a number of very important monuments on the Salisbury Plain (Fig. 4.67). To an archaeologist, this is one of the great prehistoric places, a World Heritage site, a zone of monuments, and a multitude of unanswered questions. Within a few kilometers of Stonehenge are Neolithic long barrows, huge oval and circular earthworks, dozens of Bronze Age mounds, an Iron Age hillfort, and many, many still-buried secrets.

The construction and elaboration of Stonehenge took 1,500 years, from approximately 3100 to 1600 BC, during the Neolithic and early Bronze Age. Farming had arrived in the British Isles a millennium earlier, around 4000 BC. Domesticated plants and animals, pottery, and small villages spread across the landscape as forests were felled, fields cleared, pasture opened, and population grew. In this Neolithic period a series of great constructions were erected around the Salisbury Plain. This landscape of monuments is our focus.

Following an introduction to some of the recent research that has been done in the Stonehenge region in the last decade, I consider each of the major monuments individually. It is important to remember, however, that these monuments were not separate and isolated places but part of a greater pattern of communal activity, ceremony and world view concerned at least in part with placating nature, caring for the ancestors, and dealing with death. These structures discussed below are clearly related, found within an area of less than 4 by 3 km² (2½ by 2 mi), for the most part mutually visible. Some of these monuments have been known for centuries—Stonehenge, Durrington Walls, Woodhenge, the Cursus, and the Avenue. Much that is new has been learned about these places in the last ten years as a consequence of recent

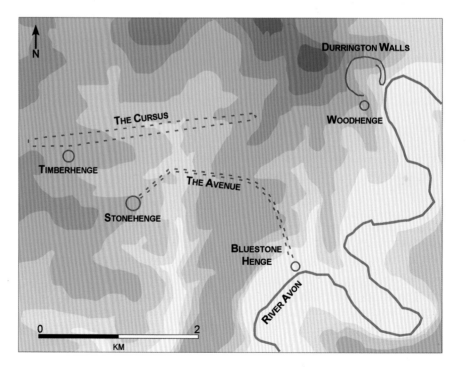

Fig. 4.67.
Plan of the Salisbury Plain with monuments mentioned in the text.

archaeological efforts in the Salisbury Plain. In addition, new monuments have been discovered—Bluestone Henge, Timberhenge—that make the landscape even richer and more intriguing. This research has revolutionized our understanding of Stonehenge and its companions on the plain.

New Projects

It may seem surprising that so much work remains to be done in a place like Stonehenge. But the reason is straightforward: virtually all previous studies have focused on a few large monuments. The area of the Salisbury Plain is extensive. Archaeological fieldwork is slow and expensive. Money for excavations is difficult to come by. So archaeologists concentrated their efforts at places where they knew something might be found. Now the scientists are starting to look beyond the major monuments.

Several projects have been ongoing in the last decade at Stonehenge and environs. Over the last ten years, the largest archaeological project ever undertaken in the UK, the Stonehenge Riverside Project, has been busy looking for new structures, digging into old ones, obtaining more precise dates, and trying to determine the relationships between the various monuments in the Stonehenge region. The main aims of the project are to evaluate the idea that Stonehenge was dedicated to the ancestors, and that Woodhenge and Durrington Walls were places of the living and more recently deceased.

The Stonehenge Riverside Project was funded at more than $1 million by the British Research Council, National Geographic, and English Heritage, among others. A consortium of universities ran the project. It was directed by Mike Parker Pearson of Sheffield University, with co-directors Josh Pollard (Bristol University), Julian Thomas (Manchester University), Kate Welham (Bournemouth University), and Colin Richards (Manchester University). It was a huge project combining the efforts of hundreds of staff, students, and volunteers in summer excavations and year-round analysis of the materials and information that the fieldwork produced.

In another Stonehenge study, Timothy Darvill and Geoffrey Wainwright have focused on the "bluestones," which come from dolerite outcrops in the Preselli Hills of southwest Wales. In 2008 Darvill and Wainwright made a small excavation within Stonehenge, digging into the outer bluestone setting. Their view is of Stonehenge as a place of healing. Finally, a third project, the most recent, involves a survey of the fields and terrain around Stonehenge and the other monuments using geophysical instrumentation to peer into the earth. Like sonar looking for submarines, georadar pings into the subsoil and records the return signals to identify harder or softer, drier or wetter places below the ground surface. Vince Gaffney, of the University of Birmingham, is leading the multimillion-euro Stonehenge Hidden Landscapes Project, projected to map 14 km² (5½ mi²) around Stonehenge in a three-year period. It is probably safe to say that almost as much has been learned about Stonehenge and its environs in the last ten years as was known prior to the start of twenty-first century. Now to the monuments themselves.

Stonehenge

Seen today, Stonehenge is a ruin, the remains of strange and elaborate structures built more than 5,000 years ago, used and expanded for more than 1,500 years, before finally being abandoned around 1600 BC (Fig. 4.68). A henge is a circular earthwork. In a number of cases around the British Isles, these henge monuments contain standing stones as part of the monument. Although Stonehenge was almost continuously rebuilt during the later Neolithic and early Bronze Age, the previous constructions remained visible and respected as part of the continuity of the monument from beginning to end.

The earliest stage of the monument was constructed around 3100 BC. It consisted of a circular bank and ditch, almost 100 m (330 ft) in diameter, cut into the chalk subsoil. The bank on the inside of the circle would have stood almost 2 m (6½ ft) high, piled up with material dug from the ditch. It is probable that a wooden palisade was erected along the bank in the fashion of other causewayed enclosures known in England at this time. Hiding the interior from view made the place even more special.

A broad entrance to the circle lay on the northeast side, with a smaller one to the south. Inside this circle and bank fifty-six "Aubrey" holes were dug, each about 1 m in diameter, regularly spaced around the perimeter, named after their seventeenth-century discoverer. These holes were intentionally filled sometime after their excavation, and their original purpose is uncertain. Recent re-excavation of one of the Aubrey holes by the Riverside Project has suggested that the bluestone sentinels may have originally been placed in these holes.

During a second stage of construction, one hundred years later, the monument was extensively remodeled, but almost none of these additions remain visible. A circle of upright timbers or posts was erected in the center of the circle. A short "avenue"

Fig. 4.68.
Stonehenge.

of wooden posts was added toward the southern entrance, and a substantial timber screen was built across that avenue to block the view to the center. Cremation burials were placed in a few of the depressions, and also in the bank and ditch areas around the perimeter of the monument. Radiocarbon dates from these cremations suggest that Stonehenge was already in use as a place of burial.

The third stage of construction involved a series of major additions between 2600 and 2300 BC. The timber circle (of the type seen in Fig. 4.70) was replaced with stone, whose arrival at Stonehenge transformed it from a rather typical monument into something unusual. Two rings of large holes were dug around the outer circle. These may have held some eighty standing stones that are now absent. Two parallel, crescent-shaped rows of standing bluestones were erected in the center of the circle, along with several other upright stones. This blue-tinted volcanic dolerite came from a source some 250 km (150 mi) distant in southern Wales. Part of the stones' journey must have been by water. More standing stones were added near the entrance and inside the periphery of the ditch.

The Avenue to the River Avon was built during this phase as well. The Heelstone may have been added at this point, or slightly later during the third stage. Next, a circle of thirty carefully shaped pillars and lintels of Sarsen sandstone was added in the center. Huge columns of this sandstone were quarried as far as 40 km (25 mi) away, shaped into pillars, and dragged to the site. Five trilithons (two upright pillars with a crosspiece on top) of Sarsen stone were erected in a horseshoe-shaped arrangement open toward the northeastern entrance and inside the larger circle of Sarsens. One of these trilithons is distinctly taller than the other four, standing 8 m (25 ft) high. The lintel on this trilithon is 5 m (16 ft) long and more than 1 m (3 ft) thick. The larger Sarsen pillars weigh as much as 50 tons (equivalent to a loaded train car) and were likely moved on oak rollers.

A system of scaffolding was probably used to raise the stones into position. The individuals involved in the various construction phases at Stonehenge must have numbered in the hundreds or thousands. Slightly later, a new circle of standing bluestones was placed inside the horseshoe of trilithons. In the next stage of construction, a ring of bluestone pillars was raised inside the Sarsen circle, but outside the horseshoe.

For a geologist, the Salisbury Plain is a hilly landscape of chalk downs, a 30 by 24 km (19 by 15 mi) tract in the south of England. The thick chalk deposit is a soft white rock that formed 700 million years ago when this area was a shallow sea. As soon as you scrape away 40 cm (15 in) or so of topsoil, the white of the chalk appears. There are few hard stones, although some of the Sarsen stones may have been found on the surface of the chalk transported by glacial ice. Certainly bluestones for the Stonehenge monuments had to be carried an extraordinary distance. Estimates suggest that 1,800 tons of Sarsen stones from 40 km or less distant and 250 tons of Bluestones from Wales (250 km, 150 mi distant) were brought to the site. The quarrying, shaping, and movement of such large stones was a major technical achievement in and of itself.

In the last major remodeling, between 2300 and 1900 BC, the bluestones were rearranged in a circle between the two rings of Sarsens and in an oval at the center of the inner ring (Fig. 4.69). The last stage of Stonehenge reflects its declining use in the period between 1600 and 1500 BC. Two concentric rings of pits were added around the stone circles in the middle of the monument. Their function is unknown. In addition, several carvings were added to the trilithons, including a depiction of a bronze dagger. After 1600 BC evidence of human activity at Stonehenge largely disappears.

The labor needed to build Stonehenge is almost unimaginable. Workers needed to be housed and fed. The logistics were huge. Millions of hours of labor are estimated to have been involved. The first stage of construction probably needed around 450 person-days of work, stage 2 around 15,000 person-days (forty years). Stonehenge 3 may have involved up to 73,000 days (or 200 years) of labor. The cutting and movement of the stones alone is estimated to have taken around 2,300 years of person-days of labor given the tools and techniques available.

Fig. 4.69.

Plan of Stonehenge with the major features identified.

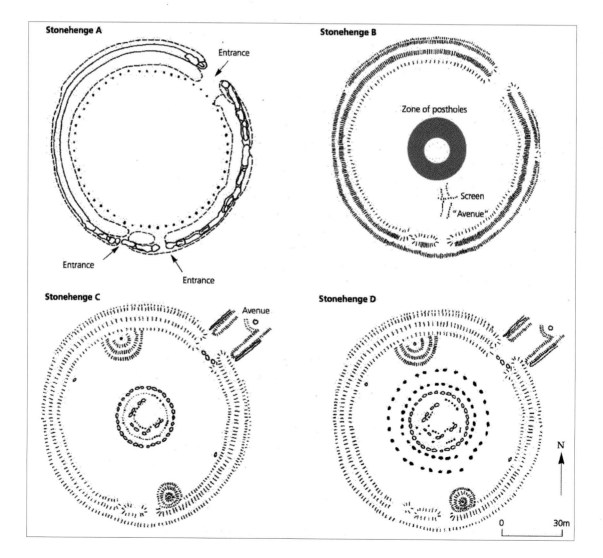

Durrington Walls

Three kilometers north of Stonehenge lies Durrington Walls, the largest of all the henges of Britain. This monument has a maximum diameter of 525 m (1,700 ft), enclosing some 12 ha (30 acres) within an immense ditch and bank. Only a small part of this site had been investigated before 2003, and the area both inside and out was assumed to be largely empty. A small timber circle just inside the southeastern entrance to Durrington Walls was reported in 1967 and designated as the Southern Circle, an arrangement of six concentric rows of timber posts some 40 m (130 ft) in diameter. A second timber feature, the Northern Circle, was also located in the same year.

Excavations by the Riverside project revealed several new features of the monument. A 30 m (100 ft) wide flint and gravel avenue was built before the construction of the henge, leading from the River Avon and aligned on the midsummer sunset. The avenue ran 170 m (550 ft) up to the Southern Circle. Further excavations inside and outside Durrington Walls led to an unexpected discovery: the Durrington Avenue and the Southern Circle were at the center of a large expanse of houses dating to ca. 2600 BC. The excavations revealed eight small structures, each about 5 m (16 ft) square, made of timber with a central hearth and a clay floor still covered with rubbish. The excavators were surprised by the amount of broken pottery and animal bones. They argue the remains are not daily waste, but rather evidence of feasting activities that may have been associated with construction and other activities at Durrington Walls. It is likely that these dwellings were used by the builders of some of the monuments at Stonehenge.

The eight houses that were uncovered came from a very small part of Durrington Walls. The excavators believe that this settlement may have consisted of several hundred houses, perhaps the largest Neolithic village in Britain. The absence of grain or quern stones in the houses and the lack of bones from neonatal pigs and cattle, together with the evidence for slaughtering pigs in the winter, suggest that occupation here was seasonal, likely during midwinter.

Woodhenge

Woodhenge, located to the south of Durrington Walls, is another timber circle, originally excavated in 1926. Woodhenge was built about the time that the large stone circles were erected at Stonehenge, less than 3 km (2 mi) to the southwest. Maud Cunnington, the excavator, found the burial of a young child in the center of a structure that consisted of six concentric rings of postholes, surrounded by a single ditch and outer bank, 85 m (280 ft) in diameter (Fig. 4.70). Most of the holes were for wooden posts, although there was evidence that several standing stones originally had been erected at the site. Based on the depth of the holes, estimates put the timber posts at having been 7.5 m (25 ft) high, the equivalent of a two-story building. These posts would have weighed up to 5 tons. Although it has been suggested that the

Fig. 4.70.
A modern reconstruction of Woodhenge.

posts and ditched enclosure supported a large circular building, there is very little convincing evidence to support this theory.

The Cursus

The Cursus is the most enigmatic monument in the Stonehenge region, a huge ditch in the shape of an elongated oval, 3 km (2 mi) in length, 100–150 m (330–500 ft) in width, and 1.6 m (5 ft) in depth. Excavations in 2006 uncovered an antler pick in the bottom of the ditch, radiocarbon dated to ca. 3500 BC, making the Cursus perhaps the earliest monumental construction in the region. Exposure of the northern ditch suggested that it may have been made up of a series of short segments, rather than a continuous trench, resembling another kind of Neolithic construction, a causewayed camp.

The Avenue

The Avenue must have been a procession path, some 3 km (2 mi) long and 15 m (50 ft) wide, flanked on either side by an earthen ditch and bank. The Avenue was constructed from the northeast corner of Stonehenge following a curved course to the River Avon. The Riverside project focused on the riverside end of the Avenue, where it reached the river as an 18 m (60 ft) wide path flanked by parallel ditches lined with timber posts. This construction led directly to

Bluestone Henge, which was first discovered during the course of the Riverside Project.

Bluestone Henge

The henge itself is 25 m (80 ft) in diameter and sits along the River Avon at the end of the Avenue from Stonehenge. Excavations in 2008 of about one-quarter of the henge recorded nine postholes, part of a central circle just under 10 m (33 ft) in diameter that may have held a total of twenty-five standing stones (Fig. 4.71). Radiocarbon dates suggest that this outer henge was built around 2400 BC, but other artifacts in the stone circle indicate that there may have been an earlier phase. If this is the case, then the stone circle was probably built before the henge itself and may represent the oldest standing stones in the area. The post holes were empty and no fragments remained; the stones had been removed intact and were not broken up in the process. The henge was then constructed with at least one entrance on the east side toward the river.

Timberhenge

The most recent major discovery at Stonehenge came in 2010, in which no excavations were done. The science of archaeological fieldwork is advancing

Fig. 4.71.
Excavations at the Bluestone Henge in 2008 exposed about one-quarter of the circular monument and a central ring of post (or stone) holes, which probably held some of the first bluestones brought to the Stonehenge area. Members of the excavation team stand in the holes left by the removal of the standing stones several thousand years ago.

fast. This was the start of a three-year project, a continuation of the Riverside work, to examine the many fields around Stonehenge. It is now possible to relatively cheaply and quickly look into the earth without digging. As georadar imaging equipment is pulled across the fields, it can map buried walls and ditches over a large area in a few days. This is archaeology without a shovel.

One of the images from the georadar reveals what appears to be a circular series of holes, 25 m (80 ft) in diameter, that were perhaps once filled with twenty-four wooden posts or standing stones. The holes are about 1 m (3 ft) in diameter. This feature, nicknamed Timberhenge, lies 900 m (3,000 ft) northwest of Stonehenge. The name Timberhenge assumes that this was a wooden henge monument, but without excavation it is impossible to say. Timberhenge appears to have been built with the same orientation as Stonehenge, with entrances to the northeast and southwest. Only detailed excavation, however, will reveal the true significance of this discovery.

New Ideas

The reasons for Stonehenge's construction remain shrouded in mystery. Many explanations have been offered over the years. Early legends in Medieval England credited Merlin, the sorcerer from the time of Arthur, as being responsible for the monument, using his magic to move the stones from Ireland. Others argued it was a Roman temple. In the seventeenth century, Aubrey, for whom the outer circle of holes are named, believed that Stonehenge was the work of the Druids, the learned priests of the Celtic Iron Age. An early English prehistorian, John Lubbock, argued at the end of the nineteenth century that Stonehenge belonged to the Bronze Age, contemporary with the many burial mounds that dot the Salisbury Plain. Over the last century, the true antiquity of Stonehenge as a Neolithic monument more than 5,000 years old has been established. The purpose and function of the construction, however, may never be known.

Stonehenge functioned in part to record the summer solstice. On the twenty-first or twenty-second of June every year, the dawn sun rises directly over the Heel Stone in line with the center of the monument. When the weather is clear, the first sunlight passes across the Heel Stone and through the double standing stones at the entrance, bisects the two horseshoes of standing stones, and reaches the altar stone in the very center of the circle. Today the sun just misses the exact top of the Heel Stone, as a result of small changes in the earth's axis since construction of the monument.

The Stonehenge Avenue, on the other hand, is aligned on the midwinter sunset. At Durrington Walls, the southern timber circle faces the midwinter sunrise, and the Durrington Avenue aligns on the midsummer sunset. According to Parker Pearson, this arrangement implies that one might make a ceremonial procession from Durrington to Stonehenge at midwinter, and in the opposite direction at midsummer.

Some have argued that Stonehenge was a sophisticated astronomical computer, used to record various lunar and stellar alignments. One of the more popular theories is that the circle of stone and holes could have been used to predict lunar eclipses. There is no evidence, however, for any alignments at Stonehenge other than the solstice.

The recent studies by the Stonehenge Riverside Project have been instrumental in rewriting our understanding of the function of the monument. Archaeologists had assumed that Stonehenge was used as a burial ground only for a short part of its history. The new investigations strongly support the idea that Stonehenge was a cemetery from the time of its creation. Although the final evidence is not yet in, there were a series of cremations excavated at Stonehenge in the 1930s, found in the Aubrey Holes and the ditch that likely date to the second half of the monument's history. The implication would be that Stonehenge was a place of burial for almost 1,000 years, most of the third millennium BC. This burial ground would have been the biggest cemetery in Britain at the time. The idea of Stonehenge as a domain of the dead, a place of ancestors, thus seems much more compelling.

Pearson, the leader of the Riverside project, makes a strong case for his ideas about the Stonehenge region as a sacred ceremonial zone for the Neolithic people. His scenario would have large groups residing in the houses at Durrington Walls during midwinter, involved in the construction and remodeling of the monument, celebrating the living, respecting the dead, worshipping the ancestors. Pearson claims that Stonehenge was linked by the River Avon and the two ceremonial avenues to the matching wooden circle at nearby Durrington Walls. The two circles with their temporary and permanent structures represented the domains of the living and the dead. "Stonehenge is a kind of spirit home to the ancestors," he says.

At midwinter, he envisions the passage from life to the place of the dead for the deceased members of society. Perhaps the dead were brought to Woodhenge, the standing tree trunks—the living world—and then transported down the River Avon in a passage to the place of the dead. The dead were then taken from Bluestone Henge along the Avenue in a procession, arriving finally at Stonehenge itself. We will never know, however, if this is the original concept or sequence of events that took place at Stonehenge. Proof is rare in archaeology. It is very difficult to understand or explain human behaviors so many millennia ago. We can only try to make sense of the evidence at hand and suggest what it might mean. At the same time, Pearson's version does give us a fascinating story that seems to fit much of the current evidence.

Stonehenge has been a problem for British archaeology for many years. Although a Mecca for tourists to England (just behind the Tower of London in popularity), the wear and tear wrought by visitors has led to careful regulation of the monument grounds. Decades of postwar tourism had dire consequences; inquisitive fingers had worn down the engravings on the stones, and the passage of millions of feet had eroded the ground down to the chalk bedrock. At the summer solstice in late June, huge festivals celebrated the summer as modern Druids welcomed the sunrise. Today, most of the monument is not directly accessible; walkways direct the visitor past the mute sentinels of the past. Although such means of protection distance the visitor from the stones, they do serve to help ensure that Stonehenge and its heritage will remain for the future as a monument to and from the ancient Britons. Plans are under way to establish better access, protection, and care.

NEWGRANGE, IRELAND, 3100 BC

This section turns to a passage grave in Ireland, a place called Newgrange in a region known as the Bend of the Boyne River. There are more than forty large passage graves in the Bend of the Boyne, an area of about 8 km² (3 mi²) in the east of Ireland, 70 km (45 mi) north of Dublin. Three of these tombs—Dowth, Knowth, and Newgrange—are truly extraordinary and the primary reason that the Bend of the Boyne is a World Heritage site (Fig. 4.72). Each of these three monuments covers about 4,000 m², an area equivalent to half a soccer pitch.

The nature of these three giant passage graves is both intriguing and complex. Dowth and Knowth both contain at least two passage graves within a single covering mound. Newgrange is a truly impressive monument consisting of a mound composed of alternating layers of loose stone and grass sods. The mound is 85 m (280 ft) in diameter and 11 m (36 ft) high. The overall impression is of a large, circular, two-story building. The monument was built between 3100 and 2900 BC.

The 19 m (60 ft) long passage at Newgrange leads to a cruciform-shaped chamber. A stone-lined opening above the entrance to the tomb allows the rising sun at the midwinter solstice to shine down the passage and fill the inner chamber with light on the shortest day of the year. The chamber is 8 m (25 ft) long, entered via the passage on the southeast side (Fig. 4.73). The ceiling of the chamber has a spectacular corbeled roof, 6 m (20 ft) high (Fig. 4.74). A partially enclosed side room makes up one part of the cruciform. On the

Fig. 4.72.
The spectacular Neolithic passage grave at Newgrange.

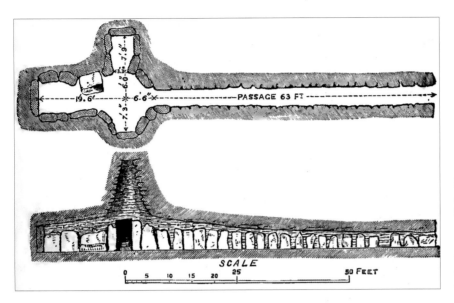

Fig. 4.73.
A plan and cross-section of Newgrange. Note the very long passage, the cruciform chamber, and the high, corbeled ceiling of the chamber.

outside of the tomb, there is a surrounding circle of free-standing stones, the largest of which is about 2.5 m (8 ft) high.

Unfortunately, the tomb was first opened in 1699 and little is known of its original contents. Extensive excavation and restoration was carried out from 1962 through 1975 by Michael J. O'Kelly of the University of Dublin. Scattered finds were encountered, including seven stone "marbles," four pendants, two beads, a used flint flake, a bone chisel, and several fragments of bone pins and points. Fragmentary human and animal bone and some cremated human remains were also recovered in the excavations, but clearly the major contents of the monument had been removed in the preceding centuries.

One of the striking aspects of the passage graves in the Bend of the Boyne region is the number of decorated stones in and around the tombs. Damage and borrowing over centuries has resulted in the loss of many of the stones, but best estimates are that a thousand decorated stones were originally in place. This is by far the largest number of any location in Neolithic Europe. These designs are largely nonrepresentational and geometric forms; circles, spirals, and lozenges were the most common motifs. Many of these stones were in the passages and chambers of the tombs, but some of the exterior standing stones were also elaborately decorated. A huge stone, 3.5 m (almost 12 ft) long, lying on its side in front of the entrance to Newgrange, has a remarkable series of engraved spirals covering the front side of the stone (Fig. 4.75). This rock has been described as "one of the most famous stones in the entire repertory of megalithic art."

The reconstruction of Newgrange by Michael J. O'Kelly in the 1970s provoked substantial debate about its authenticity. Much of this argument concerns the controversial vertical wall of white quartzite nodules that O'Kelly erected around the monument. O'Kelly argued vociferously that the

Fig. 4.74.
The interior of the Newgrange passage grave, showing the cruciform chamber and the corbeled ceiling.

monument was a one-time construction. From that perspective, the white wall should have been the final stage of the construction process. The fill of the mound involved a series of alternating layers of grass sods and loose stones, held in place by a 3 m (10 ft) high stone wall built above the circle of kerbstones around the monument.

O'Kelly believed that the wall of the monument, coated with white flint nodules, had collapsed and spread in front of the kerbstones. Critics of the white wall point out that the technology to erect a vertical retaining wall was unknown when the mound was built. They believe that the white quartzite stones formed a pavement on the ground around the entrance to the tomb that was buried when the earthen walls of the structured collapsed. It is the case that the white wall, though spectacular, is unknown elsewhere in the Neolithic. It does appear that O'Kelly may have overindulged in the restoration. The white wall looks unusual and out of place in the context of passage graves. The restorers at the nearby tomb of Knowth took a more conservative approach and retained their white quartzite stones as a pavement.

Another question concerns the single-stage construction model of O'Kelly. It can be argued that Newgrange was actually built in several stages as new materials were added to the mound. Palle Eriksen, a Danish archaeologist, has suggested that Newgrange is in fact a large passage grave with a mound that was enlarged in at least four stages over a substantial period of time.

There are various lines of evidence for several stages of construction. For example, the entrance to the passage tomb sits 16 m inside the outer entrance to the mound, as might be expected if the large mound were a later addition. Eriksen argues that the first stage of construction at Newgrange involved a passage grave with a small sod-built mound. Subsequently, both the tomb and the mound were enlarged. As noted, the mound is composed of alternating layers of sod and stone. Each sod layer represents a grass-covered surface at a particular point in the enlargement of the mound, according to Eriksen. The three sod layers thus mark the four phases of mound construction. The last phase of construction may in fact belong to the Bronze Age, which was when the outer standing stones were added.

Whatever the story on the construction phases, these tombs remain one of the more remarkable places in Neolithic Europe. Their size suggests that these early Irish farmers were both well to do and well organized. There must have

Fig. 4.75.
The engraved line
decoration on a large
stone at the entrance to
the Newgrange passage
grave. Such decorations
are unusually common
at the site and often
include large spiral
designs. The opening
above the entrance is
where the sun shines
through to the inner
chamber at the summer
solstice.

been a substantial population in the Bend of the Boyne. These stones did not come from the immediate area; building the tombs required transporting large stones weighing several tons over some distance, an enormous undertaking. Designing and managing the actual construction of the monuments must have involved specialists, early architects and engineers, to complete the task.

Megalithic structures are dramatic and enduring evidence of the impact of early agriculture on the landscapes of western Europe. Construction of monumental architecture is one clue to the increasing complexity of societies. Shortly after farming was adopted, a pronounced trend toward regionalization began. In spite of widespread belief systems and long distant trade, various local styles in material culture arose in conjunction with the fortification of settlements and increasing evidence for warfare. It appears that more distinct, delineated, and determined societies were identifying themselves across the continent. This pattern intensified into the succeeding Bronze and Iron Ages.

LOS MILLARES, SPAIN, 3200 BC

There were extraordinary events taking place around the Mediterranean as the Neolithic was coming to a close. The site of Los Millares in southeastern Spain was occupied from 3200 BC to 2300 BC, from the end of the Neolithic to the beginning of the Iberian Bronze Age, a period known as the Copper

Age (or Chalcolithic). The size, scale, and architecture of Los Millares is easily comparable with significant developments at major centers elsewhere in the Mediterranean at this point in time (Fig. 4.76).

This is an amazing archaeological site. Los Millares is located on a promontory of land between Andarax River to the north and the smaller Rambla de Huéchar to the south. Steep slopes surround the site on three sides, but a level plain without natural defenses lies to the west.

This huge settlement had four major components (Fig. 4.77). The major residential area lay to the east, enclosed in a series of massive stone walls. More than eighty corbel-vaulted tombs were situated to the west, covering an area 750 m (2,500 ft) in diameter. Thirteen ring forts dotted the hilltops around the residential and burial zones. Finally, there was an area of copper smelting and production inside the walls of the settlement. Copper was used to make weapons, ornaments, and tools. The copper mines themselves were some 15 km (10 mi) from the site.

Los Millares was discovered during building of the railway through this area in 1891. Archaeological investigations have been taking place there intermittently ever since. Clusters of the foundations of simple circular houses were found inside the walls, as well as one large building containing evidence of copper smelting. Most of the settlement area of the site has been excavated, and most archaeological activity has focused on the walls.

Fig. 4.76.
An artist's reconstruction of the settlement area of Los Millares, Spain. Note the corbeled tomb outside the elaborate gate in the outer wall in the lower right corner.

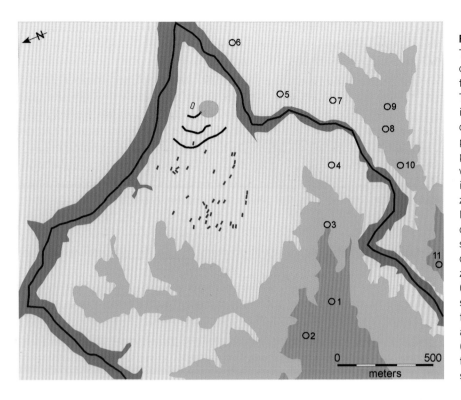

Fig. 4.77.
The area of Los Millares on a promontory next to the Rio Andarax. The settlement area is enclosed in a set of three walls that protect the end of the promontory. A copper working area lies inside the settlement zone (orange oval). More than eighty large corbeled tombs are scattered to the west of the settlement zone, not all shown (red rectangles). A series of thirteen ring forts dot the hills around the settlement (numbered circles); two to the northwest are not shown.

The walled residential portion of the site alone covers an area of 5 ha (15 acres), the equivalent of a very large city block. The population of Los Millares has been estimated at approximately 1,000 people. The settlement has three consecutive walls of large, dry stone masonry and an innermost citadel. This citadel at the top of the promontory, 50 m (165 ft) above the river, was occupied from the founding of the site; the down slope ring walls were added sequentially. The citadel, a rectangular structure, has been investigated only by means of various test trenches, which have revealed walls up to 6 m thick, confirming the importance of the structure. This may have been a special public building, or the residence of an elite family. Adjacent to the citadel there is a deep basin, which the original excavator, Siret, concluded must have been a water cistern. He also reported evidence of a water or irrigation channel at the site, but neither of these features has been confirmed.

The outer wall of the settlement area has a number of bastions and a heavily fortified entrance gate, or barbican. This wall completely restricts access to the interior of the promontory. The location of Los Millares is strategic for control of the routes leading between the Mediterranean coast and the interior areas of the country, as well as to the mines for copper ore in the nearby Sierra. The impression is one of a large, heavily defended town in a very strategic location. The thirteen ring forts are mostly to the south, protecting the access route from the coast. Most are simple circular stone walls. Excavations have focused on Fort 1, a complex construction with a central tower, two concentric stonewalls with bastions, and two external ditches. The entire structure covers an area 55 m (180 ft) in diameter. Specialized activities, including metalworking, production

Fig. 4.78.
A decorated Millares pottery vessel (16 m high) with various symbols, known also from stone figures.

of flint arrowheads, and processing and storage of cereals, have been identified inside the fort.

The pottery of the Copper Age in southeastern Spain is distinctive and includes plain and decorated wares. Some of the decorated pottery, probably funerary ware, includes various symbols also found on carved stone figures, perhaps idols, that are assumed to be symbolic of a local cult or belief system (Fig. 4.78).

In contrast to the forts, walls, and settlement area, only a few of the tombs have been investigated; many no doubt were robbed in antiquity. The majority of these so-called passage graves have an interior corbeled ceiling, but tombs without vaulted roofs also exist. In a number of cases, stone "porthole" doors lead from the entrance through the passage into an interior circular chamber (Fig. 4.79). Grave goods found in excavations included ceramics, sea shells, flint blades, stone axes, figurines, and items of ivory and ostrich-egg shell imported from Africa.

Fig. 4.80.
Grave goods from one of the corbeled passage graves. The items include ceramics, a conch shell, stone blades, figurines, stone axes, beads, and ivory.

The contents and locations of the tombs suggest status differentiation within the population (Fig. 4.80). Analysis of tomb forms, sizes, number of burials, contents, and distributions suggests that not everyone was buried in the vaulted tombs, with higher-status groups being buried in larger, richer tombs located close to the settlement.

Los Millares appears to have been finally abandoned around 2250 BC, at the same time that new settlements of Bronze Age communities were appearing in the region. The end may have involved conflict, which intensified in the late Copper Age, as seen from the level of burning and destruction at a number of sites at this time, including Los Millares.

HAL SAFLIENI, MALTA, 3600 BC

The Maltese Islands are a tiny archipelago in the center of the Mediterranean, roughly 100 km (60 mi) south of Sicily and 300 km (180 mi) north of Africa. There are a total of seven islands, three of which are inhabited, with a population today of 400,000 people. The islands cover an area of about 300 km² (120 mi²), a little more than three times the size of Manhattan. The central location of the islands in the Mediterranean is of great strategic importance. A sequence of invaders have ruled there: the Phoenicians, Greeks, Romans, Fatimids, Sicilians, the Knights of St. John, France, and Britain. The Republic of Malta gained independence from the UK in 1964 and has been a member of the European Union since 2004.

In spite of its small size and seemingly isolated location, Malta has a fascinating prehistory and history dating back thousands of years. The islands are sometimes described as a museum of archaeology because of the abundance of temples, shrines, and other ancient structures that are found everywhere (Fig. 4.81).

The earliest certain evidence of human residence on the islands dates to about 5500 BC, with the arrival of Neolithic farmers. Around 3600 BC these farming

Fig. 4.79. (opposite)
A corbeled passage grave with porthole doors at Los Millares.

Fig. 4.81.

Remains of the
Mnjandra Neolithic
Temple on Malta.

groups began to erect megalithic temples, free-standing stone buildings, using enormous blocks of stone weighing up to 20 tons. There are at least forty of these structures on the two main islands. The plan of the temples change through time, beginning with a series of nichelike spaces around an irregular open court and culminating in a symmetrical building with three pairs of apses along a common axis. They are claimed to be the oldest stone buildings in the world, built 1,000 years before the pyramids and 500 years before the start of Stonehenge. They are also among the oldest known megaliths, but they are described here at the end of the megalithic sites because of their uniqueness. Though there are many megaliths on the islands of Malta, the site of Hal Saflieni is something more.

The Hypogeum of Hal Saflieni is a World Heritage site (along with several of the other temples) and one of the more remarkable Neolithic constructions anywhere in the world. The word *hypogeum* is Greek for underground, and refers to subterranean temples and tombs from the pre-Christian period.

The underground rooms and chambers at Hal Saflieni were discovered around 1902 by a group of stonemasons building houses in the area. They had used the caverns to dump waste material until finally, after three years, the local authorities were notified. The first person to study the remains was a Jesuit priest, who unfortunately passed away without leaving any records of his activities at the site. Then Professor Temi Zammit of Malta's Museum Department took over the long and difficult project to clean out the hypogeum and recover as much of the archeology as possible.

His excavation yielded a wealth of archaeological material, including lots of pottery and human bones, personal ornaments such as beads and amulets, little carved animals, and larger figurines. The remains of 6,000 to 7,000 human bodies were discovered. The complex had been used as a burial place and sanctuary; in this way the practice was not greatly different from the megalithic tombs of western Europe, although the size and scale of the hypogeum is much, much larger.

There were some natural cavities and chambers in the limestone at the site that were used initially as catacombs for the burial of the dead beginning around 3600 BC. As these places filled with bodies over time, new chambers were cut progressively deeper into the rock (Fig. 4.82). Parts of the complex were skillfully carved in an imitation of the above-ground temple architecture.

The Hypogeum consists of halls, chambers, and passages hewn out of the living rock, an area of some 800 m² (8,500 ft², Fig. 4.83). The rock-cut chambers are of various shapes and sizes; some are very finely finished, while others are rather rough-cut. Underground, there are three levels in the complex: the upper (3600–3300 BC), middle (3300–3000 BC), and lower (3000–2400 BC). The deepest room in the lower level is 10.6 m (35 ft) below the surface.

The upper level is a large hollow area with a central passage and burial chambers cut into all the sides. One of the chambers still contains original burial deposits. The middle level contains a series of smooth walled chambers, finished to give the impression of stone-built masonry. Curvilinear and spiral paintings in red ochre are still visible in some areas. The carved façade of the "Oracle Chamber" is one of the finest examples of art in the hypogeum. Many amulets and figurines were recovered from this level, including the most famous—the so-called Sleeping Lady, a reclining figurine, perhaps meant as a representation of eternal sleep (Fig. 4.84).

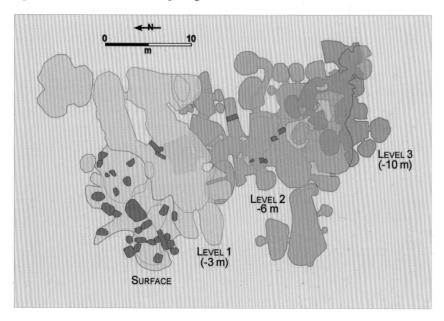

Fig. 4.82.
A plan of the Hypogeum of Hal Saflieni on Malta, showing the ninety chambers and four levels of the monument.

Fig. 4.83.
Interior view of the
Hypogeum of Hal
Saflieni.

The lowest level is entered via an ancient and uneven stairway. At the bottom of the stairs, a narrow ledge allows difficult access through a well-preserved trilithon to the right of the entrance. Most of the burials were found in this level, along with their grave goods. Today a modern museum has been built above the Hypogeum to protect the site and house and display the artifacts and information from the earlier excavations. The number of visitors to the underground is limited to a maximum of 200 per day.

ROCK ART: BARRANCO DE LA VALTORT, SPAIN, 5500 BC

Another example of rock art, this time from the Neolithic of the Spanish Levant, is the focus here. These pictographs demonstrate the problems inherent in dating rock art; they belong to the Neolithic, are reasonably well-preserved, and have extraordinary scenes of life in the Stone Age (Fig. 4.85).

Fig. 4.84.
Fired clay sculpture of
the sleeping lady from
the Hypogeum of Hal
Saflieni. The sculpture
is 7 cm high, 12 cm
long, and 6.8 cm wide.

The antiquity of rock art has always been contentious. The methods and techniques available for dating are limited because of the nature of the medium. Most of the art is on vertical faces of rock, not deposited in stratigraphic layers that can be dated. The materials used for painting and engraving are not readily amenable to dating techniques. Engraving rock removes the surface material and leaves little trace of the tools that were used. Painting leaves a thin layer of pigment on the surface of the rock. The black, white, red, and orange pigments used in most places are largely inorganic and contain very little or no carbon, which is necessary for dating. In addition, very little actual material is used for the painting and left on the rock, making traditional radiocarbon dating almost impossible. In a few cases, the tools used to produce the art or drops of pigment have been found deposited in stratigraphic position beneath the art, associated with materials that can be dated.

Because of these problems, only a few absolute dates have been available from rock art sites. The antiquity of the art in many places was unknown. Now, however, archaeological scientists, using new techniques, are dating the rock surface just beneath the painting, rather than the actual pigments. Researchers carefully collect samples of mineral salts known as oxalates just behind missing flakes of pigment on top of the paint. Oxalates form on the rock surfaces in dark, damp caves and build up over time like layers of dust. An accelerator mass spectrometer (AMS) is then used for radiocarbon-dating these salts. This

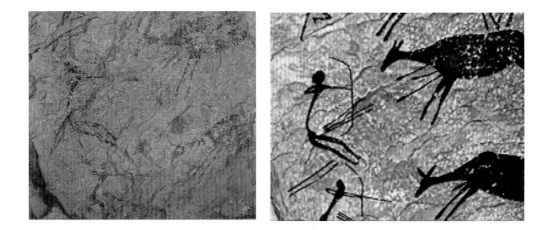

Fig. 4.85.
Two views of a scene
of deer hunting in
the Levantine style
from Cova del Cavalls,
Spain: original (left),
reconstruction (right).

method results in dates that might be a little older than the actual paintings, but presumably not by much.

The Spanish Levant holds a fascinating series of rock art, in this case pictographs—painted figures—scattered through a large part of the eastern, Mediterranean portion of Spain. These depictions appear in rock shelters and on rock outcrops across the landscape. There are more than 800 rock art sites in the Spanish Levant included in the World Heritage listing for the area.

The rock art of this region is spectacular: the human and animal figures depicted often appear to be in motion (Fig. 4.86). There are scenes with multiple figures, rather than the individual motif so often seen in other rock art. Humans are commonly the central figures, surrounded or adjacent to animals. Many depictions are shown of daily life, hunting, gathering, dancing, and more. Perhaps the most common scene is one of warriors armed with bows and arrows. It is an extraordinary repertoire of the activities of the people of this region thousands of years ago.

A fine example of the rock art from the Spanish Levant comes from the Barranco de la Valtort, near Castellon. Along a 7 km (4 mi) section of the small canyon there are a total of thirty-nine painted rock shelters. Rock Shelter 4 has a pictograph of a group of people gathering wild honey (Fig. 4.87), one of

Fig. 4.86.
A scene of running or
dancing warriors, armed
with bow and arrow.

several found in this overhang. The entire painting covers an area of approximately 55 by 30 cm (20 by 12 in). The rock surface on the back wall of the shelter is uneven, with many natural small fissures and cuplike holes. One of the holes in the wall is used to represent the bees' nest at the top of the painting. Two small, vertical, parallel fissures were painted and probably intended to portray a rock crevice containing the bees' nest. Birds or large bees are shown in the air around the nest. The top of the ladder extends down from a basket or bag that was probably used for collecting the honey. There are five human figures on the ladder and another twelve small human figures, most of whom are probably female, along with several animals on the ground below the crevice.

The exact age of these ancient paintings has been a matter of controversy and speculation for many years. When the paintings were first reported more than a century ago, they were immediately compared to the well-known cave art of the Paleolithic from France and Cantabrian Spain. The Paleolithic date was presumed to be correct for many years. Eventually it was recognized that there were significant differences. The Levantine rock art is open-air, on exposed rock surfaces. No extinct Pleistocene animals were shown in the Levantine art. The age of the paintings was then recalculated and assumed to be Mesolithic, since so many of the scenes depicted hunting and collecting activities.

It is only in the last decade that these pictographs have been scientifically dated using radiocarbon methods on the oxalates behind the paintings. The surprise was that most of the dates belong to the Spanish Neolithic period, between 5600 and 2000 B C. The textbooks have to be rewritten once again. What remains puzzling is the fact that the art is largely about hunting and gathering—yet the artists themselves were farmers.

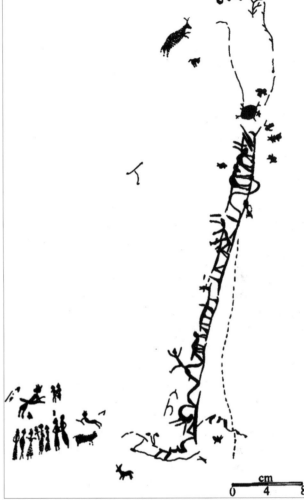

Fig. 4.87.
A pictograph from the Barranco de la Valltorta, Spain, shows wild honey gathering activities and depicts a very tall ladder in use.

SOME REFLECTIONS

The Paleolithic period witnessed the achievement of humanness, a heritage that was passed on to the inhabitants of the more recent millennia of our species' past and to the present. The major developments of the last 10,000 years would not have been possible without the population expansion, innovative technology, and development of language, social relationships, and ritual that characterized the journey of our ancestors through the Paleolithic.

The next major step in the evolution of our species required changing nature. The origins of agriculture involved domestication of plants and animals, a process that began in the ancient Near East more than 10,000 years ago. Wheat, barley, chickpeas, peas, lentils, bitter vetch, and flax were the first crops; goats, sheep, cattle and pigs furnished animal protein for the human diet. The initial spread of farming from Southwest Asia across Europe was relatively slow, taking place over a period of roughly 3,000 years. The first farming communities in Europe are known from Greece and the Aegean area and date to around 7000 BC. By 4000 BC, farming had penetrated to the coasts of western Europe and reached its climatic limits in Scandinavia and Britain. By that point in time, virtually all the cultivable areas of Europe were inhabited by farming populations, and the last hunters retreated to the more northerly and marginal areas of the continent.

As I noted, the transition to farming involved much more than domesticated foods. It also entailed major, long-term changes in the structure and organization of the societies that pursued this way of life, as well as a totally altered relationship with the environment. Along with new species of plants and animals, the Neolithic incorporated innovative tools, equipment, construction, and a new way of life—pottery and ground stone tools, construction of permanent shelter, food storage, the first wheeled vehicles, village life, new religious beliefs, and population growth.

The beginnings of domestication are generally linked in time with more permanent or fully sedentary communities, changing social and political relationships, larger and denser populations, new technologies and economies, and extensive networks of exchange and communication. Humans must have also established new relationships with one another. New roles and new rules must have emerged to structure growing communities. For long-term maintenance and survival, larger communities would have required new mechanisms for integration, dispute resolution, and decision making. Kin relationships are severely tested when decisions must be made for groups of several hundred.

Larger numbers of people also require innovations in the exchange of materials and information. Economies were probably based on barter and reciprocal exchange. More productive and storable food resources permitted larger communities and denser populations. Increased evidence for burials, ritual objects (e.g., figurines), nonresidential structures, more formal patterns of exchange, and in some cases less equal access to goods and labor would seem to reflect these very significant changes in social and political relationships.

Cultivation supported a stable economy with surplus that ultimately resulted in the formation of elite groups. A fascinating aspect of the origins of agriculture is this fundamental change in human relations. Many animal species are characterized by some form of dominance behavior. Among most groups of hunter-gatherers, however, dominance is dampened by cultural mechanisms to promote equality and small-group harmony. Egalitarian behavior is the norm.

Among farming groups, though, there are new demands for organizational structure due to increasing numbers and density of population. Agricultural surplus provides a means for the rise of hierarchical human relations. One can imagine how successful families or individuals in a farming community may have exploited an inherent tendency to dominate, to support their kin while at the same time accumulating power and wealth. The brakes on dominance behavior were released and social inequality emerged.

Some farming societies instituted more permanent, formal leadership roles. Such leaders or decision makers, in turn, may have fostered greater concentrations of resources and labor, leading to intensified production and even larger communities. Such changes in Europe may be manifest in the appearance of rare objects such as copper and gold. Sites like Varna and others with dramatic evidence of differences in wealth suggest that pronounced social inequality was present in the Neolithic of southeastern Europe.

Villages became the primary form of settlement, with multifamily communities sharing space and resources. These villages appear to be composed of household units, each with a physical representation, usually in the form a small rectangular structure. Households are the level at which social groups articulate directly with economy and ecology. The study of households offers archaeologists the opportunity to examine human adaptation at that interface. In agricultural societies, production of food and other essential materials is at the household level, in contrast to the sharing practices and group behavior of co-resident hunter-gatherers. Economies become more specialized through time, with larger groups or entire communities involved in producing specific items. The emergence of specialist groups of producers such as potters, metal smiths, and weavers marks more advanced agricultural societies.

The terms *bands, tribes, chiefdoms,* and *states* are used by some archaeologists to describe various types of human societies. The framework was defined by the anthropologist Elman Service many years ago, and it still serves as a useful heuristic device for discussing the growth and development of European society.

Tribes are larger and more sedentary than groups of hunter-gatherers and are usually involved in subsistence agriculture or pastoralism. Tribe members normally live in villages, and the entire tribe may reside in two or more such communities. At the same time, tribes remain relatively small-scale societies of farmers where relationships are generally egalitarian and family-oriented. Decision making may be consensual at the family or household level, but tribal societies often have recognized leaders or elders who are responsible for group policy. Social inequality can emerge in tribal societies as individuals gain power, authority, or wealth. As such differentiation becomes institutionalized and hereditary, tribes can evolve into what are known as chiefdoms.

New belief systems were emerging and expanding in the Neolithic. Cosmologies must have been altered by the rapid changes taking place in human life and experience. One manifestation is the appearance of megalithic tombs and monuments along the Atlantic coastline of Europe. The burial monuments themselves would have been dramatic statements of the importance of the individuals buried within them. Public architecture such as Stonehenge, Carnac, and many others were statements about societies, the worldview, and their power as a group. Certainly by this time, rituals were scheduled according to specific times of the year. The solar "computers" of myriad stone and wood circles of northwestern Europe clearly functioned for this purpose.

Sedentism, population growth, and aggregation characterize the development of the Neolithic. More people occupy the landscape as population numbers and density increase. Farmers modify the landscape, cutting forest to create fields, pasturing animals, and creating new environments. The land itself becomes domesticated as the process of agriculture expands and intensifies. Nature retreats as the ecosystem is simplified through human intervention. Villages dot the landscape and farmers take over the land. Europe gradually fills with productive farming societies.

In the later Neolithic, these earlier, widespread Neolithic societies became more focused and regionalized, following idiosyncratic trajectories but participating widely in increasing warfare, trade, and wealth. Regionalization is seen as more archaeological cultures, more names, more arrows on the archaeological map of Neolithic Europe. Styles of pottery show more restricted distributions as more distinctively identifiable groups emerge at this time. Societies are becoming larger, more populous, and more powerful. With this growth, conflict and warfare are much more visible. Settlements become fortified and defensive locations are preferred, beginning a trend that continues for millennia. This path toward hierarchical organization and conflict in the Neolithic accelerated with the introduction of bronze around 3000 BC, as warrior societies emerged across the European landscape.

The longer-term consequences of the agricultural revolution are enormous and still rippling through human culture. The transition to agriculture and sedentism occurred at the onset of a rapid succession of changes that have culminated in our modern world. The pace of these recent changes is truly remarkable when viewed from the perspective of human history. Although neither domestication nor sedentism alone is necessary or sufficient to explain the formation of towns, cities, and ancient states, permanent communities and food production are critical elements in those very significant, subsequent developments.

CHAPTER FIVE

Bronze Age Warriors

THE RISE OF METALS

The European Bronze Age took place during the third and second millennia BC. This same period witnessed the first civilizations and empires in Mesopotamia and the Nile Valley—the first cities, the first states, the first writing systems, and many other innovations. Europe unquestionably felt the impact of these changes. Partially in response to these developments, and 1,000 years before the classical civilizations of Greece, 2,000 years before Rome, the Aegean area witnessed the

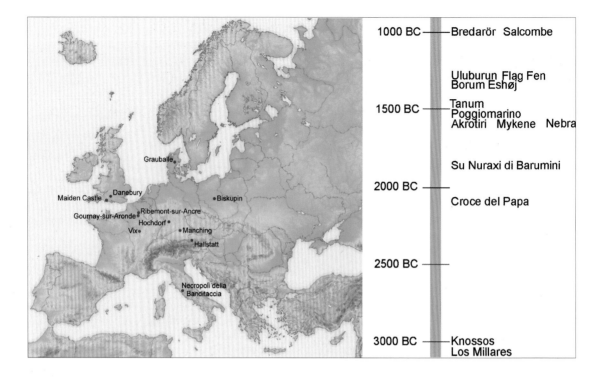

1000 BC ——— Bredarör Salcombe

Uluburun Flag Fen
Borum Eshøj

Tanum
1500 BC ——— Poggiomarino
Akrotiri Mykene Nebra

Su Nuraxi di Barumini

2000 BC ———

Croce del Papa

2500 BC ———

3000 BC ——— Knossos
Los Millares

Fig 5.1.
The location and
time scale for sites
mentioned in this
chapter.

emergence of more complex societies on Crete and the Greek mainland. The Minoan palaces and Mykenean (also known as Mycenaean) citadels were urban centers of these civilizations and the focal points of industry, commerce, religion, military power, and central accumulation. North of the Alps, there was much less political integration; societies operated on a smaller scale. This pattern continued essentially until the Roman conquest of France and much of Britain, shortly before the Common Era. More details on the developments in southern and northern Europe are provided in subsequent sections of this chapter.

Bronze defines this period and becomes the dominant metal in Europe. As noted earlier, it has several advantages over copper. Because it holds an edge much better, most of the early bronze objects were weapons: swords, daggers, spearheads, and arrowheads, in the context of continuing warfare. Bronze is an alloy of copper and tin or arsenic. Initially it was made from copper and arsenic to form arsenic bronze. Some copper ores naturally contain a good bit of arsenic, and smelting these ores may have accidentally created an early form of bronze. Copper ores are available and fairly widespread in Europe from Ireland to Bulgaria (Fig. 1.4). Sources are concentrated in mountainous regions and more often found in the Alps and to the south and east. Some of these copper sources were incredibly productive. The Mitterberg mines near Salzburg in Austria, with tunnels up to 100 m (330 m) in length, may have produced as much as 18,000 tons of copper. Bronze production in Europe began in the Aegean region with the rise of early civilizations on Crete and mainland Greece.

Some of the major trends during the Bronze Age involved intensification of patterns that had begun in a few places in the late Neolithic. Specifically, status differentiation and social inequality became pronounced in the Bronze Age. There are clear indications of substantial differences in wealth among burials in this period—a small number of very rich tombs in contrast to the simple graves of more common people. Site size also increases as population aggregation grows and the more large towns began to appear, primarily in southeastern Europe. Warfare and fortification of settlements also intensified, as conflict must have been a regular aspect of life during much of the Bronze Age. Craft specialization, particularly in metals and rare stone, also saw dramatic growth. Cottage industries developed in metals, textiles, wine, and other materials of wealth and status.

Some years ago, Andrew Sherratt proposed that some of the causes for the distinctive changes in the Bronze Age involved what he called the secondary products revolution. Sherratt pointed to what appeared to be a widespread series of innovations in farming and craft production. Domestic animals became the source for more than just meat. Wool, milk, traction, mobility by means of riding, and pack transport were renewable resources now available from domestic herds. Many of these innovations first appeared in the Near East during the fourth millennium BC and spread to Europe by the beginning of the third millennium in the form of new species (horses, donkeys), breeds (such as woolly sheep), technology (the wheel, the ard or simple plow) and technological knowledge (plowing, equestrian skills).

Since Sherratt proposed the Secondary Products Revolution a great deal of new information has pushed the arrival of several of these innovations further back in time. These changes no longer seem to be simultaneous or unique to the Bronze Age. The use of animal milk products, for example, clearly begins early in the Neolithic. Textile production using flax and wool appears to have been practiced at least by the late Neolithic, and perhaps much earlier. Evidence for the use of the ard has been found in the form of clear traces beneath Neolithic barrows. Nevertheless, the Bronze Age witnesses extraordinary changes in the lives of Europe's inhabitants.

Here I consider the highlights of the Bronze Age in two parts. The major developments that took place in the Aegean are the initial focus of discussion. Marvelous sites such as Knossos, Akrotiri, and Mykene document the spectacular nature of these early European civilizations. I also consider the remarkable Bronze Age shipwreck at Uluburun, which contained a wealth of information on trade and commerce. I then turn to Europe north of the Alps, the arrival of bronze in that region, and the important cultural changes that took place there.

THE BRONZE AGE IN THE AEGEAN

The Bronze Age marks a watershed in the prehistory of Europe. In the eastern Mediterranean, early civilizations rose in the Aegean, on mainland Greece, and later on the peninsula of Italy. These societies were literate and ruled by kings; they inhabited large towns, kept armies and navies, collected taxes, and established laws. These states controlled trade over large areas and extracted a variety of raw materials and other products from a huge area. Much of Europe was involved in the movement of materials and goods into the economic magnet of the eastern Mediterranean. These economic connections spurred development of more hierarchical societies north of the Alps, as well as the rise of wealthy and powerful Bronze Age chiefs in resource-rich and strategic parts of the continent.

The wine-dark waters of the Aegean Sea bathe the shores of Turkey to the east and Greece to the north and west. The long, mountainous island of Crete marks the southern limits of this sea (Fig. 5.2). The Aegean is dotted with small rocky and volcanic islands, actually the summits of a submerged mountain range, with thin, poor soils and a dry climate. These rugged, barren conditions may have offered hidden benefits for their early inhabitants, however; the absence of large areas of fertile farmland meant that crops other than cereals had to be cultivated. Wheat could be grown in more sheltered areas with deeper soils, but grapes, olive trees, and sheep flourished on the rocky slopes of the islands. Not only are grapes a delicious fruit, but their fermented juice turns into wine. Olives are remarkably nutritious and provide oil that can be burned, eaten, cooked, or rubbed on the skin and hair. Sheep produce meat and they yield wool for weaving. This Mediterranean triad of oil, wine, and cloth became important exports for the economies of these small islands and the foundation for their growing power in the region. The inhabitants must have also relied on the sea for fish and other foods; sailing and knowledge of watercraft and the sea would have been a fundamental part of life.

Seafaring and trade permitted movement of goods and foods between islands, and between the islands and the mainland. The strategic location of

Fig. 5.2.

A satellite view of Crete and the Aegean. The circular island of Thera is located in the right center of the photo, with Crete in the foreground.

Crete and the Aegean islands along the main avenues of sea trade enabled the inhabitants to act as middlemen in movement of materials among Egypt, the Near East, and the settlements of Europe.

Demand for wine, olive oil, pottery, textiles, and other goods enhanced the economic well-being of the people of the Aegean. This active commerce fostered the import of raw materials to be made into finished products. Craft workers used the potter's wheel and clay to make fine ceramic vessels. Others carved stone, bone, and ivory seals for marking economic transactions, sculpted figurines and bowls of marble, obsidian, and other colorful stones, or created jewelry and other luxury items. After 3000 BC, the craft workers of the Aegean also began to make objects of bronze, silver, and gold. Smiths produced bronze tools and weapons by the thousands for both local use and export. This metal was the signature material of the times, and its production was one of the primary reasons for the explosion of economic and political power in the Aegean region.

The Aegean Bronze Age dates from about 3000 to 1000 BC, ending with the beginning of the Iron Age and the eventual rise of the classical Greek civilization of Plato and Homer. There were two major centers of development and power in the Aegean Bronze Age, one on Crete and one on mainland Greece. The civilization that emerged on the island of Crete was known as the Minoan and reached its peak between 2000 and 1450 BC. During this period, the Minoans dominated the Aegean and the control of trade in the eastern Mediterranean through sea power. The seats of authority on Crete were in palaces and villas, residences of the local rulers who directed this early state. Defensive fortifications were apparently not needed by the islanders; they were protected by their ships.

The Mykeneans on mainland Greece controlled most of the Aegean between 1600 and 1100 BC and probably took over Crete after 1450 BC. The Mykenean civilization was dominated by a series of hilltop fortresses, or citadels, interconnected by roads. These citadels were ruled by powerful warrior-kings, who lived in palaces called *megara* (singular: *megaron*), and whose graves are among the richest ever uncovered in Europe. Episodic alliances among the citadels led to greater political, economic, and military power, and the Mykeneans became the major force in the Aegean around 1500 BC. The gradual collapse of Mykenean power and abandonment of the heavily fortified citadels after 1200 BC is one of the more intriguing mysteries of Aegean archaeology.

The differences between the Minoan and Mykenean civilizations are profound. Both are powerful political entities in the Aegean region, but their expressions of power and wealth take very different forms. The Minoans lived in large, rather open palaces, while Mykenean rulers occupied heavily fortified and defended citadels. Minoan art is lively and naturalistic; Mykenean art is largely martial and often involving militaristic or hunting scenes. The Mykenean royalty was buried in elaborate tombs with extraordinary wealth, while graves of the elite of Knossos are largely unknown. Written languages were in use in both area, but the Minoan Linear A has never been deciphered.

Mykenean Linear B represents an early form of Greek. In the end, the Mykeneans are often thought to have conquered Crete and the Minoans and incorporated their civilization into their own for several hundred years. Power and wealth come and go. In the following pages the sites of Knossos, Akrotiri, and Mykene are the focus of discussion, to document the major centers of these Aegean civilizations.

KNOSSOS, CRETE, GREECE, 3000 BC

Sir Arthur Evans, then keeper of the Ashmolean Museum in Oxford, England, traveled to Crete in 1894 and "discovered" an extensive group of ruins, buried under a low mound of soil and collapsed walls, at a place known as Knossos (Fig. 5.3). Of course the local people had known about these ruins for many years, but his was the first report back to the English-speaking world. Beginning in 1900, Evans spent the remaining thirty-five years of his life investigating Knossos; he purchased the entire archaeological site in order to do this. Most of the excavations were actually completed by 1905. He restored many of the areas he had excavated, rebuilding the walls and repainting the plaster in the vivid colors that had been preserved in the ruins. Today, the palace that he

Fig. 5.3.
Air photo of the Palace of Knossos on the island of Crete.

uncovered is a monument to his labor and his vision of the restoration, and one of the major tourist attractions on the island. The accuracy of the restoration is often questioned and must be understood in the context of Evan's time.

The excavations at Knossos revealed a Neolithic tell, or settlement mound, with some 7 m (23 ft) of deposits, beneath the famous Bronze Age palace. Neolithic farmers had arrived on Crete before 6500 BC and appear to have been very successful. The earliest Neolithic phase at Knossos is aceramic, perhaps similar to the pre-pottery Neolithic of Cyprus. The first houses are small, rectangular, and made from fired mudbrick. In later phases of the Neolithic settlement, the buildings are made of poured mud resting on stone foundations. Wall surfaces are regularly mud-plastered. Two large buildings from the late Neolithic were found by Evans and contained two permanent hearths, a very unusual feature. One of the buildings held fifteen rooms. The first evidence for the use of metal on Crete was found in that building in the form of a copper axe. These buildings foreshadow subsequent developments in the Bronze Age.

The Neolithic settlement of Knossos was deep and extensive. The extent of the Neolithic occupation covers a larger area than the later palace and its associated community. There was widespread trade taking place in the eastern Mediterranean from the beginning of the Neolithic, involving both utilitarian goods (stone tools and raw materials) and exotic items (prestige items of shell, stone, and later metal). Craft specialists appear to have been present, at least part-time, producing ceramics and textiles. Monumental architecture, in the form of large buildings or tombs, is missing until the Bronze Age.

The first palace at Knossos was erected around 2800 BC. A series of palaces were then built on top of one another, each larger and more elaborate, as the settlement and administrative structure grew. Knossos covers almost 25,000 m² (an area the size of a large basketball arena), in a complex of buildings and construction that included the palace itself, several surrounding mansions, and many smaller houses, connected by roads. The palace alone is 130 m (425 ft) on each side, two soccer fields side by side.

There are several palaces on the island, thought to have been the centers of independent Minoan states, laid out and built according to plan, with a large, rectangular central court surrounded by myriad rooms, numerous corridors, a maze of courtyards, grand staircases, private apartments, administrative chambers, enormous storerooms, baths, and even a sophisticated plumbing system (Fig. 5.4). The term *palace* may be misleading. Knossos, for example, was an intricate collection of more than 1,000 interlocking rooms. Functional space was carefully designed and separated according to residential, administrative, storage, religious, and manufacturing uses.

The complex of rooms and buildings housed many of the administrative functions of the government. Important craft workshops were located in the palace or housed in adjacent buildings. The palace was a multistory building with extensive storerooms. Long, narrow rooms held enormous storage jars, or *pithoi*, along the walls for oils, wine, and other liquids, and stone-lined pits in the floor were filled with wheat and other cereals. It is clear from this

Fig. 5.5. (opposite)
The Palace of Knossos,
partially restored by Sir
Arthur Evans.

arrangement that the palace complex controlled at least some of the economic activities of the state.

The palace of Knossos was at the center of a large town, covering perhaps 75 ha (185 acres) at its height and with a population estimated at 10,000–12,000 people. The palace did not control all the wealth in the town. Several grand houses have been excavated outside the palace, decorated with wall paintings and containing high-status prestige objects;. for example, a steatite bull's-head vase was found in one of these larger houses (Fig. 5.6b). Craft workshops and pottery kilns associated with these grand houses indicate that the palace did not exclusively command craft production.

Architecture, art, and engineering were highly accomplished in the Minoan civilization. High column bases were made of stone—breccia, porphyry, serpentine, and conglomerate—while the columns themselves were milled tree trunks, inverted to prevent sprouting and improve water runoff (Fig. 5.5). The palace was also designed to remove rainwater and provide fresh water to the inhabitants. To carry surface runoff and wastewater away, elaborate stone-lined drains, large enough to crawl through, were built. Flush toilets and a sewage system were installed as well.

The rooftops of the palace and other prominent areas were lined with stone *bucrania*, facsimiles of ox skulls. *Bucrania* also refers to an architectural element, in the U-shape of cow horns, which was used in various parts of the ancient Mediterranean. Frescoes and murals decorated the walls of the palace, depicting various aspects of Minoan life. Shrines are scattered throughout the palace as well, documenting the integration of church and state in the early Aegean civilizations. Much attention has been focused on the open-bodice costumes of the goddesses and the acrobatic bullfighters who are often

Fig. 5.4.
Restored interior of
the so-called Throne
Room in the Palace of
Knossos.

depicted. Religious ceremonies appear to have combined several elements, notably the bull, a sacred axe, and snakes.

The palace played a preeminent economic role, with control over production, storage, and redistribution of agricultural staples and secondary products such as hides and wool. A bureaucracy existed to manage these economic activities, and new technologies were added as part of the bookkeeping system. Clay sealings were used to close and "lock" containers with symbols that referred to ownership, amounts, and contents. The seals themselves were made from several types of stone—carnelian, agate, rock crystal, chalcedony, jasper—in rectangular and circular shapes. Clay tablets were used for recording and storing information regarding payment of taxes and movement of foods and goods around the state. The palace likely controlled crafts people and production of

Fig. 5.6.
a) Gold and amber earring from a Minoan workshop. b) Bull's Head Rython (drinking cup) from Knossos. Carved out of steatite with gilded horns, the eyes are made of red jasper and white shell or marble was used for the line around the nostrils.

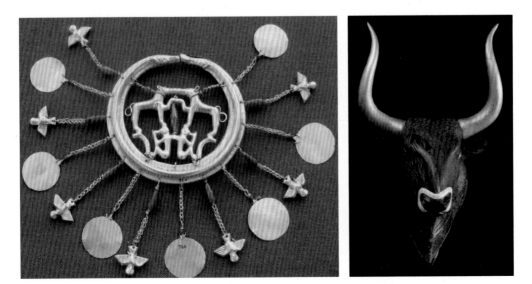

prestige goods such as textiles, fine ceramics, and jewelry (Fig. 5.6a). Textile production is one of the centerpieces of the Minoan economy, and tomb paintings in Egypt depict woolen cloth from Crete as a major import.

Bronze Age ceramics on Crete were generally colorful and with cheerful motifs, often inspired by the sea (Fig. 5.7). Earlier vessels were decorated with patterns of spirals, triangles, curved lines and crosses, fishbone designs, and the like. Naturalistic decorations of pottery came to the fore in the middle of the Minoan period, with paintings of animals, birds, and flowers; fish, squid, birds, and lilies were common motifs. Minoan potters were careful to fit their designs to the size and shape of the pot. Late Minoan ceramic design shared many features with Mykenean styles, which added a geometric simplification to the continuing naturalism of the Minoans. Several very fine ceramic wares were produced on Crete and traded to Egypt and elsewhere around the eastern Mediterranean.

Three writing systems were used on Crete, including early hieroglyphics. By 1900 BC a variety of glyphs appeared, some on three-sided clay seals, depicting an olive sprig, saffron, wheat, dog, ram, goat, snake, fish, and short- and long-horned cattle. Some appear to have been borrowed from Egypt. Around 1700 BC these glyphs blossomed into a written language known as Linear A, likely the first complete writing system in Europe. Linear A is still undeciphered. A second writing system, Linear B, has been decoded and is related to the archaic Greek language. Linear B may have developed on mainland Greece and later been introduced to Crete by the Mykeneans.

The extensive network of trade that was controlled from Knossos and other Minoan centers is evidenced by the variety of raw materials found in the palace: copper from Cyprus and Turkey, ivory, amethyst, carnelian, and gold from Egypt, lapis lazuli from Afghanistan, amber from Scandinavia. These commodities, and the Cretan ships that carried them, were the foundation of the wealth and power of the Minoan state. The Egyptians feared the "great green sea," yet the sturdy Minoan ships, with their deep keels and high prows (known from paintings and decorated pottery on Crete), weathered the storms of the Mediterranean and controlled the sea lanes.

One of the striking contrasts between the Minoan towns and the Mykenean citadels is the absence of fortifications and defensive locations on Crete. Some have argued that this peaceful posture reflects the political unification of the island and the power of the fleet to repel foreign invaders. Clearly, however, at some point such arrangements failed and Knossos and Crete fell to the Mykeneans. In fact a whole series of calamities appear to have befallen the Minoans. Natural catastrophes in the form of earthquake, fires, and volcanic eruptions played a predominant role in the prehistory of Crete.

The palace of Knossos was destroyed at least twice during its history. The first destruction, in 1700 BC, was marked by extensive wall collapse and evidence of a major fire. Many of the other palaces and villas on Crete show evidence of similar

Fig. 5.7.
A Minoan vase with a marine motif in a cartoon style, approximately 50 cm high.

destruction at the same time; it seems clear that a major earthquake must have occurred. Most of the palaces were rebuilt following this episode of destruction.

Another catastrophe was the eruption around 1625 BC of Thera, 120 km (75 mi) to the north of Crete, discussed in the section on Akrotiri. The island collapsed after a long period of eruption and exploded across the sea. The earthquakes, and likely tsunami accompanying this event, must have had major consequences for the Minoans. At the same time, there are few archaeological or architectural indications of devastation. It is often argued that this event must have wiped out much of the Minoan fleet, but this kind of information is not available in the archaeological record. Moreover, the eruption took place more than 150 years before the end of the Minoan civilization.

The second period of destruction at Knossos dates to approximately 1450 BC and marks the end of the Minoan civilization. The palace was reoccupied following this episode, but pottery and other artifacts indicate that Mykeneans had taken control. Other palaces on Crete were also destroyed at this time, but not simultaneously as in 1700 BC. The evidence appears to reflect conflict and conquest rather than natural catastrophe.

Knossos and the Minoan civilization is the stuff of legend. Many major archaeological sites are simply larger than life. That is, you can look at lots of photographs and read lots of information, but a visit to the site itself is a magical experience. At Knossos, the term *labyrinth* is the key to the ruins. The palace is a maze of hundreds of rooms, connected through various passages, stairways, and tunnels. Knossos is often cited as the home of the legend of the Minotaur. The Minotaur was a mythical creature, with the head of a bull on the body of a man, trapped in a labyrinth by King Minos of Crete. The Minoans demanded that the Athenians provide seven young men and women every year for sacrifice to the Minotaur. Eventually, using trickery, the Athenian Theseus sailed to Crete and killed the Minotaur.

Such legends likely encompass aspects of real history. The Mykeneans probably did pay tribute in some form to Crete. Evidence for human sacrifice at Knossos and other sites on Crete has recently come to light. Certainly the myth of the Minotaur has a lot to say about the relationships between the Minoans and the Mykeneans, and it may help explain the Mykenean conquest of the island.

AKROTIRI, SANTORINI, GREECE, 1626 BC

Many people know of the Roman town of Pompeii, buried by volcanic ash in AD 79. It is a classic story of disaster—the bodies of the townspeople found dead in their streets and homes as they tried to escape the fiery cloud of toxic ash. Very few people know of Akrotiri, a Minoan town on the island of Thera in the Aegean, buried deeply by volcanic ash around 1626 BC, or 1,700 years before Pompeii. It is an equally compelling story, though perhaps not quite as dramatic because in this case the townspeople escaped the island before everything exploded.

Thera, today called Santorini, is a volcanic island in the middle of the Aegean Sea, 120 km (75 mi) north of Crete and 200 km (125 mi) south and east of mainland Greece (Fig. 5.2). Seen from above, it is clearly a volcanic crater, an area ca. 12 by 7 km (7½ by 4 mi), filled with the sea from two openings in the circular caldera. The two major islands that outline the caldera have cliffs of 300 m (1,000 ft) height, almost vertical, on the caldera side that slope gradually away from the center to the Mediterranean.

The island has a long history of repeated eruptions. Immediately prior to the Minoan event, the walls of the caldera formed a nearly continuous ring of islands. The northern part of the caldera gradually filled with volcanic ash and lava, and then collapsed in a cataclysmic explosion. That eruption of Thera was one of the largest in human history. Underwater survey revealed volcanic ash to a depth of 10–80 m covering the ocean floor for 20–30 km (12–20 mi) in all directions from the island. Vulcanologists estimate an ash plume 30 km (20 mi) high, descending largely to the east and northeast. The amount of ash that reached Crete during the eruption was minimal. At the same time, the collapse and explosion of the volcano probably created a tsunami of enormous impact. Estimates suggest waves 4–10 m (13–33 ft) high or more, which would have devastated the northern coast of Crete, particularly ships and towns along the seashore (Fig. 5.8).

Dating the eruption has been a contentious issue in Mediterranean archeology for many years. Before the advent of more accurate dating techniques, archaeologists in this region dated their finds by association, using an object of known age found with undated materials to date all the items. The changes in Egyptian artifacts over time were well documented and dated using

Fig. 5.8.

The modern town of Fira on the island of Santorini perched on the remnants of the crater rim of the volcano.

the accepted calendar dates for the Egyptian dynasties; moreover, Egyptian objects were traded throughout the eastern Mediterranean. Thus finds of Egyptian pottery, jewelry, and other items on Crete, or elsewhere, could be used to date archaeological layers outside of Egypt. This method was used to suggest 1500 BC for the eruption of Thera, close to the date of 1450 BC when the Mykeneans took over the Minoan island. A nice story of environmental catastrophe and the collapse of civilization.

Various scholars over the years pointed to problems with this date and conflicts in the archaeological record. Several lines of evidence from ice cores, tree rings, and a number of radiocarbon dates suggested that the eruption was earlier. Most of these arguments were dismissed by the majority; the Egyptian chronology was thought to be infallible. However, in 2006, two studies were published lending similar strong evidence of an earlier date. One of the studies concerned an olive branch found at the base of the 60 m (200 ft) of ash left by the eruption near the center of the caldera. The scientists reasonably argued that the olive tree was killed by the eruption and that the radiocarbon date from the tree provides a date for the eruption. They dated several sets of tree rings in the branch and were able to estimate, with 95 percent confidence, that the eruption took place between 1627 and 1600 BC.

The date of the eruption has a number of important consequences for Mediterranean archaeology, in particular regarding the collapse of Minoan civilization. This question is discussed in more detail in the next section on Knossos. The eruption had more immediate consequences for the inhabitants of Thera, of course. The island was destroyed, sterilized, and rebuilt by the volcanic eruption. At the same time, there appears to have been substantial warning of the coming disaster. The town of Akrotiri, on the southern coast of the island, was abandoned before the eruption buried it under 6 m (20 ft) of volcanic ash.

The discovery of Akrotiri beneath the ash is an archaeological detective story. The detective was a Greek archaeologist named Spyridon Marinatos. In the 1930s he was digging a Minoan villa on the north shore of Crete. The villa had been partially destroyed by what he first thought was an earthquake, not uncommon in the Aegean region. Digging continued, however, and he found a layer of volcanic ash and concluded that a volcano played a role in the collapse of the villa. There were no volcanoes on Crete; the nearest was Thera. In order to prove his theory, Marinatos decided to excavate on Thera for evidence. Villagers from modern Akrotiri had reported potsherds and other artifacts from diggings near their community. Marinatos visited and in 1967 began excavations. Under two stories of volcanic ash, his hunch paid off and he found a buried Bronze Age town, proof of a major eruption during Minoan times (Fig. 5.9).

Akrotiri was probably founded during the Neolithic, around 4500 BC and continuously occupied until its abandonment. The full extent of the town is unknown, but it may have covered as much as 20 ha (about 12 city blocks). The citizens clearly had time to evacuate the town. There are no bodies in the streets, and there was little left behind in the way of valuables or personal effects. At the same time, the volcanic ash was rather gentle in the way it covered and protected the houses, furniture, and other contents of the town.

Fig. 5.9.
Part of the excavated area of Akrotiri, buried beneath several meters of volcanic ash, with a modern protective roof over the site.

An enormous canopy protects the excavations today. To enter the site is to go back in time. The central boulevard opens onto more paved streets lined with flat-roofed stone and mudbrick buildings (Fig. 5.10). Some of the buildings still stand three stories high. An elaborate drainage system runs beneath the streets, and some of the houses have indoor plumbing. At street level are the shops, workshops, and restaurants of the town, some with large ceramic storage jars and cooking areas. Above the shops are the apartments of the owners and inhabitants. A labyrinth of doorways, stairs, and passages connects rooms and buildings.

Extraordinary wall paintings and murals decorate many of the buildings. The pastel colors, large size, varied subjects, and calm mood of most of the depictions suggest a light and positive atmosphere. The subjects are highly varied and include men and women in various activities (fishing, boxing, collecting flowers), plants, animals (antelopes, monkeys, dolphins), marine scenes, ships, and more. One structure contained a lovely fresco in blue, red, orange, and yellow tints depicting vervet monkeys on the steep ocean cliffs not far Akrotiri. These monkeys come originally from the Nile region and thus confirm contact with Egypt and the people of the Upper Nile.

A description of one or two buildings may provide a sense of place. The House of the Ladies, named from the murals it contains, was three stories, connected by two staircases, one at the front entrance and another in the center of the building. This was a large structure with ten rooms, and perhaps because of the size it was furnished with a light well next to the central staircase. The House of the Ladies was likely a wealthy private residence. The north section of the building held a suite of three rooms, the middle one with wall paintings dominated by depictions of women.

The West House is the most fully explored structure at Akrotiri. It is a long, narrow building of medium size. There are two stories present for at least part of the structure, with two interior staircases. The ground floor was used for the storage and preparation of food and other workshops, as documented by the pottery and other artifacts left behind. A large central room on the second floor was probably used for weaving, given the number of loom weights found there. With the exception of one small room used as a toilet, all the rooms in the west wing of the house were decorated with wall paintings. One of these was the so-called miniature fresco, of which Figure 5.11 is a part showing ships traveling between two islands, perhaps Thera and Crete. It is a realistic, yet stylized, scene with much information about towns, the ships, and the seascape. Many other murals are also found in the West House. Various scenes and motifs appear: fishermen, a priestess, deer, flocks of animals, strings of fish, a group of warriors.

Akrotiri and Thera may also have some connections with later Greek mythology. The legendary island of Atlantis was first mentioned in 360 BC in the dialogs of Plato; he described Atlantis as a naval power lying in front of the Pillars of Hercules and told how after the Atlanteans failed to conquer Athens their island sank into the ocean "in a single day and night of misfortune." If Atlantis ever existed (there is little evidence to support the argument), then certainly Thera would be a good candidate for that missing, mystical place.

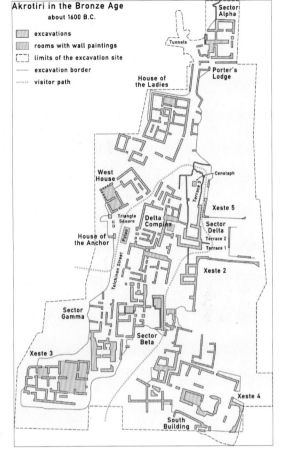

Fig. 5.10.
A plan of the excavated area, streets, and houses of Bronze Age Akrotiri.

MYKENE, GREECE, 1600 BC

The Bronze Age in Europe, and its accompanying weaponry, ushered in an era of conflict and warfare in which the skills, perspective, and power of the military

Fig. 5.11.
A mural from Akrotiri depicting sea travel in the Aegean.

seems to have become an important presence in society. A new warrior class emerged during this period; weapons and armor were often the primary burial goods, and martial and hunting scenes dominated decorative art. A military presence is strongly visible in the Mykenean citadels of southern Greece, the "halls of the heroes." These places are the roots of the myths, so vividly imagined in *The Iliad* of Homer, of the men who sailed to Troy on the west coast of Turkey and sacked the city around 1250 BC. This is the civilization of Homer's heroes Agamemnon and Ulysses. These early Greeks gradually wrested power away from Crete and the Minoans and came to dominate the Aegean, in a time known as the Mykenean period in prehistoric archaeology.

The word *Mykene* actually has several connotations. On the one hand, it refers to the time period, the Late Bronze Age, between 1600 and 1100 BC in Greece. It also refers to an archaeological culture that shares a number of similarities and dominated much of Greece and parts of the Aegean. Finally, Mykene is a specific place, an archaeological site (Fig. 5.12).

The magnificence of the Mykenean period has its beginnings in the earlier Bronze Age in Greece. From around 2000 BC, through various means—both peaceful and violent—at least five major kingdoms rose from a number of warring petty chiefdoms. These political units were centered on fortified palace towns, or citadels, with a population that included scribes, warriors, and craft and art specialists. The palace economy focused on taxes or tribute in the form of foodstuffs, textiles and animal hides, ceramic and metal artifacts, military equipment, and labor. Long-distance trade developed, more extensive than the Minoan in both scale and extent. Interaction with the eastern Mediterranean, Italy, the west Mediterranean islands, Iberia, and Europe north of the Alps intensified.

Fig. 5.12.
The Citadel of Mykene, Greece.

The citadels, of which the site of Mykene is best known, are the most visible archaeological remains of this period, located on high, defensible points on the landscape, and heavily fortified with massive stone walls, which are termed

Cyclopean because of their size. Major citadels from this period are known from Mykene itself, Tiryns, and Thebes. At Tiryns, the great walls are 15 m (50 ft) thick and have internal passages.

The citadel of Mykene still looms as a powerful statement of the might of the people who lived there more than 3,000 years ago. Mykene is located about 90 km (55 mi) southwest of Athens. It sits in the northeastern corner of the Peloponnese, the large peninsula, almost an island, in southern Greece that forms the part of the country south of the Gulf of Corinth. Mykene is perched on a strategic hilltop, controlling the natural pass from the Isthmus to the Peloponnese. The hill has a commanding view of the region and plentiful fresh water. In order to build the citadel of Mykene, the hilltop was leveled and terraced to accommodate the walls of the fortress, as well as the inhabitants of the palace and town. A long, narrow road, flanked by massive stonewalls, leads to the Lion Gate, the entrance to the citadel, so named because of the enormous stone sculpture of two lions that crowns the gate (Fig. 5.13a).

The monumental stone walls of Mykene encircle an area 1,100 m (3,500 ft) in diameter (the equivalent of two city blocks), enclosing the palace of the king, as well as a number of other structures: two groups of shaft graves (the grave circles), granaries, guardrooms, shrines, and several private dwellings. The stone wall of the outer fortifications of the citadel is preserved to a standing height of 12.5 m (40 ft) in several places. The wall was 7.5–17 m (25–55 ft) thick and required a herculean effort to construct. Almost 15,000 large stones

Fig. 5.13a.
The Lion Gate at Mykene. A person in the entrance gives scale. Note the size of the Cyclopean stones used in the construction of the gate and wall.

Fig. 5.13b.
A corbeled arch (right) compared to a true Roman arch with a keystone (left).

were used, with a minimum weight of 10 tons. Human labor might take a bit more than two days to move a single stone, 110 years to move them all; use of oxen for draft would reduce the time to some ten years. The larger stones in the wall and around the gate weighed more than 20 tons, with a few up to 100 tons.

The palace itself included a central *megaron* (meeting hall, throne room, and courtyard) with adjacent private quarters, storerooms, guard stations, and administrative rooms. There is a large cistern inside the walls of the citadel in case of siege. The water supply is accessed by a secret passage of corbeled construction that leads down ninety-nine steps into the heart of the hill, to a cistern carved out of rock 15 m below the surface. The cistern was fed by a tunnel from a spring on distant higher ground.

The Mykenean palaces combined many of the administrative, military, and manufacturing functions of the kingdom within the residence of the ruler. Workshops for crafts, guardrooms, storerooms, and kitchens were attached to the rear of the palace. There was a small postern gate at the back of the citadel. Outside the Lion Gate and massive walls of the citadel were found the private houses, workshops, public works, and other features of the lower town and the large *tholos* tombs.

The corbel architecture technique is used to construct arches and vaults, seen in Mykenean structures as well as in other areas throughout the Mediterranean. A corbeled vault or dome is built up of horizontal layers of stone (Fig. 5.13b). Every layer is slightly closer to the center of the room, its weight carried by the layer below. This is not a true Roman arch with a keystone, but instead another solution for building vaulted rooms and passages.

The early rulers of the citadel of Mykene were buried in shaft graves, straight-sided pits, cut 6–8 m (20–25 ft) deep into the soft rock of the hilltop settlement. Groups of shaft graves were enclosed in a circle of standing limestone slabs (Fig. 5.14). Two such grave circles have been excavated at Mykene. Grave Circles A and B may have been in use for only a short period between ca. 1600 and 1500 BC. The walls of the tombs were lined with stone, and the entire structure was covered with a timber roof. Several tombs were found in each shaft; the shafts were reopened several times and new tombs were added. A total of nineteen individuals were buried in the six shafts of Grave Circle A at Mykene, two to five people in each shaft. There were nine men, eight women, and two children. The individuals buried in the shaft graves were larger and taller than other individuals buried at the site.

The bodies in the shaft graves were placed on their back in an extended position. It was common to find several burials per grave, and earlier burials were pushed to the side or stacked as more recent corpses were added to the tomb. The bodies appear to have been wrapped with burial shrouds having hundreds of small gold foil leaves, flowers, butterflies, or stars sewn onto the

Fig. 5.14.
Grave Circle A, enclosing several shaft graves, at Mykene. Located inside the citadel near the Lion Gate.

cloth. Gold funeral masks were placed on six of the adult males and one child. None of the females was found with a mask.

Heinrich Schliemann, the excavator of the graves, described opening one of the shafts in a letter to a friend in 1876. He had found five tombs in the grave circle, and in the smallest were the skeletal remains of a man and a woman along with at least 5.6 kg (12.3 lb) of pure gold jewelry in the form of earrings, ornaments, two gold scepters with crystal handles, many large gold and bronze vessels, and hundreds of gold leaves scattered throughout the tomb.

Schliemann was convinced that he had found the gold death mask and body of Agamemnon (Fig. 5.15), Homer's hero who was murdered by his wife's lover when he returned from the conquest of Troy. Although this individual was probably not Agamemnon, and the mask may well have been a forgery brought in by Schliemann, the contents of the graves of Mykene vividly document the wealth of this civilization and its rulers.

The grave goods from Mykene are among the most spectacular finds from the Bronze Age and the richest finds ever made in the Aegean area. There are gold and bronze masks and drinking cups, necklaces, earrings, a crystal bowl carved in the shape of a goose, and swords and daggers with gold and lapis inlays. Amber from northern Europe, ivory from Africa, silver from Crete, glass from Egypt, and great amounts of gold were entombed along with these early rulers. One early grave contained more than 5 kg (11 lb) of gold. The graves included precious metals and stone in the form of weapons, metal vessels, stone vases, seals and signet rings, amber, and a wide range of pottery.

Fig. 5.15.
A gold funerary mask from the shaft graves at Mykene, claimed by Schliemann to be the face of Agamemnon, 30 cm high.

Ninety swords were found in the graves of three individuals. Some were decorated with incised ornamentation, and the hilts were often covered with richly decorated gold sheet. The pommels were beautifully carved blocks of ivory, alabaster, or marble. Daggers and knives were also common, some inlaid with elaborate scenes made with different colors of pure metals and their alloys (Fig. 5.16). The scenes were of hunting and nature. Bronze spearheads and arrowheads were very common and standard weapons in Mykenean Greece.

Among the metal vessels and containers in the graves, twenty-eight were made from solid gold, forty-two from silver, and more of bronze. The silver objects are carefully made and carry motifs and techniques that point to Crete as their source. The gold items are not as well made and appear to have been of local manufacture. There are numerous goblets and vats, which

must have been used for holding, serving, and drinking wine. Many of these objects are elaborately decorated with scenes of combat or hunting. Among the most spectacular are a silver bull's head *rhyton* (a drinking cup) and a stag *rhyton*, probably imported from central Anatolia. Stone vases were typical Minoan products from Crete, although there were also examples made from ostrich eggshell, produced on Crete from material imported from Africa.

Seals and signet rings, marks of ownership and identity, were made of gold and carved with scenes of warfare and the hunt. Amber from the Baltic region is found in the form of thousands of beads and small pendants in rich graves of the Mykenean period. The amount of wealth in the hands (and burials) of a few elite individuals at Mykene and elsewhere points to a society in which inequality is pronounced and concentration of power at the top is extreme.

By 1400 BC, a new kind of grave, the huge, vaulted, beehive-shaped *tholos* tomb, was constructed for the major rulers. Several of these architectural

Fig. 5.16.
A bronze dagger from the shaft graves at Mykene, hunting scenes and stylized design inlaid with precious metals. The human figures are approximately 2 cm high.

Fig. 5.17.
Entrance to the Treasury of Atreus, a tholos tomb at Mykene.

Fig. 5.18.
A Linear A tablet from Knossos along with a drawing to clarify the symbols; approximately 10 by 6 cm.

wonders still stand today. The Treasury of Atreus at Mykene is the finest example of such a *tholos* tomb (Fig. 5.17). The roof of the vault stands more than 13 m (45 ft) above the floor, which is 15 m (50 ft) in diameter. The dramatic doorway to the tomb is 5 m (16 ft) high, and the lintel across the door weighs more than 100 tons. Unfortunately, the contents of the tomb were stolen long ago.

There is a good bit of information on the economy of the Mykenean citadels. The surrounding villages supplied plant foods and meat, men and materials, to the lord of the citadel. This information comes from preserved clay tablets with Linear B script. In some instances, these soft clay tablets were accidentally burned in fires that swept the citadels and hardened the clay, thereby preserving the script (Fig. 5.18). The subjects of the texts are primarily economic, dealing with inventories, shipments, and quotas of items to be paid to the palace in tribute. At the palace of Pylos, where a major hoard of tablets was preserved, a list of occupations in the kingdom was recorded: bakers, bronzesmiths, carpenters, heralds, masons, messengers, potters, shepherds, and "unguent boilers." Many other skills are also evidenced in the artifacts and architecture of the citadel, such as delicate ivory carving, fresco painting, metal inlaying, and arms manufacturing.

The fire-hardened tablets of the Linear B archives at several Mykenean palaces document the transfer of commodities within the palace territory as part of an economic system of redistribution. The tablets list the inventories of palace resources and record the movement of these goods, land, and personnel. Four types of transactions are documented in the archives:

1. Taxes, paid in nonstaple commodities such as spices, dye plants, hides, wood, flax, oil, honey, and metal and cloth. Every community apparently owed roughly the same amounts of these materials.
2. Agricultural production. The palace itself must have had some estates where various crops and especially animals were raised. Sheep were kept primarily for wool production. The wealthy palace at Knossos, during the Mykenean period, kept records on 80,000 sheep, 60,000 of which were used for wool. Figs, olives, and grapes were other important crops raised directly by the palace.
3. Maintenance of the palace staff. At the Mykenean palace of Pylos there were some 4,000 palace retainers. About one-third (including most craftspersons and palace servants) received food; the remainder (bronzesmiths, soldiers, hunters, and planters) were given small plots of land.
4. Craft production. Craft production involved bronze, chariots, textiles, weapons, furniture, leather goods, perfumed olive oil, gold, and glass. The palace gave workers measured amounts of raw materials, along

with production targets. Detailed inventories of finished craft goods in the palace treasury were maintained.

The archaeological evidence for long-distance trade in the economy documents the extensive tentacles of the palace economy and the eastern Mediterranean interaction sphere. Large coarse-wear jars were used for moving olive oil across the Mykenean region. Shipwrecks from this period, such as the Uluburun described in the next section, yield clear evidence for the materials moving into the Mykenean region. The ship's cargo included copper and tin ingots, large jars with olives, glass beads, fine pottery, and resin for preserving wine, along with ebony logs, ostrich eggs, elephant tusk and hippo tusk ivory from Africa, glass ingots probably from Egypt, jewelry, and thousands of Baltic amber and quartz beads.

Many large and small settlements from this time period were scattered across southern Greece. A sophisticated system of graveled roads for chariots and carts, with stone bridges and culverts, connected these towns and villages. The bridge at Kazarma, for example, was constructed in the Cyclopean style, with fitted large stones and spanning a culvert with a length 22 m (75 ft), a height of 5.4 m (18 ft), and a width of 4 m (13 ft). This bridge is still in place today (Fig. 5.19).

The reason for the collapse of Mykenean civilization remains a mystery. Seemingly unrelated to drought or outside conquest, perhaps it was simply the result of a culmination of centuries of warfare and competition. The threat or reality of major conflict appears to have played a dominant role throughout much

Fig. 5.19.
The Mykenean bridge at Kazarma, Greece.

of the Mykenean period. The heavily fortified sites and the militaristic nature of the society fit such a pattern. Evidence for warfare is endemic; all the major sites experienced episodes of violent destruction between 1250 and 1200 BC.

Mykenean civilization slowly declined during the twelfth century BC as all signs of state authority, major construction, craft specialization, and literacy disappeared, to be followed by a period known in Greek history as the Dark Age. After 1100 BC, Athens began to assert more importance in Greece as the focus of the new industry of iron making, and the other centers of the Mykeneans fell into disuse. The Iron Age civilization of Greece blossomed from 600 to 300 BC, giving rise to the golden age of Athens and the foundations of much of Western civilization.

ULUBURUN, TURKEY, 1300 BC

The sea floor is one of the least explored places on earth and home to lots of intriguing archaeology. There are mammoth bones and stone tools on the floor of the North Sea (Doggerland) from when that area was dry land during the lower sea levels of the colder periods of the Paleolithic. There are submerged Mesolithic settlements around the coast of Europe from a period when human subsistence focused on the sea and shorelines were lower than today. Tybrind Vig in Denmark is such a place. The 10 m (33 ft) dugout canoe from Tybrind is one of the oldest known examples of water transport. Recently, a Bronze Age shipwreck has been found at Salcombe along the south coast of England, one of the oldest ships known anywhere in Europe. The finds from Salcombe are described later in this chapter.

Fig. 5.20.
Underwater excavations at the Uluburun wreck, off the coast of southwestern Turkey.

Several shipwrecks from the Bronze Age have been found in the Mediterranean. One was discovered in the 1980s only 60 m off the southwest coast of Turkey. This was a cargo ship 15 m (50 ft) long, found near the town of Uluburun in 50 m (165 ft) of water (Fig. 5.20). These are known to be dangerous waters and the place of numerous wrecks. This one contained the largest and richest collection of late Bronze Age materials ever found in the Mediterranean. The sailing ship was plank-built from cedar timber, using a mortise and tendon technique to join the planks, and capable of carrying 20 tons of cargo. The Uluburun wreck sank around 1306 BC, according to the tree rings in the wood on board.

The remains were discovered in 1982 by a local sponge diver who informed the research group at the Institute of Nautical Archaeology at Texas A&M University, which has a local facility in a nearby town. Underwater excavations began in 1984 and continued for ten years. The wreck lay on a steep slope and the remains were scattered across the seafloor.

The ship's intended route is uncertain, but from the cargo it can be surmised the vessel came from Cyprus and was possibly headed to Greece. The ship was carrying a remarkably varied range of materials from the eastern Mediterranean. The major part of the hold was filled with 500 copper ingots totaling some 10 tons, with another ton of tin ingots. Cyprus was a major source of smelted copper in the Bronze Age; the tin may have originated in eastern Turkey. Scattered among the ingots were hundreds of pottery vessels of various sizes—large *pithoi* 50 cm (20 in) in height, and smaller containers as well (Fig. 5.21). Several of the *pithoi* held olives, glass beads filled another, and half a dozen carried various sizes and shapes of pottery from Cyprus. Most of the storage jars contained almost one ton of resin from pistachio trees, which can be mixed with wine to prevent mold.

The ship also carried a number of other rare and exotic items, some previously unknown—testimony to the extent of trade. This part of the manifest included ebony logs, elephant ivory and hippo tusks from tropical Africa, thousands of quartz and Baltic amber beads, lavender- and turquoise-colored glass ingots probably from Egypt, large turtle shells, and ostrich eggshells. There was a remarkable series of standardized weights, in animal forms, for use with a balance, made from bronze and filled with lead. These forms included a sphinx, a lion, a lioness, bulls, cows, a calf, ducks, and frogs.

Fig. 5.21. Amphorae and copper "oxhide" ingots in a museum reconstruction of the Uluburun wreck on the sea floor.

There was a rich assemblage of jewelry and scrap gold and silver, and shell rings with bitumen adhesive from Mesopotamia. There are also Egyptian objects of gold, electrum, silver, steatite—including a gold scarab inscribed with the name of Nefertiti. There was a lovely, small bronze goddess effigy, with gold-covered head, hands, and feet (Fig. 5.22). Wooden writing boards (two thin pieces of wood with shallow recesses to hold wax to write on with a stylus) were held together by an ivory joint. There were also numerous weapons and tools, some of which were undoubtedly part of the ship's equipment. The tools included sickles, awls, drill bits, a saw, tongs, chisels, axes, a ploughshare, whetstones, and adzes. Lastly a number of stone anchors were scattered about the wreck and must have served a secondary function as ballast.

The ship also carried a good bit of food and fishing equipment. The foodstuffs included almonds, pine nuts, figs, olives, grapes, safflower, black cumin, sumac, coriander, and whole pomegranates, along with a few grains of charred wheat and barley. The fishing gear was varied: lead net sinkers, needles for making nets, fishhooks, trolling sinkers, a bronze trident, and a fishing spear.

The ship itself probably originated in the Near East, given the types of tools and personal objects found on board, including a razor and a few amulets. In addition, the stone anchors were made from a sandstone unknown in the

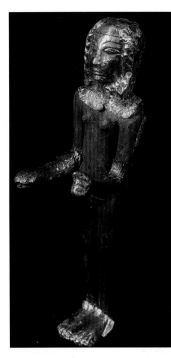

Fig. 5.22.
Bronze goddess effigy
from the wreck of the
Uluburun, ca. 10 cm
high.

Aegean and in all probability from Southwest Asia. The Near East at this time was a hot bed of large civilizations, cities, warfare, written records, and extensive long-distance trade. The Phoenicians controlled much of the maritime trade with Egypt and the eastern Aegean. The armies of the Assyrian Empire eventually conquered territory and towns as far south as modern Israel. The Egyptians fought unsuccessfully with the Assyrians, who then extended their power into the Nile valley. At the same time, in Europe outside of the Aegean region, north of the Alps, dramatic changes were underway.

THE BRONZE AGE NORTH OF THE ALPS

During the third millennium BC in Europe, major changes in technology and transportation took place, notably the manufacture of bronze weapons and jewelry, widespread adoption of the plow and the wheel, and use of horses for riding and as draft animals to pull carts and chariots. Weapons and martial motifs dominated the symbols of status in European society. Local warfare and conflict contrasted strongly with patterns of intensive craft production, long-distance trade, commerce, and cooperation. Textiles of wool and linen, metal dress pins, and amber and gold necklaces characterized the clothing of the elite. A bronze razor (for shaving) was a means to alter one's appearance as a mark of status and power.

Certainly by this time, rituals often took place at scheduled times of the year, determined by calendrical means. The solar "computer" of Stonehenge and the myriad stone and wood circles of northwestern Europe clearly functioned in this manner. North of the Alps, political and social organization seems to have involved alliances of ephemeral chiefs who cooperated in exchanging exotic materials and in warfare. As wealth accumulated and increased during the Bronze Age, there was a marked trend toward fortification. The economy and social relations were intertwined. The most notable features of the Bronze Age landscape, aside from exceptional monuments such as Stonehenge, are large earthen barrows—the tombs of the elite. There was a dramatic, no doubt intentional contrast between the massive tombs of the nobility and the flat graves of commoners.

Metals appeared later in the northern part of Europe than in the Aegean. The first bronze in Europe north of the Alps was introduced by the Bell Beaker people. *Bell Beaker* is the term used to describe a distinctive form of pottery that appears across much of Western Europe in the third millennium BC, at the transition between the Neolithic and the Bronze Age. The burials of Bell Beaker individuals contain some of the first bronze and gold in Western Europe, along with new equipment for archery and some evidence for the first domesticated horses. More information on Bell Beaker appears later in this chapter, along with the extraordinary archer's grave near Amesbury in England.

The major archaeological cultures and chronology for the Bronze Age north of the Alps are summarized in Figure 5.23. Two major cultures dominate the Bronze Age in Central Europe.

The first is Únětice, the name given to the early Bronze Age, dated from 2300 to 1600 BC; it is recognized by distinctive bronze objects such as torqs (a heavy neck ring of precious metal worn by elite individuals), axes, daggers, bracelets, pins, and rings. The Urnfield culture (ca. 1300 BC–750 BC) appears in the later Bronze Age of Central Europe. The name comes from the custom of placing the cremated ashes of the dead in ceramic urns (Fig.

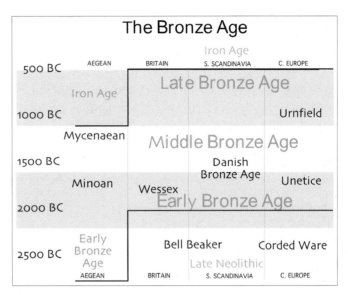

5.24), which were then buried together with others in a cemetery. Urnfield groups expanded west and south in the later Bronze Age and are often suggested to have influenced the development of Etruscan society (see Fig. 5.26).

The Bronze Age in prehistoric Europe was in large part about accumulation of wealth and power by the ruling elite. The archaeological evidence emphasizes rich tombs, trade, warriors to protect and control that trade, and distant marriages and alliances to establish stable political arrangements. Wealthy and powerful hierarchical societies arose at the centers of important trade routes and mining areas in the early Bronze Age. Tin bronze became the primary form of the metal only later in the third millennium BC. Bronze is typically around eighty-eight percent copper and twelve percent tin. Tin bronze was superior because alloying and casting were easier and the finished product was stronger. Bronze production on a significant scale first appeared north of the Alps about 2400 BC.

The Únětice culture emerged around the largest sources of tin in Europe—the Erzgebirge, or Ore Mountains, along the present-day border between Germany and the Czech Republic. The Únětice culture, best known from several "princely" burials, dominated central Europe in this period (Fig. 5.25).

The Bronze Age in Denmark and southern Sweden, funded by a wealth of amber on the beaches, was spectacular in terms of the quantity of fine metal objects. There is more bronze in southern Scandinavia from the Bronze Age than anywhere else in Europe. The demand for amber in Europe and the eastern Mediterranean was unceasing.

Amber is a remarkable material in many ways. It is translucent, it floats in saltwater, it can be

Fig. 5.23.
The Bronze Age north of the Alps: chronology and cultures.

Fig. 5.24.
Cremation vase from the Urnfield Period, found near Marburg, Hesse, Germany, c. 40 cm high.

Fig. 5.25.
Bronze axes, daggers, chisels, a stone axe, gold pins, rings, a bracelet, and a whetstone from the princely burial at Leubingen, Germany. The larger copper axe at the top of the photo is 16 cm in length.

burned as incense, it is sometimes used as a healing agent or an ingredient in perfume, and when rubbed against fur or wool it generates static electricity. Amber found in the Baltic region of northern Europe accounts for approximately 80 percent of the world supply. Pieces of amber wash up on Baltic beaches still today, eroding out of seafloor deposits during strong winter storms.

A third dominant Bronze Age culture, the Wessex in England, elaborated the construction of Stonehenge and erected hundreds of barrows across southern England. It has been suggested that the Wessex graves of the early second millennium in south-central England owe their wealth to control of the tin deposits in Cornwall. Bronze objects began to appear commonly in graves and cemeteries of farming settlements in Europe north of the Alps after 2000 BC. By this time, Minoan and Mycenaean cultures in the eastern Mediterranean had developed into powerful political entities through a combination of alliances, sea power, craft production, and control of trade.

The eastern Mediterranean was a magnet for valued raw materials from the rest of Europe. Copper, tin, and gold from sources in Ireland and England moved across the English Channel, down the Seine and Rhône rivers in France, to the Mediterranean for shipment to the Aegean. Copper ores and ingots from the Carpathian Mountains in Eastern Europe were brought overland through the Brenner Pass in the Alps to Greece. Amber from the Baltic and North Sea coasts of Poland and Denmark was imported across Europe to the Aegean. Other exports, such as furs and slaves, may have also been sent in return for finished bronze weapons, pottery vessels, and bronze and gold jewelry. In fact, much of what is known about the Bronze Age north of the Alps comes from large barrows or caches of metal objects hidden in the ground; relatively few houses or settlements have been discovered or excavated. Burials were often in the form of cremations (Fig. 5.25), and grave goods, if any, were frequently consumed in the funeral pyres. Less information is obviously available from such finds. Such information provides a biased, though spectacular, view of a small, wealthy, and powerful segment of Bronze Age society.

Metal is a powerful material, used for making effective tools and weapons, but also rare and especially suitable as a status symbol. This rarity was exacerbated by the use of tin, which was even scarcer than copper. Ownership and control of metal was thus a measure of wealth. Because copper and tin are distributed irregularly and in limited quantities, movement of raw materials bound European societies into the trade of metal. Importation of metal from

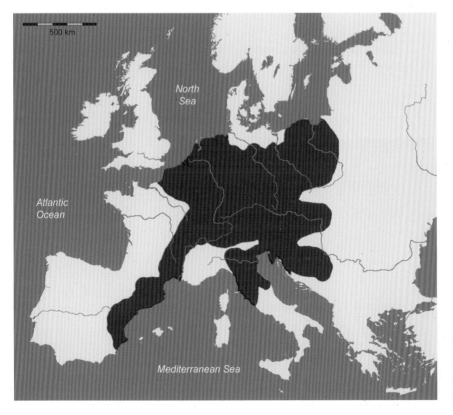

Fig. 5.26.
The distribution of Urnfield culture in the later Bronze Age of Europe.

the continent into Late Bronze Age Britain is evidenced by the cargo of the Salcombe shipwreck near the English Channel, discussed below. Control of raw materials, resources, and craft specialists became increasingly important. Late Bronze Age fortified settlements of the Urnfield period (Fig. 5.26) appear to have acted as regional metallurgical centers.

Continuing the tour, we visit a series of important sites from Bronze Age Europe in the western Mediterranean and north of the Alps, where the Aegean had less influence. The grave of the Amesbury Archer in the south of England is a rich burial from the beginnings of the Bronze Age, associated with the Bell Beaker culture. From Italy come the remains of a series of Bronze Age sites buried by the eruption of Vesuvius, long before Roman Pompeii even existed. Nebra is the find spot in eastern Germany of the most extraordinary artifact found in the last decade. Other exceptional Bronze Age finds are also described in this section.

Su Nuraxi di Barumini is one of the hundreds of Bronze Age fortresses on the island of Sardinia. Salcombe is the place in Britain where a Bronze Age shipwreck revised our understanding of long-distance trade in this period. Borum Eshøj is the rich barrow and tomb of a Bronze Age family from Denmark. Bredarör, Sweden is another barrow of a very different flavor from Northern Europe. Tanum, Sweden, with its rock art, is another of the amazing places from this time period.

BELL BEAKER

Bell Beaker describes a distinctive form of pottery that appears across much of Western Europe in the third millennium BC, crossing the boundary between the Neolithic and the Bronze Age. The Beakers are radiocarbon-dated from 2900 to 1800/1700 BC. The arrival of Bell Beakers was also associated with the introduction of metals such as copper daggers, bronze and gold jewelry, new archery equipment and arrowheads, distinctive buttons, occasional equestrian gear, and probably new beliefs. This package of new things appearing simultaneously led researchers to think about migration and the arrival of new peoples.

Fig. 5.27.
A decorated Bell Beaker from Hungary, ca. 25 cm high.

Bell Beakers are given their name because of the distinctive inverted, bell-shaped profile of their pottery (Fig. 5.27). It is well made, usually red or red-brown in color, and ornamented with horizontal bands of incised, excised, or impressed patterns. Archaeologists tend to designate the people associated with this pottery as the Bell Beaker folk. They remain one of the mysteries of European prehistory.

The origin of Bell Beaker is one part of the mystery. Bell Beaker materials are known more often from graves, largely of male individuals, which show a discontinuous distribution from Hungary to the west (Fig. 5.28).

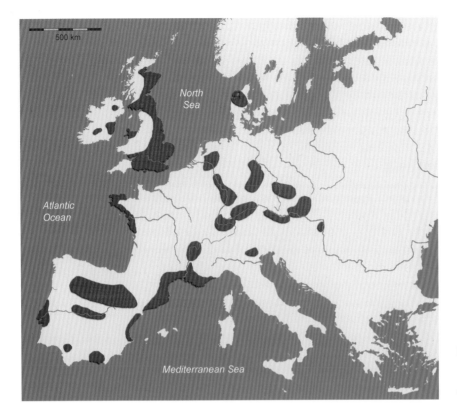

Fig. 5.28.
Distribution of Bell Beaker materials in Western Europe.

Beakers are found in higher density along routes of movement, including river fords, river valleys, and mountain passes, emphasizing the mobility of these materials and most likely the people who made them. The presence of the new metals and the evidence for mobility suggested to some that the Bell Beaker folk were metal smiths, tinkers traveling across Western Europe. Others have pointed to the evidence for beer and mead residues in some beakers and suggest that alcohol was important in the spread of the Bell Beaker folk.

A famous European prehistorian in the middle of the twentieth century, V. Gordon Childe, suggested the Beaker Folk might be similar to various kinds of mobile groups: traders, merchants, prospectors, warriors, missionaries, or a kind of gypsy folk. Still others argue that Bell Beaker is not a distinct group of people; rather, the beakers and other new objects and materials were the result of adoption of new crafts and skills by local people. This new knowledge may have come about by any combination of population movements and cultural contact. On the other hand, several lines of evidence suggest that Bell Beaker was indeed associated with the movement of people.

Comparison measurements of the dimensions of the skull and skeleton of burials indicated that the Beaker people were of a physical type different from earlier populations in the same geographic area. They were described as tall, heavy boned and with broad, short heads. Jocelyne Desideri examined the teeth in skeletons from Bell Beaker sites in Northern Spain, Southern France, Switzerland, the Czech Republic, and Hungary. Looking at inherited dental traits, she found that only in Northern Spain and the Czech Republic were there demonstrable genetic links between immediately previous populations and Bell Beaker populations; elsewhere there was genetic discontinuity. Other studies have generally confirmed this pattern. An isotopic study of strontium in tooth enamel from individuals in Bell Beaker graves in Bavaria indicated that 20–25 percent of all graves were occupied by people who came from a considerable distance outside the area. This was true of children as well as adults, indicative of significant migration in this period.

THE INDO-EUROPEANS

The place of origin of Bell Beakers is a matter of considerable debate. A number of homelands have been suggested and rejected. At present, the generally accepted origin of Bell Beaker lies in far eastern Europe and what is known as the Kurgan culture. The "Kurgan hypothesis," initially proposed by Marija Gimbutas, related the origin of the Bell Beaker Folk to groups to the east, displaced by incursions of tribes from the steppe. Her general proposition, though debated and modified, is still generally accepted. The more controversial aspect of her argument involves the spread of Indo-European languages and people.

Three billion people in the world speak Indo-European languages, which include most of the major tongues of Europe, the Iranian plateau, and South Asia, including Spanish, English, Hindi, Portuguese, Bengali, Russian, German, Marathi, French, Italian, Punjabi, and Urdu, among many others. This shared language family suggests a common origin in the distant past for its speakers.

The origin of Indo-European is one of the thorniest issues in all of European prehistory. It is a very difficult question to deal with archaeologically; language before writing is almost impossible to trace. There are also substantial political and racial issues entwined in the concept. The related term *Aryan* was originally used in academic contexts, but it was co-opted and misused by Nazi Germany in the 1930s and 1940s to promote a blond, blue-eyed race and to designate undesirables. Today the term is often used by white supremacists.

Indo-European studies in archaeology are of questionable merit, for several reasons. One, as noted, is the difficulty of identifying language in the archaeological record. Second, the questions of the origin of Indo-European languages and the origin of European peoples are not necessarily related. Third, Indo-European speakers cannot be assumed to have been a single, identifiable people or tribe. With these reservations, a brief review can continue.

Studies in Europe have focused on the Proto-Indo-European language (PIE), a reconstructed version of the prehistoric language that gave rise to so many varieties today. PIE is assumed to have been the language of peoples east of the Black Sea from the southern Ukraine and Russia. Information about PIE comes largely from historical linguistics and the study of words and terms shared among modern languages. In addition, there is some material evidence from genetics and archaeology about the changes taking place in Europe in the third millennium BC. Genetic evidence involving the Y chromosome and a haplotype designated as R1a1, reported by Spencer Wells, points toward migration of new people into Europe during the third millennium BC.

AMESBURY ARCHER, ENGLAND, 2470 BC

Archaeological excavations in the south of England in 2002, in advance of construction of a housing project, exposed a Roman cemetery. Two dark stains in the ground on the periphery of the construction area were left for last. Excavation of the larger of the two pits revealed the richest collection of Bell Beaker grave goods ever found from this period in Britain. Almost one hundred artifacts were there, including two gold hair bands. The radiocarbon date of 2470 BC from the grave confirms the Bell Beaker age and the oldest gold artifacts in Britain.

The Archer was a male, between thirty-five and forty-five years of age. He was tall and strongly built, but his left kneecap had been destroyed some years before his death, causing him to walk with a stiff leg. Near the man's head were two Beaker pots, a red deer bone used for working flints, boars tusks, a cache of flints, and a smaller copper knife (Fig. 5.29). Two more Beaker pots lay at the man's feet. By his knees there was an archer's wrist guard, another small copper knife, a shale belt ring, and the two gold hair bands.

This grave was found some 5 km (3 mi) from Stonehenge. Because of the quantity of archery equipment and the richness of the burial, the interred individual has been dubbed the Amesbury Archer and the Prince of Stonehenge (the latter at the least quite a piece of PR). The media would even like to make the archer responsible for starting construction of the stone trilithons at Stonehenge. This is nonsense. There is nothing to connect this individual to Stonehenge other than the fact that he was alive during the time that Stonehenge was in use.

The second stain turned out to be the grave of another male between twenty-five and thirty years of age, dating from same time as the Archer (Fig. 5.30). Two gold hair bands were also found with this individual. In addition he and the archer shared an unusual bone structure in their feet, suggesting that the two individuals were related.

Fig. 5.29.
Grave goods associated with the Amesbury Archer in England, one of the richest Bell Beaker graves in Europe. Flint flakes, tools and arrowheads, pottery (brown), gold earrings (yellow), bronze daggers, pins, a ring, slate wristguards, animal teeth, and shell.

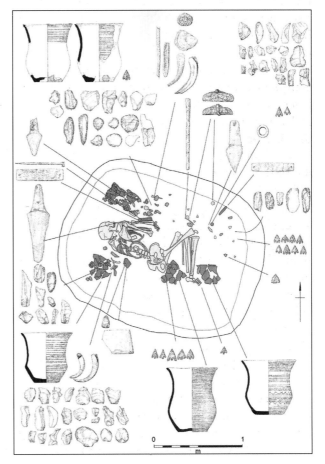

POGGIOMARINO, ITALY, 1600 BC

At the start of the twenty-first century AD, two extraordinary Bronze Age sites

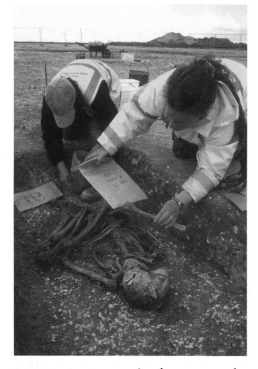

Fig. 5.30.
Excavation of the second individual, likely a relative of the Amesbury Archer.

were found just 15 km (10 mi) apart south of the city of Naples. Archaeologically, Naples is famous for the nearby ancient Roman city of Pompeii, buried in AD 79 by volcanic ash from Mount Vesuvius. Both of these new sites also lie at the foot of Vesuvius, to the east and south of volcano.

Poggiomarino is a waterlogged site with exceptional preservation discovered in 2000 during the construction of a new water treatment facility. Croce del Papa was buried in an eruption of Vesuvius and discovered near the modern town of Nola in 2001. The ash preserved the houses and many other aspects of daily life. There are in fact a number Bronze Age sites on the Campanian Plain around the base of Vesuvius. Several of these sites are still under investigation.

Poggiomarino is a large site, covering an estimated 7 ha (18 acres). The full extent of the settlement is unknown, however, as much remains to be uncovered or lies beneath modern buildings. The cultural layer is deeply buried in wetland deposits, almost 3 m (10 ft) below the modern surface. The depth of the Bronze Age layer means that excavations require removal of a thick layer of ash and earth lying over the prehistoric materials. For this reason, only a small part of the site has been excavated so far (Fig. 5.31).

The Bronze Age community of Poggiomarino was established in a wetland area. Eight small, artificial, round islands were discovered, ranging between 120 and 240 m^2 in size and connected by a navigable network of canals. Stilt houses were built on the islands. The excavator of the site, Claude Albore Livadie, nicknamed it a "Bronze Age Venice." The prehistoric settlement was occupied continuously for almost 1,000 years from the sixteenth to the sixth century BC.

The islands were created by digging canals. Bulwarks of oak trees and wooden panels were erected along the canals and the earth removed from the canal was thrown up into the area behind the bulwark to build an artificial island. Each island held a hut and a landing place for small watercraft. Some of the islands may have been connected by permanent bridges or drawbridges. The surface of these islands was usually paved with pebbles and slabs of volcanic rock quarried in the area to maintain a drier, more stable surface. Finally, a constant water level was maintained in the island settlement area by a series of drainage canals and sluices.

Poggiomarino yielded an enormous quantity of artifacts, ranging from wooden construction material to fine metal products. A large amount of well-preserved wood (mostly oak) was found in the form of posts, flat planks, worked and semiworked beams, huts, house furnishings, tools, and a few dugout canoes used in the canal system. More than 500,000 pieces of pottery and 100,000 animal bones and antlers (largely wild boar, deer, and bear) have been recovered, along with more than 600 artifacts made of bronze, lead, iron, glass, amber, bone, and antler. Important finds include unworked pieces of amber,

Fig. 5.31.
Excavations continue at Poggiomarino under the shelter of a temporary roof.

a furnace for smelting copper, and a few molds for casting bronze objects. The investigators suggest that Poggiomarino was an important industrial center, where various goods were produced and traded across southern Italy and perhaps throughout the central Mediterranean. The site was abandoned during the sixth century BC when floods and mudslides covered the area.

CROCE DEL PAPA, ITALY, 2150 BC

Croce del Papa was abandoned, and buried by ash, some 500 years before Poggiomarino came into being. The site was discovered in 2001, 3 m (10 ft) below the ground surface, during excavation of underground parking for a new shopping mall. This Bronze Age village was only 15 km (10 mi) from the active vents of the Vesuvius volcano and was buried in a pyroclastic flow during an eruption dated ca. 2150 BC. The excavations uncovered detailed evidence of a small village abandoned quickly by its occupants at the time of the eruption. The human inhabitants left the village at the moment of the eruption, leaving only footprints and the items they were unable to carry away from the site.

The details of this eruption are fairly clear. Much of this evidence comes from another Bronze Age village, Afragola, some 14 km (9 km) from the main vent on Vesuvius, and likewise buried in the same eruption (Fig. 5.32). Three separate volcanic events are recorded at Afragola in pumice, ash, and projectile deposits. Sedimentological and structural damage analyses clearly indicate that the pyroclastic flow in the Afragola area was slow-moving and of very

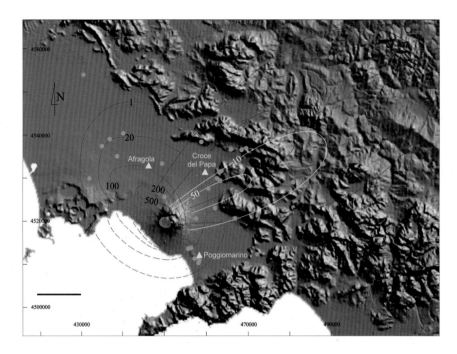

Fig. 5.32.
The area around Vesuvius and the three major eruptions in 1781 BC (red, white, and blue contours). Contour intervals mark depth of ash deposits in centimeters. Green circles mark Bronze Age villages; yellow triangles are sites mentioned in the text.

low density. It did not cause severe structural damage to the ancient village. A temperature ca. 300 °C (572 °F) is estimated for the flows when they reached the village. Those conditions would have been deadly to humans and animals, from contact or inhalation. Repeated ash fall buried the initial flow, followed by a massive eruption with large projectiles reaching this area. Substantial flooding was also caused by the eruption and ash fall, which dammed streams, burying the village in deep layers of mud.

Croce del Papa, to the east of Afragola, experienced a similar sequence of events during an earlier eruption. Croce del Papa was at the outer limit of the initial pyroclastic flow. The village escaped a shower of white-hot pumice that took place during the first five to six hours but did not avoid the subsequent fall of gray pumice and ash. Most of the construction materials of the prehistoric huts were destroyed by the eruption, but falling ash and volcanic mud hardened to create a kind of molded copy of the village (Fig. 5.33). Excavation director Giuseppe Vecchio and his team have uncovered a treasure trove of hastily abandoned objects that tell us a great deal about domestic life in the Italian Bronze Age. Abundant evidence of food production and storage has been found, including pig, sheep, goats, and cow bones, and pots full of grain. Plant remains from cereals and other vegetables are well preserved. No human remains have been found at Croce del Papa, only a few footprints preserved in the mud.

Three huts were found in the excavations, separated from one another by light stockades. Two wells were found, with frog bones in the bottom. In addition, a number of areas enclosed with fencing were identified, featuring a threshing floor. It was possible to identify different types of fences and other features such as a wooden bucket hanging on a fence. Some of these enclosures

Fig. 5.33.

Excavations at Croce del Papa, deep beneath the volcanic ash and mud, have revealed several houses from a prehistoric Bronze Age village.

were pens for livestock, as documented by the abundant tracks of cattle, sheep, and goats, often accompanied by human footprints.

The houses have a horseshoe shape with a doorway at the straight end, and a protruding canopy over the entrance. The door was a wickerwork of branches. The size of the houses varied, with the largest 15.2 m (50 ft) long, 9 m (30 ft) wide, and 5 m (16 ft) high and the smallest 7.5 m (25 ft) long, 4.5 m (15 ft) wide, 4.5 m high.

The walls were continuous up to the steep roof. They are built using vertical poles and horizontal wooden rails, lashed together with thick rope. Several central posts supported the roof. There may have been a kind of open attic in at least one of the huts, where some of the large pottery vessels were stored. Interior walls divided the house into two or three rooms. In the longest hut, a narrow opening linked the living area with a pantry space where food storage vessels were found. The living area contained a hearth and a circular cooking feature.

The mudflow that filled the site preserved the huts and other structures to a depth of 1.3 m (4.3 ft). The mud slowly covered home furnishings, ovens, heavy pottery vessels and their contents, and other objects. Lighter items were displaced and floated to the top of the mud. This mud protected the house contents, including a ladder and wooden vessels, wickerwork containers, fabrics, cords from which vessels were hanging or for lashing the wooden structure together. The straw bundles that roofed the huts, ferns, oak leaves, mushrooms, cereals, and other plant remains were also preserved in the mud.

Some of the finds left behind when the village was abandoned were cooking utensils, drinking cups, hunting tools, a hat or helmet decorated with wild boar tusks, and a pot waiting to be fired in a kiln. Remains of these boar tusk hats or helmets were found in several houses. Bronze weapons and other valuable items were removed by the inhabitants when they fled; most of the domestic animals were apparently taken as well. The two larger structures contained nearly a hundred pottery vessels, some of which still held their contents, identifiable as almonds, flour, and ears of barley and spelt.

The most spellbinding evidence is the tracks and footprints that cross the layer of fresh ash as people and animals fled the volcano (Fig. 5.34). That most people were able to leave is documented by the absence of human remains in this layer. Several other recently discovered Bronze Age villages in the region were not so lucky, and a number of their inhabitants died in the catastrophic eruption. Many of the animals at Croce del Papa were also less fortunate. Four pregnant goats and several other animals died, penned or tethered in one of the yards. Other animals were also trapped; a dog was found in one of the huts, huddled in a corner, where it had taken refuge.

Fig. 5.34.
Human footprints in the fresh volcanic ash at the site of Croce del Papa.

NEBRA, GERMANY, 1600 BC

The Bronze Age in Europe north of the Alps is in many ways an unusual period of time. Settlements are not well known; much of what is known comes from graves. The period seems to be one of movement, conflict, warriors and priests, and mystery. This discussion of Nebra is about a single artifact rather than an archaeological site. The object, however, is one of the most important finds in Europe in many years. There are a number of truly spellbinding artifacts made from the new metals of the Bronze Age that create surprise and wonder when encountered. Here I focus on the Nebra disk, but I also want to mention a few other strange finds from the shadows of the Bronze Age.

The story of the discovery and recovery of the Nebra sun disk is a remarkable tale. Nebra is a small town in the former East Germany, about 60 km (40 mi) west of Leipzig. With the fall of the Berlin Wall and reunification in Germany in the late 1980s, unscrupulous black market antiquities dealers were quick to get cheap metal detectors into the hands of looters and grave robbers. In the middle of the night in 1999, three men in the forest of the Mittelberg outside Nebra were alerted by the loud beeping of their detectors. They quickly dug into the earth and found an unusual bronze disk (Fig. 5.35), two bronze swords and axes, and several other objects. They had looted a prehistoric enclosure on top of the hill in a forest with hundreds of Bronze Age burial mounds.

Eventually the looters contacted Harald Meller, a museum archaeologist in the area, offering to sell the disk to him for almost $400,000. A meeting was finally arranged in February 2002, in Switzerland between Meller and the looters. The looters brought the disk, and Meller brought the police; the museum got the treasure and the tomb robbers got a year in prison. In addition, the precise location of the discovery was provided as part of a plea bargain. Archaeological excavations have since been conducted in and around the place to better determine the context of the finds. The prehistoric enclosure in which the disk was found appears to be astronomically oriented in line with a nearby peak to mark the solstice.

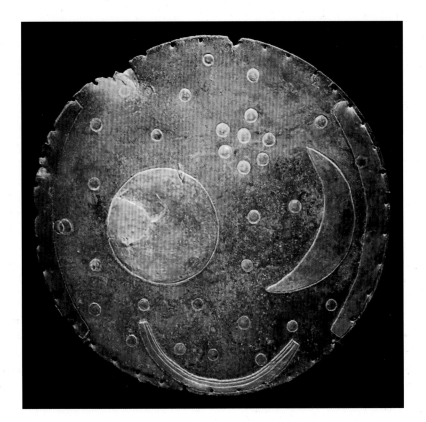

Fig. 5.35.
The Nebra disk. An enigma in bronze and gold, 32 cm in diameter.

Because of the very unusual circumstances of the discovery of the disk, and because of the extraordinary nature of the artifact itself, many archaeologists thought it was a forgery. One German archaeologist wrote to a newspaper saying that it was fake and that the green corrosion on the disk had been made by a mixture of urine and acid. It took several years and a series of in-depth investigations to convince the professional community that this disk was the real deal.

The evidence supporting the antiquity of the Nebra disk is multifold. The most convincing has to do with the orientation of objects on the disk. Measurements have revealed a precise angle of 82°. This angle, between the sunrises at the summer and winter solstice, fits only in a rather limited area of Central Europe, including Nebra. The angle increases or decreases quickly as one moves north or south.

The source of the raw materials for the disk—copper, tin, and gold—also yield some important information about the antiquity of the piece. If the sources were unknown in ancient times, it would be difficult to prove the disk was genuine. Bronze is an alloy of mostly copper and some tin, usually about 12 percent. The bronze used for the disk is a typical alloy for the Bronze Age and not produced today because of the high amount of poisonous arsenic. Lead isotopes in the copper of the Nebra bronze were used to identify its source as Mitterberg, an ancient mine near Bischofshofen in Austria.

The Nebra disk is the earliest known depiction of the night sky. The disk has been dated in two ways, by association with the swords of known date found with the disk and by radiocarbon assay. Both methods produce an age of 1600 BC, 200 years older than the oldest images of the sky found in Egypt.

The heavy bronze disk is 32 cm (12.5 in) in diameter, about the size of a dinner plate. The bronze has corroded to a bright green color. Attached to the slightly domed surface of the disk are a series of gold leaf ornaments that appear to represent the sun, the crescent moon, and the stars. On either side of the domed surface are two bands marked with engraved lines. One band contains a gold appliqué, and the other is missing. The angle between two crossing lines drawn from either end of the two bands is 82°. In addition, there is a large, upturned curve of gold on the lower edge of the disk. There are thirty-two small gold circles (one is missing) scattered on the surface of the disk. (Three of the circles are beneath the right band and cannot be seen.) Forty small holes lie around the outer edge of the disk.

The meaning of these symbols and their location on the disk was not immediately clear and subject to some debate. The motifs have been interpreted in a variety of ways. The most recent explanation seems to account for all of the features and to be the most logical. The disk was apparently used as a complex astronomical calculator for the calibration of solar and lunar calendars.

The solar calendar that we used today is based on the annual journey of the earth around the sun in 365 days. The lunar calendar is based on the phases of the moon that cycle in a little less than 30 days. A lunar year of twelve months is 354 days, eleven days shorter than the solar year. The Nebra disk was used to synchronize the lunar year with the solar year, to determine if and when a thirteenth month should be added to the lunar calendar, so that it stayed aligned with the seasons.

The small gold circles represent stars, and the group of seven should be the Pleiades constellation. The two marginal bands mark the earth's horizon. The crescent moon is important because it is the specific shape of the moon in relation to the Pleiades at the winter solstice, which meant an extra lunar month was needed, every two to three years. Bronze Age astronomers could hold the Nebra disk to the sky and observe the position of the celestial bodies to determine if the additional month was needed.

By the end of the 400-year period for which the disk was in circulation, its use had changed from calculator to cult object. The forty perforations on the edge of the disk and the curved band of gold in the lower portion of the disk were probably added late in the life history of the disk. The curved band may represent the ship that carried the sun at night, and the perforations may have been to mount or decorate the disk. It seems that the knowledge and use of the disk as a calculator may have been lost sometime before it was buried near Nebra.

One reason the Nebra disk has made such an impact in archaeology and the media is because it was so unexpected. The Bronze Age north of the Alps was thought to have been a rather barbaric period of horsemen, warriors, migration, conflict, and cults. Compared to the extraordinary civilizations of Knossos, Mykene, or Egypt, little intellectual achievement was expected from these "backward" groups, ruled by the sword. It should not be too surprising, however, because in various parts of Bronze Age Europe—central Germany, the Czech Republic, Denmark, Wessex in England—powerful chiefs emerged. These places were strategic, in terms of either access to valuable resources or positioning along major routes of transport and movement. Denmark had amber and fur; Wessex controlled the movement of copper, tin, and gold. The natural riches of central Germany—copper, salt, and fertile soils, and control of several trade routes to the Mediterranean—formed the basis of power for the resident Early Bronze Age princes, who collected and exchanged goods from all parts of Europe. Magnificent tombs, extensive bronze treasures, gold jewelry, textiles, rare foods and drink, and rich weaponry survive as their status symbols. Examples of such wealthy nobility can be seen at Børum Eshøj in Denmark, described later in this chapter.

BRONZE AGE FINDS

There are a number of spectacular and mysterious finds from the Bronze Age north of the Alps. Here I mention just a few other examples: the Trundholm Sun Chariot and the bronze lurs from Denmark, and the Golden Hat from Berlin. Like the Nebra Disk these artifacts reflect an enormous investment of wealth, labor, and aesthetic into items of religious and ceremonial significance. Spirits, cults, beliefs, and gods must have played a very important role in the lives of Bronze Age peoples. In the light of so much conflict, warfare, risk and uncertainty, perhaps the need for beliefs in powerful supernatural force was essential. For whatever reason, religion appears to have been a dominant theme in the Bronze Age.

Sun Chariot, Denmark, 1400 BC

The remarkable artifacts from the Bronze Age discussed here reveal a continuing fascination with solar or celestial objects and time. The Sun Chariot from Denmark is a model of a mare pulling the sun across the sky. The entire piece is 50 cm (17 in) long and 30 cm (12 in) high (Fig. 5.36). Dated to the early Bronze Age, ca. 1400 BC, the domesticated horse is one of the earliest representations of this animal in Europe. The sun disk has two sides; two separate disks were put together. One side is covered in gold leaf, probably to indicate the day; the other is dark bronze, perhaps representing the night (Fig. 5.37). Both disks are ornamented with intricate decorations arranged in concentric circles. The horse and sun stand on six wheels, to permit motion and symbolize the movement of the sun. The chariot could be pulled or rolled along a flat surface such as a table.

The Sun Chariot was originally discovered in 1902 when the bog called Trundholm on the Danish island of Zealand was drained and plowed for the first time. The finely made spiral decorations on the sun disk point to eastern Denmark as the place of manufacture, as such patterns are particularly well documented in this area. Certain parts of the Sun Chariot were cast in bronze using a lost-wax technique. This method permits the creation of fine details on cast objects, including the remarkable spiral designs. An exact copy of each designed part was carefully formed and decorated in wax. The wax model was carefully covered in clay and heated to harden the clay and melt the wax, which runs out the base of the mold, leaving a hollow copy of the object to be cast. The hole in the base is then closed and molten bronze is poured in through the top of the mold, filling all the spaces left by the missing wax.

Fig. 5.36.
The Trundholm Sun Chariot from the Danish Bronze Age, 50 cm long by 30 cm high.

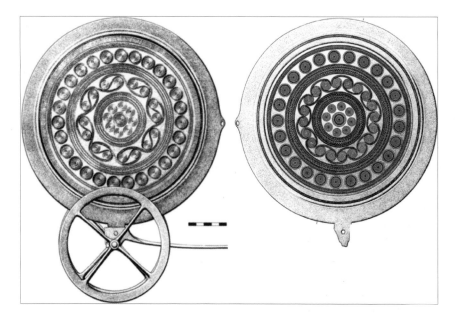

Fig. 5.37.
The two sides of the
Sun Chariot disk,
day (left) and night
(right). The scale is in
centimeters.

The sun was an important part of Bronze Age religion. The basic cosmology of existence at that time may have revolved around the journey of the sun across the vaulted heavens during the day and through the dark underworld at night. A divine horse is often depicted as pulling the sun through the sky. Ships also play an important role in this ideology, carrying the sun at night through the darkness.

Bronze Lurs, Denmark, Sweden, ca. 1000 BC

A lur is a long musical horn without finger holes, having a sound something like a trombone. It is essentially a long tube with a kettle-shaped mouthpiece at the thin end of the tube and an ornamental plate at the thick end (Fig. 5.38). Lurs can be straight, or curved in various shapes. The lost-wax casting technique was use to make bronze lurs, which probably evolved from earlier cow horn instruments. Bronze Age lurs were often found in pairs, deposited in bogs. Sixty examples are known from Denmark, southern Sweden, northern Germany, Norway, and Latvia. Thirty-seven come from Denmark alone. The instrument consists of a mouthpiece and several separate pipes that connect to the head. The total length is between 1½ and 2 m (4½ to 6½ ft). Illustrations of lurs have also been found in rock carvings across Scandinavia.

The first lurs found came from central Zealand in Denmark, found by a farmer digging peat for fuel in the Brudevælte bog in 1791. Three pairs of the lurs were recovered by the farmer. They must have been placed as sacrifice, or for safekeeping in the lake, before it dried up.

The Brudevælte lurs date to approximately 800–700 BC, toward the end of the Nordic Bronze Age. The remarkable preservation of these instruments has allowed them to be played today. They are tuned differently; one pair is in C, one in D, one in E. These instruments, designed to be played while carried,

Fig. 5.38.
A modern reproduction of a lur next to a Bronze Age rock engraving of lur players in action, from Tanum, Sweden.

must have been used in ceremonies and processions, in all likelihood activities related to the worship of the sun.

Gold Hats, Germany, ca. 1000 BC

Another spectacular category of Bronze Age finds are the gold hats worn by chiefs, priests, shamans, or seers. These hatwearers were the original coneheads. Depiction of an object resembling a conical hat on a stone slab at Bredarör, southern Sweden (described in a later section in this chapter), strongly supports their association with religion or cult. The gold hats date to the later Bronze Age, and there are at least four known examples, which in itself is rather remarkable and suggests that this kind of costume or adornment was not completely uncommon in society. The four known hats come from Central and Western Europe. They are made of gold leaf with embossed designs and were meant to be worn over some sort of felt or leather headdress.

The Berlin Gold Hat is the best-preserved example, with a long, slender conical shape and a distinctive cap and brim (Fig. 5.39). The flat brim is made of bronze strengthened by a thin twisted wire. The Berlin hat is completely decorated with various motifs applied with small stamps and wheels. The number, type, and arrangement of the designs in the bands on the hat are thought to have calendrical information, used to tabulate solar and lunar dates and calibrate between them.

The Berlin hat is 75 cm (30 in) tall and weighs almost 500 g (1 lb); it is made from a single sheet of gold, 0.6 mm (0.2 in) thin. It is decorated with twenty-one horizontal bands and rows of symbols made by fourteen stamps and three wheel or cylindrical stamps. Raised lines separate the individual bands. The designs were probably filled with darker putty made from tree resins or wax to make the them stand out more clearly.

The Berlin hat was in a private collection until 1995, when it was purchased by a Berlin museum. It is assumed to have originated in southern Germany or Switzerland, but the actual provenience of the artifact is unknown.

The remaining three hats come from Avanton near Poitiers in France, from Schifferstadt near Speyer, and from Ezelsdorf-Buch near Nuremberg, both in Germany. The last is the tallest example at almost 90 cm (nearly 3 ft). The precise age and provenance of these artifacts are not well known.

Fig. 5.39.
The gold hat from
Berlin, 75 cm high.

SU NURAXI DI BARUMINI, SARDINIA, ITALY, 1800 BC

Sardinia is the second largest island in the Mediterranean, some 200 km west of Tuscany. It belongs to Italy but is actually closer to North Africa. The island covers some 24,000 km² (9,250 mi²), 270 by 140 km (170 by 90 mi) in size, about the size of Wales or New Hampshire. The most prominent archaeological features of Sardinia are the Bronze Age towers that appear everywhere in the landscape (Fig. 5.40). A stark reminder of the past and what once was!

Nuraxi is a Sardinian term, translated as nuraghe, for a distinctive type of fortified Bronze Age settlement found throughout the island—and nowhere else. There are more than 7,000 of these structures remaining, concentrated in the northwest and south-central parts of the country (Fig. 5.41). Many more have probably disappeared over time, some incorporated into modern towns and villages.

The nuraghe were built beginning around 1800 BC and continued in use for 1,500 years or so until the rise of Rome. The sites have a number of common features. Usually situated on a prominent or strategic place in the landscape, the hallmark megalithic stone towers can be seen from some distance. The stone used is often basalt, readily available in much of the Sardinian countryside, worked into rough shape for building purposes, and erected as dry wall masonry. The design and construction of the towers was exceptional, as so many of the structures still stand today.

There are several types of nuraghe, ranging from single standing towers without associated houses to multiple tower settlements with many circular houses. These towers, built in some cases of enormous stones, are as much as 20 m (70 ft) in height and take the form of a truncated cone. The walls are up to 5 m (16 ft) thick, thinning toward the top of the building. A parapet of wood

Fig. 5.40.
A simple nuraghe in the Sardinian landscape.

or stone may have been added to the top of the tower, anchored to the large stones sometimes found there. The structure is largely rubble-filled except for the central room; the ceiling of this interior room was corbeled. In the larger nuraghe, the central core was divided horizontally, with a wooden ceiling separating the ground floor from one or even two upper rooms. A stairway sometimes circled inside the walls from the ground floor. There is often a niche off the stairway at a higher level, which may have served as an exterior entrance. There are usually several stone niches built into the walls of the circular rooms as well. A single doorway with a large lintel was built on one side of the tower, typically to the south or southeast. A triangular area above the lintel was often left open for light and ventilation.

The archaeological site Su Nuraxi di Barumini (the Nuraghe of Barumini), in south-central Sardinia, is one of the largest and best preserved of the many examples that dot the countryside (Fig. 5.42). It was added to the list of World Heritage sites in 1997 and today is one of the major tourist attractions in the country.

The main tower, originally more than 19 m (60 ft) high, was built in the latter half of the second millennium B C. That tower was later surrounded by a massive rampart with four towers. That complex was eventually enclosed in another set of seven towers, connected by a hexagonal wall probably completed around 700 B C. The floor area inside the eighteen-room fortress was approximately 200 m² (2,150 ft²).

To attack the core of the fortifications, an enemy had to achieve a single entry through the massive, 5 m (16 ft) thick stone walls. The "sky door" was more than 7 m (23 ft) above the ground in the wall of the central tower. These were mighty fortifications and imply serious conflict among the inhabitants of the island during the Bronze Age. The fact that sites are heavily fortified in the central part of the island as well indicates that this threat was not simply from foreign raiders.

Narrow tunnels open from the central fortifications into the rest of the settlement. The maze of the village packed around these walls resembles nothing more than a warren, with narrow paths connecting circular houses, wells, and meeting huts. Construction of the common village houses was simple, with lower stone walls supporting a thatched, wooden, or even stone roof. The silent stones almost do speak; it is easy to imagine a montage of people and animals boisterously filling the town streets. An estimated twenty people inhabited the bastion, and an additional ninety may have lived in the village houses, which average 16 m² (175 ft²) in size.

Toward the end of the second millennium BC, some of the nuraghe elite were able to generate substantial wealth and power. More complex compounds were erected and reflect the accumulation of wealth. Craft production was an important part of the growth of the more powerful nuraghe. Sardinia is rich in metallic ores, a source for copper, iron, lead, silver, and tin. Bronze production is seen in the settlement complexes in the form of metallurgical wastes and hordes of finished bronze objects. Lead is found commonly in the settlements and is used for a variety of purposes—pottery repair and masonry clamps, among other things. Mining and metallurgical production must have been an important part of the economy.

There are a number of imported objects from the eastern Mediterranean found in the later Bronze Age in Sardinia, among them oxhide-shaped copper ingots, Mykenean and Minoan ceramics, and bronze figurines from the Levant. The ingots of copper were in production on Cyprus between 1550 and 1200 BC. The small bronze figurines, or *bronzetti*, were made using the lost-wax casting method, probably originally invented in the Levant several centuries prior to its use on Sardinia. Introduction of eastern styled bronze figures and casting techniques was followed by local production of Nuragic *bronzetti*, made from Sardinian copper. Such materials document long-distance trade and interaction across much of the Mediterranean in this period.

There are also numerous smaller and simpler nuraghe across the landscape as well as villages without nuraghe towers or fortifications. The nuraghic site of Duos Nuraghes lies in an upland of west-central Sardinia in an area that today is overgrazed scrubland. During the Bronze Age this part of Sardinia was covered with mixed-oak forest and fields belonging to the numerous small agricultural villages of cultivators and herders. Excavated between 1985 and 1996, the settlement—as the name implies—had two separate and distinct towers surrounded by a large fortification wall enclosing the village (Fig. 5.43). The site covers at least 4,600 m² (50,000 ft²) of a low knoll, a rather small settlement. Duos Nuraghes is

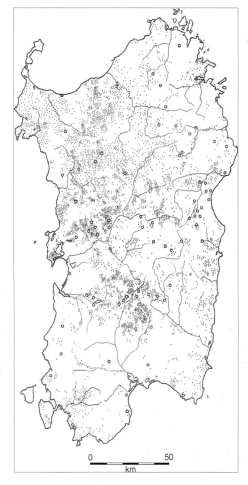

Fig. 5.41.
Distribution of ancient nuraghe in Sardinia. Dots are simple towers; circles are settlements with towers.

Fig. 5.42.

The complex nuraghe of Su Nuraxi di Barumini.

thought to represent a more typical commoners' place of residence, rather than that of an elite.

The site was in use from 1800 BC well into the Iron Age. During the Middle Bronze Age the single tower site was expanded with a second tower around 1500 BC, and a village of small, circular huts grew up around the towers during the Late Bronze Age, ca. 1250 BC. The massive stonewall around the site was added in the early Iron Age, ca. 900 BC. Excavations inside the towers indicate domestic activities and their use as a residence. The excavator, Gary Webster, believes that towers were residence for a small agro-pastoral homestead during the first 700–800 years of use. The number of co-resident individuals is unknown, but the interior living space is small (50 m², 540 ft²) and may have held six to eight individuals.

The evidence from the village huts suggests that some were used for specific functions such as cooking and eating, grain processing, and animal herding. The animal remains document the meat portion of the diet and came from sheep and goats, pigs, deer, cattle, and rabbits, along with a few birds. Hunting wild deer provided more animal food than cattle keeping, judging from the number of bones in the towers. Evidence from around the hearths included grinding stones, ceramic baking dishes, bread pans, serving cups, and bowls that would be typical of domestic use.

The nuraghe towers and villages are not the only types of sites from this period. Various kinds of burial and ceremonial locations are also known, often close to the nuraghe themselves. Most of the Nuragic burial monuments are called the so-called

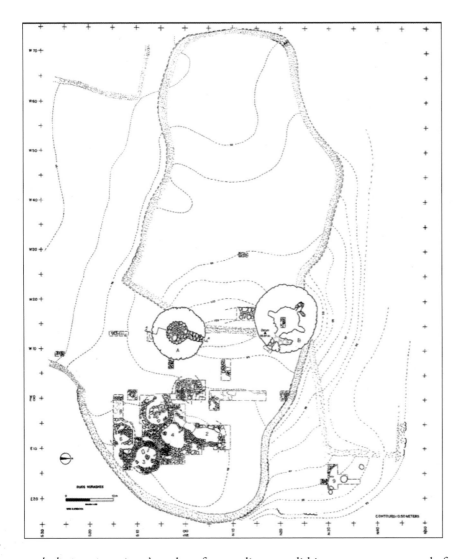

Fig. 5.43.
Plan of Duos Nuraghes with two distinct towers inside a long fortification wall.

tombedi giganti, or giants' tombs—freestanding megalithic structures composed of a rectangular chamber and semicircular forecourt. From the large number of burials found, these appear to have been communal tombs associated with a specific site or local group. At the tomb of Coddu Vecchiu the forecourt is about 12 m wide and is faced with eleven upright slabs; the tallest central stone is 4 m (13 ft) high (Fig. 5.44). The chamber itself, inside the forecourt, is almost 10 m (33 ft) long.

Collective tombs and water shrines formed part of the sacred landscape. The water shrines, or holy wells, are often exceptional architectural structures, built of finely cut basalt blocks. On the location of freshwater springs, a stone building encloses a subterranean structure and a stairway descends to the water source beneath a corbeled dome. At the site of Santa Christina, the water still emerges from the tight-fitting stone blocks during the winter and spring. The staircase faces east and is aligned so that the rising sun of the summer and fall equinox shines down the steps (Fig. 5.45). A number of the small *bronzetti* figurines have been found in these holy wells, likely deposited as offerings.

Fig. 5.44.
The giants' tomb at
Coddu Vecchiu.

Political and social parameters of the nuraghe period are not well understood.
An archaeological survey by Joe Michaels and Gary Webster in south-central
Sardinia recorded forty-seven nuraghi (thirty-seven single-tower and three
multitower complex), fourteen megalithic tombs, and one well temple in the
study area of 40 km² (more than 15 mi²). They suggested that the hierarchical
arrangement of large and smaller nuraghi indicated political integration at
the regional level. The collective tombs were generally at the periphery of the
area and may have served as territorial markers. Conflict within and among
such local political units, plus the threat of raids and conquest, may well have
been the reason for the extraordinary construction of Nuragic fortresses across
Sardinia. Certainly the militant appearance of many of the *bronzetti* figures
supports a warrior mentality on the island during this time (Fig. 5.46).

BORUM ESHØJ, DENMARK, 1350 BC

Bronze began filtering into Northern Europe from the Aegean region after
2000 BC, but regular availability of the metal is seen only after 1700 BC,
the official start of the Bronze Age in this area. The Nordic Bronze Age in
Northern Europe continues until the introduction of iron, ca. 500 BC.

But the Bronze Age is about much more than metal. The second millennium
BC in northern and western Europe witnessed a number of major innovations

Fig. 5.45.
The sacred well at
Santa Christina. The
opening leads to a
stairway down to a
spring of fresh water.

in addition to metals: the oxcart and oxen as draft animals, the horse and chariot, and new weapons. These changes accumulate in larger and more powerful societies where trade, craft, production, and growing competition are added to the foundation of village farming.

The Bronze Age witnessed the first pronounced inequality in social status and position in North European society. The elite segment of the population must have controlled most of the resources, as well as trade. Wealth differences, probably associated with ownership of land and cattle herds, were an aspect of life in the period. Slaves and captives may have been an important part of the economic means of wealthier families. Control of the amber sources around southern Scandinavia generated the exportable wealth of the region, perhaps in conjunction with furs and other commodities. Local production of textiles, oxhides, foodstuffs, and other materials led to an expanding economy at home.

Status differentiation was also expressed in individual appearance. For the first time, items of personal use such as razors, tweezers, earwax scoops, and other toiletry equipment show up in grave goods in wealthy burials. Metal objects assumed an important role in creating and maintaining individual identities relating to gender and status. High-status males carried bronze swords and daggers; wealthy females had bronze and gold jewelry, belt buckles, and other objects. These items were placed in graves to accompany elite individuals in death. During the first half of the Bronze Age in Southern Scandinavia, elite burials were placed in stone cists or hollowed oak tree trunks. Cremation ashes buried in an urn was the normal practice during the Late Bronze Age.

Fig. 5.46.
Small bronzetti
figurines often found in
the sacred wells, 5–10
cm in height.

Fig. 5.47.
Bronze Age barrows
(beneath red arrows) dot
the high points of the
landscape across much
of southern Scandinavia.

Earthen mounds (barrows) were constructed over the oak coffin graves. Bronze Age barrows dot the landscape of southern Scandinavia (Fig. 5.47); an estimated 25,000 mounds still stand from northern Germany, across Denmark and into southernmost Sweden. Bronze Age barrows were built for the wealthier members of society and placed near where the living had

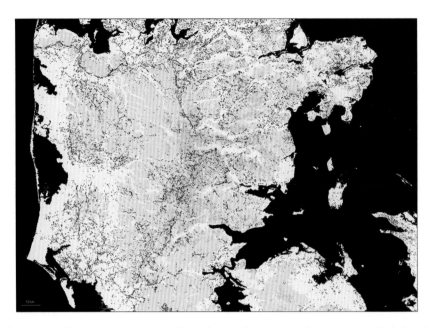

Fig. 5.48.
Distribution of
Bronze Age barrows
in Denmark. The
west-central part of
Linear arrangements
of barrows on this map
probably lay along
roads or paths. Barrows
are present, but not
mapped south of the
Danish border.

died. Most barrows in Denmark are located in areas of productive farmland, evidence of the important relationship between wealth and the control of agricultural resources. These tall, circular burial mounds were often placed dramatically on the horizon to emphasize the importance of the buried individuals.

Lines of barrows follow the high points on the landscape, often along old roads and routes of movement. The distribution of thousands of such barrows offers some information on the use of the landscape and the organization of early Bronze Age society. Figure 5.48 shows the location of Bronze Age barrows part of Denmark; clear concentrations can be seen in various areas. In addition, distinct linear arrangements of barrows can be observed, particularly in the southern half of the Jutland peninsula. The lines of barrows almost certainly lie along routes of movement and communication in the area, and the major intersections were at the residences of the wealthy.

The amount of metal (bronze and gold) in these burials is an indication of the wealth of the deceased individuals. All bronze and gold in southern Scandinavia had to be imported because the ores are not indigenous. Gold was more valuable; only 1 g of gold is found for every 1,000 g (2.2 lb) of bronze. There are pronounced differences in buried wealth between the sexes and between individuals. Male graves are more common than female graves, and they contain more wealth. Some individuals were buried with a great deal of bronze and gold and some without any, suggesting that social differentiation was pronounced. Some of these burials were looted during the Bronze Age, suggesting that less fortunate people sought buried riches, or that enemies wished to demolish the social identity and status of the deceased.

The barrows themselves were a statement about the wealth of the interred individual(s). Construction of a mound involved a huge amount of labor. The

Fig. 5.49.
A Bronze Age oak coffin in situ, excavated in the early twentieth century.

earthen barrows in southern Scandinavia were built up of layered concentric rings of grass sods. A medium-sized barrow 36 m (110 ft) in diameter and 6 m (20 ft) high would have required more than 7 ha (17 acres) of sod. (Trafalgar Square in London covers one hectare.) Removing the topsoil from such a large area would have sacrificed good farmland for decades and created a rather barren zone around the barrow for several years.

Most of the burials in the barrows from the Bronze Age have disappeared over time, robbed in antiquity or returned to nature as the coffins and organic contents disintegrated. In a few extraordinary instances, however, the contents of these barrows have survived, along with the oak coffin, and they afford a glimpse of the Bronze Age elite in southern Scandinavia (Fig. 5.49).

No more than a few dozen barrows with preserved coffins and contents are known. Most of these were excavated more than one hundred years ago, and there are reports of water flowing like a spring when some of the tombs were opened. Dressed in fine clothing and jewelry, the deceased was placed in a coffin. This coffin was then covered with a pile of stones and buried under a mound of cut sods and soil. The contents of these barrows were preserved under very specific conditions, but disturbances by tomb robbers and farmers probably caused many of them to deteriorate.

In the known cases, however, it is clear that the mounds were built in two parts, a core and an exterior, both made of stacked sods. The core was a smaller, initial mound directly over the coffin tomb. This flat-topped structure may have been built initially for ceremony or rituals associated with the funeral of the dead. It may also be the case that this core structure was intentionally filled with water prior to burial under the second, exterior mound. This process of waterlogged burial was known in the medieval period as a technique for preserving meat and may have been done intentionally by Bronze Age people to try to preserve the contents of the grave.

Whether intentional or not, the water in the tomb created the conditions for a rapid reduction-oxidation reaction that created an iron-rich hardpan around the smaller mound. The hardpan and water sealed the interior from the air. These conditions preserved both the coffins and the contents to a remarkable extent. These barrows with pronounced iron pans are known only from middle and southern Jutland in Denmark and the province of Schleswig in northernmost Germany. Tree ring studies of the oak trees used for the coffins allow precise dating of these burials, determining the year the tree was cut. Most of the mounds with preserved oak coffins were constructed within a sixty-year period, between 1389 and 1330 BC. Because of the limited time period and small geographic area in which these barrows occur, one can posit that some of the people buried in the mounds must have known each other.

As an example of one of these iron pan barrows, we can turn to Borum Eshøj, one of the largest Bronze Age barrows in Denmark, located near the modern city of Aarhus. The original mound was almost 9 m (30 ft) high, equivalent to a three-story building, and 40 m (140 ft) in diameter. The barrow was first opened in 1875 by the landowner, who began removing the rich soil of the mound to add to his fields (Fig. 5.50).

The Borum Eshøj graves are the largest single find of this kind from Denmark. This huge mound was built over three oak coffins, containing an older man and woman and a young man, who was likely their son (Fig. 5.51). Each of them had been wrapped in ox hides and buried in fine woolen clothes. Bronze and wood objects accompanied them, probably personal possessions. Two of these coffins have been dated by tree rings to around 1350 BC. All three coffins were probably buried at the same time, and the bodies were all carefully prepared. One can only wonder about the cause of death and the simultaneous burial of these three individuals in the middle of the fourteenth century BC.

Preservation in the mound was extraordinary. The body of the older male, fifty to sixty years of age, was so well preserved that it had to be dismembered for transport to Copenhagen, what with the muscles still holding the skeleton together. His hair was intact; he had been blond. He was clean-shaven and had manicured hands and nails. Lying on a cow skin and was covered with a woolen blanket, he was dressed in a domed hat with a kidney-shaped cloak, a short kilt with a rope belt, and cloth wrapped around his feet. All the textiles were wool. The only other object in the grave, apart from the clothing, was a wooden pin, attached to the collar of the cloak. Piles of wood chips around the

Fig. 5.50.
Watercolor of the original excavations of the Bronze Age mound at Borum Eshøj, 1875.

Fig. 5.51.
The older male and the log coffin from Borum Eshøj.

Fig. 5.52.
The younger male from the log coffin at Borum Eshøj.

outside of the coffin indicate that the oak tree trunk was hollowed out on the spot.

The older woman was also well preserved. She too was fifty to sixty years old and 1.57 m (5'1") in height, relatively short and stocky. Traces of muscles on her bones reveal that she had done hard physical labor. The first item found when the coffin was opened was a cowhide with the hairs still intact. Beneath the hide was a wool rug on top of the woman's body. She was buried wearing a skirt and tunic of brown wool, a tasseled belt, and a hairnet of wool thread with her long hair still inside. A comb made of horn was found next to her hair. Various bronze objects in the coffin included a pin, a dagger with a horn handle, a belt disk, two ornamental bronze plates, and rings for the fingers, arms, and neck. The grave also contained a pottery vessel and a wooden box.

The twenty-year-old man was well preserved too. Muscles and other soft parts still connected the bones, and his hair was intact in a pageboy style. The young man was dressed in a wool shirt held together by a leather belt and a wooden button, a cloak, and a kilt also of wool (Fig. 5.52). He may have been wearing a pair of leather shoes. His grave goods included a bronze dagger in a wooden sword scabbard, a horn comb, a bark box, and a bone needle.

These burial monuments from Bronze Age southern Scandinavia have a lot to say about the society that erected them. Clearly status and role in life were continued in death, commemorated with the deceased, validating the living. The massive labor, large size, strategic location, and high visibility of the mounds leave little doubt that they were reserved for people of high rank. The contents of the tombs help define the nature of social identity in the earlier part of the Bronze Age.

Personal appearance and material culture clearly were important in building social identities in terms of gender, age, and status. High-quality clothing and equipment was the mark of the elite. A bronze sword in a finely made wooden sheath was a symbol of high rank and warrior status, perhaps adulthood as well. The sword was hung at the waist or worn diagonally across the chest.

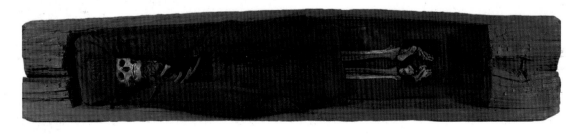

Personal equipment (razors, pins, tweezers) and objects such as birch bark buckets, decorated wooden bowls, folding wooden stools with otter skin seats, and antler spoons were also placed inside the oak coffins.

Female dress varied with position and age. A clear distinction was made when a woman reached adulthood or married. A sixteen-year-old girl in another coffin burial from Denmark wore a miniskirt of cords, whereas the older woman from Borum and adult women in other graves were dressed in long skirts. Elaborate hairstyles with a covering net or cap may also have been a marker of elite married women. A long-sleeved blouse was worn by all women. A spiral-decorated bronze belt plate worn on a belt at the waist was nearly *de rigueur* for the high-status female. Smaller, buttonlike plates, elaborate safety pins, neck collars, and various rings of gold and bronze for the ears, arms, legs, neck, or hair completed the female costume. Small personal items, such as antler combs and bronze pins, were sometimes carried in a small purse or box or attached to the belt.

BREDARÖR, SWEDEN, 1000 BC

The Bronze Age cairn known as Bredarör is located near the present town of Kivik in southernmost Sweden (Fig. 5.53). A cairn is simply a heap of stones piled up as a memorial or landmark. Bredarör is one of the largest burial monuments in northern Europe. The name means broad cairn in Swedish (the monument is 75 m in diameter). The restored height is 3.5 m (12 ft), but the original rock mound was probably between 7 and 15 m (from 25 to 50 ft) high. Stones have been quarried from the cairn for centuries, and the tomb inside was looted in 1748, according to historical records.

Archaeological excavations took place in 1931, and the tomb chamber and cairn were then restored. This monument is also known as the King's Grave,

Fig. 5.53.
The Bronze Age cairn of Bredarör in southern Sweden. The person in the photo stands in the path to the entrance.

in reference to the tomb inside the cairn. There is a path partially through the mound, leading to a massive stone entrance. The monument likely dates to ca. 1000 BC during the Nordic Bronze Age. This stone cairn is the Swedish equivalent of the earthen barrows of Bronze Age Denmark, such as Borum Eshøj.

Bredarör is justifiably famous for the size of the cairn enclosing the tomb. But the tomb itself is remarkable. Inside the chamber, there is a large stone cist (a stone box) with elaborate rock art. Some human bone, remains of cremations, and fragments of bronze grave goods that survived the looting were also found in the cist. Ten slabs formed the inner sides of the 4 by 1½ m (13 by 5 ft) m stone cist and are decorated with petroglyphs (Fig. 5.54). The images carved into the stones depict people, animals (including birds and fish), ships, lurs being played, symbols, and a chariot or cart with four-spoke wheels, drawn by two horses. These images may relate to the funeral procession and ceremony.

In fact, it appears there were originally two cists in the tomb. At the south end of the large cist, there was another set of raised stone slabs, 1.2 x 0.65 m (4 x 2 ft) in size, that probably contained a second individual. Recent examinations of the surviving bones indicate there were several individuals buried in the grave later in the Bronze Age. Because of the early quarrying and looting, little is known about the original contents of the tomb.

SALCOMBE, ENGLAND, 1000 BC

Fig. 5.54.
The engraved plaques from the Bredarör grave.

Salcombe is a fishing and shipbuilding port near Plymouth in the southwest corner of England, with a fine sheltered harbor and thriving crab industry. The waters around Salcombe hold a number of important shipwrecks. In

2009, divers working on the very rich Salcombe Cannon Wreck, a seventeenth-century ship with 400 Moroccan gold coins, expanded their search around the ship and began to encounter even older materials, eventually identifying a new wreck from the Bronze Age (Fig. 5.55).

This new site, known as Moor Sand, or Salcombe B, contains a 3,000-year-old ship, dated to the Bronze Age. This was a plank-built ship about 13 m (42 ft) long and 2 m (6½ ft) wide. The ship probably held a crew of fifteen and was powered by paddles. There is no evidence of a sail onboard.

Fig. 5.55.
Underwater archaeology with a metal detector at the Salcombe wreck, southern England.

The cargo of the ship, however, documents long-distance voyages and crossing of the English Channel. The cargo recovered from the sea floor includes more than 250 copper ingots and at least twenty-seven tin ingots (Fig. 5.56) along with a bronze sword, several slingshot stones, and three gold bracelets. These items were apparently being brought to Britain when the ship sank before landing. The ship appears to have been a trading vessel carrying materials for making bronze, an alloy of copper and tin. The copper ingots probably came from the Alps region in Central Europe. The tin ingots are the earliest known in Britain and may be from eastern Germany.

Copyright © 2010 South West Maritime Archaeological Group

Fig. 5.56.
Ingots of copper and tin from the Salcombe wreck. (Courtesy of the Southwest Maritime Archaeological Group)

An even earlier Bronze Age boat, dating to 1550 BC, was found in 1992 some 6 m beneath the streets of the city of Dover, in southeasternmost England, during road construction. The vessel is estimated to have been 12 m (40 ft) in length (part of the front portion had been removed in the past) and 2.3 m (8 ft) wide. The boat was made from at least six long oak planks lashed together with thin branches of yew; all the joints were reinforced with thin sheets of oak, pressing against the moss and fat pushed into the joints for waterproofing. The original logs were probably 12 m (40 ft) long and 1.1 m (4 ft) in diameter and came from three straight-grained oak trees, well over 300 years old when felled. A boat of this size could cross the channel with about three tons of materials, livestock, or passengers. It was probably rowed by at least sixteen individuals. The Dover boat had been abandoned, and no cargo remained on board.

The Salcombe wreck and other finds of boats from the Bronze Age document the importance of long-distance trade in the Bronze Age. A new technology of shipbuilding created craft that could carry cargo across wide stretches of the sea. A major investment in materials supply was required to maintain the forests for such special timber. Many more craftspersons must have been involved to build and operate the ships and to produce the goods and materials for trade. These developments reflect the growing power of the elite in Bronze Age society, wealthy and powerful individuals for whom the products of trade and craft were intended.

FLAG FEN, ENGLAND, 1350 BC

The Fens, near the modern city of Peterborough in eastern England, were the largest area of natural wetlands in what is now the United Kingdom until they were drained several hundred years ago. One of the more intriguing monuments in all of Bronze Age Europe was found on the western margin of the Fens, at a place called Flag Fen. Flag Fen itself is a basin of low-lying land. The area of higher, drier land to the west is known as Fengate; these two areas have produced a fascinating set of evidence on Bronze Age farming practices and ceremonial activities.

As the city of Peterborough expanded toward Fengate during the latter half of the twentieth century, archaeological investigations ahead of construction revealed a series of fields marked by peripheral ditches. Finds in the ditches came from the Bronze Age and indicated the fields had been in use from 2500 to 900 BC. The fields were connected by lanes, known as droveways, with more ditches on either side. These were paths or roads for moving animals. The droveways often lead to the edge of Flag Fen, which during the Bronze Age was flooded in the winter months.

The archaeologists believe that the ditched fields were pasture lands, intended for grazing herds of sheep and cattle, rather than for cultivation. The animals were taken from the fields to feed in the wetland pastures of Flag Fen during the drier, summer months when the water receded, and they then returned to the higher ditched fields for the winter. Land that was flooded in winter provided lush hay and grazing for sheep and cattle during the summer. In addition to the fields and paths, there were Bronze Age houses scattered through this landscape—large circular structures likely with conical, thatched roofs. These houses had a front porch facing the fields and may have been some of the first livestock farms in Britain.

In the center of the field system there was a complex of lanes, yards, and paddocks for the animals around the largest track in the system. This area appears to be a communal stockyard for the field systems. A large droveway led from this stockyard to the edge of Flag Fen.

Surveying modern drainage ditches at the edge of the fen in 1982, archaeologist Francis Pryor came upon a series of waterlogged oak timbers with old carpentry joins made by a small axe. That was the beginning of a fifteen-year project of excavation at Flag Fen, which eventually uncovered a huge set of timber constructions. The waterlogged conditions meant these materials have been preserved to the present.

There are two major features at Flag Fen. A causeway of vertical wooden posts with a timber roadway led from the end of the main droveway at Fengate across Flag Fen for more than 1.2 km (4,000 ft; Fig. 5.57). This structure was built and rebuilt a number of times between 1350 and 950 BC. The posts were set in five upright rows with a wicker fence along the north side of the causeway; they may have risen more than 3 m (10 ft) above the surface, perhaps being used to mark the causeway in periods of high water. The horizontal timbers of the causeway were pegged into position, and coarse sand and fine gravel was spread on the surface to provide more traction. It's estimated there were more than 60,000 vertical timbers and

Fig. 5.57.
An artist's reconstruction of the Bronze Age landscape at Flag Fen, with the livestock farms of Fengate, the timber causeway, the artificial timber platform, and the mysteries of Northey Island.

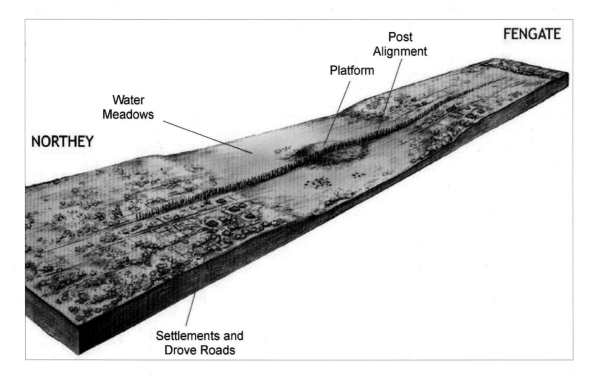

250,000 horizontal pieces of wood in the structure, all worked and shaped with bronze tools. This trackway or alignment crossed the wetlands of the fen to dry ground of Northey Island and may have been intended for moving cattle across the marsh.

But there seems to be much more. Bronze Age people committed many thousands of hours to building this structure. The alignment isolates the northern part of the fen from the outside and may have served as a boundary and defense to protect the rich pasture lands. In addition, some divisions of the causeway into segments 5–6 m long with timber and wattle partitions were observed. Offerings of weapons, grinding stones, and other materials were found among the timbers in these segments. There may have been sacrificial and ritual activities associated with the causeway as well.

But there is more. The second major feature at Flag Fen is an artificial timber platform (Fig. 5.58) in the middle of the trackway with a circumference of 1 km (3,300 ft), the size of Wembley Stadium in London. This late Bronze Age structure is contemporary with the causeway. The precise plan of the platform is unknown because much of the structure still lies beneath almost 2 m (6 ft) of peaty alluvium. Within the excavated area of the platform, a large timber structure has been uncovered. Vertical timbers in this area were supports for eaves, walls, and roof for a massive rectangular building approximately 6–6.5 m (ca. 20 ft) wide and perhaps 18–20 m (ca. 60 ft) long. It is possible that a number of such large structures were built on the artificial island.

Fig. 5.58.
Part of the excavated posts and platform at Flag Fen.

The construction of the walls and eaves of the large building was quite sophisticated, expertly worked and built of high-quality, slow-grown oak. The multitude of vertical posts indicates that the building had been repaired, rebuilt, and modified over many years. The refuse on and below the floor is unusual, including a large number of unbroken pots, only a small number of animal bones, the remains of several dogs, and a limited amount of "domestic" waste. This structure was not a simple dwelling but rather some type of special building, perhaps with religious or ceremonial connotations. Some 275 offerings of metal objects clearly demonstrated the importance of ritual at Flag Fen. The bronze and tin objects included weaponry, ornaments, and several continental imports (mainly from France and central Europe). There was evidence that many of the items had been deliberately smashed or broken before being placed in the water. Ceremonial use of this place continued into the Iron Age.

A second major concentration of artifacts was found at the end of the causeway in Fengate. The materials on the Fengate end were composed of more normal domestic remains that likely came from nearby settlements.

The causeway and platform at Flag Fen are extraordinary monuments in terms of size and construction. In addition, the finds from the excavations include the oldest wooden wheel in England, wooden axe handles, metal workers' tools, a marvelous collection of Bronze Age swords and daggers, and a set of bronze shears in their original wooden case (Fig. 5.59).

The opposite end of the timber alignment at Northey Island remains something of a mystery. There are several small barrows on the island. Excavations have produced some evidence of cremations and burial goods, suggesting this was perhaps an island for the dead; but the real purpose or purposes of Northey Island, the timber causeway, and the artificial platform at Flag Fen are still not clear. The Bronze Age often seems a strange and unusual period in European prehistory.

Fig. 5.59.
Iron shears and wooden case among the offerings at Flag Fen.

Francis Pryor became the director of the Flag Fen Laboratories and Bronze Age Centre and has spent many years studying, developing, and protecting the monument. Keeping such an enterprise above water financially is always a challenge because public funds are rarely sufficient. Other problems also arise. In January 2000, fire broke out in a large research building at Flag Fen that housed thousands of slides and archives, as well as some recent Bronze Age finds. Fire crews were able to carry out several of the badly charred filing cabinets, but approximately ninety-five percent of the records were lost.

ROCK ART: TANUM, SWEDEN, 1500 BC

The World Heritage site at Tanum, Sweden, covers approximately 45 km² (17 mi²) and contains 430 known locations with Bronze Age petroglyphs, dating between ca. 1700 and 500 BC (Fig. 5.60). At that time this area, which today is 25 m (80 ft) above sea level, was on the seashore.

The west coast of Sweden from Göteborg north is one of the loveliest places on earth. Archipelagos of bare rock reach far out into the Kattegat like lines of huge hump-backed whales breaching the surface. Bare rock, scoured by the passage of many glaciers, gleams along the coast and hillsides. This area between Göteborg and Oslo is lightly populated. The Swedish forest covers places with soil and the rocks shine through where the forest cannot grow.

In this particular region of Sweden, rock art— in the form of petroglyphs—is found everywhere. The landscape is the gallery (Fig. 5.61). New rock art is being discovered every year, most of it from the Bronze Age. The motifs include human figures, ships, weapons, fishing nets, the sun, bulls, horses, deer, birds, and scenes of daily life. Certain themes are repeated, especially human figures and ships. Human figures are sometimes grouped into what appear to be processions, perhaps capturing one aspect of this art as ceremonial or religious in origin. One depiction of a human figure over 2 m (6½ ft) tall carrying a spear is the largest petroglyph of a person in Europe; it is sometimes interpreted as the Norse God of War, Odin.

The Vitlycke panel at Tanum is one of Sweden's most remarkable. The surface is smooth and sloping, and the rock is light in color. The panel is 22 m (75 ft) long and 6 m (20 ft) wide; water flows over parts of the carved surface. This very famous panel consists of nearly 300 figures, including 170 cup marks (small, circular depressions). There are a variety of scenes and motifs. One of the more famous is the so-called bridal couple, with a male, with a huge phallus, raising an axe. Other special and interesting images are the worshiper in front of a huge snake, a "devil-like" human figure in a chariot, and a kneeling female figure beside a tall man lying down. Many of the cup marks are arranged in a line, and men are depicted fighting on both sides of that line. There are numerous ships of different sizes, some double-lined, with or without crew. There are a series of warriors

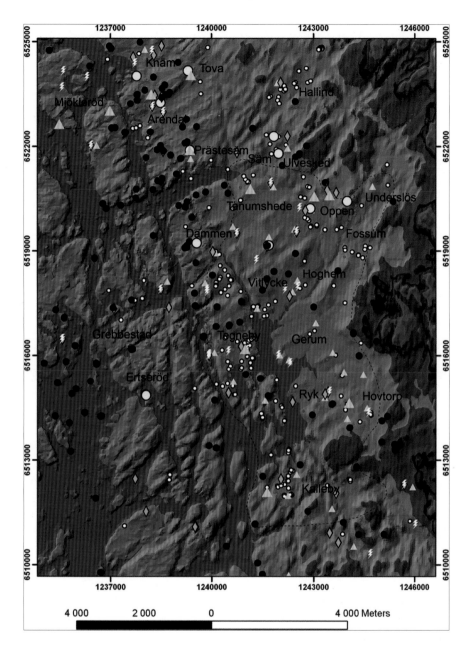

Fig. 5.60.
The Tanum area, Sweden, in the Bronze Age showing the shoreline 13–14 m above sea level; red dots = rock art sites; white dots = cup mark sites; black dots = cairns; large light brown triangles = settlement finds (carbon dates, ceramics, or other features) dated to the Bronze Age; small light brown triangles = indicative settlement sites from the Bronze Age; yellow dots = bronze items; blue diamonds = daggers from LNI-EBA II; white flashes = sickles from LNI–EBA II.

equipped with axes and swords, some with a circle-shaped body, which may represent a shield.

Rock art varies greatly in time and place. The Bronze Age rock art of northern Europe, known largely from Scandinavia, exhibits specific themes in a distinctive style. Human figures in a variety of activities are common, and ships play an important role in the art. The specific purpose of these engravings on the smooth rock surfaces of Scandinavia is not clear. Perhaps they can be thought of as prayers or offerings to the gods, spirits, or forces of nature. But we can never really know.

Fig. 5.61.
Bronze Age Rock
Art from Tanum.
Petroglyphs are
outlined with red paint
today to make them
more visible for visitors.

SOME REFLECTIONS

Changes in sociopolitical organization are well documented in later prehistoric
Europe. Chiefdoms and states are larger societies where relationships are
defined by inequality. Organization is hierarchical, with a permanent political
structure. Agriculture is usually intensive, and relations with other societies
often conflictual. Status is hereditary and assigned by birth order (rank) in
chiefdoms or class affiliation (stratification) in states. Chiefdoms and states
are normally associated with monumental architecture in the form of massive
earthworks and construction such as pyramids, ziggurats, platforms, and
palaces. Towns and cities are often found in chiefdoms and states, respectively.
States are also territorial and can be distinguished from chiefdoms by greater
population, size, complexity, and a permanent bureaucracy. Robert Carniero
provided a useful working definition of a *state* as an autonomous political unit
with various member communities within its territory, having a centralized

government with the power to collect taxes, draft men for work or war, and decree and enforce laws.

The third and second millennia B C saw the rise of early states and empires in Mesopotamia, the Nile Valley, and the Aegean. Before the literate civilizations of classical Greece and Rome, the Aegean area witnessed the emergence of state-level societies on Crete and the Greek mainland. The Minoan palaces and Mykenean citadels were the urban centers of these civilizations and the focal points of industry, commerce, religion, military power, and central accumulation.

Economic systems have three components: production, distribution, and consumption. Production can be generalized or specialized. Marshall Sahlins defined the "domestic mode," a generalized form of production in which households make the materials and items that they need to continue. Craft specialization, on the other hand, is a way to more efficiently organize production. Specialization can take many forms and at different scales: individual, household, workshop, community, industrial. Cathy Costin coined the term *attached specialization* to describe craft production controlled and managed by elite or state institutions. In the Bronze Age, for example, craft workshops are often found in the shadow of the palaces in the Aegean or with the places of power in Europe north of the Alps. Much of the production at this time involved metals, weapons, jewelry, rare stones, and other materials.

The Bronze Age was in many ways an unusual period in European prehistory. Several terms might be used to define Bronze Age society: mobile, martial, and wealth. This was a period of movement, of transience, of change. Both individuals and large groups were on the move. Kristian Kristiansen and Thomas Larsson have reviewed the Bronze Age connections among northern Europe, the Aegean, and the Near East. They argue for an "heroic age of travels, cultural transmissions, and social transformations throughout the whole region." Active travel and trade between these areas was arranged through the movement of elite individuals who bring back new materials and ideas from the Mediterranean and Aegean regions.

Groups and whole societies were also mobile at this time. The start of the Bronze Age, marked by the expansion of the Bell Beaker folk, was a sign of the times. In the same period, some argue, the Indo-European peoples moved into parts of Europe. The end of the Bronze Age saw the Urnfield culture expanding across central Europe and the eastern Mediterranean, giving rise to Etruscan and other important Iron Age societies. Mobile also includes objects as trade and interaction between Europe and the eastern Mediterranean moved materials and foodstuffs across great distance.

Weapons and warfare were preeminent as warrior societies appeared across the continent in the Bronze Age. The technology of conflict expands rapidly as fortifications, new weapons, new strategies, and a whole new scale of warfare emerge in this time. The battles raged as larger societies sought land, slaves, and wealth from their neighbors.

Relatively few Bronze Age settlements were known in Europe until the last two decades, with large rescue excavations and discoveries such as Croce del

Papa. Most of our knowledge came from burials, and these in the form of the large barrows that dot the landscape of northern and western Europe and the kurgans of the east. These very visible monuments have been the target of tomb robbers and landowners in the past, and archaeologists in recent decades. These are the graves of the elite, furnished with the riches of the upper class. Evidence for mobility comes from the grave goods, which included weapons, jewelry, and even furniture either directly or indirectly from the Aegean and Near East. These were chiefs and nobles, powerful families of elite individuals in Bronze Age society. But little was (and in fact remains) known of the common people in these societies. Information comes to light as more settlements are discovered, but our fundamental view of the Bronze Age is most definitely biased toward the rich and famous.

One of the reasons for the reduced visibility of Bronze Age settlement and the biased view of this period may lie in the nature of subsistence and wealth. It appears that pastoralism played a larger role in food production at this time; cattle herding may have been the preeminent form in large parts of northern and western Europe. Cattle were food, traction, and wealth. Cattle pastoralism may well have been a rather mobile activity, moving larger herds from place to place as pasture and fodder were available. Instead of a landscape of small farming villages and fields, more open areas of pasture and more ephemeral settlements may have been the dominant mode.

CHAPTER SIX

Centers of Power, Weapons of Iron

AT THE EDGE OF HISTORY

The introduction of iron after 1000 BC brought new tools and weapons to Europe. Smelting technology and higher furnace temperatures were likely the key to iron production, which is generally thought to have originated in Anatolia around 1400 BC among the Hittites, but there are a few earlier examples of iron artifacts as old as 2300 BC in Turkey. Iron produced sharper, more readily available implements and was in great demand. In contrast to copper and tin, whose sources were limited, iron was found in a variety of forms in many places across the continent. Veins of iron ore were exploited in Iberia, Britain, the Alps, the Carpathian Mountains, and elsewhere. Bog iron was exploited in northern Europe. Carbonate sources of iron in other areas enabled local groups to obtain the raw materials necessary for producing this important material.

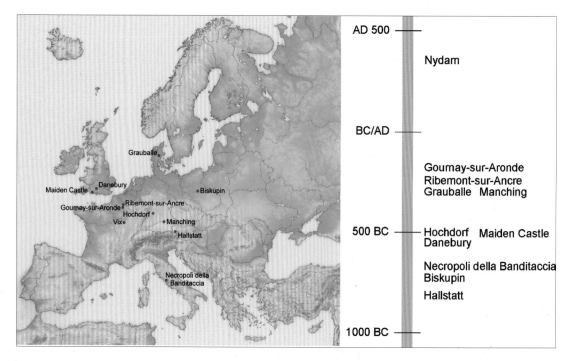

Fig. 6.1.
The location and time scale for sites mentioned in this chapter.

At the same time, the collapse of the dominant Bronze Age civilizations of the Aegean changed the flow of raw materials and finished products across Europe. Greece fell into a Dark Age following the demise of the Mycenaean city-states. The Etruscans were on the rise in Italy. Rome was a small town at the border of the Etruscan region. Soon, however, new centers of power in classic Greece and Rome emerged, bringing writing and, with it, history to Europe. Again, we can observe important and dramatic differences between the "classic" areas of the Mediterranean and the northern parts of "barbarian" Europe.

The chronology for the Iron Age in much of Europe is portrayed in Figure 6.2. The Iron Age begins earlier in the Mediterranean area, ca. 900 BC, where the Classical civilizations of Greece, the Etruscans, and eventually Rome emerge in the first millennium BC. Rome and its empire expanded rapidly, conquering much of western Europe in a few decades before the beginning of the Common Era and Britain around AD 43, effectively ending the prehistoric Iron Age in these parts of the continent. The Iron Age begins somewhat later in Scandinavia, around 500 BC.

The arrival of iron coincides with the emerging identities of what are often called

IRON AGE				
AEGEAN	ITALY	C. EUROPE	BRITAIN	S. SCANDINAVIA
Rome	Rome	Rome	Rome	Roman Iron Age
			Late Iron Age	
		La Tené	Middle Iron Age	Pre-Roman Iron Age
Classical Greece (Athens)	Rome			
Archaic Greece			Early Iron Age	
		Hallstatt		Late Bronze Age
Geometric Period	Etruscans			
			Late Bronze Age	
Bronze Age				

(AD/BC, 200 BC, 400 BC, 600 BC, 800 BC, 1000 BC)

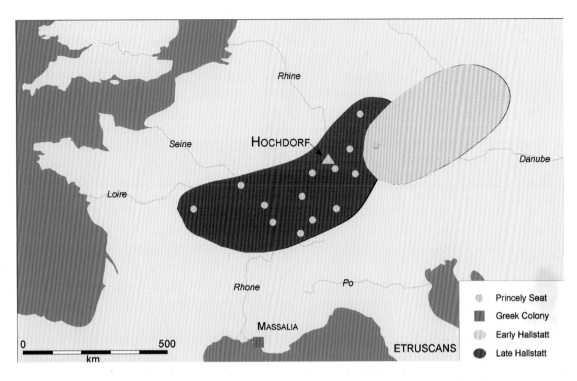

Princely Seat
Greek Colony
Early Hallstatt
Late Hallstatt

Fig. 6.3.
Distribution of Early and Late Hallstatt in Central Europe. The red dots show princely seats of power in the Early Hallstatt period. Note also the location of Massilia, a trading center founded by the Greeks in 600 BC, beneath modern Marseille, France.

Celtic societies. The term *Celtic* is a generic rubric for the various diverse societies in central Europe who spoke related languages. Over time, some of these groups moved to the west and south, across the Rhine and Alps, where they were eventually encountered by Caesar and the Romans, who lumped them together as the Gaul, or Celts. Celtic culture has its origins in the Iron Age of Europe, but the term has many other connotations.

The Iron Age—the time of the "Celtic" tribes—can be divided into two phases: Hallstatt and La Tène. La Tène is often treated as synonymous with Celtic, although La Tène is a specific period of time with a distinctive material culture. Hallstatt, the earlier part of the Iron Age, dates from approximately 900 to 450 BC and was centered in Austria, southern Germany, and the Czech Republic (Fig. 6.3). During the early Iron Age, salt and iron mines in these regions led to economic boom times. The tombs of the elite are the best-known finds from this period. The riches of the Hochdorf grave, for example, described in this chapter, document the wealth and power concentrated in the hands of these chiefs.

A distinctive art style developed throughout much of Western Europe during the pre-Roman Iron Age. Both Hallstatt and La Tène are defined primarily by artistic motifs and by specific types of pottery. Complex patterns of concentric circles, spirals and meanders, and a variety of bird and animal figures appear on metal, ceramic, and other objects. Disembodied heads with almond-shaped eyes and fierce mustaches, long and fanciful horse heads, and willowy statues of women characterize this tradition. Weapons, tools, jewelry, ceremonial paraphernalia, and everyday equipment were ornamented in this characteristic art style.

Fig. 6.2. (opposite)
Chronological framework for the European Iron Age.

Fig. 6.4.

Three large stone statues from the Iron Age probably depicting individual chiefs or rulers.

Hallstatt settlements were sometimes fortified and situated on hilltops, and they often housed workshops for bronze-, silver-, and goldsmiths. In the central Hallstatt region toward the end of the period, rich graves of high-status individuals under large tumuli (earthen mounds) are found near the fortified hilltop settlements. The tombs often contain wagons and horses as well. Elaborate jewelry of bronze and gold, and stone statues of chiefs and warriors, have been found in this context (Fig. 6.4). Typical sites are the Heuneburg on the upper Danube, surrounded by nine very large grave tumuli; Mont Lassois in eastern France, with the very rich grave at Vix (described later in this chapter); and the hill fort at Molpír in Slovakia.

The La Tène period followed Hallstatt, from ca. 500 BC until the Roman conquest. Italy and the eastern Mediterranean were flourishing at this time with the rise of Etruscan civilization and the classical Greek civilization of Socrates and Pericles. The name La Tène for the later Iron Age in Central Europe is taken from a site on the north side of Lake Neuchâtel in Switzerland. The largest concentration of sites from this time is found in eastern France, Switzerland, southern Germany, and the Czech Republic. By the early La Tène period, Celtic groups had expanded to the British Isles, Iberia, and across parts of the Balkan Peninsula to Anatolia. Elaborate burials also reveal a wide network of trade. Exports from La Tène to the Mediterranean cultures included salt, tin and copper, amber, wool, leather, furs, and gold.

The *oppida* are the characteristic sites of the La Tène period. These hilltop fortresses and chiefly towns occurred across Central Europe from western France to the Czech Republic. The *oppida* were established and abandoned during the final centuries BC. Although there is substantial variability among these ancient towns, there are also a number of similarities. The *oppida* are large—sometimes hundreds of hectares, fortified with massive earth and timber ditch and rampart walls, located on naturally defensible or elevated features of the landscape, contained areas for production of iron tools, weapons, pottery, and other items, and were often located in places where trade routes intersected.

The Celtic Iron Age came to an end in most of Western Europe around 50 BC with the Roman conquest, led by Julius Caesar. The emperor Claudius conquered most of England shortly thereafter. Remnants of Celtic traditions continued in Ireland for centuries, however, largely untouched by the Roman

Empire. Germanic tribes in central and northern Europe remained in the Iron Age, outside of the control of Rome for 1,000 years, essentially until the arrival of Christianity. The Roman conquest effectively ended prehistory in southern Europe and Britain; the spread of Christianity marked the beginning of the historic period in much of Europe north of the Alps.

THE CELTS

The Celts and the Germans are terms often used to describe the societies living across much of western and central Europe during the time of the Roman Empire, after ca. 50 BC. These terms in large part reflect a Roman view of the world and how they named those around them. Celtic is used more generically to refer to the people of Iron Age Europe who lived largely north and west of the Alps, through France and into the British Isles. These were the societies that for the most part fell to Rome and, with some exceptions, adopted Romance languages, losing their own.

People referred to as Celts are first mentioned historically in Greek texts during the pre-Roman Iron Age. The Greek geographer Strabo described the Celts as "war mad, high spirited and quick to battle but otherwise straightforward and not of evil character." These are the peoples that Julius Caesar called the Gauls, who had earlier sacked Rome. The word *Celtic* is used today for peoples whose present or former native tongues are related to those of the ancient Celts. Most present Celtic-speaking peoples live in the Britain and Ireland.

Defining exactly who the Celts were is challenging. The concept was created by the Romans for political and social reasons. Celtic societies were numerous and highly varied, both geographically and culturally; they possessed vibrant cultures, shared languages and religious beliefs, and developed a superb artistic style, at the same time both flamboyant and hypnotic (Fig. 6.5).

Most Celtic groups were headed by powerful leaders and organized along similar lines. Some had elected magistrates. Julius Caesar, who encountered these groups in battle and in negotiations, wrote of their social structure, describing three major groups below the king or chief: an aristocratic class of warriors and priests, the common people, and slaves—a stratified society (Fig. 6.6). But beyond features of an art style and a generic warrior society based on herding with some cultivation, it is difficult to capture the diversity of peoples and practices that defined Iron Age Europe before the Romans.

Fig. 6.5.
A tiny Pegasus, a winged horse, decoration at the terminus of a heavy, gold Celtic torq, buried in the princess grave at the site of Vix, France. The horse is about 1 cm long.

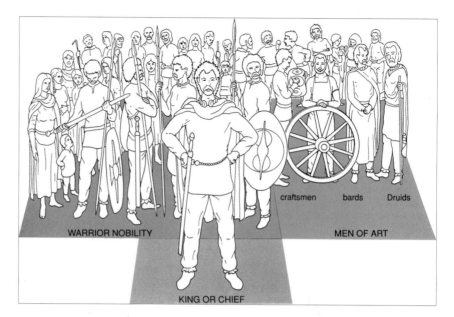

Fig. 6.6.
Levels of authority and power in Celtic society. The common people stand in the rear of this group.

In the third century BC, during their maximum expansion, the Celtic peoples had spread from their homelands as far west as Ireland and east to Turkey's central plain, as far north as Belgium and south to Cadiz in Spain. They crossed the Alps and conquered the armies of the Etruscan empire, occupied Rome, and invaded Greece. In addition to their prowess as formidable warriors, these peoples also invented new farming techniques, laid the first roadways through deep European forests, and displayed extraordinary skill in their crafts: metalwork, monumental stone carvings, glassware, and jewelry. And they survive today in various parts of Europe.

THE GERMANS

The Germanic peoples are a linguistic and ethnic branch of Indo-European origin in Northern Europe, identified by their use of the Germanic languages. Archeological evidence from around 750 BC suggests related Germanic peoples were located across northern Germany and southern Scandinavia, from the Netherlands to the Vistula and across Denmark into southern Sweden. By the first century AD, Roman authors described Germanic-speaking peoples in four tribal regions centered in Poland, the lower Rhine, the Elbe River, and Jutland and the Danish islands.

Julius Caesar described the Germans in his *Commentarii De Bello Gallico*, written at some point in the middle of the first century BC:

> Their whole life is occupied in hunting and in the pursuits of the military art; from childhood they devote themselves to fatigue and hardships. Those who have remained chaste for the longest time, receive the greatest commendation among their people; they think that by this the growth

Fig. 6.7. (opposite)
An artist's reconstruction of a fortified princely estate from the site of Pohansko in Slovakia. The presence of the church documents the arrival of Christianity. A cemetery is adjacent to the church.

is promoted, by this the physical powers are increased and the sinews are strengthened. And to have had knowledge of a woman before the twentieth year they reckon among the most disgraceful acts; of which matter there is no concealment, because they bathe promiscuously in the rivers and [only] use skins or small cloaks of deer's hides, a large portion of the body being in consequence naked.

Migrating Germanic groups spread throughout Europe between AD 300 and 600 mingling with existing Celtic and other groups across the continent. Europe's Germanic peoples, such as the Franks, Saxons, Vandals, Angles, Lombards, Burgundians, and Goths, transformed the Roman Empire into Medieval Europe. Today, Germanic languages are spoken through much of the world, represented principally by German, Dutch, the Scandinavian dialects, and English. In addition, they created the runic writing system, adapted from the Romans.

These democratic warrior societies developed more hierarchical political structures with aristocratic classes among the warriors and nobility as they came in contact with the Romans and Romanized Celts. The most powerful component of Germanic social structure was the *comitatus*, a retinue of warriors who voluntarily attached themselves to a lord or king. Through oaths of loyalty, the *comitatus* militarily protected the ruler. The ruler, in turn, granted individuals the protection of the *comitatus* and rewarded them with wealth. The *comitatus* was a sophisticated military organization built on the economic principle of reciprocity.

Germanic settlements were usually small, often less than ten households, frequently located at clearings in the forest. A variety of timber buildings have been found in these small villages: farmhouses along with smaller structures such as granaries, workshops, and storage rooms. Cattle and humans lived together in the same house. Larger settlements are also known, along with stand-alone princely estates that included part of the ruler's retinue at a magnate farm. The ruling class was distinguished by possession of large farms (Fig. 6.7) and rich equipment and clothing such as weapons for the men and silver objects for the women, imported earthenware, and items of Celtic origin. A number of cemeteries are known from this time. In some cremation graves, Celtic brooches and swords have been found together with wagons, Roman cauldrons, and drinking vessels.

The Germans were farmers involved in agriculture and animal husbandry. Cattle herding was extremely important both as a source of dairy products and meat and as a basis for wealth and social status, measured by the size of one's herd. Barley and wheat were the most common agricultural products, used for baking a certain flat type of bread as well as brewing beer. Forest game also contributed to the larder. Clothing styles are known from the remarkably well-preserved corpses that have been found in bogs in Denmark; they included woolen garments and brooches for women and trousers and leather caps for men (Fig. 6.8). Important craft industries produced textiles, leather goods, pottery, and iron tools and weapons.

Fig. 6.8.
Clothing from the Huldremose woman, a bog body from the second century BC in Denmark. The clothing includes a plaid woolen skirt, a plaid woolen scarf, and two skin capes.

THE SCYTHIANS

I briefly mention the Scythians here, not as a specifically European phenomenon but because of their widespread impact across Eurasia during the first millennium BC. The

Scythians were nomadic pastoralists— "horse archer" warriors—probably originating in Iran, who dominated the Pontic-Caspian steppe for a millennium after 900 BC, during the European Iron Age and the rise of Rome. The Scythian realm stretched from the Don in the east to the Danube River in the west. Scythian influences were felt far beyond its borders.

Much of what we known about the Scythians comes from the writings of Herodotus, the Greek historian (ca. 440 BC), in his *Histories*, and Ovid in his poems. Archaeologically, extraordinary information on the Scythians is found in the depictions of Scythian life in exquisite gold work from southern Russia and the Ukraine. The best-known remains of the Scythians come from the contents of their tombs in large earthen mounds known as kurgans (some more than 20 m or 65 ft high) that are seen across the Pontic steppes. These tombs can be all the more spectacular because they are on occasion found wrapped in permafrost with remarkably preserved organic contents. Graves in these tombs range from simple interments to extraordinarily rich royal burials with weapons, horse equipment, gold, silk, animal sacrifices, and more.

Fig. 6.9.
Detail of the gold work on a Scythian necklace.

The gold work of the Scythians was both abundant in quantity and extraordinary in rendition. The discovery of an undisturbed royal kurgan in 2001 in southern Siberia revealed 20 kg (44 lb) of gold jewelry and equipment. The Scythians produced jewelry with Central-Asian animal motifs along the lines of the Greek style of realism: winged gryphons attacking horses (Fig. 6.9), battling stags, deer, and eagles, combined with everyday motifs such as milking ewes.

MAKING IRON

Iron has a melting temperature of 1,536 °C (2,797 °F). Sophisticated furnaces and smelting techniques are required for reducing the ore. Iron making was discovered in Turkey shortly before 2000 BC. The new metal was used initially to make stronger, more durable weapons and later for making more practical tools and equipment. The technology—involving furnaces and high temperatures for smelting iron ores—was probably a well-guarded secret for some time, to gain military advantage. Iron came to Europe around the beginning of the first millennium BC, slightly earlier in the eastern Mediterranean and slightly later in the northwestern part of the continent.

Iron is not as hard as bronze, but the ores are more widely available. Sources for iron occur in several forms. Red ochre, which is hydrated iron oxide, was used as a pigment in the late Paleolithic and Mesolithic. Meteoric iron was used early for making simple jewelry and artifacts by cold hammering. Iron mining and production is a bit more complicated. Iron ores are found in many parts of central and southern Europe, as well as the British Isles. More important sources occur in the eastern Alps, in the Holy Cross Mountains of Poland, the Hunsrück-Eifel region of Germany, and Etruria in Italy. Most iron could be obtained from the surface by open pit mining, but there were shaft mines in the Alps and elsewhere. Bog iron—thin layers of iron nodules that accumulate in some wetlands—provided a source of ore for the smelting furnaces of northern Europe.

Furnace temperatures were not sufficient for casting the metal in the European Iron Age; objects were made of wrought iron. Wrought iron is inferior to bronze in terms of strength and durability, so a process known as carburization—heating iron in the presence of carbon, usually charcoal—was used to harden the edges of tools and weapons.

Iron production is an expensive process, involving large quantities of wood, ore, and labor. Reduction techniques are used to speed the process. Layers of iron ore and charcoal are placed in a shaft furnace and maintained at a temperature of more than 1,500 °C (2,732 °F) for several hours (Fig. 6.10). The actual reduction of the ore to the metal can take only a few minutes if optimal temperature and conditions are present. After the furnace cools, it is broken apart and the bloom, a spongy mass of impure iron, is removed. This mass had to be heated and hammered repeatedly to produce usable iron. Production of 1 kg (2.2 lb) of iron required approximately 10 kg (22 lb) of charcoal and 25 hours of labor.

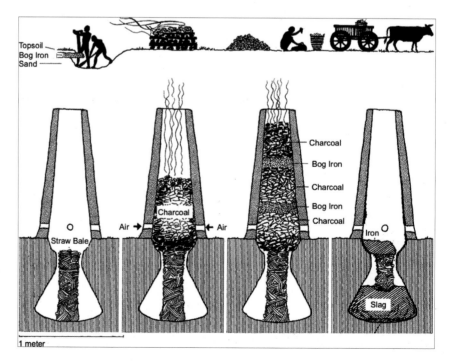

Fig. 6.10.
Stages of iron production using bog ore. In the upper panel, bog iron is collected from natural deposits, burned to remove impurities, and broken into small pieces and transported to the furnace. The clay shaft furnace is loaded with fuel, charcoal, and bog iron and fired to temperatures around 1,536 °C. The iron ore melts into bloom iron, a type of spongy slag ready for the forge.

BISKUPIN, POLAND, 738 BC

The fortified Iron Age settlement of Biskupin is one of the most famous archaeological sites in Central Europe. Its size and location and the preservation of the buildings are truly remarkable. The settlement was constructed in a very short time on a lake in western Poland. It essentially covered the end of a small peninsula, turning the naturally protected point of land into a heavily defended fortress and town. In fact, construction of the settlement may have converted several small islands near the shore into this peninsula.

The settlement was surrounded with a massive wooden rampart inside a timber breakwater at the water's edge (Fig. 6.11). The oval rampart was 550 m in circumference, 3.5 m wide (12 ft), and 3 m (10 ft) high, enclosing an area of 2.4 ha, more than half a city block. The wall was constructed as a series of massive timber boxes filled with earth and stone. Inside the rampart a ring road ran around the settlement.

A two-story tower and fortified gate dominated the entrance. Inside the gate was a town square surrounded by thirteen rows of 105 timber houses, uniformly arranged along eleven wooden corduroy streets (Fig. 6.12). Each house was about 8 x 10 m (25 x 33 ft). The houses were packed closely together, with one roof for every three houses. Biskupin had an estimated population of 800–1000 inhabitants.

The site has been dated by both radiocarbon and tree ring methods. The oak timbers for the first major building project were cut down between 747 and 722 BC, but more than half of the trees were felled in the course of one winter, in the years 738–737 BC. The tree ring dates are very consistent and suggest that

Fig. 6.11.
The site of Biskupin today, with the reconstructed rampart and tower on the peninsula on Lake Biskupin.

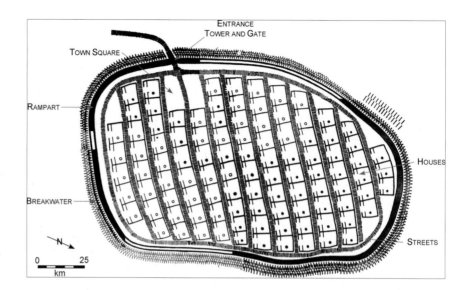

Fig. 6.12.
The fortress of Biskupin, with major features identified.

most of the wood construction was put in place during that winter and stood for more than one hundred years. The radiocarbon determinations indicated an initial settlement at the site around 720 B C and a later occupation at 560 B C. The earlier radiocarbon age corresponds well with the tree ring dates. The primary settlement at Biskupin belongs to the Hallstatt period of the early Iron Age.

The history of research at Bisupin is an interesting story, and a lesson in the politics of archaeology. Biskupin was discovered in 1933 by Walenty Szwajcer, a teacher at a local school, who took his students to the lake on an excursion and noticed large wooden timbers along the edge of the peninsula. He thought the timbers might be parts of ancient houses and notified the local authorities. Professor Józef Kostrzewski arrived from the nearby city of Posnan to examine the peninsula. He decided to begin excavations as soon as possible. His project began in 1934 and very soon became the largest archaeological excavation in Polish history; almost 2,500 m² (27,000 ft²) were excavated by the end of 1938. Very advanced methods for the time were employed, including underwater archaeology and balloon photography (Fig. 6.13). The first scientific report on the excavations was published in 1936.

Biskupin, an ancient fortress only 70 km (40 mi) from the German border, became a popular symbol for the strength and resistance of the ancestors of the Poles against foreign invaders. The German blitzkrieg that conquered Poland in the fall of 1939 at the start of World War II ended the Polish excavations at Biskupin. The Germans immediately incorporated Biskupin into their own ideology. The site was located in what the Germans called Warthegau, a region claimed to have been Germanic since the Iron Age or even earlier.

The Nazis sought to "Germanize" this area of the Warthegau, meaning its complete political, cultural, social, and economic assimilation into the German Reich. Cities, towns, and streets were renamed. Thousands of Polish businesses, from large to small, were confiscated without payment to the owners. Nearly half a million German citizens were resettled in western Poland by 1945 and an equal number of local residents forcibly evacuated.

Fig. 6.13.
A balloon photograph of the excavations at Biskupin in the 1930s. The plan of the timber town and oval fortress is easily visible. Two lines rising to the balloon and camera can be seen in the lower right of the photo.

The site of Biskupin was renamed "Urstädt," meaning original, or early, town. Excavations were resumed there in 1940 by the Germans under the direction of the SS (Schutzstaffel), an all-powerful political and military force in Germany, and the patronage of its commander, Heinrich Himmler. The German archaeologist at the site excavated for three years and published only two short popular accounts explaining how Germanic tribes overran the small settlement of Biskupin. When the Germans retreated, the site was intentionally flooded, an act that had quite positive effects for good preservation until the Polish excavations resumed after the war in 1946. At that point, direction of the project was passed to Zdzisław Rajewski, the former assistant at the site.

Excavations continued until 1974; Biskupin became a focal point of archaeological research once again in Poland. Field training for Polish archaeology students was centered there, and most of the next generation of archaeologists got at least some of their field experience at the site. Various smaller projects investigating the local environment and other details at the site continued into the 1990s, and small-scale studies continue today.

One of the major concerns at Biskupin, of course, is preservation. Because of its waterlogged conditions, the wood was very well preserved. Preservation meant recovery of exceptional information, but it also created problems of conservation, primarily for the structural timbers. Smaller finds and artifacts were relatively easy to remove, treat, and conserve. Large pieces of wood were difficult, requiring special facilities, lots of time, and expense.

The archaeologists and conservators today are devoting most of their energy to protecting and preserving the remaining structures. The water table in much of Europe has been lowered by modern agricultural practices and water consumption. The drying of the timbers due to lower water levels can oxidize and destroy them. To help prevent this, a dam has been built at the outlet

Fig. 6.14.
The reconstructed fortress entrance and gate at Biskupin, Poland.

of the lake to raise the water level by 50 cm (1.6 ft) and ensure that much of the site remains waterlogged. Most of the earlier excavations were filled in to protect the remains.

Biskupin has become a major attraction, bringing more than 450,000 tourists a year to the area. A number of houses, the gateway, and a section of the palisaded rampart have been reconstructed at the site (Fig. 6.14). In addition to the reconstructed fortress, there is an annual archaeological festival. The small nearby town is overrun with hordes of tourists for a few days every year during the festival. The stronghold itself was built to protect its inhabitants and succeeded for perhaps a century, before an earlier horde fell on the fortress and sacked it.

THE ETRUSCANS

The Etruscan civilization came into being around 700 BC, from antecedents in the Urnfield period of the late Bronze Age. Many of the most characteristic features of Etruscan society—settlement in towns, distinctive burial customs, production of goods for regional and long-distance trade and exchange—were present in incipient form. Early Etruscans were influenced by Greek, Phoenician, and other Mediterranean societies.

Excavations in Etruscan towns from this period have revealed evidence of urban planning and public works, such as streets, drainage channels, reservoirs, retaining walls, fortifications, and large sanctuaries (Fig. 6.15). By 600 BC, the Etruscans were the rulers of Rome, building some of the first streets, temples,

Fig. 6.15.
The Etruscan gate and city wall from the ancient city of Perugia. There are later additions to the top of the wall, but the base is originally Etruscan.

and a water system. The oldest known documents in the Etruscan language appeared along with their first towns and cities. The language remains undeciphered.

The Etruscans came before Rome. They emerged in Tuscany in west central Italy in the first millennium BC during the pre-Roman Iron Age (Fig. 6.16). Theirs was the first major civilization in Italy, built on a series of powerful, fortified city-states across the region. The magnificent walls that still surround old Tuscan towns—Sienna, Perugia, Veii, Tarquinia, and many others—are not Roman, but Etruscan.

Some say they taught the French to make wine and the Romans to build roads. They employed the first writing system in Europe beyond the eastern Mediterranean (Fig. 6.17). The Latin alphabet has its origins in the Etruscan writing system. Their influence expanded across most of northern Italy and west to the island of Corsica. Eventually, their power and influence declined, and they were absorbed in the growth of the Roman Empire around 80 BC.

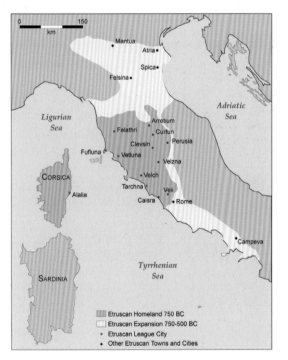

Fig. 6.16.
Distribution of the Etruscan civilization around 750 BC, an area of expansion between 750 and 500 BC, and the major cities of the Etruscans.

The Etruscans were skillful sailors and masters of metallurgy. They mined Italy's rich mineral resources and traded raw copper, iron, and bronze for perfume, ivory, amber, and fine ceramics from the eastern Mediterranean. Etruscan bronze products were exported widely, throughout the Mediterranean and beyond the Alps. Etruria was famous for jewelry production, particularly ornaments decorated

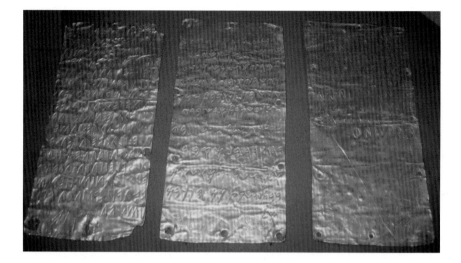

Fig. 6.17.
Etruscan writing preserved on three gold sheets, known as the Pyrgi tablets after the place of discovery. The tablets are approximately 20 by 10 cm in size.

with gold granulation (using fine beads of gold) and filigree (using fine spirals of gold and silver wire). Etruscans probably learned these techniques from the Syrians or the Phoenicians.

Trade grew steadily. Beginning in the eighth century BC, Etruscans developed extensive trade contact with the eastern Mediterranean, notably Greece and Phoenicia. Recovered shipwrecks were loaded with Etruscan trade goods: pottery and other crafts and amphorae filled with agricultural products, such as pine nuts, wine, and olives. In exchange, the Etruscans imported the eastern luxury goods found in such abundance in aristocratic graves. Etruscan trade was not administered centrally; instead, many small political units, controlled by the elite, competed on more or less equal terms. The Greeks also established trade towns on the coast of southern Etruria, and Greek craftsmen settled permanently to work in Etruria.

Etruscan art is extraordinary. Many media were employed and a very distinctive style developed—charming, ornate, and wonderfully made. Their artwork was highly animated and very fluid. Particularly distinctive in the Etruscan tradition were figurative sculptures in terracotta (particularly life-size sarcophagi and figures on temples; Fig. 6.18), cast bronze, wall paintings, and metalworking (e.g., engraved bronze mirrors). In addition to scenes of daily life, Etruscan art is dominated by religious depictions. Because of the preservation of the tombs, we know that much of this art is related to funerary practices.

NECROPOLI DELLA BANDITACCIA, ITALY, 650 BC

Cemeteries were built at the edge of Etruscan towns. There were several cemeteries around the former Etruscan town of Caere (now modern Cerveteri). The Necropoli della Banditaccia is a World Heritage Site, along with several other cemeteries in the area. It is one of the largest ancient burial grounds in the Mediterranean, covering an area of 400 ha (1,000 acres). Ten hectares (25 acres) and approximately 1,000 tombs are open to the public. The tombs date

from the ninth century to the late third century BC. The oldest were simple pits that housed the ashes of the dead.

The two common types of tombs are mounds (Fig. 6.19) and what are called dice—square tombs built in long rows along roads in the cemetery. The mounds are circular structures and can be as large as 30–40 m (100–130 ft) in diameter and 12–15 m (40–50 ft) high. A single door at the side of the mound leads to the interior. The inside of the mounds, often carved from the living volcanic rock, was a reconstruction of the home of the deceased, including a corridor, a central hall, and several rooms. Our knowledge of Etruscan daily life is largely based on the decorative details and finds from such tombs.

The most famous of these mounds is the Tomba dei Rilievi (Tomb of the Reliefs), from the third century BC (Fig. 6.20). An inscription informs us that the tomb belonged to one Matunas. Inside are a series of marvelous frescoes, bas-reliefs, and sculptures portraying a large set of tools, equipment, and other household items. Many of the finds excavated at Cerveteri are housed in the National Etruscan Museum in Rome.

Social inequality is evident in the Etruscan cemeteries. The tombs show distinct differentiation based on gender, socioeconomic status, and place of origin. The elite built elaborate chamber tombs covered with tumuli (the

Fig. 6.18.
The sarcophagus of a reclining couple from Necropoli della Banditaccia, ca. 520 BC, painted terracotta, 1.1 m high.

Fig. 6.19.
Round and dice-shaped tombs in the Etruscan cemetery at Necropoli della Banditaccia.

Fig. 6.20.
The interior of an Etruscan tomb, carved into the living rock, a soft volcanic tuff. The tomb interior is a copy of an Etruscan home.

mound tombs). A particularly grand example is the Tomb of the Chariots at the cemetery of Populonium. Within a mound 28 m (90 ft) in diameter, the tomb contained funerary beds for four occupants. At least one female, with gold jewelry, was buried in the tomb. She was accompanied by three males, who were buried with a chariot and a two-wheeled carriage.

The Tomb of the Five Chairs at Cerveteri, from the second half of the seventh century BC, provides some additional information on burial rites and beliefs. The main chamber of the tomb held two bodies, while a side chamber offered space for mourners to worship as part of an ancestor cult. Five chairs were carved from rock to hold terracotta statues representing these ancestors, two women and three men. The ancestor statues sat before rock-carved tables laden with food offerings. A nearby altar held their drinks. Two empty chairs were present, for the buried couple to join their ancestors at the feast.

HALLSTATT, AUSTRIA, 800 BC

Modern Hallstatt is one of those impossibly picturesque mountain villages, located on a lake with the same name, high in the Austrian Alps (Fig. 6.21). The name comes from *hall,* a term for salt, referring to the Iron Age salt mines in the local mountains. Salt was a valuable resource for preserving meat and fish in the Iron Age; it furnished the economic wealth for this town and its inhabitants. The mines are still active today.

The Iron Age mining operations were remarkable. The shafts and tunnels went deeper and deeper from one level to the next, a total of twenty-one levels, as the ancient miners followed the salt deposits in the mountain. The total depth of the mine was 215 m (700 ft). Today each level is connected to the next by a large wooden slide for a speedy trip down (the longest was 64 m or 200 ft). Iron Age mining tools of wood and antler were preserved by the salt and dry conditions in the mine. The well-preserved body of a miner with clothes and tools was found in the eighteenth century.

Fig. 6.21.
The modern village of Hallstatt in the Austrian Alps.

The modern village shares its name with the early Iron Age Hallstatt culture. The Iron Age of Central and Western Europe, prior to the Roman conquest, is divided into two major periods: Hallstatt from 900–450 BC, and La Tène from 450 BC until the arrival of the Romans in the second half of the first century BC. Hallstatt gained archaeological fame not because of the salt mines but because of a major cemetery of wealthy graves found near the town.

In 1846, Johann Georg Ramsauer, manager of the Hallstatt mine, discovered a large prehistoric graveyard between the lake and the salt mines, 450 m (1,500 ft) above the modern town. His careful excavations over many years yielded a total of 1,045 burials, many of which were carefully recorded in a series of remarkable painted illustrations (Fig. 6.22). Most of the burials in the prehistoric cemetery are dated between 800 and 450 BC. The style and

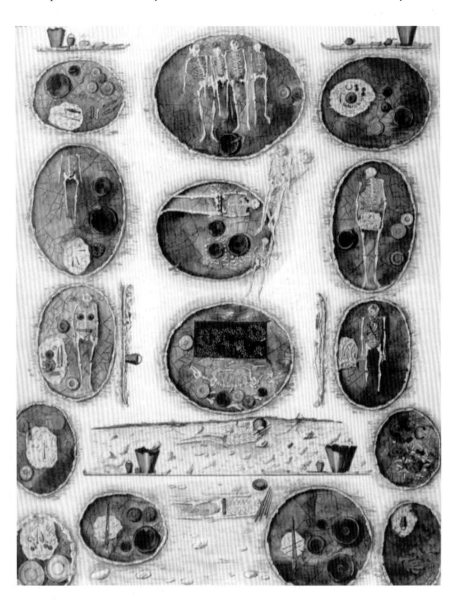

Fig. 6.22.
Original drawings of the graves from the excavations of the Hallstatt cemetery in the 1850s.

decoration of the grave goods found in the cemetery are distinctive and directly linked to the Hallstatt culture.

Approximately 55 percent of the burials were simple inhumations, usually with elaborate grave goods. The remaining were cremations, ashes and burnt bone heaped under the grave goods, which included weapons and objects of personal adornment, surrounded by pottery and other offerings. Weapons at Hallstatt are of bronze and iron; among them are long and short swords found with both male and female burials. One-fourth of the buried individuals appear to be males, with a full complement of weapons, interpreted as warrior graves. The cemetery includes children of all ages.

The Hallstatt graves excavated by Ramsauer were exceptionally rich, with an extraordinary number of large bronze vessels, other metal objects, glass, and amber. The cremation graves were the richest of all. The wealth of the graves suggested that only the upper level of society was buried here. More recent excavations have demonstrated that the cemetery was in fact much larger, containing perhaps 5,000 or more graves, and many of the new burials lack the metal objects and are supplied only with pottery vessels as grave gifts.

HOCHDORF, GERMANY, 530 BC

Fürstensitz, or prince's seat, is the German name for the residential citadels of Iron Age chiefs in southern Germany, Switzerland, and eastern France during the first part of the Iron Age, the Hallstatt period. These places were heavily fortified hilltop towns, centers of political, economic, and military power under the rule of a powerful chief. These were the first urban settlements, true towns, in Europe north of the Alps, called *oppida* by the Romans. At the *oppidum* of Heidengraben in southwest Germany, for example, the massive fortifications enclosed an area of almost 17 km² (6½ mi²), about five times the size of Central Park in Manhattan.

Large earthen mounds cover the tombs of the elite from these towns in the early Iron Age. There are some forty known rich, elaborate tombs from the Hallstatt period (Fig. 6.23). Most were robbed in antiquity via tunnels into the center of the mound, where the primary grave was located. Excavations of these mounds today usually recover only minor items left behind by the looters and sometimes fragments of lavish burial goods. An exception was found near the village of Hochdorf, not far from Stuttgart in southwestern Germany.

The tomb at Hochdorf, remarkably, had not been plundered. One reason may be that not much was left of the earthen mound after 2,500 years of agricultural activity. Plowing over the centuries had reduced the mound to a mere 1.5 m rise in a wheat field. In fact, the tomb was not even known until 1977, when an amateur archaeologist, known for her site-finding skills, reported the place to the regional professional, Jörg Biel. The amateur had noticed a circular line of stones around the edge of the rise and thought they might mark something of interest. Rescue excavations by the state agency in 1978–79 exposed this ring of large stones to be 60 m (200 ft) in diameter and

Fig. 6.23.
The restored Iron Age barrow at Hochdorf, Germany.

marking the outside of the tumulus, which they estimated originally stood 8–10 m (ca. 30 ft) high.

The excavations also revealed a second reason that tomb robbers may have been unsuccessful at Hochdorf. The builders of the grave had constructed a remarkably strong and resistant chamber, probably in anticipation of looting, to house the deceased and his food, equipment, and valuables in the afterlife. At the center, before the mound was built, a large square pit, 11 by 11 m (36 ft) and 2.5 m (8 ft) deep, was dug into the ground. A very unusual and massive construction was added to protect the contents of the grave. A square chamber 7.5 m (25 ft) on a side, built of huge oak timbers, was assembled in the pit. Inside that chamber, like a smaller box inside a larger one, was another oak chamber 4.7 m (15.5 ft) on a side. The space between the chambers and especially above the outer chamber was packed with huge stones weighing a total of 50 metric tons. Finally, four layers of heavy timbers were placed on top of the stones. No one entered that tomb until the archaeologists arrived.

The archaeologists removed the earthen mound and exposed the chamber. The stone ceiling had collapsed into the interior box and crushed the contents. At the same time, the tomb had not been robbed or disturbed in antiquity; the massive construction had done the job and protected the prince of Hochdorf over the centuries. This was the first princely grave in Germany that had not been looted. The archaeologists were ecstatic.

The excavators slowly removed the heavy stones from the burial chamber. Near the bottom of the tomb, they began to encounter the remarkable contents of the grave. Slowly the scatter of broken and crushed fragments began to make sense. The layout of the burial and grave goods demonstrated the careful arrangement of the tomb. The skeleton of the chief was found on the west side of the inner chamber, dressed in finery. The man was about forty years old and 1.83 m (6 ft) in height, 20 cm (8 in) taller than the average male in the Hallstatt period. The remaining pieces of material indicated that his clothing was made from richly patterned cloth, embroidered with Chinese silk.

Pieces of gold jewelry adorned his remains, including a gold torq, or neck ring, a hallmark of high status in Celtic society. Gold brooches held his clothing together, and a gold band was part of his belt. A dagger with a golden hilt lay at his waist and a gold armband encircled his arm. Even his shoes had fine strips of gold woven into the leather (Fig. 6.24). A conical birchbark hat was near his head; a leather bag held a wooden comb, nail clippers, a razor, and a few fishhooks. A leather quiver with bronze and iron tipped arrows had been hung on the wall behind the couch. Nine large drinking horns with gold bands, one made of iron and eight from the horns of aurochs—huge wild cattle—hung on the south wall of the chamber.

This wealthy chief was laid to rest on a bronze couch, 2.5 m (8 ft) long, sitting on eight legs with wheels so that the furniture could be easily moved. The legs of the couch were cast bronze figures of standing females holding the bed of the sofa. The high bronze back of the couch was embossed using a punch technique with dancing figures and two horses pulling a four-wheeled cart.

Fig. 6.24.
Some of the chief's clothing, weapons, and jewelry, along with the conical birchbark hat.

Food and drink for the afterworld was provided. In the northwest corner of the chamber was an enormous, ornate bronze cauldron that originally held 400 liters (a bathtub full) of mead (a fermented honey liquor) and a gold drinking bowl. The round caldron itself, 1 m (3 ft) in diameter and 70 cm (2 ft) high, was decorated with three small bronze lions around the mouth of the vessel. The style of these ornaments and the cauldron itself point to its manufacture in mainland Greece.

On the east side of the chamber was a four-wheeled cart stacked with various items (Fig. 6.25). The cart itself was elaborately decorated with iron figures and chains. The harness and leather gear for the horses was also with the wagon. Nine bronze plates and three platters had been placed on

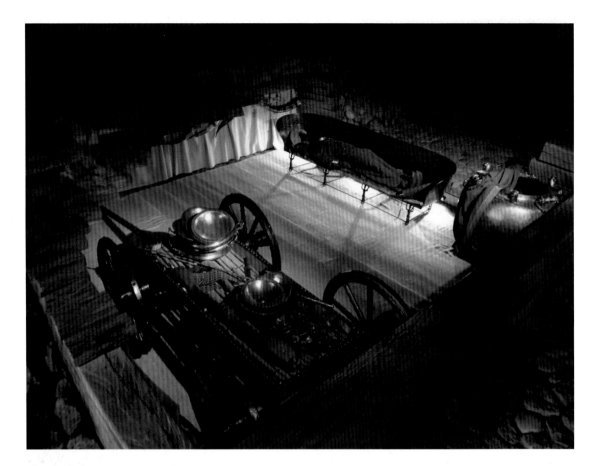

Fig. 6.25.
A modern reconstruction of the burial chamber at Hochdorf.

the bed of the wagon along with knives, an axe, and other tools, probably to slaughter and butcher animals.

The walls and floor of the chamber were covered in rich fabrics, fragments of which have survived. These pieces were held together with iron clasps and bronze brooches, one of which furnished a date for the tomb of 530 BC. Textile specialists have identified bright red and blue dyes, often in complex geometrical patterns, in the fabrics on the chamber walls, the wrapping around the man's body, and covering the couch, the cauldron, and the wagon. The remains of the cloth and other fabrics in the tomb constitute the richest find of textiles from this period in Europe.

After excavations were completed and the artifacts and other materials removed from the tomb, the conservators needed many years to reconstruct and restore these decayed, broken, and flattened objects to their original condition. Study of the contents of the Hochdorf tomb continues today to enlighten our knowledge of the Iron Age. The mound, itself an archaeological monument, was restored to its original height and topped with a stone stela. A fine museum was built nearby to house the finds from Hochdorf. In the earth underneath the museum, a reconstruction of the prince's grave affords a glimpse of the tomb and its contents as they may have looked 2,500 years ago on the day of burial. The sheen of precious metals, the vibrant colors of cloth, the magnificence of the wagon and bronze cauldron speak vibrantly to the power and wealth of the chief who had been buried.

VIX, FRANCE, 480 BC

The tombs of the elite of Celtic society are among the best-known finds from this period. The grave at Vix was excavated in 1953 by René Joffroy at the foot of an Iron Age hillfort (an *oppida*; Fig. 6.26). The hillfort is known as Mont Lassois, located about 200 km (120 mi) southeast of Paris, along the headwaters of the Seine River in northern France. A woman was buried there beneath an earthen mound in 480 BC; she is often referred to as the Princess of Vix. Although her true status is unknown, the wealth with which she was buried clearly points to important status in life.

Analysis of the skeletal remains of this woman have revealed valuable information. Her age was thought to have been between thirty-five and forty. Her stature was estimated to have been only around 160 cm (5'3") tall, according to the length of her femur. Substantial problems with her hip joints and an asymmetric head shape suggest that she would have had a waddling gait, and her head would have been held tilted to the right and her face somewhat twisted. These traits may be a consequence of either congenital conditions or childhood stress due to disease or malnutrition, or both. In sum, the woman buried in this elaborate tomb at Vix would have had an unusual appearance.

Fig. 6.26.
Aerial photo of Mont Lassois in the Seine River valley, France.

Her distinctive form in combination with the uncommon objects in the tomb have led some archaeologists to suggest that the princess was in fact a seer, ritual healer, or shaman.

The tomb consisted of a timber mortuary house with a central room 3.1 by 2.75 m (10 by 9 ft), covered with a layer of protective stone and encased in an earthen mound, originally 42 m (140 ft) in diameter and perhaps 5 m (16 ft) high. The body had been placed on the bed of a ceremonial cart or hearse in the center of the grave (Fig. 6.27). The wheels of the cart were removed and stacked against the sides of the tomb. The corpse was covered with a leather blanket, and a bronze-headed staff was placed across her torso. She was buried with a heavy gold collar of foreign manufacture and wore Baltic amber beads, locally made bronze brooches, and other pins and jewelry.

The uniquely ornamented gold neck ring was of exceptionally fine workmanship and weighed 480 grams. At the two bulbous ends were lion paws, tiny winged horses, and intricately incised ornamentation (see Fig. 6.5). The style of ornamentation suggests connections with Greek and Scythian traditions. The other personal equipment was more typical of elite female graves in the Early Iron Age, but there were more and more highly decorated objects in the

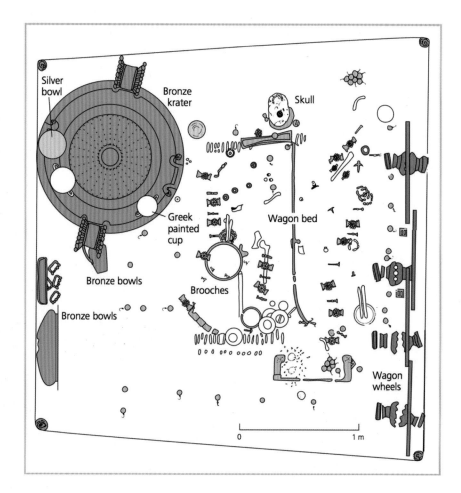

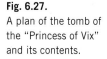

Fig. 6.27.
A plan of the tomb of the "Princess of Vix" and its contents.

Fig. 6.28.
Detail of the rim of the bronze krater from the "princess" grave at Vix.

Vix tomb. Three bracelets of schist and one of thin bronze were found on each wrist; a necklace of amber, diorite, and serpentine beads was around her neck. On each ankle was a hollow bronze ring. Although textiles had disappeared, the pins and brooches she wore remained. There were eight fibulae (ornamental brooches) used to fasten garments and for decoration. Two were of iron and the other six of bronze, some ornamented with gold, amber, and coral.

The tomb was filled with a wealth of exotic, funerary offerings but lacks the weapons common in most male graves from this period (Fig. 6.28). On the western side was an extraordinary assemblage of ceramic, bronze, and silver vessels. A huge bronze *krater*, a vessel for mixing and storing wine, more than 1.5 m (5 ft) high, weighing 208 kg (450 lb), with a volume of more than 1,000 liters (1,500 bottles of wine), was set in one corner of the grave. It was crafted using the lost-wax technique in a Greek bronze workshop, probably located in southern Italy. It is the most spectacular piece of classical Greek metalwork to survive anywhere (Fig. 6.29). The *krater* was designed to be dismantled for transport, and the assembly instructions were labeled with Greek letters. The design around its rim depicts Greek warriors and horse-drawn chariots. A number of bronze, silver, and gold bowls were placed alongside, including a

Fig. 6.29.
A museum reconstruction of the contents of the "princess" burial at Vix.

bronze flagon from Italy and two painted pottery cups from the luxury ceramic industry in Athens. Other feasting equipment in the grave included eight vessels, at least six of them imports from the Greek and Etruscan worlds. A bronze jug and three basins all may have come from Etruscan workshops in Italy.

The origins of the materials found in the princess burial at Vix indicate the extensive trade taking place in Europe at that time and emphasize the importance of the major rivers as transportation routes. The Rhône, the largest river in Europe that joins the Mediterranean, served as a major corridor from the south into temperate Europe. The modern city of Marseilles, at the mouth of the Rhône in southern France, was originally a Greek colony called Massilia, founded in 600 BC. Wine from the Aegean was sent to Massilia for shipment into western Europe. Various goods and materials from the interior of the continent were exported through this colony to the eastern Mediterranean. Fragments of a garment of Chinese silk, found in the Hochdorf tomb in Germany, are one example of the extent of trade at this time. The quantity of materials flowing through Massilia must have been remarkable.

Subsequent excavations southwest of the Vix burial in the early 1990s uncovered a square enclosure 23 m (75 ft) on a side, bounded by a ditch. An opening in the ditch 1.2 m (4 ft) wide at the center of one side faces the fortified hilltop settlement on Mont Lassois. Animal bones and remains of ceramic bowls in the ditch suggest that rituals associated with funeral rites were conducted in the enclosure. In the ditch just east of the opening were two almost life-size limestone sculptures of seated humans: a woman is wearing a neck ring resembling the one in the rich female tomb, and a man is wearing a sword and holding a shield. Apparently these figures were placed at either side of the entrance into the enclosure.

The town of Mont Lassois, directly above the grave at Vix, was one of the major political and commercial centers of late Hallstatt Europe. A number of burial mounds surround the base of the mountain, and the flat top is a place of residence. Excavation on the summit of Mont Lassois revealed extensive fortifications, with ditches and walls up to 8 m (26 ft) thick. Excavation inside the enclosure revealed a variety of buildings, including post houses, pit dwellings, hearths, and storage units built on stilts. Geophysical work shows a large planned settlement, with a central north-south axis and several phases of buildings.

Excavations in 2006 revealed an unusual structure at the center of the site. It is a complex of two or three buildings, the largest 35 by 21 m (115 by 70 ft), with an estimated height of 12 m (40 ft), the dimensions of a modern church. This large hall had an apse at the back and a front porch. Overall, the central unit resembles a megaron construction used in early Greek architecture. Such a find is unprecedented in early Celtic Europe. Artifacts and other materials in and around the structures suggest domestic or feasting activities. The structure has been described by some as the "Palace" of the Princess of Vix.

Mont Lassois has all the features of a high-status settlement: large fortifications, the presence of a citadel, a lower town, rare and fine imported materials, and numerous rich burial mounds. Mont Lassois dominates the upper Seine Valley at the spot where the river becomes navigable and flows west to the Atlantic. The Rhône and its tributaries lie just to the east. Thus Mont Lassois is at a strategic point in the main route of commerce between the western Mediterranean and the Atlantic coast of western France, the English Channel, and the British Isles. Iron ore and forests for wood to make charcoal for reducing the ore were also available in the area. The richness of the offerings in the tomb of the princess at Vix, some 500 km (300 mi) north of the Greek colony of Massilia, suggests that the Greeks were giving gifts to the elite of Celtic society in order to obtain favorable trading status and to secure commerce.

DANEBURY, ENGLAND, 550 BC

Danebury is one of the largest and most completely excavated Iron Age hillforts in all of Britain. Dating from the first half of the first millennium BC, roughly contemporary with Maiden Castle (later in this chapter) and many of the Celtic *oppida* in Western and Central Europe, this type of site epitomizes the warlike nature of Iron Age society and the constant threat of conflict that kept the population inside heavily fortified walls. There were in fact hundreds of hillforts across the landscape of southern Britain during the first millennium BC.

Danebury is a small, low hill some 20 km (12 mi) northwest of the modern city of Winchester in the chalk downs of southeast England (Fig. 6.30). Three

Fig. 6.30.
Aerial view of Danebury hillfort and the encircling ditches in southern England.

massive earth walls and ditches mark the site today, enclosing an area of 5 ha (12½ acres) that was at one time one of the larger towns in England. Although the hill of Danebury is only 40 m (130 ft) above the surrounding plain, the white chalk ramparts of the fortifications would have been visible for many kilometers. The site would have dominated the landscape.

Barry Cunliffe of Oxford University conducted excavations at Danebury for twenty years, from 1968 to 1989. In that period, the gates and parts of the walls and the interior were examined in detail. Almost 40 percent of the interior of the citadel was uncovered. Artifacts at the site included some 160,000 pieces of pottery, 240,000 bits of animal bone, many stone objects such as querns, bone tools used for weaving, and lots of iron and bronze artifacts. The number of features inside the walls was staggering: approximately 2,400 pits were excavated, 10,000 postholes, and more than 500 smaller rectangular structures.

Within the enclosure, houses (both rectangular and circular in form) were aligned along streets extending more or less east to west across the interior—but not all were contemporary. Numerous small square or rectangular structures, which may have been grain silos, were also revealed. In the center were four unusual, small rectangular structures, which might have been temples or shrines of some kind. The hillfort may well have been the seat of a ruler or chieftain and his family, retinue, and craftsmen, as well as a farming community. There are traces of craft and industry on a large scale.

Posts, burned mud daub, and house floors marked the hundred or so round houses made of timber, mud, and wattle. There were also some 500 smaller, rectangular storage structures inside the walls. Oak and hazel were particularly common in construction. Oak was used for larger posts and frameworks; hazel was used for wattle to build walls, fences, and other structures. The hazel was grown and coppiced by the inhabitants in order to get long, straight branches. Clay was brought into the site from some distance for making daub for the mud walls and other objects. Thatch from nearby wetlands would have been available for roofing and other purposes.

The typical house was a circular, one-door structure, 6–9 m (20–30 ft) in diameter. Walls were either of wattle and daub or vertical planks, caulked with moss and resin. The floors of the houses were made by a rammed chalk technique, packing down the surface of the chalk to make a smooth surface. The houses often had one or more large, deep pits inside (Fig. 6.31). The opening of these pits on the house floor was only 50 cm (1.6 ft) in diameter and could have been covered with a board or wicker lid. These were storage facilities for grain and other materials. In some cases, when these pits were abandoned they were reused for burial of human or animal remains. In some instances this practice seems to be normal internment or disposal of animal carcasses, and in others there appears to be some ceremonial or ritual involved in the placement of the remains.

One of the most intriguing finds at Danebury was evidence for grain storage on a prodigious scale. The enormous storage capacity seems far in excess of the needs of the occupants of the site itself, who were estimated to have been

Fig. 6.31.
Excavations at
Danebury revealed a
Swiss cheese of pits,
posts, and trenches on
the surface of the chalk
subsoil.

between 200 and 350 at any one time. It has been suggested that the primary function of Danebury was to act as a central place for storage and protection of grain supplies for the people in the surrounding landscape.

Plant and animal remains were abundant in the pits and elsewhere at Danebury. Important crops were spelt wheat and six-row barley, both winter-sown varieties. Winter sowing meant an early crop at a time when stored supplies may have been running low. Some forty species of weeds were also found among the cereals, revealing the soil types and field conditions in which the domestic crops were raised. The primary food species were cattle, sheep, and pigs.

Craft production took place on two levels at Danebury. The household likely produced much of its own domestic equipment. Raw materials for many items were readily available: clay, chalk, wood, bone, antler, leather, sinew, wool, straw, horn, reeds. Other materials such as iron, bronze, and stone had to be imported.

Pottery is abundant at Danebury. There are more than 100,000 sherds from the first decade of excavations alone. Two kinds of pottery were made, simple undecorated vessels of sandy clay and finely made bowls with shoulder decorations. Specialists were likely responsible for these finely made bowls and attest to the second level of craft production at the site. There were probably specialists in several other crafts such as carpentry and blacksmithing, along with production of textiles, leather, and baskets and mats. Cloth production is evidenced by numerous spindle whorls, loom weights, and weaving combs. Spindle whorls are perforated clay disks placed on one end of a wooden spindle for spinning yarn. The whorl acts like a flywheel to maintain the momentum of the turning spindle. Weights of stone or ceramic are hung on the vertical warp of a loom to keep tension on the threads.

Apart from the practical aspects of the finds from Danebury, there are a number of intriguing and difficult-to-understand bits of evidence for the beliefs and rituals that must have been embedded in life and death at the site.

Fig. 6.32.
The ramparts of Danebury in winter.

There are repeated burials of horses, dogs, birds (particularly ravens) and humans in the storage pits. This pattern suggests perhaps that some or all of these animals, as well as humans, were sacrificed as part of the offerings or beliefs of the inhabitants. Along with the buildings that likely served as shrines, we must imagine that religion played a large role in the rhythm of days at Danebury.

The defenses of Danebury were remodeled several times during the occupation of the site between 550 and 100 BC (Fig. 6.32). The first defensive structure was a single wall and ditch. This region has chalk bedrock very close to the surface, a material that is relatively easy to dig. The chalk from the ditch was used to fill large, rectangular timber containers to build up a 4 m (13 ft) high rampart, or wall, along the inside of the trench. The defensive nature of the structure is emphasized by the find of thousands of round sling stones that would have been hurled at attackers. The east gate was an opening 4 m (13 ft) wide in the rampart, with a fortified timber gatehouse.

Fifty years or so later, the fortifications were enhanced. The ramparts were raised higher and the east gateway was widened to 9 m (30 ft). A century after that, the rampart was raised again and the V-shaped ditch deepened until it was 6 m deep and around 12 m (40 ft) wide. A stone wall was likely erected on top of the rampart to heighten the defenses once again. The distance from the bottom of the ditch to the top of the rampart was about 16 m (50 ft). The east gateway was strengthened twice by making it longer and constructing earthworks on either side of the entrance. Eventually a second ditch was dug outside the first, doubling the size of the enclosure.

Around 100 BC the eastern entrance was burned down. The burning of the gates was probably the result of an attack. Charnel pits near the gate contain almost one hundred bodies of men, women, and children, many with injuries that appear to have been inflicted by weapons such as spears and swords. This event marked the end of significant human settlement at Danebury, and the site was largely abandoned from that point in time.

GRAUBALLE, DENMARK, 300 BC

Archaeologists rarely find flesh on the bones of the past. Much of what we know about our ancestors and their lives comes from piecing together information from fragments of pots and tools, discarded bones and buried skeletons—the broken, forgotten, and hidden remnants of what human society once created. Unusual situations, especially in the case of human bodies preserved from the past, immediately capture our attention. These discoveries spotlight the fragile nature of the human condition. Ötzi the Iceman was a striking example of such a find.

Among the most remarkable of preserved prehistoric bodies are the "bog people" from northern Europe. Hundreds of individuals have been found in the peat bogs of northern Germany and southern Scandinavia, dating largely to the centuries around the birth of Christ. These bogs have marvelous preservative powers. The accumulation of peat and organic detritus that fills these swamps and mires contains tannin from the leaves and bark of oak trees. Tannin, used for tanning hides, is one essential factor in preservation of the skin of the bog bodies. A second is the waterlogged condition of the bogs, an oxygen-free environment free of the bacteria that would break down soft tissues.

These bogs in northern Europe have been used as a source of fuel for many hundreds of years. The organic matter in the bog is peat, which, when dried, burns slowly and produces heat, making it an important fuel in areas where forests had been largely decimated by the expansion of agriculture and the growth of industry. Until the twentieth century, peat was cut from bogs by hand, the blocks laid out to dry and sold for fuel. The peat cutters who worked in the bogs often encountered various ancient objects that had ended up in these former lakes.

The bog bodies are usually not the result of accidental drowning or disappearance. Some of these individuals may have been executed for their

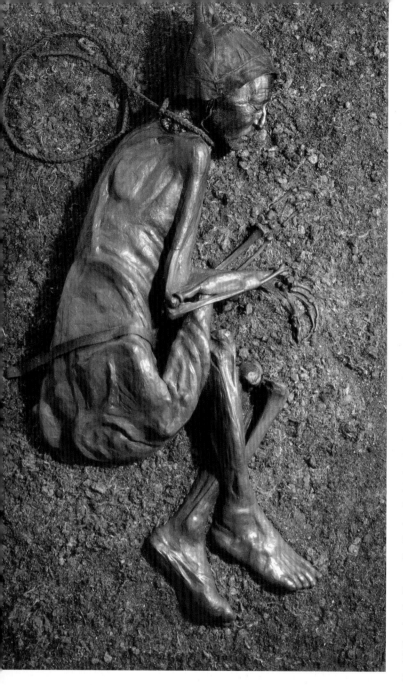

crimes, but others were there as a consequence of the religious beliefs and practices of early Iron Age society. These people viewed certain lakes and bogs as sacred places where sacrifices were to be made to the gods. Long braids of human hair were cut off and thrown into the bogs as one form of offering. Offerings of food were made in the form of sacrificed animals and pots filled with various fare. Weapons and jewelry of bronze, iron, and gold were also placed in the mire to appease the gods. And men and women were sometimes intentionally sacrificed in these sacred places.

One of the best-known examples is Tollund Man, exhumed from the bogs of Denmark by the late P. V. Glob of the Danish National Museum. Tollund Man was placed in the murky waters of a peat bog in central Denmark almost 2,000 years ago. As Glob described it, the body was very well preserved; even his eyelashes and beard were readily visible. Tollund Man had been strangled; a thin leather garrote was still tightly wound around his neck (Fig. 6.33). He was naked except for a small leather cap and a belt around his waist. Tollund Man was well groomed when he died, and his hands were soft and uncalloused, not used for hard labor. His last meal was a gruel of many kinds of seeds and grains. His execution in the spring of the year may have been related to the rituals of Iron Age society that required sacrifice and offerings for the resurrection of the year and the bounty of the earth.

Most of the human remains from the bogs have been examined in detail, as the bodies are an encyclopedia of information about the past and a source of great human interest. One of the best-studied examples comes from a place called Grauballe in Denmark. Grauballe Man, as he is known, was a thirty-to-thirty-five-year-old male whose throat had been slashed before he was placed in a small bog sometime around 300 BC. He had been put into a small pit in the bog created by removal of peat for fuel some years earlier.

After more than 2,000 years, his body came to light again in 1952. Several men cutting peat in the Grauballe bog exposed the body about one meter (3.3 ft) below the surface of the ground. The local doctor and an archaeologist were called in to remove one of the most important finds in Danish prehistory from its resting place.

The body was excavated *en bloc*. A wooden frame was placed completely around the corpse and the material in which it was buried, so that a rectangular block of peat along with the body were removed *in situ* from the bog. The block was carefully moved to the Moesgaard Museum, near the city of Aarhus, for further excavation, cleaning, and study. The body underwent extensive examination and conservation for three years, before becoming a focus of great public interest in the museum exhibit in 1955.

Conservation of a complete bog body had not really been attempted before. Only the head of the Tollund Man, discovered two years before Grauballe, had been prepared for exhibit. A good bit of care went into determining the best methods for preservation. Eventually it was decided to tan the skin of Grauballe Man like fine leather. The interior cavities in the body were filled with small chips of oak bark.

On the fiftieth anniversary of the discovery, a new series of investigations were done, taking advantage of the new technologies and methods that had come into archaeology in the intervening period. The second round of studies involved many disciplines, more than forty scientists, and many new methods, among them radiological examinations, CT scanning and 3D visualization, stereolithography, an endoscopic exam, isotope studies of the hair, new AMS dating, magnetic resonance imaging and spectroscopy of the intestines, botanical study of their contents, and a forensic reconstruction of the face. That's quite a litany of techniques, but the amount of new information obtained is remarkable.

Examination of the body permitted an estimate of the height of Grauballe Man of 165–170 cm (5'7"), about average stature for the period. His hair was in place on his head, and he had a reddish stubble of whiskers remaining on his face (Fig. 6.34). His hair was 15 cm (6 in) long with straight-cut ends, indicating that scissors were used. He was originally found with a short beard and moustache, which were lost during the conservation process. The eyes, nose, and mouth were well preserved. He had bad teeth, heavily worn from a diet of coarsely ground grain, probably mixed with some grit. He must have suffered from toothaches due to active infection in two of his teeth at the time of death. Careful examination of his teeth revealed dark, horizontal rings in the enamel, a symptom of stress, disease, or poor nutrition.

His arms, legs, feet, and hands were particularly well preserved. The nails on his fingers and even his fingerprints were intact. It was suggested after the discovery that the absence of calluses on his hands indicated an easy life, but it is also possible that immersion in the bog had softened the skin and disguised any evidence of hard labor.

The insides of Grauballe Man were also well preserved, so the contents of his intestines could be studied in detail to learn about his diet. The gut

Fig.6.34.
The body of Grauballe Man as he was found in the bog.

contained the remains of several meals before his death, likely from a gruel or soup composed of the seeds of sixty types of weeds along with about 20 percent domesticated cereals (rye, oats, barley, and two types of wheat). The botanists who examined this material suggested the gut contents were the by-product of grain processing, the material left after threshing and collecting the grains themselves. There were also small pieces of charcoal and sand consumed with the meals. Such residual material from the threshing floor is usually food for the poor or fodder for animals. The absence of fresh herbs or berries in the gut contents argues for the winter or early spring season as the time of death.

One part of the new study of the Grauballe Man involved a forensic reconstruction. The skull was scanned by MRI and a copy made in plastic. A specialist in England, Caroline Wilkinson, used the copy of the skull to rebuild the muscles and soft tissues of the face and added skin to re-create his face. Such specialists have made detailed studies of how tissues attach to bone in the face. These methods are used in criminal cases today to reconstruct the victim of a crime where only the skeleton remains. Relatives of victims have been able to identify them from forensic reconstructions, which suggests they are generally accurate and reliable. The reconstruction (Fig. 6.35) has not been painted and remains the brown color of the plasticine used to mold the features.

MANCHING, GERMANY, 300 BC

Manching was a large commercial center and *oppidum* in the La Tène Iron Age. The town was located on a level plain adjacent to the Danube River in Bavaria, Germany. In contrast to many of the larger settlements from this time, Manching was not in a high defensive position; nor was the town initially fortified. The site was founded around 300 BC and quickly developed as an important center of trade, craft, finance, and political power. The town was likely an important place for markets and fairs. Manching controlled a major east-west route through central Europe, running along the Danube. A period of unrest around 100 BC led to construction of a city wall that also enclosed some agricultural land. Manching was eventually abandoned, by 50 BC.

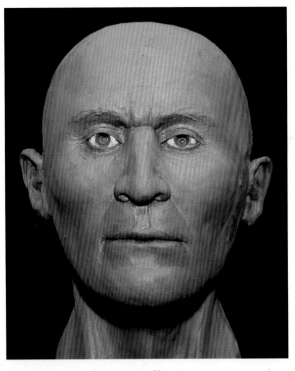

Fig. 6.35.
Forensic reconstruction of the face of Grauballe Man.

The city wall had a circumference of 7 km (4 mi), enclosing 380 ha (940 acres), most of which was settled with houses and other buildings. Today, only sections of the ramparts and two projecting gate towers are visible. The wall may have originally been built to display the importance of the town as a focal point for commercial activities, and only later did it take on a defensive nature. There were a number of buried individuals found at the site who died from injuries sustained in battle. A second stage of construction reinforced the entire length of the enclosure. Excavations also revealed a harbor area at the river's edge, adjacent to the settlement.

The town of Manching had an extensive planned street system following a grid, with residential areas, sanctuaries, and other official and commercial facilities (Fig. 6.36). Structures include rows of stalls, homes, and even warehouses for the agricultural produce that made up the bulk of exchanged goods. The archaeological remains from the town indicate an armed elite in residence, specialized craftsmen, a mint for producing coins, and evidence of abundant imported goods. The appearance of mints and currency imply the operation of market economies in the Iron Age. Market economies are, of course, commonplace today but emerged to replace barter and trade. Market economies use money and prices to regulate the exchange of goods and services, depending on supply and demand.

The central part of the site was organized to facilitate trade and production. These activities included collection of raw materials and manufacture of finished products. Manching is exceptional for the wealth and diversity of

Fig. 6.36.
Reconstruction of part of the interior of Manching.

material evidence collected there. Raw materials used in producing glass, pottery, iron, and bronze indicate that Manching was a thriving center for craft production. Different areas of the site may have had their own specialized industries. The excavations have revealed a dense cluster of small workshops along the main east-west road, apparently occupied by specialists in textile production. One of the palisaded enclosures contained a dense concentration of fragments of coin molds for gold and silver coins.

Slag from iron is fairly widely scattered over the settlement. The abundant finds of iron objects at Manching and other sites document enormous growth in iron production at this time. Iron objects found in the excavations include keys, personal ornaments, swords, spears, and shield bosses, as well as a wide range of specialist tools, among them various types of hammer, files, compasses, drills, plowshares, wagon fittings, and sickles. Iron bars found in the settlement suggest that iron was also traded in large quantities. Indeed, the abundant bog ore deposits in the local wetlands may have been an important reason for the location and growth of Manching.

Handicrafts were established as independent professions in Celtic towns. Objects for daily use were produced in quantity and sold as part of an extensive domestic economy. Pottery production and trade was an important industry at Manching; imported pottery, fine graphite ceramics, coarse wares, smooth wheel-thrown pottery, and painted pottery were all used in this period. Forty-eight amphorae that originally contained Mediterranean wine are among the items imported to the site. Fine graphite cooking pots were made with a special clay that contained graphite imported from 200 km down the Danube. Various products were traded across central and southern Germany, and beyond, reaching central France. The potter's wheel was introduced to central Europe in the fifth century BC and allowed mass production of ceramics; wheel-thrown pottery could be produced quickly in large quantities. Fine painted wares and wheel-turned and handmade domestic and storage vessels were also mass-produced.

Religious or ceremonial activities are also in evidence at the site. Several examples of a distinctive quadrangular enclosure with a central structure have been found that resemble the cult shrines seen at Gournay-sur-Aronde (discussed below) and elsewhere in Celtic Europe. Excavations in 1984 turned up a cult tree with a wooden trunk, covered in gold leaf, and a side branch with bronze leaves, along with gilded acorns (Fig. 6.37). It was found in a wooden box, also decorated with gold leaf. An iron horse sculpture from the second century BC at the site may also be a cult statue.

The reasons for the demise of Manching are unclear; the site was abandoned before the Roman conquest in 15 BC. Some scholars have suggested that Germanic invaders destroyed the town. Other information indicates the town may have moved to the north of its original location.

MAIDEN CASTLE, ENGLAND, 43 BC

Maiden Castle is a storehouse for the later prehistory of Great Britain. Situated atop a high, saddleback hill in the downs of Dorset, near the southern coast of England, Maiden

Fig. 6.37.
The golden tree found at Manching. The leaves are 2–3 cm in length.

Castle dominated its Iron Age landscape and was probably the largest hillfort in all of Europe (Fig. 6.38). The massive ramparts enclose an area of 18 ha (90 acres), the equivalent of fifty soccer fields.

The major settlements from the Iron Age in Europe are these defended hilltops, found throughout southern Germany, France, and Britain. The fortresses and their inhabitants were formidable; the Romans frequently remarked on the strength of the walls that surrounded these hilltops. Roman writers reported on the ferocity of the warriors, describing the bold *gaesatae,* spearmen who went naked into battle. Roman statuary commemorated the valor of the Celts as fair-haired warriors with drooping moustaches. In a famous sculpture, a defiant yet defeated Celt puts himself to the sword rather than surrender to the Romans. That the Romans should so admire the character of their boisterous and aggressive enemy is itself a remarkable statement about the Celts.

Sir Mortimer Wheeler excavated parts of the site from 1934 through 1937, and more recent excavations were undertaken during the 1980s. Wheeler was a major figure in British archaeology, highly respected for both the quality of his work and his concern with the education of archaeologists. Wheeler's forte was the stratigraphic section, excavation of trenches and squares across manmade features to reveal the sequence and methods of construction. This vertical wall, or profile, of excavated trenches and squares provides information

Fig. 6.38.
Aerial photo of Maiden Castle near the south coast of England.

essential to understanding the history of a site. Recording these sections in photographs and drawings creates a permanent record of the sequence of events for the archaeologist to interpret. Wheeler's precise excavations and recording methods have revealed much about the prehistory of Maiden Castle, from the Neolithic to the Roman conquest of Britain.

The hilltop was first used around 3700 B C as a Neolithic camp; an enormous barrow was erected here during the same period, overlooking the adjacent valley. This Neolithic long barrow ran for more than 550 m (1,800 ft) across the hilltop, marked by two parallel ditches, each 5 m wide (16 ft), 15 m (50 ft) apart. Maiden Castle was the center of an elaborate landscape of henge monuments, timber settings, and causewayed camps.

In the Iron Age, around 500 B C, fortifications were first constructed around a growing market center on the hilltop. The first fort at Maiden Castle was univallate (having one wall) and enclosed some 6 hectares. Large hillforts such as Maiden Castle appear to have had administrative, religious, economic, and residential functions in a proto-urban context.

There are several distinct areas within Maiden Castle. An Iron Age shrine or temple was uncovered on the most prominent part of the hilltop. This structure was later replaced by a Roman temple, documenting the continuity of religious significance and focus. The hilltop served as a residence as well as a fortified storehouse for the agricultural surplus from the rich farmlands. Residential structures dot the hilltop; evidence of dense occupation suggests that as many as 2,000–4,000 people lived there. Large pits were dug into the chalk, up to 3 m (10 ft) deep, used for storage, water reservoirs, and other purposes. Excavations also revealed the parallel ruts of wagon wheels crossing the defended interior; the standard wheel-to-wheel distance in the later Iron Age was 1.46 m (almost 5 ft). More recent excavations have uncovered numerous structures and an enormous quantity of refuse in the form of pottery, bronze and iron artifacts, and animal bones. Most of the animal bones were from sheep, and several showed signs of malnutrition.

By 50 B C, shortly before the first Roman invasion of Britain, the fortifications were expanded and the enclosed area inside the hillfort tripled in size (Fig. 6.39). The final set of fortifications consisted of a set of three enormous concentric banks and two ditches; a fourth bank was built at the south end for additional protection. The term *multivallate* describes large hillforts with complex defenses of multiple ditches and ramparts. Some of the walls at Maiden Castle still stand as high as 20 m (65 ft) today. These walls had a stone foundation 4 m (13 ft) high and a massive wooden palisade on top. A narrow, serpentine, and dangerous path leads to the entrance at the eastern end of the hilltop. At the entrance were wooden gates 4 m (13 ft) wide. Some 22,000 sling stones were found in caches near the walls, for one of the important defensive weapons in use during that period.

In spite of its massive defenses against attack, Maiden Castle fell to the Roman legions and their siege artillery in A D 43. One dramatic find near the entrance to the fortifications was an iron spear head from the Roman war machines, lodged in the backbone of a defender (Fig. 6.40).

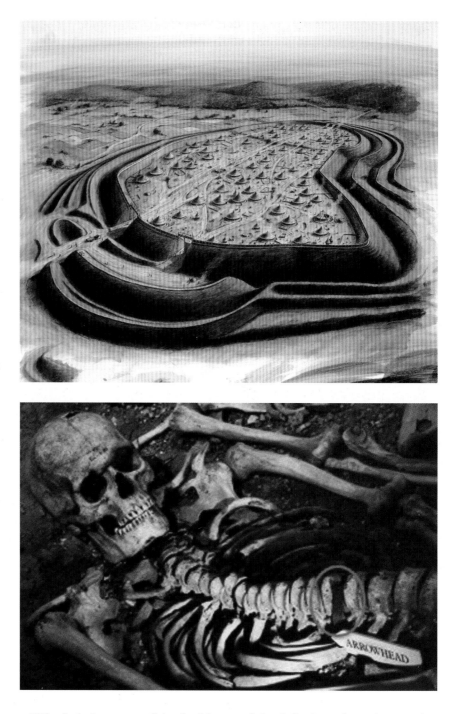

Fig. 6.39.
An artist's reconstruction of the multivallate ditches, rampart fortifications, western entrance, and the Iron Age settlement at Maiden Castle.

Fig. 6.40.
A Roman ballista iron arrowhead lodged in the back of one of the defenders of Maiden Castle.

Wheeler's depiction of the final hours of the defenders of Maiden Castle is a masterpiece of archaeological interpretation and prose:

> Before the close fighting began, the regiment of catapults or *ballistæ,* which habitually accompanied a legion on campaign, put down a barrage across the gateway, causing casualties at the outset. Following

the barrage, the Roman infantry advanced up the slope, cutting its way from rampart to rampart, tower to tower. In the innermost bay of the entrance, a number of huts had been recently built; these were now set alight, and under the rising clouds of smoke the gates were stormed. But resistance had been obstinate and the attack was pushed home with every savagery. The scene became that of a massacre in which the wounded were not spared. Finally, the gates were demolished and the stone walls which flank them reduced to the lowly and ruinous condition in which we found them, nineteen centuries later [Wheeler, 1943, p. 47].

GOURNAY-SUR-ARONDE/RIBEMONT-SUR-ANCRE, FRANCE, 260 BC

A little over three decades ago, very little was known about the religion of the Celts except for the largely Roman historical sources, which described various practices of these peoples. These reports are informative, but they may also be biased by personal or political convictions. The Celts were thought to be barbarians—uncivilized people, who deserved to be conquered in order to be taught certain basic values and behaviors.

The archaeological breakthrough in regard to Celtic religion came from aerial photography in northern France. Air photographs taken during dry years in the early 1970s revealed the location of a number of distinctive structures that were thought to be pre-Roman Celtic sanctuaries (Fig. 6.41). Two of them, Gournay-sur-Aronde and Ribemont-sur-Ancre, are discussed in this section. These constructions have largely the same layout with two square structures, one inside the other. The structures were built from timber and mudbrick. The interior square is the temple itself, in which the god or altar was placed. The inner structure was surrounded by a square ditch and palisade with a large timber gate. The outer square was a courtyard or gallery surrounding the temple, where worshippers could venerate the gods, conduct sacrifices and feasts, and celebrate victories. The entrance to the temple area was oriented at the rising sun on the summer solstice. The entire area was 14–18 m (45–60 ft) on a side.

The excavations at Gournay-sur-Aronde took place from 1975 to 1984, under the

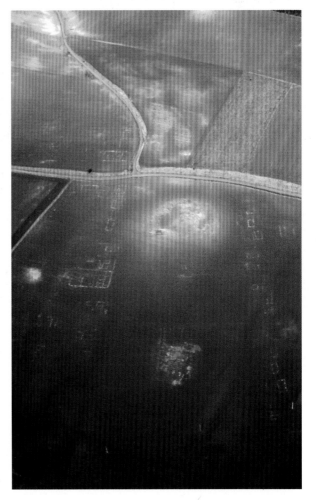

Fig. 6.41. Aerial photo revealing the site of Ribemont-sur-Ancre. The pre-Roman Celtic sanctuary is the structure I the lower center of the photo. The other features seen in the photo are from later Roman use of the area.

direction of Jean-Louis Brunaux, and exposed the first example of a Celtic shrine (Fig. 6.42). Those excavations provided a model for finding similar sites, and a few years later, in 1990, the sanctuary at Ribemont-sur-Ancre became the focus of excavations, again led by Brunaux.

The excavations at Gournay-sur-Aronde, Ribemont-sur-Ancre, and elsewhere have demonstrated that the Celts built permanent ritual sites, that religious practice was not simply spontaneous. Dated to the beginning of the third century BC, these cult centers were likely the work of the Belgae, a Celtic tribe thought to have moved to northern Gaul from central Europe. The rituals performed at Gournay-sur-Aronde and Ribemont-sur-Ancre involved both animal sacrifice and triumphant display of the remains of enemies killed in battle or sacrificed to the gods of the underworld, from whom the Celts believed they themselves were descended.

At Gournay-sur-Aronde, a massive timber palisade with a ditch on either side formed the outer square and enclosed the inner sanctuary. A single entrance, facing east, was marked by a monumental gateway (Fig. 6.43). A square inner structure, 15 m (50 ft) on a side, covered a large pit, described as a sunken altar. The bodies of sacrificed animals were placed in this pit to decompose; the skulls were nailed to the gate. Also in the enclosure there were tall wooden posts with collections of weapon trophies—helmets, shields, spears, and swords—displayed at the top. Finally there were several large trees growing inside the enclosure, probably related to the Celtic reverence

Fig. 6.42.

Plan of the excavations at Gournay-sur-Aronde with the outer trench and palisade, littered with weapons and human sacrifices, and the inner sanctum and large pit or altar. Several stages of construction are shown.

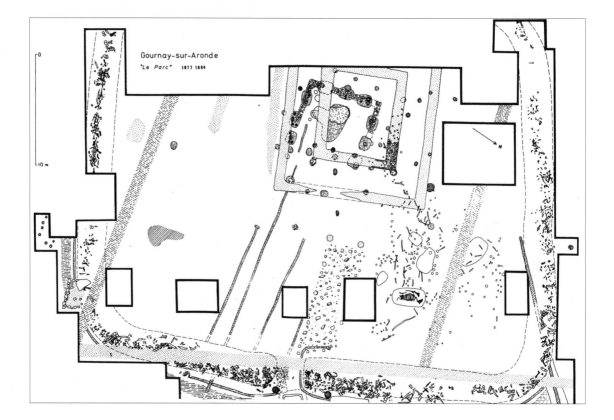

Fig. 6.43.
An artist's
reconstruction of the
sanctuary at Gournay-
sur-Aronde.

for nature and sacred trees. Two thousand weapons and pieces of armor were found in the ditch surrounding the enclosure. These war trophies were the equipment of some 500 individuals and may originally been on the top of posts or arranged on a platform near the monumental gateway.

The important site of Ribemont-sur-Ancre is located about 50 km (30 mi) to the north of Gournay-sur-Aronde. It was discovered from the air in 1963. The site itself is large and contains archaeological material from several time periods. Much of the site belongs to a large Roman villa, which included baths, auxiliary buildings, a 3,000-seat theater, and a sanctuary on the highest part of the hill. The sanctuary was here before the villa and continued in use in various forms after the arrival of the Romans. The first sanctuary was probably built in 260 BC. The archaeological materials from the sanctuary represent trophies of battle, the remains of hundreds of individuals, and thousands of shields, spear points, and a few iron swords. These weapons were likely war booty and represent the largest collection of Celtic weapons in Europe.

The sacrificially crushed and burned bones of nearly 1,000 enemies were found in the inner precinct at Ribemont-sur-Ancre. War trophies at this site also included beheaded corpses and piles of long bones (Fig. 6.44). The headless skeletons of eighty individuals were found along one wall of the enclosure, thrown together with weapons and other equipment. These individuals were probably displayed along with their weapons on a platform inside the shrine before the bodies completely decomposed.

The Roman author Diodorus Siculus, in his first-century *History,* described Celtic head-hunting as follows:

> They cut off the heads of enemies slain in battle and attach them to the necks of their horses. The bloodstained spoils they hand over to their attendants and... they nail up these first fruits upon their houses, just as do those who lay low wild animals in certain kinds of hunting.

Fig. 6.44.
The mass of human
bone found at
Ribemont-sur-Ancre,
war trophies in the
Celtic shrine.

They embalm in cedar oil the heads of the most distinguished enemies, and preserve them carefully in a chest, and display them with pride to strangers.

It seems a bit hypocritical to read the Romans criticizing the barbaric practices of others. At the same time, the description by Diodorus rings true. The headless corpses in the sanctuary at Ribemont-sur-Ancre seem to confirm the head-taking practices of the Celtic warriors. These sanctuaries appear to have a dual role, both martial and religious. The displays of bodies, war booty, and crushed and burned bones must have been the stuff of legends to their enemies. No doubt these were also places of victory and celebration, as well as cultic practice. The bodies of the animals and enemies can also be seen as offerings to the important Celtic gods of the underworld from whom the power of the warriors derived.

CELTIC RELIGION

Celtic peoples left no written records about their religion, and relatively little is known about their beliefs and practices. Only a few distinctly ceremonial objects have survived from the period (Fig. 6.45). Modern historians, relying on reports by Caesar and others, have characterized the religion of the Celts in Gaul as spontaneous, in contrast to the well-planned cultic practices of the Greeks and Romans. Religious practices and places of worship have been generally ignored by the historians. A few Roman authors, however, did describe sacred enclosures or temples of the Celts.

The Celts had a pantheon of more than 200 gods and goddesses and a powerful clerical hierarchy (soothsayers, priests, singers, and the like). According to Greek and Roman accounts, there was a priestly caste of religious specialists called the druids, although very little is known about them. The Celts

Fig. 6.45.
The Strettweg cult wagon with various human and animal figures, about 30 cm high. There was likely a large bronze bowl attached to the raised platform on the wagon.

worshipped nature and its forces and did not have anthropomorphic deities. They venerated their gods in various ways, sometimes through votive offerings and sacrifices of both animals and humans. The numerous bones of sacrificed animals that have been excavated come exclusively from domesticated species; wild animals do not appear to have been sacrificed.

Two types of sacrifice seem to have been practiced, judging by the animal remains. Young pigs and lambs were killed in the spring or early summer and consumed at feasts inside the ritual structures. A second form of animal sacrifice involved cattle: bulls, oxen, and cows. The animal would be killed and the body placed in a large pit inside the enclosure of the shrine to rot. The remains of at least fifty cattle have been found in such a context.

There is substantial archaeological evidence that human sacrifice was an important aspect of the religious practices of these Iron Age Celts. Mass graves have been unearthed both Gournay-sur-Aronde and Ribemont-sur-Ancre; the excavator of these sites interpreted them as places of human sacrifice in devotion to a war god. Various scholars believe that the Celts gave reverence to the power of the human head. Ownership and display of the heads of enemies allowed warriors and chiefs to retain and control the power of the deceased.

SOME REFLECTIONS

Several events marked the beginning of the La Tène period of the Iron Age in Northern Europe, between 500 BC and the birth of Christ. The collapse of trade with the Mediterranean, rapid population increase, and conflict led to expansion and a series of migrations to the south and east of the Celtic heartland. People known as the Gauls moved into northern Italy and the

Po River Valley, farther east into Romania, and eventually Anatolia in Asia Minor. Around 390 BC, the Gauls sacked Rome.

With the decline of long-distance trade, local craftsmanship improved, and a spectacular, powerful style of art and decoration predominated among the Celts. These crafts, along with many other aspects of society, were concentrated in towns in the Celtic areas of Europe. These towns most often occupied *oppida*, the heavily walled and fortified centers of political and economic power. Maiden Castle is just one of many examples of these centers that eventually fell to the Romans as their empire expanded.

A very different sequence of events characterized the Mediterranean. By 800 BC, the effects of growing population and urbanization led to the emergence of Greek city-states as major powers. Conquest and continuing population expansion brought Greek colonization of several areas to the east and west of the homeland. Colonies appeared in Sicily, southern Italy, southern France, and Spain, as the eastern Mediterranean could not contain the growing numbers of Greeks, Phoenicians, and Carthaginians. Local demand for Greek goods was high in the west. At one site in Spain, for example, 1,400 Greek pottery vessels were found in a single, small excavation. A single grave at an Iron Age cemetery in Spain held gold jewelry that included a seal from Syria and an earring from Egypt.

Fig. 6.46.

The maximum extent of the Roman Empire, ca. AD 116.

Trade and colonization during the earlier half of the Iron Age, the first millennium BC, changed to warfare after 400 BC as the dynamics of power shifted to the Italian peninsula. The Greeks, and later the Romans, encoded

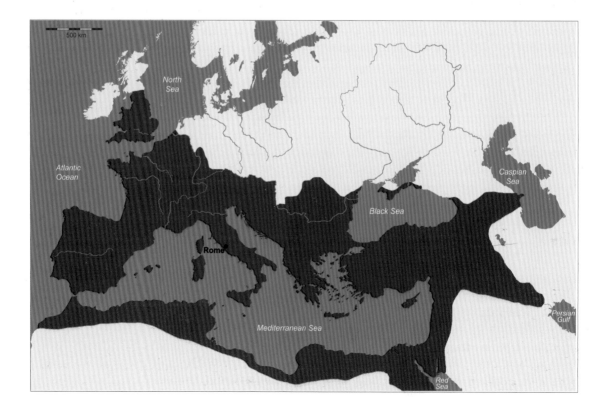

Fig. 6.47.
The limits of Rome. Hadrian's Wall in Northumberland marked the border of empire. The wall ran 120 km from the east to the west coast of northern England; it was originally 3 m wide and 5–6 m in height.

systems of law, military drafts, and elaborate bureaucracies, characteristics of high-level state societies. As classical Greece declined in power, Rome began to build its empire (Fig. 6.46). The Macedonians under Philip, and later Alexander the Great (356–323 BC), had turned to the east, setting out against Asia. By 290 BC. the Romans had spread into most of Italy, and by 140 BC they had eliminated their major rivals at Corinth in Greece and Carthage in North Africa. Rome controlled the Mediterranean and then turned toward the interior of Europe. Roman trade and colonization at first focused on Spain as an important source of raw materials.

Soon, however, trade routes and the wealth of northern Europe captured the attention of the Romans. Julius Caesar led the legions against the Gauls who occupied France, the Britons in the British Isles, and other groups in parts of central and eastern Europe. From 59 to 51 BC, Caesar pushed the boundaries of the Roman Empire across France to the Rhine River, largely destroying indigenous society in the process. In one instance, following the siege and conquest of the town of Cenabrum (modern Orleans in northern France), the Romans killed all but 300 of the 40,000 men, women, and children taking refuge in the fortress. By the birth of Christ, Rome controlled virtually all of southern and western Europe. A few decades later, the empire extended across the Channel into much of England (Fig. 6.47). A few pockets of indigenous Iron Age peoples remained in Ireland and Scotland and on some of the Atlantic and Channel islands.

Fig. 6.48.
An Iron Age village reconstructed at Sagnland Lejre, Denmark.

North of the Rhine, the Germanic tribes resisted and eventually outlasted the Roman Empire. The Germanic Iron Age followed the Roman period and extended from the birth of Christ through most of the first millennium AD. In this area of Germany, Scandinavia, and eastern Europe, warrior societies continued and flourished. These groups consisted of small, yet highly productive, agricultural communities (Fig. 6.48). Society was largely egalitarian, and authority was vested in individuals of demonstrated strength and wit. Through time, these communities grew larger and more powerful, gradually forming alliances and creating larger polities.

Past and Present—Lessons from Prehistoric Europe

Europe before Rome

Significance

Relevance

Preservation

Appreciation

THIS CHAPTER concludes the story. I want to do several things here, all briefly. A quick summary of the prehistory of Europe may serve to remind you of the remarkable changes that have taken place in the last million years on the continent. I want to say something about the significance and relevance of the past, about why society should place value in learning of our prehistory, and about the importance of preserving it. I feel strongly that antiquity holds a salient message for both the present and the future that we are just beginning to comprehend. We need to keep some of that past intact for future generations. A final comment involves appreciation, recognition of the importance and beauty of what has been preserved in the archaeological record.

EUROPE BEFORE ROME

A summary of European prehistory in a few paragraphs is almost an impossibility, perhaps comparable to touring Paris in a quarter of an hour. Nevertheless, we can simplify the task by moving quickly through large blocks of time and recording only major developments. Our time scale starts in hundreds of thousands of years and compresses to millennia as we come closer to the present and more evidence accumulates.

Back to the beginning. One of the many species of Miocene apes in Africa, six to seven million years ago, began to walk constantly on two feet, as the climate warmed and dried and forests shrank and grasslands expanded. Some of their descendants turned into the earliest members of the genus *Homo* around 2.5 mya and moved, for the first time, out of Africa, shortly after 2 mya. These individuals arrived in Europe by at least 1.3 mya in a form known as *Homo antecessor*. The evidence from Atapuerca, Spain, and other sites indicates that they were meat eaters, and sometimes they ate each other. A few of their characteristic handaxe stone tools were also present.

By 500,000 BP *antecessor* evolved into *heidelbergensis* and humans were becoming better hunters. Places like Boxgrove and Schöningen hold dramatic evidence of both the weapons and the prey that were successfully taken. Fire enters the technological repertoire of our ancestors and provides warmth, protection, cooked food, and a focal point for the group. Closer human relations must have been forged by the warmth of the hearth. Neanderthals take over the line of human ancestry in Europe sometime after 250,000 years ago and hold the stage there until the arrival of modern humans around 40,000 years ago. The Neanderthals began to exhibit more human behaviors, such as caring for the weak and elderly. They covered their bodies with furs or skins. They buried some of their dead, occasionally with gifts, and must have imagined some existence after death.

Conflict and romance probably defined Neanderthals' relationships with the newly arrived *Homo sapiens* in Europe between 40,000 and 30,000 years ago. This new species displayed a creativity not seen before in the human past. Innovations included new hunting equipment, such as the spearthrower and the bow and arrow; domestication of the dog; shaping new materials such as bone, wood, shell, and ivory into more complex composite tools; transport or exchange of raw materials such as flint and shell over long distances; and sewn clothing, counting, crude calendars, and the first art. Figurines, cave paintings, engravings, and myriad decorations of other objects reflect this creative explosion that characterized Upper Paleolithic achievement. The first incontrovertible evidence of residential structures and camplike settlements appears in this period. These human groups in the Upper Paleolithic resemble the hunter-gatherers known from ethnographic accounts in historical times: small-scale societies composed of mobile groups of a few families each, with more or less egalitarian social relationships and food-sharing economies, dependent on the wild foods of the land.

The Pleistocene and the Upper Paleolithic came to an end some 10,000 years ago. The ice sheets retreated as warmer temperatures prevailed at the beginning of the Holocene epoch. This was the time of the Mesolithic, the last hunters in the warmer and more hospitable environments of the European continent, when humans began exploiting a broad spectrum of plants and animals from a wide range of habitats, prior to the arrival of farming and the Neolithic. Particularly notable is the use of marine and other aquatic resources in substantial quantities. Human groups appear to be well adapted, and evidence of more sedentary behavior appears in a variety of places across Europe.

In the ancient Near East certain human groups began to cultivate wild plants and herd wild animals toward the end of the Pleistocene, domesticating a number of species in the process. But the transition to farming was more than simple herding and cultivation. It entailed major, long-term changes in the structure and organization of the societies that adopted this new way of life, as well as a totally new relationship with the environment. Whereas hunter-gatherers largely lived off the land in an extensive fashion, generally exploiting a diversity of resources over a broad area, farmers intensively use a smaller portion of the landscape and modify the environment to create a milieu that suits their needs. With the transition to agriculture, truly humans began to manipulate the earth.

Most Mesolithic hunting and gathering societies disappear with the introduction of agriculture between 7000 and 4000 BC, starting in the southeast corner of Europe and moving to the north and west across the continent. The archaeology of Europe changed dramatically with the arrival of agriculture and the Neolithic. Small farming villages began to appear in Greece and on the Aegean islands after 7000 BC as farmers with domesticated plants and animals expanded from their place of origin in Southwest Asia. From this initial beachhead in Greece, agriculture took two routes as the spread continued. One was coastal, along the north shore of the Mediterranean; many of the islands were colonized for the first time in this period, and at the same time farming groups were spreading along the coastline. A second route went inland through Southeastern Europe as the Neolithic expanded into Central Europe. Pottery became a common feature of Neolithic sites, and residential architecture is more visible as new construction materials and methods permit more substantial structures. Settlements were larger and contained more people for longer periods of time. The economic changes that accompanied the Neolithic transformation were major. Long-distance trade became commonplace, and commodities in the form of raw materials, axes, pottery, foods, rare stones, and other materials traveled substantial distances. By 4000 BC, small farming villages had reached Britain and Scandinavia; domesticated plants and animals could be found almost everywhere in Europe within the limits of cultivation.

The introduction of metals began in the Neolithic with copper and gold, mined and melted primarily in southeastern Europe. This material was used largely for jewelry and axes and can be understood as a premonition of the coming Bronze Age. Bronze arrived in Europe after 3000 BC, earlier in the eastern Mediterranean, later in northwestern Europe. The Bronze Age witnessed major changes, initially and most spectacularly in the southeastern part of the continent. The Aegean area was the center of this development, first on the island of Crete and shortly thereafter on the Greek mainland. The Minoans on Crete and later the Mykeneans controlled the eastern Mediterranean of Europe and dominated trade with the rest of the continent. Crete and the Aegean became a magnet for the raw materials of Europe; metal ores of gold, copper, silver, and tin; amber, furs, and many other materials were funneled along major trade routes, rivers, and passes to the Aegean. There, craft specialists produced an abundance of finished products, including jewelry, metal weapons, cloth, wine, and oil, that were traded for additional wealth and power.

Along the trade routes in the interior of the continent, powerful societies emerged in places rich in resources or in control of strategic routes of trade and transport. Archaeological materials in Wessex in England, Bohemia in the

Czech Republic, and Denmark in Scandinavia document a wealthy Bronze Age culture with a rich entombed elite, buried with the treasures of the age. Weapons of bronze, martial motifs, fortifications, and evidence of warfare chronicle the rise of conflict and discord in this period, as wealth was unevenly distributed across the European landscape and power backed by military force became an essential component of politics.

The arrival of iron and its associated technology in Europe around 1000 BC intensified trends initiated earlier during the late Neolithic and Bronze Age. The classic civilizations of Greece and Rome arose in the last millennium before Christ, during the early Iron Age in Europe. From the sixth to fourth centuries, the eastern Mediterranean was dominated by Greek city-states such as Athens and Sparta, which were responsible for forging many of the features of Western civilization. At the same time, Etruscan civilization took hold in the northern Italian peninsula, leaving a lasting influence in art and architecture.

North of the Alps, prehistory continued. In temperate western Europe, "Celtic" and Germanic tribes with distinctive traditions and art styles were thriving. The fortresses of these warrior societies (known by their Roman name, *oppida*) dotted the landscape of western Europe. The tombs of nobles document the wealth and reach of those elites. Sacrifices and executions preserved in the bogs of the north offer a startling glimpse of some of the less fortunate inhabitants of that region.

The discipline and strength of the Roman legions finally overwhelmed many of these societies in France, Spain, and elsewhere, as Julius Caesar and his successors carried the legacy of Rome to western Europe. The Iron Age fortress of Maiden Castle in southern England was razed by the Romans in AD 43. By AD 125, the Romans had extended Hadrian's Wall across the northern border of England. Only those areas north and east of the Rhine River remained free of Roman rule and continued a tribal way of life for a short while longer. Eventually, during the first millennium AD, the spread of Christianity brought new religion, and a literate priesthood recorded history, closing the prehistoric aspect of Europe's past.

The first millennium AD in northern Europe was a time of great change and growth as both population and political organization increased. Village farming was the basic unit of subsistence and organization, and the development of such communities can be traced in some detail through this period. Urbanization was slow to reach the north; the first towns do not appear until the seventh century AD, functioning initially as important commercial centers.

The departure of the Romans brought new invaders to the British Isles. The Anglo-Saxons, originally Germanic peoples, established small kingdoms in what is now England and Scotland and introduced the Old English language. Meanwhile in Scandinavia, myriad late Iron Age groups grew in size and strength and began to expand to the east, south, and west. Raids by these groups, known as the Vikings, began after AD 750, and eventually Scandinavian settlers occupied large parts of what are now England and Scotland. The Vikings also colonized the islands of the North Atlantic and

Greenland, and they visited eastern North America for a brief period around AD 1000. In the tenth century AD, the Kingdom of England emerged from unification of the various Anglo-Saxon domains.

The spread of Christianity marked the beginning of the historic period in much of continental Europe north of the Alps. Charlemagne (ca. AD 742–814) unified the Franks and expanded the Frankish kingdom into an empire that incorporated much of Western Europe. His reign was associated with a flowering of art, religion, and culture through the medium of the Catholic Church. With his conquests and internal reforms, Charlemagne helped define both Western Europe and the Middle Ages. Christianity reached Britain in the fifth century AD and Scandinavia by 1000 AD, bringing more involvement with the rest of Europe, along with large towns and cities, kings and peasants, and almost constant medieval warfare. Europe was becoming distinctly European.

After AD 1000, much of Europe entered the Dark Ages, followed by the Renaissance, the Industrial Era, and today. We are only a millennium or two removed from a time when Europe was a totally different place, but even then the materials were available and the processes were under way for the emergence of European civilization.

SIGNIFICANCE

European prehistory is a story of spectacular change over time. Because of a long history of research and the richness of prehistoric remains, Europe is archaeologically one of the best-known places on Earth. There has been more research going on for a longer period than anywhere else on earth. The prehistory of Europe can be viewed as a model for the evolution of human society, from small bands of foragers and hunter-gatherers in the Pleistocene and early Holocene through the first hierarchical societies of the Neolithic to the powerful states of the Bronze and Iron Age. There are other models and different trajectories through the past in other places, but in Europe we see more of the details.

There are many big questions to consider in the archaeology of Europe. When did we become human? When did we become hunter-gatherers? What happened to the Neanderthals? What was responsible for the creative explosion that took place during the Upper Paleolithic? Why did hunters become farmers? How and why did social inequality emerge? Why are metals so important in human society? Why so much warfare and conflict? When did towns and cities appear in Europe, and why?

Answers to some of these questions are emerging in the study of European prehistory. Many of the what, where, and when questions have been resolved or at least penciled in. The how and why questions are much more difficult to answer. Some of these are big, existential issues that certainly have more than a single, simple solution. One of the exciting aspects of archaeology is the continuing pursuit of the answers.

There is, of course, excitement and mystery involved in unearthing treasures and learning about past lifeways. But beyond that, archaeology also tells us about ourselves and how we got to be the way we are. Ultimately, archaeology's greatest importance lies in the lessons it teaches about our past. The human condition is one that has changed and will change over time. To know our place and to have confidence about where we are going are essential for the success of our species.

RELEVANCE

There is no question that archaeology has significance and meaning in our modern world beyond its value in building human knowledge. In the twenty-first century, it seems that everything needs currency—that is, relevance to the present—and needs to contribute to the quality of life. Important issues today include climate change, social inclusion, environmental protection, and sustainable development. These are areas for which archaeology has decoded messages from the past. There is much to be learned from how our ancestors confronted these issues. We are not the first generation to deal with global warming, rising sea levels, or overpopulation. Archaeology reveals how humans, over thousands and millions of years, have survived and succeeded in the face of the difficult challenges of changing environments and competitive neighbors. We learn how past societies dealt with issues such as climate change, overpopulation, political competition, and success and failure.

Archaeology documents many instances of the problems of climatic and environmental changes that human groups have faced over the millennia. Archaeology records the climate changes and natural catastrophes and permits insight on their incidence and severity. Archaeology tells us what the human environment was like in the past and how changes have affected human societies. Information on terrain stability, flood hazards, changes in sea level, wildlife population dynamics, and the nature and distribution of plant and animal communities in the past are subjects of archaeological study. In the Netherlands, for example, archaeological studies of settlement and land use in prehistory have been an essential ingredient in planning and constructing the dikes and drainage systems that enclose much of the country. Sea level change is of great interest in an era of global warming; archaeologists have developed extensive records on the human use of coasts and changes in those coastlines over time. Climatic change and its effects on culture can be seen dramatically in studies of the past.

Catastrophic events and their destructive nature are widely evidenced in archaeology; Pompeii, Akrotiri, and a number of other places document past volcanic activity and its effect on human settlements. Earthquakes in the past are often recorded in archaeological sites and yield information on the incidence and consequences of these events. The sightings of celestial phenomena such as supernovas, comets, and eclipses have been recorded in archaeological objects and structures, creating an archive of the periodicity of such events.

Archaeology is also about diversity. It is very clear from the times and places in the past that we as humans have created many ways of solving the problems of survival and of improving the quality of life. The variety of ideas, technologies, and peoples that exist on the planet has ensured an increase in numbers, geographic expansion, and our success as a species. Archaeology allows us to see the variety of human societies and gain an appreciation of how humans are both different and alike through time and across geographic space.

Archaeology documents the diversity of our human past, while at the same time making clear that we are in fact all one, descended from our earliest human ancestors, mothered by an African Eve. Perhaps more than any other discipline, archaeology tells us that we are all members of the same family, traveling together on a miraculous journey through time. As the astronomer Carl Sagan put it, we are all composed of that original *star stuff* that spewed from the Big Bang across a new universe to form the stars and planets and life.

PRESERVATION

If we are to learn more about the past, then we must realize there is a note (or rather, a crescendo) of urgency in our quest. I have tried to point out in the preceding chapters how certain archaeological places are being protected for the future. But for every site that is saved, there are hundreds that are being destroyed. The archaeological record, under attack from expanding populations and global economies, is rapidly disappearing in many areas. The growth of modern cities and transportation networks is covering the earth's surface with concrete, asphalt, and mountains of trash from our consumer society. The industrialization of agriculture results in deep plowing through the earth, mixing layers of soil, and the lowering of the groundwater table, eradicating ancient organic materials that might remain in the ground. If we are to have archaeology in the future, it is essential that the fundamental information of our past that remains be recorded and protected, before nothing is left for us to study.

In 1992 the Council of Europe ratified a most important agreement regarding archaeological places and things. The Valletta Convention on the Protection of the Archaeological Heritage is a comprehensive response to the challenges of modern development and a model that can be used elsewhere. Archaeological heritage is defined, and basic principles established for European Union states to deal appropriately with that heritage. Although this convention stipulates the basic principles of developer-funded rescue archaeology, its implementation among the European nations varies dramatically. There is also EU legislation pertaining to archaeological remains. Though most of this legislation deals with return of cultural properties, there are also rules in place aimed at curation and management of archaeological and historical resources. Protection of archaeological sites in Europe is ultimately, however, the responsibility of the heritage agencies of the individual countries, and national practices vary considerably.

In 1974, Bill Lipe proposed an important working definition of archaeological places and things: "All cultural materials, including cultural landscapes, that have survived from the past, are potentially cultural resources—that is, have some potential value or use in the present or future." The distinction of cultural *resources*, with the larger connotation of materials that can be exhausted and lost, like endangered species or environments, is critical in raising public awareness and concern about these places and things.

At the same time, there are fewer than forty archaeological sites in Europe included in the U.N.'s World Heritage list. Much, much more needs to be done to protect these precious resources from the past. The urgency of this challenge should be a focus of concern and action in the twenty-first century.

APPRECIATION

Appreciation, as I intend it here, involves many aspects of archaeology. It is important to know about the difficulties of doing archaeology—the time, energy, money, and negotiations that are needed to get research done. The process is slow, expensive, and demanding. Archaeological projects often take many years, as detailed excavations slowly peel away the layers and remove the deposits of the past. A number of the sites we have visited on this tour of European prehistory involved decades of fieldwork. Spectacular finds often occur by chance, but archaeological knowledge of the past increases incrementally from many projects, large and small.

Archaeology is difficult and painstaking because so few broken bits and pieces have survived from the past. Determining the meaning and significance of such clues is a challenge. Occasionally, remarkably well-preserved finds such as Ötzi the Iceman or the prehistoric lake dwellings at Arbon-Bleiche 3 offer up a staggeringly rich glimpse of a moment in time, but such discoveries are few and far between.

Maybe one of the most important lessons of archaeology is that we are only building on what has gone before. I have a huge appreciation for the people who have created archaeological knowledge over many generations. A great deal has been learned. At the same time, it is an endeavor without visible end; there is no light at the end of the tunnel. The accumulation of archaeological knowledge will take generations before we have a reasonable and thorough understanding of the human past. There is so much to learn, so much unknown.

Appreciation also concerns the appeal of the past. These remarkable places that have survived from prehistory are often hauntingly beautiful. The tall stone towers in Sardinia stand as sentinels in the silver moonlight. The carved art of Tanum on the flat surfaces of ancient rocks amid the grandeur of the Swedish forest is unforgettable. The standing stones of the Orkney Isles leave a lasting impression—a powerful, albeit enigmatic, human statement placed on a spectacular barren landscape (Fig. E.1). The combination of location and meaning at many prehistoric sites offers a powerful experience and a sense of wonder and appreciation.

Fig. E.1.
The Standing Stones of Stenness, Orkney Islands, England.

Perhaps the final lesson of archaeology is a lingering sense of hope about the future. My strongest sense from what I have learned as an archaeologist remains a basic optimism for our species. In every way, we are artifacts, manufactured over a very long period of time, created by the actions and experiences of our ancestors. We have been on the planet for several million years. In that time, we have evolved from chimpanzeelike apes to humans capable of exploring outer space. We have expanded geographically and survived under a wide range of difficult conditions. There is an unusual quality about the human species—an enormous potential in the human intellect, with its remarkable inventiveness for coping with change. A large brain and creativity managed to get us through that very long and difficult journey in the past. For this very reason, the future should be just as exciting.

Our ancestors left remnants of an extraordinary heritage across the European landscape. These places are often memorable if not haunting, thought-provoking if not inspirational, striking if not beautiful. I have been more than fortunate in my life to pursue a career in European archaeology and to have visited many of the remarkable places found in this book. I hope it will be your fortune as well to go to, appreciate, and ruminate upon these fascinating remnants of our past.

FURTHER READING

Chapter One   Frameworks for Europe's Past

Biehl, P. F., A. Gramsch, and A. Marciniak. 2002. *Archäologien Europas: Geschichte, Methoden und Theorien* [Archaeologies of Europe: History, Methods and Theories]. Tübinger Archäologische Taschenbücher 3. Münster: Waxmann.

Bogucki, Peter (ed.). 1993. *Case Studies in European Prehistory.* Boca Raton, FL: CRC Press.

———, and Pam Crabtree (eds.). 2003. *Ancient Europe 8000 B.C.–A.D. 1000: Encyclopedia of the Barbarian World.* Farmington Hills, MI: Scribner/Gale Group.

Bradley, Richard. 2005. *Ritual and Domestic Life in Prehistoric Europe.* London: Routledge.

Champion, Timothy, Clive Gamble, Stephen Shennan, and Alisdair Whittle. 1984. *Prehistoric Europe.* New York: Academic Press.

Cunliffe, Barry W. (ed.). 2001. *The Oxford Illustrated History of Prehistoric Europe.* Oxford: Oxford University Press.

———. 2008. *Europe Between the Oceans: 9000 BC–AD 1000.* New Haven: Yale University Press.

Daniel, Glyn. 1976. *A Hundred and Fifty Years of Archaeology.* Cambridge, MA: Harvard University Press.

———. 1981. *A Short History of Archaeology.* London: Thames and Hudson.

Harding, Anthony. 2009. Towards a European Archaeology. *World Archaeology,* 41: 629–640.

Hodder, I. (ed.). 1991. *Archaeological Theory in Europe: The Last Three Decades.* London: Routledge.

Jaroslav, Malina, and Zdenek Vasicek. 1990. *Archaeology Yesterday and Today: The Development of Archaeology in the Sciences and Humanities.* Cambridge: Cambridge University Press.

Jones, Andrew. 2009. *Prehistoric Europe: Theory and Practice.* Oxford: Wiley-Blackwell.

Kienlin, T. L., and B. W. Roberts (eds.). 2009. *Metals and Societies: Studies in Honour of Barbara S. Ottaway.* Bonn: Habelt.

Klein, Sabine, Gerhard Peter Brey, Soodabeh Durali-Müller, and Yann Lahaye. 2010. Characterisation of the Raw Metal Sources Used for the Production of Copper and Copper-Based Objects with Copper Isotopes. *Archaeological and Anthropological Sciences* 2: 45–56.

Kristiansen, Kristian. 2000. *Europe Before History.* Cambridge: Cambridge University Press.

———. 2009. Contract Archaeology in Europe: An Experiment in Diversity. *World Archaeology* 41: 641–648.

Maggi, Roberto, and Mark Pearce. 2005. Mid Fourth-Millennium Copper Mining in Liguria, North-West Italy: The Earliest Known Copper Mines in Western Europe. *Antiquity* 79: 66–77.

Milisauskas, Sarunas (ed.). 2002. *European Prehistory: A Survey.* New York: Springer.

Morteani, Giulio, and Jeremy P. Northover (eds.). 1995. *Prehistoric Gold in Europe.* New York: Springer.

Nokleberg, Warren J., Walter J. Bawiec, Jeff L. Doebrich, Bruce R. Lipin, Robert J. Miller, Greta J. Orris, and Michael L. Zientek. 2005. *Geology and Nonfuel Mineral Deposits of*

Greenland, Europe, Russia, and Northern Central Asia. Open File Report 2005–1294D. Washington, DC: U.S. Department of the Interior, U.S. Geological Survey.

Ottaway, B. S., and B. W. Roberts. 2008. The Emergence of Metalworking. In *Prehistoric Europe,* A. Jones (ed.), pp. 193–225. London: Blackwell.

Piggott, Stuart. 1985. *Ancient Europe.* Chicago: Aldine.

Plant, J. A., A. Whittaker, A. Demetriades, B. De Vivo, and J. Lexa. 2006. The Geological and Tectonic Framework of Europe. In *Geochemical Atlas of Europe. Part 1—Background Information, Methodology, and Maps,* R. Salminen (ed.). Helsinki: Geological Survey of Finland.

Radivojevi, Miljana, Thilo Rehrena, Ernst Pernick, Dusan Sljivar, Michael Brauns, and Dusan Boric. 2010. On the Origins of Extractive Metallurgy: New Evidence from Europe. *Journal of Archaeological Science* 37: 2775–2787.

Roberts, B. W. 2008. The Bronze Age. In *The Handbook of British Archaeology,* L. Atkins, R. Atkins, and V. Leitch (eds.), pp. 60–91. London: Constable and Robinson.

———. 2008. Creating Traditions and Shaping Technologies: Understanding the Emergence of Metallurgy in Western Europe c. 3500–2000 BC. *World Archaeology* 40: 354–372.

Scarre, Chris. 1999. *Exploring Prehistoric Europe.* Oxford: Oxford University Press.

Schnapp, A. 1993. *La Conquète du passé: Aux origines de l'archéologie.* Paris: Éditions Carré.

Thornton, C. P., and B. W. Roberts. 2009. Introduction: The Beginnings of Metallurgy in Global Perspective. *Journal of World Prehistory* 2: 181–184.

Trigger, Bruce G. 1989. *History of Archaeological Interpretation.* Cambridge: Cambridge University Press.

Willems, Willem J. H. 1998. Archaeology and Heritage Management in Europe: Trends and Developments. *European Journal of Archaeology* 1: 293–311.

———. 1999. *The Future of European Archaeology.* Oxford: Oxbow Books.

———. 2009. European and world archaeologies. *World Archaeology* 41: 649–658.

Chapter Two   The First Europeans

Ahern, James C. M., Ivor Karavani, Maja Paunovl, Ivor Jankovic, and Fred H. Smith. 2004. New Discoveries and Interpretations of Hominid Fossils and Artifacts from Vindija Cave, Croatia. *Journal of Human Evolution* 46: 27–67.

Aiello, Leslie C., and R. I. M. Dunbar. 1993. Neocortex Size, Group Size, and the Evolution of Language. *Current Anthropology* 34: 184–193.

Aiello, Leslie C., and J. C. K. Wells. 2002. Energetics and the Evolution of the Genus *Homo. Annual Review of Anthropology* 31: 323–338.

Aiello, Leslie C., and P. Wheeler. 1995. The Expensive-Tissue Hypothesis: The Brain and the Digestive System in Human and Primate Evolution. *Current Anthropology* 36: 199–221.

Alperson-Afil, Nira, and Naama Goren-Inbar. 2010. *The Acheulian Site of Gesher Benor Ya'aqov. II. Ancient Flames and Controlled Use of Fire.* New York: Springer.

Ambrose, Stanley H. 2010. Coevolution of Composite-Tool Technology, Constructive Memory, and Language Implications for the Evolution of Modern Human Behavior. *Current Anthropology* 51: S135–S147.

Appenzeller, Tim. 1998. Art: Evolution or Revolution? *Science* 282: 1451.

Arsuaga, J. L., Bermúdez de Castro, J. M., and Carbonell, E. (eds.). 1997. The Sima de los Huesos Hominid Site. *Journal of Human Evolution* 33: 105–421.

Austin, L. A., C. A. Bergman, M. B. Roberts, and K. L. Wilhelmsen. 1999. Archaeology of Excavated Areas. In *Boxgrove: A Middle Pleistocene Hominid Site at Eartham Quarry, Boxgrove, West Sussex,* M. B. Roberts and S. A. Parfitt (eds.), pp. 420–423. London: English Heritage.

Bahn, P. G. 1998. Neanderthals Emancipated. *Nature* 394: 719–720.

Bailey, S. E., and J.-J. Hublin. 2006. Dental Remains from the Grotte du Renne at Arcy-sur-Cure (Yonne). *Journal of Human Evolution* 50: 485–508.

Baker, T. 2006. The Acheulean Handaxe. http://www.ele.net/acheulean/handaxe.htm, accessed February 1, 2007.

Bastir, M., et al. 2010. Comparative Morphology and Morphometric Assessment of the Neandertal Occipital Remains from the El Sidrón site (Asturias, Spain: years 2000–2008). *Journal of Human Evolution* 58: 68–78.

Berger, Thomas D., and Erik Trinkaus. 1995. Patterns of Trauma Among the Neandertals. *Journal of Archaeological Science* 22: 841–852.

Bermúdez de Castro, J. M., Carbonell, E., and Arsuaga, J. L. (eds.). 1999. The Gran Dolina Site: TD6 Aurora Stratum (Atapuerca, Burgos, Spain). *Journal of Human Evolution* 37: 309–700.

Bingham, Paul M. 1999. Human Uniqueness: A General Theory. *The Quarterly Review of Biology* 74: 133–169.

Bischoff, James L., Ross W. Williams, Robert J. Rosenbauer, Arantza Aramburu, Juan Luis Arsuaga, Nuria García, and Gloria Cuenca-Bescós. 2007. High-Resolution U-Series Dates from the Sima de los Huesos Hominids Yields 600±66 kyrs: Implications for the Evolution of the Early Neanderthal Lineage. *Journal of Archaeological Science* 34: 763–770.

Blockley, S. P. E., C. Bronk Ramsey, and T. F. G. Higham. 2008. The Middle to Upper Paleolithic Transition: Dating, Stratigraphy, and Isochronous Markers. *Journal of Human Evolution* 55: 764–771.

Bordes, Francois. 1967. *The Old Stone Age*. New York: McGraw-Hill.

Brantingham, P. Jeffrey, Steven L. Kuhn, and Kristopher W. Kerry. 2004. *The Early Upper Paleolithic Beyond Western Europe*. Berkeley: University of California Press.

Burbano, H. A., et al. 2010. Targeted Investigation of the Neandertal Genome by Array-Based Sequence Capture. *Science* 238: 723–725.

Busch, R., and H. Schwabedissen (eds.). 1991. *Der alt-steinzeitliche Fundplatz Salzgitter-Lebenstedt. Teil II. Naturwissenschaftliche Untersuchungen*. Koln: Böhlau Verlag.

Carbonell, Eudald, José M. Bermúdez de Castro, Josep M. Parés, Alfredo Pérez-González, Gloria Cuenca-Bescós, Andreu Ollé, et al. 2008. The First Hominin of Europe. *Nature* 208: 465–469.

Carbonell, Eudald, Isabel Cáceres, Ma5rina Lozano, Palmira Saladié, Jordi Rosell, Carlos Lorenzo, Josep Vallverdú, Rosa Huguet, Antoni Canals, and José María Bermúdez de Castro. 2010. Cultural Cannibalism as a Paleoeconomic System in the European Lower Pleistocene. *Current Anthropology* 51: 539–549.

Carbonell, Eudald, and Marina Mosquera. 2006. The Emergence of a Symbolic Behaviour: The Sepulchral Pit of Sima de los Huesos, Sierra de Atapuerca, Burgos, Spain. *Comptes Rendus Palevol 5:* 155–160.

Carbonell, E., et al. 2005. An Early Pleistocene Hominin Mandible from Atapuerca-TD6, Spain. *Proceedings of the National Academy of Science* 102: 5674–5678.

Caron, F., F. D'Errico, P. Del Moral, F. Santos, and J. Zilhão. 2011. The Reality of Neandertal Symbolic Behavior at the Grotte du Renne, Arcy-sur-Cure, France. *PLoS ONE* 6(6): e21545.

Chu, Wei. 2009. A Functional Approach to Palaeolithic Open-Air Habitation Structures. *World Archaeology* 41: 348–362.

David, F, V. D'Iatchenko, J. G. Enloe, M. Girard, M. Hardy, V. Lhomme, A. Roblin-Jouve, A. M. Tillier, and C. Tolmie. 2009. New Neandertal Remains from the Grotte du Bison at Arcy-sur-Cure, France. *Journal of Human Evolution* 57: 805–809.

Debénath, André, and Harold Lewis Dibble. 1994. *Handbook of Paleolithic Typology: Lower and Middle Paleolithic of Europe*. Philadelphia: University Museum.

Defleur, A., O. Dutour, H. Valladas, and B. Vandermeersch. 1993. Cannibalism Among the Neanderthals? *Nature* 362: 214.

Dennell, R. 1997. The World's Oldest Spears. *Nature* 385: 767–768.

D'Errico, F., J. Zilhão, M. Julien, D. Baffier, and J. Pelegrin. 1998. The Middle to Upper Paleolithic Transition at Arcy-sur-Cure. *Current Anthropology* 39: 1–44.

Dibble, Harold L., and Paul Mellars. 2003. *The Middle Paleolithic: Adaptation, Behavior, and Variability.* Philadelphia: University Museum.

Dickson, D. Bruce. 1990. *The Dawn of Belief: Religion in the Upper Paleolithic of Southwestern Europe.* Tucson: University of Arizona Press.

Dunbar, R. I. M. 1998. The Social Brain Hypothesis. *Evolutionary Anthropology* 6: 178–186.

Dusseldorp, G. L. 2006. *A View to a Kill: Investigating Middle Palaeolithic Subsistence Using an Optimal Foraging Perspective.* Leiden: Sidestone Press.

Féblot-Augustins, J. 1997. Middle and Upper Paleolithic Raw Material Transfers in Western and Central Europe: Assessing the Pace of Change. *Journal of Middle Atlantic Archaeology* 13: 57–90.

Findlayson, C. 2004. *Neanderthals and Modern Humans: An Ecological and Evolutionary Perspective.* Cambridge: Cambridge University Press.

Fortea, J, et al. 2003. La Cueva de El Sidrón (Borines, Piloña, Asturias): Primeros Resultados. *Estudios Geológicos* 59: 159–179.

Frayer, David W., Ivana Fiore, Carles Lalueza-Fox, Jakov Radović, and Luca Bondioli. 2010. Right Handed Neandertals: Vindija and Beyond. *Journal of Anthropological Sciences* 88: 113–127.

Gamble, Clive. 1999. *The Palaeolithic Societies of Europe.* Cambridge: Cambridge University Press.

———, and Sabine Gaudzinski. 2007. Bones and Powerful Individuals: Faunal Case Studies from the Arctic and the European Middle Paleolithic. In *Hominid Individual in Context: Archaeological Investigations of Lower and Middle Palaeolithic Landscapes, Locales and Artefacts*, Clive Gamble and Martin Porr (eds.), pp. 154–175. London: Routledge.

Gamble, Clive, and Martin Porr, (eds.). 2005. *Hominid Individuals in Context: Archaeological Investigations of Lower and Middle Palaeolithic Landscapes, Locales and Artefacts.* London: Routledge.

Gaudzinski, S. 1999. Middle Palaeolithic Bone Tools from the Open-Air Site Salzgitter-Lebenstedt (Germany). *Journal of Archaeological Science* 26: 125–141.

———. 2000. On the Variability of Middle Palaeolithic Procurement Tactics: The Case of Salzgitter Lebenstedt, Northern Germany. *International Journal of Osteoarchaeology* 10: 396–406.

———, and W. Roebroeks. 2000. Adults Only: Reindeer Hunting at the Middle Palaeolithic Site Salzgitter Lebenstedt, Northern Germany. *Journal of Human Evolution* 38: 497–521.

Gorjanovi-Kramberger, D. 1913. Zivot i kultura diluvijalnoga covjeka iz Krapine u Hrvatskoj (Homo diluvialis de Krapina in Croatia, vita et cultura). *Djela Jugoslavenske akademije znanosti i umjetnosti* 23: 1–54.

Gowlett, J. A. J. 2006. The Early Settlement of Northern Europe: Fire History in the Context of Climate Change and the Social Brain. *Comptes Rendus—Palevol* 5: 299–310.

Gravina, Brad, Paul Mellars, and Christopher Bronk Ramsey. 2005. Radiocarbon Dating of Interstratified Neanderthal and Early Modern Human Occupations at the Chatelperronian Type-Site. *Nature* 483: 51–57.

Green, Richard E., et al. 2006. Analysis of One Million Base Pairs of Neanderthal DNA. *Nature* 444: 330–336.

———. 2010. A Draft Sequence of the Neandertal Genome. *Science* 328: 710–722.

Harvati, K., and T. Harrison (eds.). 2007. *Neanderthals Revisited: New Approaches and Perspectives.* New York: Springer.

Higham, Thomas, Roger Jacobi, Michèle Julien, Francine David, Laura Basell, Rachel Wood, William Davies, and Christopher Bronk Ramsey. 2010. Chronology of the Grotte du Renne (France) and Implications for the Context of Ornaments and Human Remains Within the Châtelperronian. *Proceedings of the National Academy of Science USA* 107: 20234–20239.

Higham, Tom, et al. 2006. Revised Direct Radiocarbon Dating of the Vindija G1 Upper Paleolithic Neandertals. *Proceedings of the National Academy of Sciences* 10: 553–557.

Hoffecker, J. F. 2002. *Desolate Landscapes: Ice-Age Settlement in Eastern Europe.* New Brunswick, NJ: Rutgers University Press.

Hublein, Jean-Jacques, and Michael P. Richards (eds.). 2009. *The Evolution of Hominin Diets: Integrating Approaches to the Study of Palaeolithic Subsistence.* New York: Springer.

Hublin, J.-J., et al. 1996. A Late Neanderthal Associated with Upper Palaeolithic Artefacts. *Nature* 381: 224–226.

Jankovic, Ivor, Ivor Karavani, James C. M. Ahern, Dejana Brajkovi, Jadranka Mauch Lenardi, and Fred H. Smith. 2006. Vindija Cave and the Modern Human Peopling of Europe. *Collegium Antropologicum* 30: 457–466.

Jöris, O., and D. S. Adler. 2008. Setting the Record Straight: Toward a Systematic Chronological Understanding of the Middle to Upper Paleolithic Boundary in Eurasia. *Journal of Human Evolution* 55: 761–763.

Karavanić, Ivor, and Marylène Patou-Mathis. 2009. Middle/Upper Paleolithic Interface in Vindija Cave (Croatia): New Results and Interpretations. In *Sourcebook of Paleolithic Transitions*, Marta Camps and Parth Chauhan (eds.), pp. 397–406. New York: Springer.

Kittler, Ralf, Manfred Kayser, and Mark Stoneking. 2003. Molecular Evolution of *Pediculus humanus* and the Origin of Clothing. *Current Biology* 13: 1414–1417.

Klein, Richard. 2002. *The Dawn of Human Culture.* New York: Wiley.

Kolen, J. 1999. Hominids without Homes: On the Nature of Middle Paleolithic Settlement in Europe. In *The Middle Paleolithic Occupation of Europe*, W. Roebroeks and C. Gamble (eds.), pp. 139–175. Leiden: University of Leiden Press.

Kricun, M., J. Monge, A. Mann, G. Finkel, M. Lampl, and J. Radovčić. 1999. *The Krapina Hominids: A Radiographic Atlas of the Skeletal Collection.* Zagreb: Hrvatski prirodoslovni muzej.

Kuhn, S. L. 1992. On Planning and Curated Technologies in the Middle Paleolithic. *Journal of Anthropological Research* 48: 185–214.

———, and M. C. Stiner. 2001. The Antiquity of Hunter-Gatherers. In *Hunter-Gatherers: Interdisciplinary Perspectives*, C. Panter-Brick, R. H. Layton, and P. A. Rowley-Conwy (eds.), pp. 99–142. Cambridge: Cambridge University Press.

Kvavadze, Eliso, Ofer Bar-Yosef, Anna Belfer-Cohen, Elisabetta Boaretto, Nino Jakeli, Zinovi Matskevich, and Tengiz Meshveliani. 2009. 30,000-Year-Old Wild Flax Fibers. *Science* 325: 1359.

Leroi-Gourhan, A. 1958. La galerie moustérienne de la grotte du Renne. Arcy-sur-Cure. *Bull. Societé amicale Préhistoire Archéologique Arcy-sur-Cure*: 5: 2–12.

———. 1961. Les fouilles d'Arcy-sur-Cure (Yonne). *Gallia Préhistoire* 4: 3–16.

Lozano, M., J. M. Bermúdez de Castro, E. Carbonell, and J. L. Arsuaga. 2008. Non-Masticatory Uses of Anterior Teeth of Sima de los Huesos Individuals Sierra de Atapuerca, Spain. *Journal of Human Evolution* 55: 713–728.

MacDonald, Katherine, Wil Roebroeks, and A. Verpoorte. 2009. An Energetics Perspective on the Neandertal Record. In *Evolution of Hominid Diets: Integrating Approaches to the Study of Palaeolithic Subsistence,* J.-J. Hublin and M. P. Richards (eds.), pp. 211–220. New York: Springer.

Martínez-Navarro, B., A. Turq, J. Agustí, and O. Oms. 1997. Fuente Nueva-3 (Orce, Granada, Spain) and the First Human Occupation of Europe. *Journal of Human Evolution* 33: 611–620.

McNabb, John. 2000. Review of *Boxgrove*, edited by M. B. Roberts and S. A. Parfitt. *Antiquity* 74: 439–441.

———. 2007. *The British Lower Paleolithic.* London: Routledge.

Mellars, Paul, and Jennifer C. French. 2011. Tenfold Population Increase in Western Europe at the Neandertal–to–Modern Human Transition. *Science* 333: 623–627.

Monge J., A. Mann, D. Frayer, and J. Radovčić (eds.). 2008. *New Insights on the Krapina Neanderthals: 100 Years Since Gorjanović-Kramberger.* Zagreb: Croatian Natural History Museum.

Morin, Eugene. 2010. *Palaeolithic Foragers at Saint-Cesaire, France: A Faunal Perspective on the Origins of Modern Humans.* Oxford: Oxbow Books.

Muller, Stephanie, and Friedemann Shrenk. 2008. *The Neanderthals.* London: Routledge.

Newcomer, Mark H. 1971. Some Quantitative Experiments in Handaxe Manufacture. *World Archaeology* 3: 85–94.

Oms, O., J. M. Parés, B. Martínez-Navarro, J. Agustí, I. Toro, G. Martínez-Fernández, and A. Turq. 2000. Early Human Occupation of Western Europe: Paleomagnetic Dates for Two Paleolithic Sites in Spain. *Proceedings of the National Academy of Science* 97: 10666–10670.

Orschiedt, J. 1999. *Manipulationen an menschlichen Skelet- tresten. Taphonomische Prozesse, Sekundärbestattungen oder Anthropophagie.* Urgeschichtliche Materialhefte 13. Tübingen: MoVince.

———. 2008. Der Fall Krapina—Neue Ergebnisse zur Frage von Kannibalismus beim Neandertaler. *Quartär* 55: 63–81.

Parés, J. M., et al. 2006. Matuyama-Age Lithic Tools from the Sima del Elefante Site, Atapuerca (Northern Spain). *Journal of Human Evolution* 50: 163–169.

Pastoors, A. 2001. *Die mittelpaläolithische Freilandstation von Salzgitter-Lebenstedtl: Genese der fundstelle und Systematik der Steinbearbitung.* Salzgitter Forschungen 3. Salzgitter.

Pettitt, Paul. 2011. *The Palaeolithic Origins of Human Burial.* London: Routledge.

———, and Mark White. 2012. *The British Paleolithic: Human Societies at the Edge of the Pleistocene World.* London: Routledge.

Pitts, Mike, and Mark Roberts. 1997. *Fairweather Eden: Life in Britain Half a Million Years Ago as Revealed by the Excavations at Boxgrove.* London: Century.

Radovcic, J., F. H. Smith, E. Trinkaus, and M. H. Wolpoff. 1988. *The Krapina hominids: an Illustrated Catalog of Skeletal Collection.* Zagreb: Mladost Press and the Croatian Natural History Museum.

Ramirez Rozzi, Fernando V., and José Maria Bermudez de Castro. 2004. Surprisingly Rapid Growth in Neanderthals. *Nature* 428: 936–939.

Richards, Michael P., Paul B. Pettitt, Erik Trinkaus, Fred H. Smith, Maja Paunovic, and Ivor Karavanic. 2000. Neanderthal Diet at Vindija and Neanderthal Predation: The Evidence from Stable Isotopes. *Proceedings of the National Academy of Science* 97: 7663–7666.

Roberts, M. B. 1999. Concluding Remarks and Discussion. In *Boxgrove: A Middle Pleistocene hominid site at Eartham Quarry, Boxgrove, West Sussex,* M. B. Roberts and S. A. Parfitt (eds.), pp. 420–423. London: English Heritage..

———, C. S. Gamble, and D. R. Bridgland. 1995. The Earliest Occupation of Europe: The British Isles. In *The Earliest Occupation of Europe,* W. Roebroeks and T. van Kolfschoten (eds.), pp. 165–192. Leiden: University of Leiden.

Roberts, Mark B., and S. A. Parfitt (eds.). 1999. *Boxgrove: A Middle Pleistocene hominid site at Eartham Quarry, Boxgrove, West Sussex.* London: English Heritage.

———, M. I. Pope, and F. F. Wenban-Smith. 1997. Boxgrove, West Sussex: Rescue Excavations of a Lower Palaeolithic Land Surface (Boxgrove Project B 1989–1991). *Proceedings of the Prehistoric Society* 63: 303–358.

Roebroeks, W. 2001. Hominid Behaviour and the Earliest Occupation of Europe: An Exploration. *Journal of Human Evolution* 41: 437–461.

———. 2008. Time for the Middle to Upper Paleolithic Transition in Europe. *Journal of Human Evolution* 55: 918–926.

Roebroeks, W., N. J. Conard, and T. Van Kolfschoten. 1992. Dense Forests, Cold Steppes, and the Palaeolithic Settlement of Northern Europe. *Current Anthropology* 33: 551–586.

Roebroeks, Wil, and Paola Villa. 2011. On the Earliest Evidence for Habitual Use of Fire in Europe. *Proceedings of the National Academy of Science* 108: 5209–5214.

Rosas, A., et al. 2006. Paleobiology and Comparative Morphology of a Late Neandertal Sample from El Sidrón, Asturias, Spain. *Proceedings of the National Academy of Sciences* 103: 19266–19271.

Santamaría, D., et al. 2010. The Technological and Typological Behaviour of a Neanderthal Group from El Sidron Cave (Asturias, Spain). *Oxford Journal of Archaeology* 29: 119–148.

Schoch, W. H. 1995. Hölzer aus der Fundschicht 1 des altpaläolithischen Fundplatzes Schöningen 12 (Reinsdorf-Interglazial). In *Archäologische Ausgrabungen im Braunkohlentagebau Schöningen, Landkreis Helmstedt,* H. Thieme and R. Maier (eds.), pp. 73–84. Hannover: Hahnsche.

Scott, Gary R., and Luis Gibert. 2009. The Oldest Hand-axes in Europe. *Nature* 461: 82–85.

Serre, David, et al. 2004. No Evidence of Neandertal mtDNA Contribution to Early Modern Humans. *PLoS Biology* 2(3): 313–317.

Smith, F. H. 1976. *The Neandertal Remains from Krapina: A Descriptive and Comparative Study.* University of Tennessee, Department of Anthropology Reports of Investigations 15:1–359.

Stapert, Dick. 1990. Middle Palaeolithic Dwellings: Fact of Fiction? Some Applications of the Ring and Sector Method. *Palaeohistoria* 32: 1–19.

Stringer, C. B., and E. Trinkaus. 1999. The Human Tibia from Boxgrove. In *Boxgrove: A Middle Pleistocene hominid site at Eartham Quarry, Boxgrove, West Sussex,* M. B. Roberts and S. A. Parfitt (eds.), pp. 420–423. London: English Heritage.

Stringer, Chris, and Clive Gamble. 1993. *In Search of Neanderthals: Solving the Puzzle of Human Origins.* London: Thames and Hudson.

Tattersall, I. 1999. *The Last Neanderthal: The Rise, Success, and Mysterious Extinction of Our Closest Human Relatives.* Boulder, CO: Westview Press.

———, and J. H. Schwartz. 2001. *Extinct humans.* Boulder, CO: Westview Press.

Thieme, H. 1997. Lower Palaeolithic Hunting Spears from Germany. *Nature* 385: 807–810.

———. 1999. Lower Palaeolithic Throwing Spears and Other Wooden Implements from Schöningen, Germany. In *Hominid Evolution: Lifestyles and Survival Strategies,* H. Ullrich (ed.), pp. 383–395. Gelsenkirchen/Schwelm: Edition Archaea.

———. 2005. The Lower Palaeolithic Art of Hunting: The Case of Schöningen 13 II-4, Lower Saxony, Germany. In *The Hominid Individual in Context: Archaeological Investigations of Lower and Middle Palaeolithic Landscapes, Locales and Artefacts,* C. Gamble and M. Porr (eds.), pp. 115–132. Oxford: Oxford University Press.

Tode, A. 1982. *Der altsteinzeitliche Fundplatz Salzgitter-Lebenstedt I. Archäologischer Teil.* Fundamenta A 11/1. Köln: Bohlau Verlag.

Trinkaus, Erik. 1975. The Neandertals from Krapina, Northern Yugoslavia: An Inventory of the Lower Limb Remains. *Zeitschrift für Morphologie und Anthropologie* 67: 44–59.

———. 1985. Cannibalism and Burial at Krapina. *Journal of Human Evolution* 14: 203–216.

———. 1995. Neanderthal Mortality Patterns. *Journal of Archaeological Science* 22: 121–142.

———. 2006. Modern Human Versus Neandertal Evolutionary Distinctiveness. *Current Anthropology* 47: 597–620.

———, Christopher B. Ruff, Steven E. Churchill, and Bernard Vandermeersch. 1998. Locomotion and Body Proportions of the Saint-Césaire 1 Châtelperronian Neandertal. *Proceedings of the National Academy of Science* 95: 5836–5840.

Ullrich, H. 1978. Kannibalismus und Leichenzerstückelung beim Neandertaler von Krapina. In *Krapinski pracovjek i evolucija hominida,* M. Malez (ed.), pp. 293–318. Zagreb: Jugoslavenska akademija znanosti i umjetnosti.

———. 1988. Krapina and Vindija—Mortuary Practices, Burials or Cannibalism? *Collegium Antropologicum* (Supplement) 12: 348.

———. 2004. Patterns of Skeletal Representation, Manipulations on Human Corpses and Bones, Mortuary Practices and the Question of Cannibalism in the European Paleolithic: An Anthropological Approach. *Opus* 3: 24–40.

Vaquero, M., J. M. Rando, and M. G. Chacón. 2004. Neanderthal Spatial Behavior and Social Structure: Hearth-Related Assemblages from the Abric Romaní Middle

Palaeolithic Site. In *Settlement Dynamics of the Middle Paleolithic and Middle Stone Age II*, N. J. Conard (ed.), pp. 367–392. Tübingen: Kerns Verlag.

Villa, P. 1992. Cannibalism in Prehistoric Europe. *Evolutionary Anthropology* 1: 93–104.

Voormolen, Boudewijn. 2008. *Ancient Hunters, Modern Butchers: Schöningen 13II—4, A Kill-Butchery Site Dating from the Northwest European Lower Palaeolithic.* Ph.D. Thesis, Department of Archaeology, University of Leiden.

Weaver, Timothy D., Charles C. Roseman, and Chris B. Stringer. 2008. Close Correspondence Between Quantitative- and Molecular-Genetic Divergence Times for Neandertals and Modern Humans. *Proceedings of the National Academy of Science* 105: 4645–4649.

White, R. 1993. Technological and Social Dimensions of "Aurignacian-age" Body Ornaments Across Europe. In *Before Lascaux: The Complex Record of the Early Upper Paleolithic*, H. Knecht, A. Pike-Tay, and R. White (eds.), pp. 277–299. Boca Raton, FL: CRC Press.

———, and Y. Taborin. 1998. The Personal Ornaments from Arcy-sur-Cure (Yonne) France: Technological and Evolutional Perspectives. *Journal of Human Evolution* 34(3): 1–24.

Wobst, Martin. 1976. Locational Relationships in Paleolithic Society. *Journal of Human Evolution* 5: 49–58.

Wolpoff, Milford H. 1979. The Krapina Dental Remains. *American Journal of Physical Anthropology* 50: 67–114.

———, Fred H. Smith, Mirko Malez, Jakov Radovcic, and Darko Rukavina. 1981. Upper Pleistocene Human Remains from Vindija Cave, Croatia, Yugoslavia. *American Journal of Physical Anthropology* 54: 499–545.

Wrangham, Richard. 2009. *Catching Fire: How Cooking Made Us.* New York: Basic Books.

Wymer, John. 1982. *The Palaeolithic Age.* London: Palgrave Macmillan.

Chapter Three   The Creative Explosion

Absolon, K. 1938. *Die Erforschung der diluvialen Mammutjäger–Station von Unter Wisternitz in Mähre n. Arbeitsbericht über das zweite Jahr 1925.* Brünn: Vastes.

Adams, J. M., and H. Faure (eds.). 1997. *Review and Atlas of Palaeovegetation: Preliminary Land Ecosystem Maps of the World Since the Last Glacial Maximum.* Oak Ridge National Laboratory, TN, USA. http://www.esd.ornl.gov/projects/qen/adams1.html. (visited 9/2/2011)

Albrethsen, S. E., and E. Brinch Petersen. 1977. Excavation of a Mesolithic Cemetery at Vedbæk, Denmark. *Acta Archaeologica* 47: 1–28.

Alley, Richard B. 2000. The Younger Dryas Cold Interval as Viewed from Central Greenland. *Quaternary Science Reviews* 19: 213–226.

Álvarez Fernández, Esteban. 1999. Las Perlas de Madera Fósil del Terciario y Los Objetos de Adorno-Colgantes sobre Dientes de Zorro y Ciervo del Magdaleniense de Gonnersdorf y de Andernach-Martinsberg-2 (Neuwied, Rheinland Pfalz, Alemania). *Zephyrus* 52: 79–106.

Andersen, S. H. 1980. Tybrind Vig. Foreløbig meddelelse om en undersøisk stenalderboplads ved Lillebælt. *Antikvariske Studier* 4.. København: Fredningsstyrelsen.

———. 1983. En stenalderbåd fra Tybrind Vig. *Antikvariske Studier* 6.. København: Fredningsstyrelsen.

———. 1984. Mønstrede Åreblade fra Tybrind Vig. *Kuml* 1982–1983.

———. 1985. Tybrind Vig. A Preliminary Report on a Submerged Ertebølle Settlement on the West Coast of Fyn. *Journal of Danish Archaeology* 4: 52–69.

———. 1987. Mesolithic Dug-outs and Paddles from Tybrind Vig, Denmark. *Acta Archaeologica* 57. København.

———. 1987. Tybrind Vig: A Submerged Ertebølle Settlement in Denmark. In *European Wetlands in Prehistory*, J. M. Coles and J. L. Lawson (eds.), pp. 253–280. Oxford: Oxford University Press.

Anikovich, M. V., et al. 2007. Early Upper Paleolithic in Eastern Europe and Implications for the Dispersal of Modern Humans. *Science* 315: 223–226.

Arrhenius, B., and K. Lidén. 1989. Fisksoppa eller vegetabilisk gröt? Diskussion kring matresterna från Tybrind Vig. *Laborativ arkeologi* 3: 6–15.

Audouze, Françoise. 1987. The Paris Basin in Magdalenian Times. In *The Pleistocene Old World: Regional Perspectives*, O. Soffer (ed.), pp. 183–200. New York: Plenum.

———, and J. Enloe. 1991. Subsistence Strategies and Economy in the Magdalenian of the Paris Basin, France. In *The Late Glacial in North-West Europe: Human Adaptation and Change at the end of the Pleistocene*, N. Barton, A. J. Roberts, and D. A. Roe (eds.), pp. 63–71. Oxford: Alden Press.

Baffier, Dominique. 1992. Les sanctuaires d'Arcy. Figures pariétales de la grotte du Cheval et de la Grande Grotte. *Bulletin de Liaison S.R.A. Bourgogne* 13: 21–24.

———. 2004, March. Le premier art paléolithique: Mammouths et Rhinocéros. *Dossiers d'archéologie* 291: 82–87.

———, F. David, G. Gaucher, M. Julien, C. Karlin, A. Leroi-Gourhan, and M. Orliac. 1982. Les occupations magdaléniennes de Pincevent: problèmes de durée. In *Les habitats du Paléolithique supérieur: Colloque international en hommage au professeur André Leroi-Gourhan*, L. Monnier (ed.), pp. 243–271. Paris: CNRS.

Baffier, Dominique, and Michel Girard. 1992. Découvertes de peintures paléolithiques dans la Grande Grotte d'Arcy-sur-Cure (Yonne), France. *International Newsletter on Rock Art* 2: 2–3.

———. 2003. *Les Cavernes d'Arcy-sur-Cure*. Paris: La Maison des Roches.

Bahn, Paul G. 1983. Archaeology: New Finds at Pincevent. *Nature* 304: 682–683.

———, and Jean Vertut. 1988. *Images of the Ice Age*. London: Windward.

Bailey, Geoff, and Penny Spikins (eds.). 2010. *Mesolithic Europe*. Cambridge: Cambridge University Press.

Bakka, E. 1975. Geologically Dated Rock Carvings at Hammer near Steinkjær in Nord–Trøndelag. *Arkeologiske skrifter fra Historisk Museum i Bergen* 1975(2): 7–49.

Bar-Yosef, Ofer. 2002. The Upper Paleolithic Revolution. *Annual Review of Anthropology* 31: 363–393.

Bettinger, R. L. 2009. *Hunter-Gatherer Foraging: Five Simple Models*. Clinton Corners, NY: Eliot Werner.

Bicho, Nuno F. 1994. The End of the Paleolithic and Mesolithic in Portugal. *Current Anthropology* 35: 664–674.

Binford, Lewis R. 1980. Willow Smoke and Dogs' Tails: Hunter-Gatherer Settlement Systems and Archaeological Site Formation. *American Antiquity* 45: 4–20.

———. 1984. Butchering, Sharing, and the Archaeological Record. *Journal of Anthropological Archaeology* 3: 235–257.

———. 1990. Mobility, Housing and Environment: A Comparative Study. *Journal of Anthropological Research* 46(2): 119–152.

Bosinski, G. 1979. Die Ausgrabungen in Gönnersdorf 1968–1976 und die Siedlungsbefunde der Grabung 1968. In *Der Magdalénien-Fundplatz Gönnersdorf*, Vol. 3. Frankurt: Franz Steiner Verlag.

———. 1995. Gönnersdorf. In *The Palaeolithic and Mesolithic of the Rhineland*. G. Bosinski, M. Street, and M. Baales. (eds.). Munich: F. Pfeil.

———. 2007. Gönnersdorf und Andernach-Martinsberg. Späteiszeitliche Siedlungsplätze am Mittelrhein. Mit Beiträgen von Hannelore Bosinski zu den Rondellen und zum Schmuck. *Archäologie an Mittelrhein und Mosel* 19. Koblenz: Rheinischen Landesmuseums Trier.

———. 2008. Tierdarstellungen von Gönnersdorf. Nachträge zu Mammut und Pferd sowie die übrigen Tierdarstellungen. In *Der Magdalénien-Fundplatz Gönnersdorf, 9.*

Monographien der Römisch-Germanischen Zentralmuseums Band 72. Mainz: Verlag des Römisch-Germanischen Zentralmuseums.

Bradley, R. 1997. *Rock Art and the Prehistory of Atlantic Europe.* London: Routledge.

Brantingham, P. Jeffrey, Steven L. Kuhn, and Kristopher W. Kerry (eds.). 2004. *The Early Upper Paleolithic Beyond Western Europe.* Berkeley: University of California Press.

Breuil, H., and R. Robert. 1951. Les baguettes demi-rondes de la grotte de la Vache (Ariège). *Bulletin de la Société préhistorique française* 48: 453–457.

Chauvet, Jean-Marie, Eliette Brunel Deschamps, and Christian Hillaire. 1996. *Dawn of Art: The Chauvet Cave.* New York: Abrams.

Chippindale, Christopher, and George Nash (eds.). 2002. *European Landscapes of Rock-Art.* London: Routledge.

Clark, Peter U., Arthur S. Dyke, Jeremy D. Shakun, Anders E. Carlson, Jorie Clark, Barbara Wohlfarth, Jerry X. Mitrovica, Steven W. Hostetler, and A. Marshall McCabe. 2009. The Last Glacial Maximum. *Science* 325: 710–714.

Clottes, Jean. (August 2001). France's Magical Ice Age Art. *National Geographic* 200 (2).

———. 2003. *Chauvet Cave: The Art of Earliest Times.* Salt Lake City: University of Utah Press.

———. 2008. *Cave Art.* London: Phaidon Press.

———, and Henri Delporte. 2004. *La Grotte de La Vache (Ariège): Fouilles Romain Robert.* Paris: Éditions du CTHS.

Clottes, Jean, and David Lewis-Williams. 1998. *The Shamans of Prehistory: Trance and Magic in the Painted Caves.* London: Abrams.

Coles, B. J. 1998. Doggerland: A Speculative Survey. *Proceedings of the Prehistoric Society* 64: 45–81.

Conard, Nicholas. 2009. A Female Figurine from the Basal Aurignacian of Hohle Fels Cave in Southwestern Germany. *Nature* 459: 248–252.

Conkey, Margaret. 1980. The Identification of Prehistoric Hunter-Gatherer Aggregation Sites: The Case of Altamira. *Current Anthropology* 21: 609–630.

Conneller, C., and G. Warren. 2006. *Mesolithic Britain and Ireland: New Approaches.* Stroud, England: Tempus.

Craig, O. E., M. Forster, S. H. Andersen, E. Koch, P. Crombé, N. J. Milner, B. Stern, G. N. Bailey, and C. P. Heron. 2007. Molecular and Isotopic Demonstration of the Processing of Aquatic Products in Northern European Prehistoric Pottery. *Archaeometry* 49: 135–152.

Cullen, Tracey. 1995. Mesolithic Mortuary Ritual at Franchthi Cave. *Antiquity* 69: 270–289.

Curtis, Gregory. 2007. *The Cave Painters: Probing the Mysteries of the World's First Artists.* New York: Knopf.

David, F. 1994. La faune de mammifères de Pincevent et Verberie. In *Environnements et habitats magdaléniens dans le centre du Bassin parisien*, Y. Taborin (ed.), pp. 105–111. Paris: Editions de la Maison des sciences de l'homme.

———, Nelly Connet, Michel Girard, Jean-Claude Miskovsky, Cécile Mourer-Chauviré, and Annie Roblin-Jouve. 2005. Les niveaux du Paléolithique supérieur à la grotte du Bison (Arcy-sur-Cure, Yonne): couches a à d. *Revue archéologique de l'Est* 54.

———, and M. Orliac. 1994. Pincevent. In *Environnements et habitats magdaléniens dans le centre du Bassin parisien*, Y. Taborin (ed.), pp. 154–167. Paris: Editions de la Maison des sciences de l'homme.

Delporte, H. 1993. L'art mobilier de la Grotte de la Vache: premier essai de vue générale, *Bulletin de la Société préhistorique française* 90(2): 131–136.

Demoule, Jean-Paul, and Catherine Perlès. 1993. The Greek Neolithic: A New Review. *Journal of World Prehistory* 7: 355–416.

Enloe, J. G., and F. David. 1992. Food Sharing in the Paleolithic: Carcass Refitting at Pincevent. In *Piecing Together the Past: Applications of Refitting Studies in Archaeology*, J. L. Hofman and J. G. Enloe (eds.), pp. 296–315. BAR International Series 578. Oxford: Hadrian Books.

———. 1997. *Rangifer* Herd Behavior: Seasonality of Hunting in the Magdalenian of the Paris Basin. In *Caribou and Reindeer Hunters of the Northern Hemisphere,* L. J. Jackson and P. T. Thacker (eds.), pp. 52–68. Avebury: Ashgate.

Enloe, J. G., F. David, and T.S. Hare. 1994. Patterns of Faunal Processing at Section 27 of Pincevent: The Use of Spatial Analysis and Ethnoarchaeological Data in the Interpretation of Archaeological Site Structure. *Journal of Anthropological Archaeology* 13: 105–124.

Florineth, D., and C. Schlüchter. 2000. Alpine Evidence for Atmospheric Circulation Patterns in Europe During the Last Glacial Maximum. *Quaternary Research* 54: 295–308.

Gaffney, Vincent, Simon Fitch, and David Smith. 2009. *The Rediscovery of Doggerland.* London: Council for British Archaeology.

Gaffney, V., K. Thomson, and S. Fitch (eds.). 2007. *Mapping Doggerland: The Mesolithic Landscapes of the Southern North Sea.* Oxford: Archaeopress.

Gailli, R. 2008. *La Grotte Préhistorique de la Vache.* Toulouse: Éditions Larrey.

Galanidou, Nena, and Catherine Perlés (eds.). 2003. New Research on the Mesolithic Period in Greece. In *The Greek Mesolithic: Problems and Perspectives.* London: British School at Athens.

Gamble, C. 1982. Culture and Society in the Upper Paleolithic of Europe. In *Hunter-Gatherer Economy in Prehistory,* Geoff Bailey (ed.), pp. 201–219. Cambridge: Cambridge University Press.

Guthrie, R. Dale. 2008. *The Nature of Paleolithic Art.* Chicago: University of Chicago Press.

Hahn, Joachim. 1978. New Aspects of the Magdalenian in Central Europe. *Reviews in Anthropology* 5: 313–331.

Hansen, Julie M. 1991. *The Palaeoethnobotany of Franchthi Cave.* Excavations at Franchthi Cave, Greece, fascicle 7. Bloomington: Indiana University Press.

Helskog, K. 1988. *Helleristningene i Alta. Spor etter ritualer og dagligliv i Finnmarks forhistorie.* Trondheim, Norway: Alta.

———. 2000. *Changing Rock Carvings: Changing Societies? A Case from Arctic Norway.* Adoranten. Scandinavian Society for Prehistoric Art, Tanum Hällristningsmuseum, Underslös.

Hood, B. 1988. Sacred Pictures, Sacred Rocks: Ideological and Social Space in the North Norwegian Stone Age. *Norwegian Archaeological Review* 21: 65–84.

Hublin, Jean-Jacques, Darlene Weston, Philipp Gunz, Mike Richards, Wil Roebroeks, Jan Glimmerveen, and Luc Anthonis. 2009. Out of the North Sea: The Zeeland Ridges Neandertal. *Journal of Human Evolution* 57: 777–785.

Humphrey, Nicholas. 1998. Cave Art, Autism, and the Evolution of the Human Mind. *Cambridge Archaeological Journal* 8: 165–191.

Jackes, M. 2004. Osteological Evidence for Mesolithic and Neolithic Violence: Problems of Interpretation. In *Violent Interactions in the Mesolithic: Evidence and Meaning,* M. Roksandic (ed.), pp. 23–39. Oxford: BAR International Series 1237.

Jackes, M., and P. Alvim. 2006. Reconstructing Moita do Sebastião, the First Step. In *Complexo Mesolítico de Muge: Passado, Presente et Futuro. Proceedings of the IV Congresso de Arqueologia Peninsular,* J. Rolão (ed.), pp. 13–25. Faro: Universidade do Algarve.

Jacobsen, Thomas W. 1981. Franchthi Cave and the Beginning of Settled Village Life in Greece. *Hesperia* 50: 303–319.

———, and William R. Farrand. 1988. *Franchthi Cave and Paralia: Maps, Plans, and Sections.* Excavations at Franchthi Cave, Greece, fascicle 1. Bloomington: Indiana University Press.

Jöris, O., and Th. Terberger. 2001. Zur Rekonstruktion eines Zeltes mit trapezförmigem Grundriß am Magdalénien-Fundplatz Gönnersdorf/Mittelrhein. *Archäologisches Korrespondenzblatt* 31: 163–172.

Kelly, R. L. 1995. *The Foraging Spectrum: Diversity in Hunter-Gatherer Lifeways.* Washington, DC: Smithsonian Institution Press.

Kilikoglou, V., Y. Bassiakos, R. C. Doonan, and J. Stratis. 1997. NAA and ICP analysis of Obsidian from Central Europe and the Aegean: Source Characterisation and Provenance Determination. *Journal of Radioanalytical and Nuclear Chemistry* 216: 87–93.

Klein, Richard G. 2002. *The Dawn of Human Culture*. New York: Wiley.

Klima, B. 1962. The First Ground-Plan of an Upper Paleolithic Loess Settlement in Middle Europe and Its Meaning. In *Courses Toward Urban Life*, R. J. Brianwood and G. R. Willey (eds.), pp. 193–210. Chicago: Aldine.

———. 1995. *Dolní Vestonice II. Ein Mammutjägerplatz und seine Bestattungen. ERAUL* 73/*Dol. Vest. stud.* 3.

Kotsakis, Kosta. 2001. Mesolithic to Neolithic in Greece: Continuity, Discontinuity, or Change of Course. *Documenta Praehistorica* 28: 63–73.

Kubiak-Martens, L. 1999. The Plant Food Component of the Diet at the Late Mesolithic (Ertebølle) Settlement at Tybrind Vig, Denmark. *Vegetation History and Archaeobotany* 8: 117–127.

Lanting, J. N., B. W. Kooi, W. A. Casparie, and R. van Hinte. 1999. Bows from the Netherlands. *Journal of the Society of Archer-Antiquaries* 42: 7–10.

Leroi-Gourhan, André. 1972. Les huttes châtelperroniennes d'Arcy-sur-Cure et les tentes de Pincevent. In *Analyse des structures d'habitat: problèmes de techniques et d'interprétation*, A. Leroi-Gourhan and M. Brezillon (eds.), pp. 134–161. Paris: Collège de France.

———. 1984. *Pincevent: Campement magdalénien de chasseurs de rennes*. Paris: Guides archéologiques de la France, Ministeé re de la Culture, Imprimerie Nationale.

———, and M. Brézillon. 1972. Fouilles de Pincevent: essai d'analyse ethnographique d'un habitat magdalénien (la section 36), 1. *Gallia préhistoire*, Supplement 7. Paris : CNRS.

Lewis-Williams, D. J. 2002. *The Mind in the Cave: Consciousness and the Origins of Art*. London: Thames and Hudson.

Lødøen, Trond, and Gro Mandt. 2010. *The Rock Art of Norway*. Oxford: Windgather Press.

Louwe Kooijmans, L. P. (ed.). 2001. *Hardinxveld-Giessendam Polderweg. Een mesolithisch jachtkamp in het revierengebied (5500–5000 u.Chr.)*. Amersfoort: Rapportage Archeologische Monumentenzorg 83.

———. 2003. Hardinxveld Sites in the Rhine/Meuse Delta, the Netherlands, 5500–4500 cal B.C. In *Mesolithic on the Move: Papers Presented at the Sixth International Conference on the Mesolithic in Europe, Stockholm 2000*. Lars Larsson et al. (eds.), pp. 608–624. Oxford: Oxbow Books.

———. 2007. The Gradual Transition to Farming in the Lower Rhine Basin. *Proceedings of the British Academy* 144: 287–309.

Lubell, David, Mary Jackes, Henry Schwarcz, Martin Knyf, and Chris Meiklejohn. 1994. The Mesolithic/Neolithic Transition in Portugal: Isotopic and Dental Evidence of Diet. *Journal of Archaeological Science* 21: 201–216.

Mason, S., J. Hather, and G. Hillman. 1994. Preliminary Investigation of the Plant Macro-Remains from Dolní Vestonice II and Its Implications for the Role of Plant Foods in Palaeolithic and Mesolithic Europe. *Antiquity* 68: 48–57.

McCartan, Sinead, Rick Schulting, Graeme Warren, and Peter Woodman (eds.). 2009. *Mesolithic Horizons*. Oxford: Oxbow Books.

Mellars, Paul A. 2006. A New Radiocarbon Revolution and the Dispersal of Modern Humans in Eurasia. *Nature* 439: 931–993.

———, K. Boyle, O. Bar-Yosef, and C. H. R. Stringer (eds.). 2007. *Rethinking the Human Revolution: New Behavioural and Biological Perspectives on the Origin and Dispersal of Modern Humans*. Cambridge: UK McDonald Institute Monographs. McDonald Institute of Archaeological Research.

Menu, Michael. 2009. L'analyse de l'art préhistorique. *L'Anthropologie* 113: 547–558.

Milner, Nicky, and Peter Woodman (eds.). 2005. *Mesolithic Studies at the Beginning of the 21st Century*. Oxford: Oxbow Books.

Mol, Dick, Klaas Post, Jelle W. F. Reumer, Johannes van der Plicht, John de Vos, Bas van Geel, Guido van Reenen, Jan Peter Pals, and Jan Glimmerveen. 2006. The Eurogeul:

First Report of the Palaeontological, Palynological and Archaeological Investigations of this Part of the North Sea. *Quaternary International* 142–143: 178–185.

Møller, Jakob J. 1987. Shoreline Relation and Prehistoric Settlement in Northern Norway. *Norwegian Journal of Geography* 41: 45–60.

Moss, Emily H. 1987. Function and Spatial Distribution of Flint Artifacts from Pincevent Section 36 Level IV 40. *Oxford Journal of Archaeology* 6: 165–184.

Out, Welmoed A. 2009. *Sowing the Seed? Human Impact and Plant Subsistence in Dutch Wetlands During the Late Mesolithic and Early and Middle Neolithic (5500–3400 cal BC)*. Ph.D. Department of Archaeology, University of Leiden.

———. 2010. Firewood Collection Strategies at Dutch Wetland Sites in the Process of Neolithisation. *The Holocene* 20: 191–204.

Ovodov, N. D., S. J. Crockford, Y. V. Kuzmin, T. F. G. Higham, G. W. L. Hodgins, and J. van der Plicht. 2011. A 33,000-Year-Old Incipient Dog from the Altai Mountains of Siberia: Evidence of the Earliest Domestication Disrupted by the Last Glacial Maximum. *PLoS ONE* 6(7): e22821.

Pailhaugue, N. 1998. Faune et saisons d'occupation de la salle Monique au Magdalénien Pyrénéen, Grotte de la Vache (Alliat, Ariège, France), *Quaternaire* 9: 385–400.

Pales, Leon. 1969. *Les Gravures de la Marche: Felins et Ours. 1.* Bordeaux: Imprimeries Delmas.

Payne, Sebastian. 1975. Faunal Change at Franchthi Cave from 20,000 BC to 3,000 BC. In *Archaeozoological Studies,* A. T. Clason (ed.), pp. 120–131. Amsterdam: North-Holland and American Elsevier.

Perlès, Catherine. 2001. *The Early Neolithic in Greece: The First Farming Communities in Europe.* Cambridge: Cambridge University Press.

———. 2003. An Alternate (and Old-Fashioned View) of Neolithisation in Greece. *Documenta Praehistorica* 30: 99–113.

Pettitt, Paul. 2008. Art and the Middle-to-Upper Paleolithic Transition in Europe: Comments on the Archaeological Arguments for an Early Upper Paleolithic Antiquity of the Grotte Chauvet Art. *Journal of Human Evolution* 55: 908–917.

———, and Paul Bahn. 2003. Current Problems in Dating Palaeolithic Cave Art: Candamo and Chauvet. *Antiquity* 77: 134–141.

Pinçon, G., Ph. Walter, M. Menu, and D. Buisson. 1989. Les objets colorés du Paléolithique supérieur: cas de la grotte de La Vache (Ariège). *Bulletin de la Société préhistorique française* 86(6): 183–192.

Poplin, F. 1976. *Les grands vertébrés de Gönnersdorf.* Fouilles 1968. Der Magdalenien-Fundplatz Gönnersdorf 2. Frankurt: Franz Steiner Verlag.

Price, T. Douglas, and Erik Brinch Petersen. 1987, March. Prehistoric Coastal Settlement in Mesolithic Denmark. *Scientific American,* 112–121.

Ramstein, G., M. Kageyama, J. Guiot, H. Wu, C. Hély, G. Krinner, and S. Brewer. 2007. How Cold Was Europe at the Last Glacial Maximum? A Synthesis of the Progress Achieved Since the First PMIP Model-Data Comparison. *Climates of the Past Discussions* 3: 197–220.

Rensink, E. 1995. On Magdalenian Mobility and Land Use in North-West Europe. *Archaeological Dialogues* 2(2): 85–119.

Revedina, Anna, Biancamaria Arangurenb, Roberto Becattinia, Laura Longoc, Emanuele Marconid, Marta Mariotti Lippie, Natalia Skakunf, Andrey Sinitsynf, Elena Spiridonovag, and Jiří Svoboda. 2010. Thirty Thousand-year-old Evidence of Plant Food Processing. *Proceedings of the National Academy of Science* 107: 18815–18819.

Richards, M. P., and R. E. M. Hedges. 1999. Stable Isotope Evidence for Similarities in the Types of Marine Foods Used by Late Mesolithic Humans at Sites Along the Atlantic Coast of Europe. *Journal of Archaeological Science* 26: 717–722.

Riede, Felix. 2008. The Laacher See-eruption (12,920 BP) and Material Culture Change at the End of the Allerød in Northern Europe. *Journal of Archaeological Science* 35: 591–599.

Roche, Jean. 1963. Le gisement mésolithique de Moita do Sebastiao à Muge (Portugal). Les traces d'habitation et d'organisation sociale. *Bulletin de la Société Préhistorique Française* 60: 68–73.

Roche, J. 1972. Les amas coquilliers (concheiros) mésolithique de Muge (Portugal). *Die Anfänge des Neolithikums vom Orient bis Nordeuropa Westliches Mittelmeergebiet und Britische Inseln. Fundamenta* 8: 72–107.

Roche, J. 1972. *Le gisement mésolithique de Moita do Sebastião: Muge, Portugal.* Lisbon: Instituto de Alta Cultura.

Roebroeks, W., M. Mussi, J. Svoboda, and K. Fennema. 2000. *Hunters of the Golden Age. The Mid Upper Palaeolithic of Eurasia 30,000–20,000 BP.* Institute of Archaeology Leiden, University of Leiden.

Roksandic, Mirjana. 2006. Analysis of Burials from the New Excavations of the Sites Cabeço da Amoreira and Arruda (Muge, Portugal). In *Do Epipapelolítico ao Calcolítico na Península Ibérica. Actas do IV Congresso de Arqueologia Peninsular*, N. Bicho and N. H. Veríssimo (eds.), pp. 43–54. Faro: University of Algarve Press.

Rolao, J. M. and M. Roksandic. 2007. The Muge Mesolithic Complex: New results from the Excavations of Cabeco da Amoreira, 2001–2003. In *Shell Middens in Atlantic Europe*, N. Milner, O. E. Craig and G. N. Bailey (eds.), pp. 78–85. Oxford: Oxbow Books.

Sampson, C. Garth. 1988. *Stylistic Boundaries Among Mobile Hunter-Foragers.* Washington, DC: Smithsonian Institutional Press.

Schmider, B. 1971. Les industries lithiques du Paleolithique superieur en Ile-de-France. *Gallia Prehistoire*, suppl. 6.

Schmider, Beatrice. 1982. The Magdalenian Culture of the Paris River-Basin and Its Relationship with the Nordic Cultures of the Late Old Stone Age. *World Archaeology* 14: 259–269.

———. 2002. *L'Aurignacien de la grotte du Renne: Les Fouilles d'André Leroi-Gourhan à Arcy-sur-Cure (Yonne).* Paris: CNRS.

———, B. Valentin, D. Baffier, F. David, M. Julien, Arl. Leroi-Gourhan, C. Mourer-Chauvire, Th. Poulain, A. Roblin-Jouve, and Y. Taborin. 1995. L'abri du Lagopède (fouilles Leroi-Gourhan) et le Magdalénien des grottes de la Cure (Yonne). *Gallia Préhistoire* 37: 55–114.

Schwartz, Jeffrey H., and Ian Tattersall. 2010. Fossil Evidence for the Origin of *Homo sapiens. Yearbook of Physical Anthropology* 53: 94–121.

Smits, E., and L. P. Louwe Kooijmans. 2001. De menselijke skeletresten. In *Hardinxveld-Giessendam, Polderweg. Een jachtkamp uit het Laat-Mesolithicum, 5500–5000 v. Chr.*, L. P. Louwe Kooijmans (ed.), pp. 419–440. Amersfoort: Rapportage Archeologische Monumentenzorg 83.

Smits, E., A. R. Millard, G. Nowell, and D. G. Pearson. 2008. Isotopic Investigation of Diet and Residential Mobility in the Neolithic of the Lower Rhine Basin. *European Journal of Archaeology* 13: 5–31.

Smits, E., and J. van der Plicht. 2009. Mesolithic and Neolithic Human Remains in the Netherlands: Physical Anthropological and Stable Isotope Investigations. *Journal of Archaeology in the Low Countries* 1: 55–85.

Soffer, O., J. M. Adovasio, and D.C. Hyland. 2000. The "Venus" Figurines: Textiles, Basketry, and Status in the Upper Paleolithic. *Current Anthropology* 41: 511–537.

Sognnes, K. 2001. *Prehistoric Imagery and Landscapes: Rock Art in Stjørdal, Trøndelag, Norway.* BAR International Series 998. Oxford: Archaeopress.

———. 2003. On Shoreline Dating of Rock Art. *Acta Archaeologica* 74: 189–209.

Stapert, D., and Th. Terberger. 1989: Gönnersdorf Concentration III: Investigating the Possibility of Multiple Occupations. *Palaeohistoria* 31: 59–95.

Stevens, Rhiannon E., Tamsin C. O'Connell, Robert E. M. Hedges, and Martin Street. 2009. Radiocarbon and Stable Isotope Investigations at the Central Rhineland Sites of Gönnersdorf and Andernach-Martinsberg, Germany. *Journal of Human Evolution* 57: 131–148.

Street, M. 1998. The Archaeology of the Pleistocene-Holocene Transition in the Northern Rhineland, Germany. *Quaternary International* 49/50: 45–67.

Svoboda, Jiří A. 2007. The Gravettian on the Middle Danube. *Paleo* 19: 203–220.

———, and L. Sedláčková (eds.). 2004. *The Gravettian Along the Danube. Dolni Vestonice Studies* 11. Brno: Institute of Archeology.

Svoboda, J., V. Lozek, and E. Vlcek. 1996. *Hunters Between East and West: The Paleolithic of Moravia*. New York: Plenum.

Terberger, Th. 1997. *Die Siedlungsbefunde des Magdalénien-Fundplatzes Gönnersdorf— Konzentrationen III und IV*. Der Magdalénien-Fundplatz Gönnersdorf 6. Stuttgart: Franz Steiner.

Testart, A. 1982. The Significance of Food Storage Among Hunter-Gatherers: Residence Patterns, Population Densities and Social Inequalities. *Current Anthropology* 23: 523–545.

Teyssandier, Nicolas. 2008. Revolution or Evolution: The Emergence of the Upper Paleolithic in Europe. *World Archaeology* 40: 493–519.

Trinkaus, Erik. 2005. Early Modern Humans. *Annual Review of Anthropology* 34: 207–230.

———, O. Moldovan, Ş. Milota, A. Bîlgăr, L. Sarcina, S. Athreya, S. E. Bailey, R. Rodrigo, M. Gherase, T. Higham, C. Bronk Ramsey, and J. Van Der Plicht. 2003. An Early Modern Human from Peştera cu Oase, Romania. *Proceedings of the National Academy of Science U.S.A.* 100 :11231–11236.

Trinkaus, Erik, and Jiří Svoboda. 2005. *Early Modern Human Evolution in Central Europe. The People of Dolní Věstonice and Pavlov*. Oxford: Oxford University Press.

Trinkaus, E., J. Zilhão, H. Rougier, R. Rodrigo, S. Milota, M. Gherase, L. Sarcinā, O. Moldovan, I. Băltean, V. Codrea, S. E. Bailey, R. G. Franciscus, M. Ponce de Léon, and C. P. E. Zollikofer. 2006. The Peştera cu Oase and Early Modern Humans in Southeastern Europe. In *When Neanderthals and Modern Humans Met*, N. J. Conard (ed.), pp. 145–164. Tübingen: Kerns Verlag.

Valoch, K. 1996. *Le Paléolithique en Tchéquie et en Slovaquie. Préhistoire d'Europe* 3. Grenoble: Jerôme Millon.

Van Gijn, Annelou. 2008. Exotic Flint and the Negotiation of a New Identity in the 'Margins' of the Agricultural World: The Case of the Rhine-Meuse Delta. In *Between Foraging and Farming*, H. Fokkens, B. J. Coles, A. L. Van Gijn, J. P. Kleijne, H. H. Ponjee, and C. G. Slappendel (eds.), *Analecta Praehistorica Leidensia* 40, pp. 193–202. Leiden.

Van Wijngaarden-Bakker, Louise H. 2002. Winter in a Wetland: The Bird Remains from a Late Mesolithic Camp Site at Polderweg, Municipality Hardinxveld-Giessendam. *Acta zoologica cracoviensia* 45: 55–64.

Weinstock, Jaco. 2002. Reindeer Hunting in the Upper Palaeolithic: Sex Ratios as a Reflection of Different Procurement Strategies. *Journal of Archaeological Science* 29: 365–377.

Weninger, Bernhard, Rick Schulting, Marcel Bradtmöller, Lee Clare, Mark Collard, Kevan Edinborough, Johanna Hilpert, Olaf Jöris, Marcel Niekus, Eelco J. Rohling, and Bernd Wagner. 2008. The Catastrophic Final Flooding of Doggerland by the Storegga Slide Tsunami. *Documenta Praehistorica* 35: 1–24.

White, Randall. 1986. *Dark Cave, Bright Visions: Life in Ice Age Europe*. New York: Norton.

Whittle, Alasdair, and Vicki Cummings (eds.). 2008. *Going Over: The Mesolithic-Neolithic Transition in North West Europe*. Oxford: Oxford University Press.

Wiessner, Polly. 1984. Reconsidering the Behavioral Basis for Style: A Case Study Among the Kalahari San. *Journal of Anthropological Archaeology* 3: 190–234.

Wobst, M. 1974. Boundary Conditions for Paleolithic Social Systems: A Simulation Approach. *American Antiquity* 29: 147–78.

Woodburn, J. 1982. Egalitarian Societies. *Man* 17: 431–451.

Woodman, P. C. 1978. *The Mesolithic in Ireland: Hunter-Gatherers in an Insular Environment*. BAR British Series 58. Oxford: Archaeopress.

———. 1985. *Excavations at Mount Sandel 1973–77: County Londonderry*. Belfast: Stationery Office Books.

———, E. Anderson and N. Finlay (eds.). 1999. *Excavations at Ferriter's Cove, 1983–95: Last Foragers, First Farmers in the Dingle Peninsula*. Bray: Wordwell.

Zelinkova, M. 2007. Bone and Antler Industry from Dolní Věstonice I. *Acta Musei Moraviae*. 92: 9–51.

Zilhao, Joao. 1995. The Age of the Coa Valley (Portugal) Rock-Art: Validation of Archaeological Dating to the Palaeolithic and Refutation of 'Scientific' Dating to Historic or Proto-Historic Times. *Antiquity* 69: 883–901.

———. 2004. Muge Shell Middens. In *Ancient Europe 8000 BC–AD 1000, Encyclopedia of the Barbarian World*, P. Bogucki and P. Crabtree (eds.), pp. 164–166. New York: Scribner.

———. 2007. Oase Cave: The Discovery of Europe's Oldest Modern Humans. *Current Archaeology* 24: 32–41.

———, Thierry Aubry, Antonio F. Carvalho, Antonio M. Baptista, Mario V. Gomes, and Jose Meireles. 1997. The Rock Art of the Coa Valley (Portugal) and Its Archaeological Context: First Results of Current Research. *Journal of European Archaeology* 5: 7–49.

Zilhao, J., E. Trinkaus, S. Constantin, S. Milota, M. Gherase, L. Sarcina, A. Q. Danuciu, H. Rougier, J. Quilès, and R. Rodrigo. 2007. The Pestera cu Oase People, Europe's Earliest Modern Humans. In *Rethinking the Human Revolution: New Behavioural and Biological Perspectives on the Origin and Dispersal of Modern Humans*, P. Mellars, K. Boyle, O. Bar-Yosef, and C. H. R. Stringer (eds.), pp. 249–262. Cambridge: McDonald Institute Monographs.

Zubrow, Ezra, Francoise Audouze, and James G. Enloe (eds.). 2010. *The Magdalenian Household: Unraveling Domesticity*. Albany: State University of New York Press.

Zvelebil, Marek (ed.). 1986. *Hunters in Transition: Mesolithic Societies of Temperate Eurasia and Their Transition to Farming*. Cambridge: Cambridge University Press.

Chapter Four   The First Farmers

Agius, A. J. 1959. *The Hal Saflieni Hypogeum*. Malta: Union Press.

Akeret, Örni, Jean Nicolas Haas, Urs Leuzinger, and Stefanie Jacomet. 1999. Plant Macrofossils and Pollen in Goat/Sheep Faeces from the Neolithic Lake-Shore Settlement Arbon Bleiche 3, Switzerland. *Holocene* 9: 175–182.

Allard, Pierre, Francoise Bostyn, Francois Giligny, and Jacek Lech (eds.). 2009. *Flint Mining in Prehistoric Europe*. British Archaeological Reports S1891.

Allard, Pierre, and Laurence Burnez-Lanotte. 2009. An Economy of Surplus Production in the Early Neolithic of Hesbaye (Belgium): Bandkeramik blade debitate at Verlaine "Petit Paradis." In *Flint Mining in Prehistoric Europe,* Pierre Allard, Francoise Bostyn, Francois Giligny, and Jacek Lech (eds.), pp. 31–40. British Archaeological Reports S1891.

Allison, Penelope (ed.). 1999. *The Archaeology of Household Activities*. London: Routledge.

Ammerman, Albert, and Paolo Biagi. 2003. *Widening Harvest: The Neolithic Transition in Europe*. New York: AIA Colloquia and Conference Papers.

Anthony, David. 2010. The Rise and Fall of Old Europe. In *The Lost World of Old Europe,* David Anthony (ed.), pp. 28–57. Princeton: Princeton University Press.

———, and Jennifer Chi. 2010. *The Lost World of Old Europe: The Danube Valley, 5000–3500 BC*. Princeton: Princeton University Press.

Arbogast, R.-M., S. Jacomet, M. Magny, and J. Schibler. 2006. The Significance of Climate Fluctuations for Lake Level Changes and Shifts in Subsistence Economy During the Late Neolithic (4300–244 BC) in Central Europe. *Vegetation History and Archaeobotany* 15: 403–418.

Arribas, A., F. Molina, F. Carrión, Contreras, G. Martínez, A. Ramos, L. Sáez, F. De La Torre, I. Blanco, and J. Martínez. 1987. Informe preliminar de los resultados obtenidos durante la VI campaña de excavaciones en el poblado de Los Millares (Santa Fe de Mondújar, Almería), 1985. *Anuario Arqueológico de Andalucía* 1985 II: 245–262.

Bailey, Douglass. 2000. *Balkan Prehistory*. London: Routledge.

———. 2004. Varna. In *Ancient Europe 8000 B.C.–A.D. 1000. Vol. 1. The Mesolithic to Copper Age (c. 8000–2000 B.C.),* P. Bogucki and P. J. Crabtree (eds.), pp. 341–344. New York: Scribner.

———. 2005. *Prehistoric Figurines: Representation and Corporeality in the Neolithic.* London: Routledge.

———. 2010. The Figurines of Old Europe. In *The Lost World of Old Europe,* David Anthony (ed.), pp. 112–127. Princeton: Princeton University Press.

———, Alasdair Whittle, and Dani Hofmann (eds.). 2008. *Living Well Together? Settlement and Materiality in the Neolithic of South-East and Central Europe.* Oxford: Oxbow Books.

Banning, E. B. 1998. The Neolithic Period: Triumphs of Architecture, Agriculture, and Art. *Near Eastern Archaeology* 61(4): 188–237.

Bar-Yosef, Ofer. 2011. Climatic Fluctuations and Early Farming in West and East Asia. In *The Beginnings of Agriculture: New Data, New Ideas.* O. Bar-Yosef and T. D. Price (eds.). *Current Anthropology* 52, Suppl. 4: S175–S193.

Barker, Graeme. 1985. *Prehistoric Farming in Europe.* Cambridge: Cambridge University Press.

———. 2009. *The Agricultural Revolution in Prehistory.* Oxford: Oxford University Press.

Barnett, William. 2000. Cardial Pottery and the Agricultural Transition in Mediterranean Europe. In *Europe's First Farmers,* T. Douglas Price (ed.), pp. 93–116. Cambridge: Cambridge University Press.

Belfer-Cohen, Anna, and A. Nigel Goring-Morris. 2011. Becoming Farmers, the Inside Story. In *The Beginnings of Agriculture: New Data, New Ideas.* O. Bar-Yosef and T. D. Price (eds.). *Current Anthropology* 52, Suppl. 4: S195–S208.

Beltran, Antonio. 1982. *Rock Art of the Spanish Levant.* Cambridge: Cambridge University Press.

Bentley, A., R. Krause, T. D. Price, and B. Kaufmann. 2003. Human Mobility at the Early Neolithic Settlement of Vaihingen, Germany: Evidence from Strontium Isotope Analysis. *Archaeometry* 45: 471–486.

Bentley, R. Alexander, and Corina Knipper. 2005. Transhumance at the Early Neolithic Settlement at Vaihingen (Germany). *Antiquity* 79: 306–315.

Bogaard, Amy. 2004. *Neolithic Farming in Central Europe: An Archaeobotanical Study of Crop Husbandry.* London: Routledge.

Bogaard, Amy, Rüdiger Krause, and Hans-Christoph Strien. 2011. Towards a Social Geography of Cultivation and Plant Use in an Early Farming Community: Vaihingen an der Enz, South-West Germany. *Antiquity* 85: 417–433.

Bogucki, Peter. 1988. *Forest Farmers and Stock Breeders: Early Agriculture and Its Consequences in North-Central Europe.* Cambridge: Cambridge University Press.

———. 1993. Animal Traction and Household Economies in Neolithic Europe. *Antiquity* 67: 492–503.

———. 2000. How Agriculture Came to North-Central Europe. In *Europe's First Farmers,* T. D. Price (ed.), pp. 197–218. Cambridge: Cambridge University Press.

———, and Pam Crabtree (eds.). 2003. *Ancient Europe 8000 B.C.—A.D. 1000: Encyclopedia of the Barbarian World.* Farmington Hills, MI: Scribner.

Bonanno, A., T. Gouder, C. Malone, and S. Stoddart. 1990. Monuments in an Island Society: The Maltese Context. *World Archaeology* 22: 190–205.

Bonsall C., G. Cook, R. Lennon, D. Harkness, M. Scott, L. Bartosiewicz, and K. McSweeney. 2000. Stable Isotopes, Radiocarbon and the Mesolithic-Neolithic Transition in the Iron Gate. *Documenta Praehistorica* 27: 119–132.

Boríç, Dusan. 2002. The Lepenski Vir Conundrum: Reinterpretation of the Mesolithic and Neolithic Sequences in the Danube Gorges. *Antiquity* 76: 1026–1039.

———. 2009. Absolute Dating of Metallurgical Innovations in the Vinča Culture of the Balkans. In *Metals and Societies: Studies in honour of Barbara S. Ottaway,* T. L. Kienlin and Ben W. Roberts (eds.), pp. 191–245. Bonn: Verlag Dr. Rudolf Habelt GMBH.

———, and Vesna Dimitrijevíc. 2007. When Did the 'Neolithic Package' Reach Lepenski Vir: Radiometric and Faunal Evidence. *Documenta Praehistorica* 34: 53–72.

Bortenschlager, Sigmar, and Klaus Oeggl (eds.). 2000. *The Iceman and His Natural Environment: Palaeobotanical Results*. New York: Springer.

Bosch, A., J. Chinchilla, J. Tarrús, et al. 2000. *El poblat lacustre neolític de la Draga. Excavacions de 1990–1998*. Girona: Monografies del CASC 2.

———. 2006. *Els objectes de fusta del poblat neolític de la Draga. Excavacions de 1995–2005*. Girona: Monografies del CASC 6.

Boulestin, B., A. Zeeb-Lanz, Ch. Jeunesse, F. Haack, R.-M. Arbogast, and A. Denaire. 2009. Cannibalism in the Linear Pottery Culture at Herxheim (Palatinate, Germany). *Antiquity* 83: 968–982.

Bradford, J. S. P. 1949. Buried Landscapes in Southern Italy. *Antiquity* 23: 58–72.

———, and P. R. Williams Hunt. 1946. Siticulosa Apulia. *Antiquity* 20: 191–200.

Bradley, Richard. 1998. *The Significance of Monuments: Shaping the Human Experience in Neolithic and Bronze Age Europe*. London: Routledge.

———. 2007. *Ritual and Domestic Life in Prehistoric Europe*. London: Taylor and Francis.

Bramanti, B., M. G. Thomas, W. Haak, M. Unterlaender, P. Jores, K. Tambets, I. Antanaitis-Jacobs, M. N. Haidle, R. Jankauskas, C.-J. Kind, F. Lueth, T. Terberger, J. Hiller, S. Matsumura, P. Forster, and J. Burger. 2009. Genetic Discontinuity Between Local Hunter-Gatherers and Central Europe's First Farmers. *Science* 326: 137–140.

Budja, Mihael. 2003. Seals, Contracts, and Tokens in the Balkans Early Neolithic: Where in the Puzzle. *Documenta Praehistorica* 30: 115–130.

Burl, Aubrey. 1995. *A Guide to the Stone Circles of Britain, Ireland, and Brittany*. New Haven: Yale University Press.

Card, Nick. 2010. Ness of Brodgar. *Current Archaeology* 241: 12–19.

Cauvin, Jacques. 2000. *The Birth of the Gods and the Origins of Agriculture*. Cambridge: Cambridge University Press. Translated from the French.

Chapman, John. 1981. *The Vinča Culture of South-East Europe: Studies in Chronology, Economy and Society*. Oxford: BAR International Series. 117.

———. 1990. Social Inequality on Bulgarian Tells and the Varna Problem. In *The Social Archaeology of Houses*, R. Samson (ed.), pp. 49–98. Edinburgh: Edinburgh University Press.

———. 1991. The Creation of Social Arenas in the Neolithic and Copper Age of S.E. Europe: The Case of Varna. In *Sacred and Profane*, Paul Garwood, David Jennings, Robin Skeates, and Judith Toms (eds.), pp. 152–170.

———. 1994. The Origins of Farming in South East Europe. *Préhistoire Européenne* 6: 133–156.

———. 2000. *Fragmentation in Archaeology: People, Places and Broken Objects in the Prehistory of South Eastern Europe*. London: Routledge.

———, Bisserka Gaydarska, Ana Raduncheva, and Bistra Koleva. 2007. *Parts and Wholes: Fragmentation in Prehistoric Context*. Oxford: Oxbow Books.

Chapman, J., B. Gaydarska, and V. Slavchev. 2008. The Life Histories of Spondylus Shell Rings from the Varna I Eneolithic Cemetery (Northeast Bulgaria): Transformation, Revelation, Fragmentation and Deposition. *Acta Musei Varnaensis* 6: 139–162.

Chapman, J., T. Higham, B. Gaydarska, V. Slavchev, and N. Honch. 2006. The Social Context of the Emergence, Development and Abandonment of the Varna Cemetery, Bulgaria. *European Journal of Archaeology* 9: 159–183.

Chapman, R. W. 1990. *Emerging Complexity: The Later Prehistory of Southeast Spain, Iberia and the West Mediterranean*. Cambridge: Cambridge University Press.

———. 1995. Ten Years After: Megaliths, Mortuary Practices, and the Territorial Model. In *Regional Approaches to Mortuary Analysis*, L. A. Beck, (ed.), pp. 29–51. New York: Springer.

———. 2005. Food Systems, Power Structures and Social Differentiation: Case Studies from the Prehistoric Mediterranean. In *Social and Economic Dynamics Among New World and Old World Middle-Range Societies: Changing Food Systems and New Power Structures*, I. Kuijt and W. C. Prentiss (eds.), pp. 231–249. Tucson: University of Arizona Press.

———. 2008. Producing Inequalities: Regional Sequences in Later Prehistoric Southern Spain. *Journal of World Prehistory* 21: 195–260.

Chernykh, E. N. 1978. Aibunar: A Balkan Copper Mine of the Fourth Millennium B.C. *Proceedings of the Prehistoric Society* 44: 203–217.

Cherry, J. F. 1990. The First Colonization of the Mediterranean Islands: A Review of Recent Research. *Journal of Mediterranean Archaeology* 3: 145–221.

Childe, V. Gordon. 1931. *Skara Brae, a Pictish Village in Orkney.* Meeting held in London: monograph of the Royal Commission on the Ancient and Historical Monuments of Scotland.

———, and D. V. Clarke. 1983. *Skara Brae.* Edinburgh: Her Majesty's Stationery Office.

Chippindale, Christopher. 1983. *Stonehenge Complete.* London: Thames and Hudson.

Clarke, D. V., and Niall Sharples. 1985. *Settlements and Subsistence in the Third Millennium BC.* In *The Prehistory of Orkney BC 4000–1000 AD,* Colin Renfrew (ed.), pp. 201–234, Edinburgh: Edinburgh University Press.

Cleal, Rosamund M. J., K. E. Walker, and R. Montague. 1995. *Stonehenge in Its Landscape: Twentieth-Century Excavations.* London: English Heritage.

Collet, Hélène, Anne Hauzeur, and Jacek Lech. 2008. The Prehistoric Flint Mining Complex at Spiennes (Belgium) on the Occasion of Its Discovery 140 Years Ago. In *Flint Mining in Prehistoric Europe,* Pierre Allard, Francoise Bostyn, Francois Giligny, and Jacek Lech (eds.), pp. 41–57. British Archaeological Reports S1891.

Conneller, Chantal. 2010. *An Archaeology of Materials: Substantial Transformations in Early Prehistoric Europe.* London: Routledge.

Cooney, George. 2000. Coping with Death, Changing the Landscape. In *Neolithic Orkney in Its European Context*, A. Ritchie (ed.), pp. 247–258. Cambridge: McDonald Institute Monographs.

Craig, Oliver E., John Chapman, Carl Heron, Laura H. Willis, László Bartosiewicz, Gillian Taylor, Alasdair Whittle, and Matthew Collins. 2005. Did the First Farmers of Central and Eastern Europe Produce Dairy Foods? *Antiquity* 79: 882–894.

Cruz Berrocal, María, and Juan Vicent García. 2007. Rock Art as an Archaeological and Social Indicator: The Neolithisation of the Iberian Peninsula. *Journal of Anthropological Archaeology* 26: 676–697.

Cullen, T. (ed.). 2001. *Aegean Prehistory: A Review.* Boston: Archaeological Institute of America.

Cunliffe, Barry. 2008. *Europe Between the Oceans: 9000 BC–AD 1000.* New Haven: Yale University Press.

———, and Colin Renfrew. 1997. *Science and Stonehenge.* Oxford: Oxford University Press.

Dams, M., and L. Dams. 1977. Spanish Rock Art Depicting Honey Gathering During the Mesolithic. *Nature* 268: 228–230.

Daniel, Glynn E. 1963. *The Megalith Builders of Western Europe.* Baltimore: Penguin.

De Capitani, Annick, Sabine Deschler-Erb, Urs Leuzinger, Elisabeth Marti-Grädel, and Jörg Schibler. 2002. *Die jungsteinzeitliche Seeufersiedlung Arbon Bleiche 3: Funde.* Archäologie im Thurgau, no. 11. Frauenfeld, Switzerland: Amt für Archäologie Kanton Thurgau.

Demoule, J.-P., and C. Perlès. 1993. The Greek Neolithic: A New Review. *Journal of World Prehistory* 7: 355–416.

Dimitrijevic, V., and C. Tripkovic. 2006. Spondylus and Glycymeris Bracelets: Trade Reflections at Neolithic Vinca-Belo Brdo. *Documenta Praehistorica* 33: 1–16.

Dolukhanov, P., A. Shukurov, D. Gronenborn, D. Sokoloff, V. Timofeev, and G. Zaitseva. 2005. The Chronology of Neolithic Dispersal in Central and Eastern Europe. *Journal of Archaeological Science* 32: 1441–1458.

Edmonds, Marc. 1995. *Ancestral Geographies of the Neolithic: Landscape, Monuments and Memory.* London: Routledge.

Eriksen, Palle. 2008. The Great Mound of Newgrange. An Irish Multi-Period Mound Spanning from the Megalithic Tomb Period to the Early Bronze Age. *Acta Archaeologica* 79: 250–273.

Esquivel, J. A., and E. Navas. 2007. Geometric Architectural Pattern and Constructive Energy Analysis at Los Millares Copper Age Settlement (Santa Fe de Mondújar, Almería, Andalusia). *Journal of Archaeological Science* 34: 894–904.

Fairén, Sara. 2004. Rock-Art and the Transition to Farming: The Neolithic Landscape of the Central Mediterranean Coast of Spain. *Oxford Journal of Archaeology* 23: 1–19.

Fol, Alexander, and Jan Lichardus (eds.). 1988. *Macht, Herrschaft und Gold.* Moderne Galerie des Saarland-Museums. Saarbrüken: Krüger.

Fowler, Brenda. 2000. *Iceman: Uncovering the Life and Times of a Prehistoric Man Found in an Alpine Glacier.* New York: Random House.

Gallis, K. 1992. *Atlas proistorikon oikosmon tis anatolikis Thessalikis pediadas.* Larisa: Etairia istorikon ereunon Thessalias.

Gimbutas, M. 1974. *The Gods and Goddesses of Old Europe.* Berkeley: University of California Press.

———. 1977, Summer. Varna: A Sensationally Rich Cemetery at the Karanovo Civilization: About 4500 B.C. *Expedition*, 39–47.

Goring-Morris, Nigel. 2005. Life, Death, and the Emergence of Differential Status in the Near Eastern Neolithic: Evidence from Kfar Hahoresh, Lower Galilee, Israel. In *Archaeological Perspectives on the Transmission and Transformation of Culture in the Eastern Mediterranea,* J. Clarke (ed.), pp. 89–105. Oakville, CT: Council for British Research in the Levant and Oxbow.

Greenfield, Haskel J. 2010. The Secondary Products Revolution: The Past, the Present and the Future. *World Archaeology* 42: 129–54.

Gregg, Susan A. 1988. *Foragers and Farmers: Population Interaction and Agricultural Expansion in Prehistoric Europe.* Chicago: University of Chicago Press.

Groenenborn, Detlef. 1999. A Variation on a Basic Theme: The Transition to Farming in Southern Central Europe. *Journal of World Prehistory* 13: 123–210.

———. 2007. Beyond the Models: "Neolithisation" in Central Europe. *Proceedings of the British Academy* 144: 73–98.

Guilaine, Jean. 2010. *Shillourokambos: Volume 1, Un village néolithique précéramique à Chypre.* Lyon, France: Editions Errance.

———, François Briois, Jean-Denis Vigne, I. Carrère, G. Willcox, and S. Duchesne. 2000. L'habitat néolithique de Shillourokambos (Parekklisha, Chypre). *Bulletin de Correspondance Hellénique* 124: 589–594.

Guilaine, Jean, and A. Le Brun. 2003. Le Néolithique de Chypre. *Bulletin de Correspondance Hellénique*, Supplément 43.

Haak, Wolfgang, Peter Forster, Barbara Bramanti, Shuichi Matsumura, Guido Brandt, Marc Tänzer, Richard Villems, Colin Renfrew, Detlef Gronenborn, Kurt Werner Alt, and Joachim Burger. 2005. Ancient DNA from the First European Farmers in 7500-Year-Old Neolithic Sites. *Science* 310: 1016–1018.

Halstead, P. (ed.). 1999. *Neolithic Society in Greece. Sheffield Studies in Aegean Archaeology 2.* Sheffield, UK: University of Sheffield.

Hansen, Peter V., and Bo. Madsen. 1983. Flint Ax Manufacture in the Neolithic: An Experimental Investigation of a Flint Ax Manufacture Site at Hastrup Vænget, East Zealand. *Journal of Danish Archaeology* 2: 43–59.

Hansen, Svend. 2005. Neolithic Figurines: East-West. In *How Did Farming Reach Europe?* C. Lichter (ed.), pp. 195–212. *Byzas* 2. Berlin: Deutsches Archäologisches Institut.

———. 2007. *Bilder vom Menschen der Steinzeit: Untersuchungen zur anthropomorphen Plastik der Jungsteinzeit und Kupferzeit in Südosteuropa.* Mainz: Philipp von Zabern. Archäologie in Eurasien 20.

Harris, David R. 1996. *The Origins and Spread of Agriculture and Pastoralism in Eurasia.* Washington, DC: Smithsonian Institution Press.

Harrison, R. J., and G. Moreno López. 1985. El policultivo ganadero o la revolución de los productos secundarios. *Trabajos de Prehistoria* 42: 51–82.

Hayden, Brian. 1990. Nimrods, Piscators, Pluckers, and Planters: The Emergence of Food Production. *Journal of Anthropological Archaeology* 2: 931–969.

Hendon, Julia. 1996. Archaeological Approaches to the Organization of Domestic Labor: Household Practice and Domestic Relations. *Annual Review of Anthropology* 25: 45–61.

Hernández, M. S. 2005. Del Alto Segura al Turia: Arte rupestre postpaleolítico en el Arco Mediterráneo. In *Arte rupestre en la España Mediterránea*, M. S. Hernández and J. A. Soler (eds.), pp. 45–70. Alicante: Dipt. Provincial de Alicante, C.A.M.

Hernández Pérez, M.-S., P. Ferrer Marset, and E. Catalá Ferrer. 1988. *Arte rupestre en Alicante.* Alicante: Fundación Banco Exterior.

———. 2002. El Abrigo del Tío Modesto (Henarejos, Cuenca). *Panel* 1: 106–119.

Higham, T., J. Chapman, V. Slavchev, B. Gaydarska, N. Honch, Y. Yordanov, and B. Dimitrova. 2007. New Perspectives on the Varna Cemetery (Bulgaria): AMS Dates and Social Implications. *Antiquity* 81: 640–651.

Hodder, Ian. 1990. *The Domestication of Europe: Structure and Contingency in Neolithic Societies.* Oxford: Blackwell.

Höneisen, Markus (ed.). 1990. *Die ersten Bauern.* Zurich: Schweizerisches Landesmuseum.

Hood, M. S. F. 1967. The Tartaria Tablets. *Antiquity* 41: 99–114.

———. 1968, May. The Tartaria Tablets. *Scientific American* 218, 30–37.

Hosch, Sabine, and Stefanie Jacomet. 2001. New Aspects of Archaeobotanical Research in Central European Neolithic Lake Dwelling Sites. *Environmental Archaeology* 6: 59–71.

Hubert, F. 1978. Une minière néolithique à silex au Camp-à-Cayaux de Spiennes. *Archaeologia Belgica* 210.

———. 1980. Zum Silexbergbau von Spiennes (B1). In *5000 Jahre Feuersteinbergbau,* G. Weisgerber (ed.), pp. 124–139. Bochum: Bergbau-Museum Bochum.

Hüster-Plogmann, Heidemarie, Jörg Schibler, and Karlheinz Steppan. 1999. The Relationship Between Wild Mammal Exploitation, Climatic Fluctuations, and Economic Adaptations: A Transdisciplinary Study on Neolithic Sites from Lake Zurich Region, Southwest Germany, and Bavaria. In *Historia animalium ex ossibus,* C. Becker, H. Manhart, J. Peters, and J. Schibler (eds.), pp. 189–200. Rahden, Germany: Leidorf.

Ivanov, Ivan. 1977. *Treasures of the Varna Chalcolithic Necropolis.* Sofia: Agató.

———. 1988. Die Ausgrabungen des Gräberfeldes von Varna. In *Macht, Herrschaft und Gold,* A. Fol and J. Lichardus (eds.), pp. 67–78. Moderne-Galerie des Saarlands-Museum. Saarbrüken: Krüger.

———, and M. Avramova. 2000. *Varna Necropolis: The Dawn of European Civilization.* Sofia: Agató.

Iversen, J. 1956. Forest Clearance in the Stone Age. *Scientific American* 194: 36–41.

Jacomet, Stefanie, Urs Leuzinger, and Jorg Schibler. 2004. *Die jungsteinzeitliche Seeufersiedlung Arbon Bleiche 3: Umwelt und Wirtschaft.* Archaologie im Thurgau 12. Frauenfeld, Switzerland: Amt für Archaeologie des Kantons Thurgau.

Johnson, Anthony. 2008. *Solving Stonehenge: The New Key to an Ancient Enigma.* London: Thames and Hudson.

Jones, G. D. B. 1987. *Apulia 1: Neolithic Settlement in the Tavoliere.* London: Thames and Hudson.

Jørgensen, Svend. 1985. *Tree-Felling with Original Neolithic Flint Axes in Draved Wood.* Copenhagen: National Museum of Denmark.

Joussaume, Roger. 1988. *Dolmens for the Dead.* London: Batsford.

Jovanović, B. 1978, Fall. The Oldest Copper Metallurgy in the Balkans. *Expedition,* 9–17.

———. 1980. The Origins of Copper Mining in Europe. *Scientific American* 242(5): 152–167.

———. 1982. *Rudna Glava: Najstarije rudarstvo bakra na Centralnom Balkanu* [Rudna Glava: The Oldest Copper Mine in the Central Balkans]. Belgrade, Serbia: Arheološki Institut.

Kienlin, Tobias L., and Ben W. Roberts. 2009. *Metals and Societies: Studies in honour of Barbara S. Ottaway.* Bonn: Verlag Dr. Rudolf Habelt GMBH.

Knapp, A. Bernard. 2010. Cyprus's Earliest Prehistory: Seafarers, Foragers and Settlers. *Journal of World Prehistory* 23: 79–120.

Kotsakis, K. 1999. What Tells Can Tell Us: Social Space and Settlement in the Greek Neolithic. In *Neolithic Society in Greece,* P. Halstead (ed.), pp. 66–76. Sheffield: *Sheffield Studies in Aegean Archaeology 2.*

Krause, Rüdiger. 1997. Bandkeramische Grabenwerke im Neckarland: Überraschende neue Erkenntnisse durch Ausgrabungen bei Vaihingen an der Enz, Kreis Ludwigsburg. *Niederbayerischer Archäologentag Deggendorf* 15: 89–118.

———. 1997. Un village rubané avec fossé d'anciente et nécropole près de Vaihingen/Enz, dept. Ludwigsburg. In *Neolithique Danubien et ses marges entre Rhin et Seine*, C. Jeunesse (ed.), pp. 45–56. Strasbourg: Actes du 22éme Colloque Interrégional sur le Néolithique.

———. 1998. Bandkeramische Siedlung mit Grabenwerk. *Archäologie in Deutschland* 4: 6–11.

———, R.-M. Arbogast, S. Hönscheidt, J. Lienemann, S. Papadopoulos, M. Rösch, I. Sidéra, H. W. Smettan, H.-C. Strien, and K. Welge. 2000. Die bandkeramischen Siedlungsgrabungen bei Vaihingen an der Enz (Baden-Württemberg): Ein Vorbericht zu den Ausgrabungen von 1994–1997. *Bericht der Römisch–Germanischen Kommission* 79: 5–105.

Larson G., et al. 2007. Ancient DNA, Pig Domestication, and the Spread of the Neolithic into Europe. *Proceedings of the National Academy of Science USA* 104: 15276–15281.

Laslett, P., and R. Wall (eds.). 1972. *Household and Family in Past Time.* Cambridge: Cambridge University Press.

Lazarovici, Gh., C.-M. Lazarovici, and M. Merlini (eds.). 2011. *Tărtăria and the Sacred Tablets.* Cluj-Napoca, Romania: Editura Mega.

Le Bailly, M., U. Leuzinger, and F. Bouchet. 2003. Dioctophymidae Eggs in Coprolites from Neolithic Site of Arbon-Bleiche 3. *Journal of Parasitology* 89: 1073–1076.

Letica, Z. 1964. The Neolithic Figurines from Vinča. *Archaeology* 17(1): 26–32.

Leuzinger, Urs. 2000. *Die jungsteinzeitliche Seeufersiedlung Arbon Bleiche 3:* Befunde. Archäologie im Thurgau, no. 9. Frauenfeld, Switzerland: Departement für Erziehung und Kultur des Kantons Thurgau.

———. 2004. Experimental and Applied Archaeology in Lake Dwelling Research. In *Living on the Lake in Prehistoric Europe: 150 Years of Lake-Dwelling Research*, Francesco Menotti (ed.), pp. 237–251. London: Routledge.

Lüning, Jens. 2000. Steinzeitliche Bauern in Deutschland: Die Landwirtschaft im Neolithikum. *Universitätsforschungen zur Prähistorischen Archäologie*, 58.

———, U. Kloos, and S. Albert. 1989. Westliche Nachbarn der bandkeramischen Kultur: La Hoguette und Limburg. *Germania* 67: 355–393.

Macko, S., G. Lubec, M. Teschler-Nicola, V. Rusevich, and M. Engel. 1999. The Ice Man's Diet as Reflected by the Stable Nitrogen and Carbon Isotopic Composition of His Hair. *The FASEB Journal* 13: 559–562.

Madsen, B. 1984. Flint Axe Manufacture in the Neolithic: Experiments with Grinding and Polishing of Thin-Butted Axes. *Journal of Danish Archaeology* 3: 47–62.

———. 1993. Flint Extraction, Manufacture, and Distribution. In *Digging into the Past: 25 Years of Archaeology in Denmark,* S. Hvass and B. Storgaard (eds.), pp. 126–131. Arhus: The Royal Society of Northern Antiquaries.

Makkay, J. 1984. *Early Stamp Seals in South-East Europe.* Budapest: Akademiai Kiado.

Malone, Caroline. 2003. The Italian Neolithic: A Synthesis of Research. *Journal of World Prehistory* 17: 235–312.

———, S. Stoddart, A. Bonanno, T. Gouder, and D. Trump. (eds.). 1995. Mortuary Ritual of Fourth Millennium BC Malta: The Zebbug Tomb from the Brochtorff Circle (Gozo). *Proceedings of the Prehistoric Society* 61: 303–345.

Malone, C., S. Stoddart, and A. Townsend. 1995. The Landscape of the Island Goddess? A Maltese Perspective of the Central Mediterranean. *Caeculus* 2: 1–15.

Malone, C. A. T., S. K. F. Stoddart, and D. Trump. 1988. A House for the Temple Builders: Recent Investigations on Gozo, Malta. *Antiquity* 62: 297–301.

Manning, S. W., C. McCartney, B. Kromer, and S. T. Seward. 2010. Recognition and Dating of Pre-Pottery Neolithic A Occupation on Cyprus. *Antiquity* 84: 693–706.

Mathieu, James R., and Daniel A. Meyer. 1997. Comparing Axe Heads of Stone, Bronze, and Steel: Studies in Experimental Archaeology. *Journal of Field Archaeology* 24: 333–351.

McClure, Sarah B., Lluis Molina Balaguer, and Joan Bernabeu Auban. 2008. Neolithic Rock Art in Context: Landscape History and the Transition to Agriculture in Mediterranean Spain. *Journal of Anthropological Archaeology* 27: 326–337.

Merkyte, Inga. 2007. Ezero-Kale: From the Copper Age to the Bronze Age in the Southern Balkans. *Acta Archaeologica* 78(2): 1–78.

Merlini, Marco, and Gheorghe Lazarovici. 2008. Settling Discovery Circumstances, Dating and Utilization of the Tărtăria Tablets. *Acta Terrae Septemcastrensis Journal* 7: 111–195. Special Issue: Proceedings of the International Colloquium: The Carpathian Basin and its Role in the Neolithisation of the Balkan Peninsula.

Midgeley, Magdalena. 1992. *TRB Culture: The First Farmers of the North European Plain.* Edinburgh: Edinburgh University Press.

———. 2008. *The Megaliths of Northern Europe.* London: Routledge.

Mohen, Jean-Pierre. 1990. *The World of Megaliths.* New York: Facts on File.

Molina, F. J. 2004. La ocupacion del territorio desde el Paleolítico Medio hasta La Edad del Bronce en el area oriental de las comarcas de l'Alcoia´y el Comtat (Alicante). *Archivo de Prehistoria Levantina* 25: 91–135.

———, and J. A. Cámara. 2005. *Los Millares: Guía del yacimiento arqueológico.* Sevilla: Junta de Andalucia.

———, J. Capel, T. Nájera, and L. Sáez. 2004. Los Millares y la periodización de la prehistoria reciente del sureste. In *II–III Simposios de Prehistoria. Cueva de Nerja*, pp. 142–158. Nerja: Fundación Cueva de Nerja.

Molina, F., F. Contreras, A. Ramos, V. Mérida, F. Ortíz, and V. Ruíz. 1986. Programa de recuperación del registro arqueológico del Fortín I de los Millares. *Arqueología Espacial* 8: 175–201.

Müller, Wolfgang, Henry Fricke, Alex N. Halliday, Malcolm T. McCulloch, and Jo-Anne Wartho. 2003. Origin and Migration of the Alpine Iceman. *Science* 302: 862–866.

Navas, E., J. A. Esquivel, and F. Molina. 2005. La distribución espacial de los restos faunísticos en Los Millares (Santa Fe de Mondújar, Almería). *Complutum* 16: 89–104.

———. 2008. Butchering Patterns and Spatial Distribution of Faunal Animal Remains Consumed at the Los Millares Chalcolithic Settlement (Santa Fe de Mondújar, Almería, Spain). *Oxford Journal of Archaeology* 27: 325–339.

O'Kelly, M. J. 1982. *Newgrange: Archaeology, Art, and Legend.* London: Thames and Hudson.

Ó'Ríordáin, Seán P., and Glynn Daniel. 1964. *New Grange and the Bend of the Boyne.* London: Praeger and Hudson.

Palomo, A., R. Piqué, A. Bosch, J. Chinchilla, J. F. Gibaja, M. Saña, J. Tarrús. 2005. La caza en el yacimiento neolítico de La Draga (Banyoles-Giro- na). *III Congreso del Neolítico Peninsular (Santander)*, 2003, pp. 135–144.

Papathanasopoulos, G. A. (ed.). 1996. *Neolithic Culture in Greece.* Athens: Museum of Cycladic Art.

Parker Pearson, Mike, Andrew Chamberlain, Mandy Jay, Peter Marchall, Josh Pollard, Colin Richards, Julian Thomas, Chris Tilley, and Kate Welham. 2009. Who Was Buried at Stonehenge? *Antiquity* 83: 23–29.

Parker Pearson, Mike, Josh Pollard, Colin Richards, Julian Thomas, Chris Tilley, and Kate Welham. 2008. The Stonehenge Riverside Project: Exploring the Neolithic Landscape of Stonehenge. *Documenta Praehistorica* 35: 153–167.

Parker Pearson, Mike, Josh Pollard, Colin Richards, Julian Thomas, Chris Tilley, Kate Welham, and Umberto Albarella. 2006. Materializing Stonehenge: The Stonehenge Riverside Project and New Discoveries. *Journal of Material Culture* 11: 227–261.

Peltenburg, Edgar (ed.) 2003. *The Colonisation and Settlement of Cyprus: Investigations At Kissonerga–Mylouthkia, 1976–1996.* Såvedalen, Sweden: Paul Åströms Förlag.

———, Sue Colledge, Paul Croft, Adam Jackson, Carole McCartney, and M. A. Murray. 2000. Agro-pastoralist colonization of Cyprus in the 10th millennium BP: initial assessments. *Antiquity* 74: 844–853.

Peltenburg, E., and A. Wasse (eds.). 2004. *Neolithic Revolution! New Discoveries in the Neolithic of Cyprus.* Oxford: Oxbow Books.

Pericot García, L., and E. Ripoll Perelló (eds.). 1964. *Prehistoric art of the Western Mediterranean and the Sahara.* New York: Wenner-Gren Foundation for Anthropological Research.

Perlès, Catherine. 2001. *The Early Neolithic in Greece: The First Farming Communities in Europe.* Cambridge: Cambridge University Press.

Pernicka, Ernst, and David W. Anthony. The Invention of Copper Metallurgy and the Copper Age of Old Europe. In *The Lost World of Old Europe,* David Anthony (ed.), pp. 162–178. Princeton: Princeton University Press.

Pernicka, Ernst, Friedrich Begemann, Sigrid Schmitt-Strecker, Günther Adolf Wagner. 1993. Eneolithic and Early Bronze Age Copper Artefacts from the Balkans and Their Relation to Serbian Copper Ores. *Praehistorisch Zeitschrift* 68: 1–54.

Peters, J., and A. Von Den Driesch. 1990. Archäozoologische Untersuchung der Tierreste aus der Kupferzeitlichen Siedlung von Los Millares. *Studien über frühe Tierknochenfunde von der Iberischen Halbinsel* 12: 49–120.

Piggott, Stuart. 1935. The Early Bronze Age in Wessex. *Proceedings of the Prehistoric Society* 4: 52–106.

———. 1954. *Neolithic Cultures of the British Isles.* Cambridge: Cambridge University Press.

Price, T. Douglas. 2000. *Europe's First Farmers.* Cambridge: Cambridge University Press.

———, R. Alexander Bentley, Jens Lüning, Detlef Gronenborn, and Joachim Wahl. 2001. Prehistoric Human Migration in the Linearbandkeramik of Central Europe. *Antiquity* 75: 593–603.

Price, T. Douglas, Joachim Wahl, and R. Bentley. 2006. Isotopic Evidence for Mobility and Group Organization Among Neolithic Farmers at Talheim, Germany, 5000 BC. *European Journal of Archaeology* 9: 259–284.

Price, T. Douglas, & Ofer Bar-Yosef (eds.) 2011. The Origins of Agriculture: New Data, New Ideas. Current Anthropology, Supplementary Volume 4.

Pyke, Gilian, and Paraskevi Yiouni. 1996. *Nea Nikomedeia 1: Excavation & Ceramic Assemblage.* British School at Athens.

Radivojevi, Miljana, Thilo Rehren, Ernst Pernicka, Dusan Sljivar, Michael Brauns, and Dusan Boric. 2010. On the Origins of Extractive Metallurgy: New Evidence from Europe. *Journal of Archaeological Science* 37: 2775–2787.

Radovanovi, I. 1996. *The Iron Gates Mesolithic.* Ann Arbor, MI: International Monographs in Prehistory.

Renfrew, C. 1978. Varna and the Social Context of Early Metallurgy. *Antiquity* 52: 197–203.

———. 1986. Varna and the Emergence of Wealth in Prehistoric Europe. In *The Social Life of Things: Commodities in Cultural Per*spective, A. Appadurai (ed.), pp. 141–168. Cambridge: Cambridge University Press.

Richards, C. (ed.). 2005. *Dwelling Among the Monuments: The Neolithic Village of Barnhouse, Maeshowe Passage Grave and Surrounding Monuments at Stenness, Orkney.* Cambridge: McDonald Institute..

Richards, Julian. 1990. *The Stonehenge Environs Project.* London: Historic Buildings and Monuments Commission for England.

———. 1991. *The English Heritage Book of Stonehenge.* London: Batsford.

Richards, Martin. 2003. The Neolithic invasion of Europe. *Annual Review of Anthropology* 32: 135–162.

Ritchie, Anna. 1995. *Prehistoric Orkney.* London: B. T. Batsford.

Robb, John. 2007. *The Early Mediterranean Village. Agency, Material Culture, and Social Change in Neolithic Italy.* Cambridge: Cambridge University Press.

Rodden, R. J. 1965. An Early Neolithic Village in Greece. *Scientific American* 212(4): 83–92.

———, and K. A. Wardle. 1996. *Nea Nikomedeia: The Excavation of an Early Neolithic Village in Northern Greece, 1961–1964*. London: British School at Athens.

Rollo, F, M. Ubaldi, L. Ermini, I. Marota. 2002. Ötzi's Last Meals: DNA Analysis of the Intestinal Content of the Neolithic Glacier Mummy from the Alps. *Proceedings of the National Academy of Sciences* 99: 12594–12599.

Rowley-Conwy, Peter. 2011. Westward Ho! The Spread of Agriculture from Central Europe to the Atlantic. In *The Beginnings of Agriculture: New Data, New Ideas*. O. Bar-Yosef and T. D. Price (eds.), *Current Anthropology* 52: S431–S451.

Ruiz, Juan Francisco, Martí Mas, Antonio Hernanz, José María Gavira, Marvin W. Rowe, and Karen L. Steelman. 2006. First Radiocarbon Dating of Oxalate Crusts Over Spanish Prehistoric Rock Art. *International Newsletter of Rock Art* 46, 5–8.

Scarre, C. (ed.). 2002. *Monuments and Landscape in Atlantic Europe: Perception and Society During Neolithic and Early Bronze Age*. London: Routledge.

———. 2005. *Monuments megalithique de Grande-Bretagne et d'Irland*. Paris: Editions Errance.

Schibler, Jörg, Heidemarie Hüster-Plogmann, Stefanie Jacomet, Christoph Brombacher, Eduard Gross-Klee, and Antoinette Rast-Eicher. 1997. *Ökonomie und Ökologie neolithischer und bronzezeitlicher Ufersiedlungen am Zürichsee: Ergebnisse der Ausgrabungen Mozartstrasse, Kanalisationssanierung Seefeld, AKAD/Pressehaus und Mythenschloss in Zürich*. Monographien der Kantonsarchäologie Zürich, no. 20. Zurich, Switzerland: Direktion der Öffentlichen Bauten des Kantons Zürich, Hochbauamt, Abt. Kantonsarchäologie.

Schibler, Jörg, Stefanie Jacomet, Heidemarie Hüster-Plogmann, and Christoph Brombacher. 1997. Economic Crash during the 37th and 36th centuries BC in Neolithic Lake Shore Sites in Switzerland. *Anthropozoologica* 25–26: 553–570.

Schlichtherle, Helmut. 1997. *Pfahlbauten rund um die Alpen*. Stuttgart: Konrad Theiss Verlag.

Séfériadès. Michel Louis. 2010. Spondylus and Long-Distance Race in Prehistoric Europe. In *The Lost World of Old Europe*, David Anthony (ed.), pp. 178–191. Princeton: Princeton University Press.

Shee Twohig, E. 1981. *Megalithic Art of Western Europe*. Oxford: Clarendon Press.

Shennan, Stephen. 2007. Prehistoric Population History: From the Late Glacial to the Late Neolithic in Central and Northern Europe. *Journal of Archaeological Science* 34: 1339–1345.

Shepherd, R. 1994. Mining in Europe During the Neolithic and the Chalcolithic. In *History of Humanity*, Vol. I, Z. J. De Laet (ed.), pp. 616–626. London: Routledge.

Sherratt, Andrew. 1990. The Genesis of Megaliths: Monumentality, Ethnicity and Social Complexity in Neolithic North-West Europe. *World Archaeology* 22: 147–167.

Simmons, Alan H. 1988. Extinct Pygmy Hippopotamus and Early Man in Cyprus. *Nature* 333: 554–557.

———. 2000. *Faunal Extinction in an Island Society. Pygmy Hippopotamus Hunters of Cyprus*. New York: Kluwer.

———. 2007. *The Neolithic Revolution in the Near East*. Tucson: University of Arizona Press.

Skeates, Robin. 2000. The Social Dynamics of Enclosures in the Neolithic of the Tavoliere, South-East Italy. *Journal of Mediterranean Archaeology* 13(2): 155–188.

———. 2002. The Neolithic Enclosures of the Tavoliere, South-East Italy. In *Enclosures in Neolithic Europe: Essays on Causewayed and Non-Causewayed Sites*, G. Varndell and P. Topping (eds.), pp. 51–58. Oxford: Oxbow Books.

———. 2003. Radiocarbon Dating and Interpretations of the Mesolithic-Neolithic Transition in Italy. In *The Widening Harvest: The Neolithic Transition in Europe*, A. J. Ammerman and P. Biagi (eds.), pp. 157–187. Boston: Archaeological Institute of America.

———. 2005. *Visual Culture and Archaeology: Art and Social Life in Prehistoric South-East Italy*. London: Duckworth.

———. 2008. Making Sense of the Maltese Temple Period: An Archaeology of Sensory Experience and Perception. *Time and Mind: The Journal of Archaeology, Consciousness and Culture* 1(2): 207–238.

———. 2010. *An Archaeology of the Senses: Prehistoric Malta*. Oxford: Oxford University Press.

Slavchev, Vladimir. 2010. The Varna Eneolithic Cemetery in the Context of the Late Copper Age in the East Balkans. In *The Lost World of Old Europe,* David Anthony (ed.), pp. 192–211. Princeton: Princeton University Press.

Smith, Catherine Delano. 1967. Ancient Landscapes of the Tavoliere, Apulia. *Transactions of the Institute of British Geographers* 41: 203–208

Souden, David. 1987. *Stonehenge: Mysteries of the Stones and Landscape.* London: Collins and Brown.

Souvatzi, Stella G. 2008. *A Social Archaeology of Households in Neolithic Greece: An Anthropological Approach.* Cambridge: Cambridge University Press.

Spangenberg, Jorge E., Stefanie Jacomet, and Jörg Schibler. 2006. Chemical Analyses of Organic Residues in Archaeological Pottery from Arbon Bleiche 3, Switzerland: Evidence for Dairying in the Late Neolithic. *Journal of Archaeological Science* 33: 1–13.

Spielmann, Katherine A. 2002. Feasting, Craft Specialization, and the Ritual Mode of Production in Small-Scale Societies. *American Anthropologist* 104: 195–207.

Spindler, Konrad. 2001. *The Man in the Ice: The Preserved Body of a Neolithic Man Reveals the Secrets of the Stone Age.* London: Phoenix.

Srejovic, D. 1969. *Lepenski Vir: Nova praistorijska kultura u Podunavlju.* Beograd: Srpska knjiʃevna zadruga.

———. 1972. *Europe's First Monumental Sculpture: New Discoveries at Lepenski Vir.* London: Thames and Hudson.

Steelman, K.-L., M.-W. Rowe, F.-C. Ramírez, R.-F. Valcarce, and T. Guilderson. 2005. Direct Radiocarbon Dating of Megalithic Paints from Northwest Iberia. *Antiquity* 79: 1–11.

Stoddart, S., A. Bonanno, T. Gouder, C. Malone, and D. Trump. 1993. Cult in an Island Society: Prehistoric Malta in the Tarxien Period. *Cambridge Archaeological Journal* 3(1): 3–19.

Strien, H.-C. 2000. *Untersuchungen zur Bandkeramik in Württemberg.* Universitätsforschungen zur Prähistorischen Archäologie 69.

Tarrús, Josep. 2008. La Draga (Banyoles, Catalonia), an Early Neolithic Lakeside Village in Mediterranean Europe. *Catalan Historical Review* 1: 17–33.

———, M. Saña, J. Chinchilla, and A. Bosch. 2006. La Draga (Banyoles, Catalogne): traction animale à la fin du VIè millénaire? In *Premiers chariots, premiers araires: La diffusion de la traction animale en Europe pendant les IVè et IIIè millénaires avant notre ère,* pp. 25–30. *Table Ronde de Frasnois,* June 12–15, 2002. Paris: CNRS.

Tasic, Nikola, Dragoslav Srejovic, and Bratislav Stojanovic. 1990. *Vinca: Centre of the Neolithic culture of the Danubian region.* Belgrade, Serbia: Centre for Archaeological Research Faculty of Philosophy.

Theocharis, D. (ed.) 1973. *Neolithic Greece.* Athens: Bank of Greece.

Thomas, Julian. 2003. Thoughts on the "Repacked" Neolithic Revolution. *Antiquity* 77: 67–74.

Thorpe, I. J. 1998. *The Origins of Agriculture in Europe.* London: Routledge.

Tilley, C. 1996. *An Ethnography of the Neolithic.* Cambridge: Cambridge University Press.

———, C. Richards, W. Bennett, and D. Field. 2007. Stonehenge: Its Landscape and Architecture: A Re-analysis. In *From Stonehenge to the Baltic,* M. Larsson and M. Parker Pearson (eds.), pp. 183–204. British Archaeological Reports. International Series 1692. Oxford: Archaeopress.

Tinè, D. Santo 1983. *Passo di Corvo e la civiltà neolitica del Tavoliere.* Genoa: Sagep.

Tringham, Ruth. 2001. Household Archaeology. In *International Encyclopedia of Social and Behavioral Sciences,* N. J. Smelser, James Wright, and P. B. Baltes (eds.), pp. 6225–6229. New York: Elsevier.

Trump, D., and D. Cilia. 2002. *Malta: Prehistory and Temples.* Malta: Midsea Books.

Turck, R., B. Kober, J. Kontny, F. Haack, and A. Zeeb-Lanz. 2012. "Widely Travelled People. Herxheim, Sr-isotopes as Indicators of Mobility." Population Dynamics in Pre- and Early History. New Approaches by Using Stable Isotopes and Genetics, E. Kaiser, J. Burger, and W. Schier (eds.) pp. 151–166. Berlin: De Gruyter.

Van Andel, T. H., and C. N. Runnels. 1995. The Earliest Farmers in Europe. *Antiquity* 69: 481–500.

Vigne, J.-D., J. Guilaine, K. Debue, L. Haye, and P. Gérard. 2004. Early Taming of the Cat in Cyprus. *Science* 304: 259.

Vigne, Jean-Denis, Isabelle Carrère, François Briois, and Jean Guilaine. 2011. New Evidence from the Pre-Neolithic and Pre-Pottery Neolithic in Cyprus. In *The Beginnings of Agriculture: New Data, New Ideas*. O. Bar-Yosef and T. D. Price (eds.). *Current Anthropology* 52, Suppl. 4: S255–S271.

Vigne, Jean-Denis, Antoine Zazzoa, Jean-François Saliègea, Françis Poplina, Jean Guilainec, and Alan Simmons. 2009. Pre-Neolithic Wild Boar Management and Introduction to Cyprus More than 11,400 Years Ago. *Proceedings of the National Academy of Science* 106: 16135–16138.

Wahl, J., and H. G. König, 1987. Anthropologisch-traumatologische Untersuchung der menschlichen Skelettreste aus dem Bandkeramischen Massengrab bei Talheim, Kreis Heilbronn. *Fundberichte aus Baden-Württemberg* 12: 65–193.

Wainwright, G. J. 1970. Woodhenges. *Scientific American* 223: 30–37.

Walker, Michael. 1971. Spanish Levantine Rock Art. *Man* 6: 553–589.

Weisberger, Gerd. 1980. *5000 Jahre Feuersteinbergbau: Die Suche nach dem Stahl der Steinzeit*. Bochum: Deutschen Bergbar-Museum.

Whitehouse, R. 1968. The Early Neolithic of Southern Italy. *Antiquity* 42: 188–193.

———, and S. Hamilton. 2006. Three Senses of Dwelling: Beginning to Socialise the Neolithic Ditched Villages of the Tavoliere, Southeast Italy. *Journal of Iberian Archaeology* 8: 159–184.

Whittle, A. 1996. *Europe in the Neolithic: The Creation of New Worlds*. Cambridge: Cambridge University Press.

Whittle, Alasdair, and Vicki Cummings (eds.). 2007. *Going Over: The Mesolithic-Neolithic Transition in Northwest Europe*. Oxford: Oxford University Press.

Wilkie, N. C., and M. E. Savina. 1997. The Earliest Farmers in Macedonia. *Antiquity* 71: 201–207.

Willcox, G. 2003. The Origins of Cypriot Farming. In *Le Néolithique de Chypre: Actes du Colloque International Organisé par le Département des Antiquités de Chypre et l'Ecole Française d'Athènes. Nicosie 17–19 mai 2001,* Jean Guilaine and Alain Le Brun (eds.). *Bulletin de Correspondance Hellénique* Supplement 43: 231–238.

Winn, Shan M. M. 1981. *Pre-Writing in Southeast Europe: The Sign System of the Vinca culture*. Calgary, Alberta: Western.

Woodward, Ann. 2000. *British Barrows: A Matter of Life and Death*. Stroud, UK: Tempus.

Żammit, Sir T., and K. Mayrhofer. 1995. *The Prehistoric Temples of Malta and Gozo*. Malta S. Masterson.

Zeder, Melinda. 2011. The Origins of Agriculture in the Near East. In *The Beginnings of Agriculture: New Data, New Ideas*. O. Bar-Yosef and T. D. Price (eds.). *Current Anthropology* 52 Supplement 2: S221-S235.

Zeeb-Lanz, A., B. Boulestin, F. Haack, and Ch. Jeunesse, 2009. Außergewöhnliche Totenbehandlung—Überraschendes aus der bandkeramischen Anlage von Herxheim bei Landau (Südpfalz). *Mitt. Berliner Ges. f. Anthropologie, Ethnologie und Urgeschichte* 30: 115–126.

Zilhao, Joao. 2001. Radiocarbon Evidence for Maritime Pioneer Colonization at the Origins of Farming in West Mediterranean Europe. *Proceedings of the National Academy of Sciences* 98: 14180–14185.

Chapter Five   The Rise of Metals

Almgren, B. 1987. *Die Datierung Bronzezeitlicher Felszeichnungen in Westschweden*. Uppsala: Uppsala Universitets Museum för Nordiska fornsaker.

Almgren, O. 1927. *Hällristningar och kultbruk.* Stockholm: Kungl. Vitterhets.

Aner, E., and K. Kersten (eds.). 1973. *Die Funde der älteren Bronzezeit des Nordischen Kreises in Dänemark, Schleswig-Holstein und Niedersachsen.* København: Nationalmuseet.

Anonymous. 2011. Bare Bones: "The 'Amesbury Archer' and the Boscombe Bowmen." *Current Archaeology* 251: 12–19.

Anthony, David W. 2007. *The Horse, the Wheel, and Language: How Bronze-Age Riders from the Eurasian Steppes Shaped the Modern World.* Princeton: Princeton University Press.

Asouti, E. 2003. Wood Charcoal from Santorini (Thera): New Evidence for Climate, Vegetation, and Timber Imports in the Aegean Bronze Age. *Antiquity* 77: 471–484.

Bakker, Jan Albert, Janusz Kruk, Albert E. Lanting, and Sarunas Milisauskas. 1999. The Earliest Evidence of Wheeled Vehicles in Europe and the Near East. *Antiquity* 73: 778–790.

Balmuth, Miriam S., and Robert J. Rowland, Jr. (eds.). 1984. *Studies in Sardinian Archaeology.* Ann Arbor: University of Michigan.

Bass, George F. 1986. A Bronze Age Shipwreck at Ulu Burun (Kay): 1984 Campaign. *American Journal of Archaeology* 90: 269–296.

———. 1987. Splendors of the Bronze Age. *National Geographic Magazine* 172(6): 692–733.

———, D. A. Frey, and C. Pulak. 1984. A Late Bronze Age Shipwreck at Kay, Turkey. *International Journal of Nautical Archaeology* 13: 271–279.

Bergerbrant, S. 2005. Female Interaction During the Early and Middle Bronze Age Europe, with Special Focus on Bronze Tubes on Dress. *British Archaeological Reports* 142: 13–24.

Bertilsson, U. 1987. *The Rock Carvings of Northern Bohuslän: Spatial Structures and Social Symbols.* Stockholm: Stockholm Studies in Archaeology 7.

Betancourt, Philip P. 1985. *The History of Minoan Pottery.* Princeton: Princeton University Press.

Biehl, Peter. 2007. Enclosing Places: A Contextual Approach to Cult and Religion in Neolithic Central Europe. In *Cult in Context: Comparative Approaches to Prehistoric and Ethnographic Religious Practices,* C. Malone (ed.), pp. 173–182. Oxford: Oxbow Books.

Blake, Emma. 2001. Constructing a Nuragic Locale: The Spatial Relationship Between Tombs and Towers in Bronze Age Sardinia. *American Journal of Archaeology* 105: 145–161.

Bond, A., and R. S. J. Sparks. 1976. The Minoan Eruption of Santorini, Greece. *Journal of the Geological Society of London* 132: 1–16.

Bradley, Richard. 1998. *The Passage of Arms: An Archaeological Analysis of Prehistoric Hoards and Votive Deposits.* Oxford: Oxbow Books.

———. 2007. *The Prehistory of Britain and Ireland.* Cambridge: Cambridge University Press.

Cadogan, G., E. Hatzaki, and A. Vasilakis (eds.) 2004. *Knossos: Palace, City, State.* London: British School of Archaeology Studies 12.

Callender, G. 1999. *The Minoans and the Mykeneans: Aegean Society in the Bronze Age.* Oxford: Oxford University Press.

Carancini, Gian Luigi, and Renato Peroni. 1999. *L'età del bronzo in Italia: Per una cronologia della produzione metallurgica.* Perugia: Alieno.

Carneiro, Robert L. 1970. A Theory of the Origin of the State. *Science* 169: 733–738.

———. 2000. The Transition from Quantity to Quality: A Neglected Causal Mechanism in Accounting for Social Evolution. *Proceedings of the National Academy of Science* 97: 12926–12931.

Case, Humphrey. 2001. The Beaker Culture in Britain and Ireland: Groups, European Contacts, and Chronology. In *Bell Beakers Today: Pottery, People, Culture, Symbols in Prehistoric Europe,* F. Nicolis (ed.), pp. 361–377. Torento: Servizio Beni Culturali Ufficio Beni Archeologici.

Castleden, Rodney. 2005. *The Mycenaeans.* London: Routledge.

Cavanagh, W. G., R. R. Laxton, S. Bafico, and G. Rossi. 1987. An Investigation into the Construction of Sardinian Nuraghi. *Papers of the British School at Rome* 55: 1–74.

Chadwick, John. 1976. *The Mykenean World.* Cambridge: Cambridge University Press,

Cherry, John F. 1986. Polities and Palaces: Some Problems in Minoan State Formation. In *Peer Polity Interaction and Socio-Political Change,* Colin Renfrew and John F. Cherry (eds.), pp. 19–45. Cambridge: Cambridge University Press.

———. 2009. Sorting Out Crete's Prepalatial Off-Island Interactions. In *Archaic State Interaction: The Eastern Mediterranean in the Bronze Age,* William A. Parkinson and Michael L. Galaty (eds.), pp. 107–140. Santa Fe: SAR Press.

Chippindale, C., and Francis M. M. Pryor (eds.). 1992. Special Section: Current Research at Flag Fen, Peterborough. *Antiquity* 66: 439–531.

Clark, Peter. 2004. *The Dover Bronze Age Boat.* Swindon: English Heritage.

———. 2009. *Bronze Age Connections: Cultural Contact in Prehistoric Europe.* Oxford: Oxbow Books.

Cline, Eric. 2010. *The Oxford Handbook of the Bronze Age Aegean.* New York: Oxford University Press.

Coles, J. M. 2003. And on They Went … Processions in Scandinavian Bronze Age Rock Carvings. *Acta Archaeologica* 74: 211–250.

———. 2005. *Shadows of a Northern Past: Rock Carvings of Bohuslän and Østfold.* Oxford: Oxbow Books.

———, and A. F. Harding. 1979. *The Bronze Age in Europe.* London: Methuen.

Conneller, Chantal. 2010. *An Archaeology of Materials: Substantial Transformations in Early Prehistoric Europe.* London: Routledge.

Copley, M. S., R. Berstan, S. N. Dudd, G. Docherty, A. J. Mukherjee, V. Straker, S. Payne, and R. P. Evershed. 2003. Direct Chemical Evidence for Widespread Dairying in Prehistoric Britain. *Proceedings of the National Academy of Science* 100: 1524–1529.

Costin, Cathy L. 1991. Craft Specialization: Issues in Defining, Documenting, and Explaining the Organization of Production. *Archaeological Method and Theory* 1: 1–56.

Cottrell, Leonard. 1955. *The Bull of Minos.* London: Pan Books.

Cullen, Tracey (ed.). 2001. *Aegean Prehistory: A Review.* Boston: Archaeological Institute of America.

Desideri, Jaqualine, and Marie Besse. 2010. Swiss Bell Beaker Population Dynamics: Eastern or Southern Influences? *Archaeological and Anthropological Sciences* 2: 157–173.

Di Vito, Mauro A., Elena Zanella, Lucia Gurioli, Roberto Lanza, Roberto Sulpizio, Jim Bishop, Evdokia Tema, Giuliana Boenzi, and Elena Laforgia. 2009. The Afragola Settlement near Vesuvius, Italy: The Destruction and Abandonment of a Bronze Age Village Revealed by Archaeology, Volcanology and Rock-Magnetism. *Earth and Planetary Science Letters* 277: 408–421.

Dickinson, Oliver. 1994. *The Aegean Bronze Age.* Cambridge: Cambridge University Press.

———. 2006. *The Aegean from Bronze Age to Iron Age.* London: Routledge.

Doumas, Christos G. 1983. *Thera: Pompeii of the Ancient Aegean.* London: Thames & Hudson.

———. 1991. *The Wall Paintings of Thera.* Athens: Thera Foundation–Petros M. Nomikos.

———, and H. C. Puchelt (eds.). 1978. *Thera and the Aegean World.* London: Thera Foundation.

Dyson, Stephen L., and Robert J. Rowland. 2007. *Archaeology and History in Sardinia from the Stone Age to the Middle Ages.* Philadelphia: University of Pennsylvania Press.

Earle, Timothy. 1997. *How Chiefs Come to Power: The Political Economy in Prehistory.* Palo Alto: Stanford University Press.

———, and Kristian Kristiansen. 2010. *Organizing Bronze Age Societies: The Mediterranean, Central Europe, and Scandinavia Compared.* Cambridge: Cambridge University Press.

Evans, Arthur J. 1921–1936. *The Palace of Minos: A Comparative Account of the Successive Stages of the Early Cretan Civilization as Illustrated by the Discoveries at Knossos.* London: Macmillan.

Evans, Robert K. 1978. Early Craft Specialization: An Example from the Balkan Chalcolithic. In *Social Archaeology: Beyond Subsistence and Dating*, Charles L. Redman, et al. (eds.), pp. 113–129. New York: Academic Press.

Evely, Don, Helen Hughes-Brock, and Nicoletta Momigliano (eds.). 1994. *Knossos: A Labyrinth of History.* Oxford: Oxbow Books and British School at Athens.

Fitton, J. Lesley. 2002. *Minoans.* London: British Museum Press.

Fitzpatrick, A. P. 2002. "The Amesbury Archer": A Well-Furnished Early Bronze Age Burial in Southern England. *Antiquity* 76: 626–630.

———. 2009. In His Hands and in His Head: The Amesbury Archer as a Metalworker. In *Bronze Age Connections: Cultural Contact in Prehistoric Europe*, P. Clark (ed.), pp. 176–188. Oxford: Oxbow Books.

———. 2011. *Amesbury Archer and Boscombe Bowmen: Early Beaker Burials at Boscombe Down, Amesbury, Wiltshire, Great Britain. Excavations at Boscombe Down*, Vol. 1. Salisbury, England: Wessex Archaeology.

Flanagan, Laurence. 1998. *Ancient Ireland, Life Before the Celts.* Dublin: Gil & MacMillan.

Forsyth, P. Y. 1997. *Thera in the Bronze Age.* New York: Peter Lang.

Friedrich, W. L. 1999. *Fire in the Sea, the Santorini Volcano: Natural History and the Legend of Atlantis.* Cambridge: Cambridge University Press.

———, Bernd Kromer, Michael Friedrich, Jan Heinemeier, Tom Pfeiffer, and Sahra Talamo. 2006. Santorini Eruption Radiocarbon Dated to 1627–1600 BC. *Science* 312: 548.

Fuls, Andreas. 2007. Analysis of Circular Symbols on Golden Hats (Bronze Age). *Astronomische Nachrichten* 7: 328.

Galaty, Michael L., Dimitri Nakassis, and William A. Parkinson (eds.). 2011. Redistribution in Aegean Palatial Societies. Forum. *American Journal of Archaeology* 115, 2.

Galaty, Michael L., and William A. Parkinson (eds.). 2007. Rethinking Mykenean Palaces II: Revised and Expanded Edition. Monograph Series, Number 60. Los Angeles: UCLA Cotsen Institute of Archaeology Press.

Gates, Charles. 2003. *Ancient Cities: The Archaeology of Urban Life in the Ancient Near East and Greek and Roman Worlds.* London: Routledge.

Gaucher, Gilles. 1988. *Peuples de bronze: Anthropologie de la France à l'âge du bronze.* Paris: Hachette.

Glob, P. V. 1970. *The Mound People.* Ithaca, NY: Cornell University Press.

Goldhahn, Joakim. 2009. Bredarör on Kivik: A Monumental Cairn and the History of Its Interpretation. *Antiquity* 83: 359–371.

Greenfield, Haskel J. 2010. The Secondary Products Revolution: The Past, the Present and the Future. *World Archaeology* 42: 129–54.

Guilaine, Jean. 1984. *L'Age du Cuivre Européen: Les Civilizations á Vases Campaniformes.* Paris: CNRS.

Hägg, Robin, and Nanno Marinatos (eds.). 1987. *The Function of Minoan Palaces.* Stockholm: Swedish School at Athens.

Haldane, C. 1993. Direct Evidence for Organic Cargoes in the Late Bronze Age. *World Archaeology* 24: 348–360.

Halstead, Paul. 1992. The Mykenean Palatial Economy: Making the Most of the Gaps in the Evidence. *Proceedings of the Cambridge Philological Society* 38: 57–86.

Harding, Anthony F. 2000. *European Societies in the Bronze Age.* Cambridge: Cambridge University Press.

———. 2007. *Warriors and Weapons in Bronze Age Europe.* Budapest: Archaeolingua.

———, Helen Hughes-Brock, and Curt W. Beck. 1974. Amber in the Mykenean World. *The Annual of the British School at Athens* 69: 145–172.

Harrison, Richard J. 1980. *The Beaker Folk: Copper Age Archaeology in Western Europe.* London: Thames and Hudson.

Haustein, M., C. Gillis, and E. Pernicka. 2010. Tin Isotopy: A New Method for Solving Old Questions. *Archaeometry* 52: 816–832.

Holst, Mads Kahler, Henrik Breuning-Madsen, and Marianne Rasmussen. 2001. The South Scandinavian Barrows with Well-Preserved Oak-Log Coffins. *Antiquity* 75: 126–136.

Hood, Sinclair, and William Taylor. 1981. *The Bronze Age Palace at Knossos: Plans and Sections.* Supplement of the British School at Athens, no. 13. London: British School at Athens.

Hruby, Zachary X., and Rowan K. Flad (eds.). 2010. *Rethinking Craft Specialization in Complex Societies: Archaeological Analyses of the Social Meaning of Production.* Archeological Papers of the American Anthropological Association 17. New York: Wiley-Blackwell.

Hvass, Steen, and Birger Storgaard (eds.). 1993. *Digging into the Past: 25 Years of Archaeology in Denmark.* Copenhagen, Denmark: Royal Society of Northern Antiquaries.

Johansen, Kasper Lambert, Steffen Terp Laursen, and Mads Kähler Holst. 2004. Spatial Patterns of Social Organization in the Early Bronze Age of South Scandinavia. *Journal of Anthropological Archaeology* 23: 33–55.

Johansson, Per-Olof, Ole Høegh Post, and Birthe Skovholm (eds.). 2005. Brudevæltelurerne—verdens første og største lurfund. Alleroed, Denmark: LAFAK.

Kaufholz, Ute. 2004. *Sonne, Mond und Sterne: Das Geheimnis der Himmelsscheibe.* Anderbeck, Germany: Anderbeck Verlag.

Kaul, Fleming. 2004. Bronzealderens religion: Studier af den nordiske bronzealders ikonografi. *Nordiske Fortidsminder*, Serie B, 22.

Kristiansen, Kristian. 2000. *Europe Before History.* Cambridge: Cambridge University Press.

———, K. 2002. Langfærder og helleristninger: Rock Art, Ships, and Long Distance Travels in Scandinavia? *In Situ* 2002: 67–80.

———, and Thomas B. Larsson. 2005. *The Rise of Bronze Age Society: Travels, Transmissions and Transformations.* Cambridge: Cambridge University Press.

Landesamt für Archäologie Sachsen-Anhalt und Archäologische Gesellschaft in Sachsen-Anhalt e.V. (ed.). 2002. *Archäologie in Sachsen-Anhalt, Sonderdruck: Die Himmelsscheibe von Nebra.* Halle: Landesamt für Archäologie Sachsen-Anhalt.

Lanting, J. N., and J. D. van der Waals (eds.). 1976. *Glockenbechersimposion Oberried.* Bussum-Haarlem: Uniehoek.

Lilliu, G. 2006. *Sardegna Nuragica.* Nuoro, Sardinia: Edizioni Maestrali.

Lindow, John. 2002. *Norse Mythology: A Guide to Gods, Heroes, Rituals, and Beliefs.* Oxford: Oxford University Press.

Ling, J. 2004. Beyond Transgressive Earths and Forgotten Seas: Towards a Maritime Understanding of Rock Art in Bohuslän. *Current Swedish Archaeology* 12: 121–140.

———. 2008. *Elevated Rock Art: Towards a Maritime Understanding of Bronze Age Rock Art in Northern Bohuslän, Sweden.* GOTARC Serie B. Gothenburg Archaeological Thesis 49.

Livadie, C. Albore. 2002. A First Pompeii: The Early Bronze Age Village of Nola-Croce del Papa (Palma Campania Phase). *Antiquity* 76: 941–942.

———, and G. Vecchio. 2005. Un Villagio del Bronzo Antico a Nola—Croce del Papa (Campania). In *Papers in Italian Archaeology IV*, Peter Attema, Albert Nijbor, and Andrea Zifferero (eds.), pp. 581–587. Oxford: Archaeopress. British Archaeological Reports IS 1452 (II).

MacGillivray, J. Alexander. 2001. *Minotaur: Sir Arthur Evans and the Archaeology of the Minoan Myth.* New York: Pimlico.

Mallory, J. P. 1989. *In Search of the Indo-Europeans: Language, Archaeology, and Myth.* London: Thames and Hudson.

Manning, S. W. 1999. *A Test of Time: The Volcano of Thera and the Chronology and History of the Aegean and East Mediterranean in the Mid-Second Millennium BC.* Oxford: Oxbow Books.

———. 2001. *The Absolute Chronology of the Aegean Early Bronze Age: Archaeology, History, and Radiocarbon.* Monographs in Mediterranean Archaeology 1. Sheffield: Sheffield Academic Press.

———, Christopher Bronk Ramsey, Walter Kutschera, Thomas Higham, Bernd Kromer, Peter Steier, and Eva M. Wild. 2006. Chronology for the Aegean Late Bronze Age 1700–1400 BC. *Science* 312: 565–569.

Marcus, Joyce. 2008. The Archaeological Evidence for Social Evolution. *Annual Review of Anthropology* 37: 251–266.

Marinatos, N. 1984. *Art and Religion in Thera: Reconstructing a Bronze Age Society.* Athens: D. & I. Mathioulakis.

Mastrolorenzo, Giuseppe, Pierpaolo Petrone, Lucia Pappalardo, and Michael F. Sheridan. 2006. The Avellino 3780-yr-B.P. Catastrophe as a Worst-Case Scenario for a Future Eruption at Vesuvius. *Proceedings of the National Academy of Science* 103: 4366–4370.

McCoy, Floyd W. 2010. Tsunami Generated by the Late Bronze Age Eruption of Thera (Santorini), Greece. *Pure and Applied Geophysics* 57: 1227–1256.

———, and Grant Heiken. 2000. *Volcanic Hazards and Disasters in Human Antiquity.* Washington DC: Geological Society of America.

McGovern, Patrick E. 2010. *Uncorking the Past: The Quest for Wine, Beer, and Other Alcoholic Beverages.* Berkeley: University of California Press.

Mee, Christopher. 1995. *No. 42, The Ulu Burun Shipwreck.* In *100 Great Archaeological Discoveries,* Paul Bahn (ed.). New York: Barnes and Noble Books.

Melis, Paolo. 2003. *The Nuragic Civilization.* Italy: Carlo Delfino.

Meller, H. 2004, January. Star Search. *National Geographic* 76–78.

Menghin, Wilfried. 2000. Der Berliner Goldhut und die goldenen Kalendarien der alteuropäischen Bronzezeit. *Acta Praehistorica et Archaeologica* 32: 31–108. Potsdam.

———. 2010. *Der Berliner Goldhut: Macht, Magie und Mathematik in der Bronzezeit.* Regensburg: Schnell und Steiner.

Menotti, Francesco. 1999. The Abandonment of the ZH-Mozartstrasse Early Bronze Age Lake-Settlement: GIS Computer Simulations of the Lake-Level Fluctuation Hypothesis. *Oxford Journal of Archaeology* 18: 143–155.

———. 2001. *The "Missing Period": Middle Bronze Age Lake-Dwellings in the Alps.* BAR International Series, no. 968. Oxford: Archeopress.

———. 2002. Climatic Change, Flooding, and Occupational Hiatus in the Lake-Dwelling Central European Bronze Age. In *Natural Disasters and Cultural Change,* Robin Torrence and John Grattan (eds.), pp. 235–249. London: Routledge.

Michels, J. W., and G. S. Webster. 1987. *Studies in Nuragic Archaeology: Village Excavations at Nuraghe Urpes and Nuraghe Toscono in West-Central Sardinia.* Oxford: British Archaeological Reports.

Milstreu, G., and H. Prohl (eds.). 1996. *Dokumentation och registrering av hällristningar i Tanum. No. 1. Aseberget.* Tanumshede, Sweden: Tanums Hällristningsmuseum Underslös.

Mohen, Jean-Pierre, and Christiane Eluere. 2000. *Discoveries: The Bronze Age in Europe.* New York: Abrams.

Money, J. 1973. The Destruction of Acrotiri. *Antiquity* 47: 50–53.

Morteani, Giulio, and Jeremy P. Northover. 2010. *Prehistoric Gold in Europe: Mines, Metallurgy and Manufacture.* Brussels: NATO Science Series E.

Muller, J., and S. van Willigen. 2001. New Radiocarbon Evidence for European Bell Beakers and the Consequences for the Diffusion of the Bell Beaker Phenomenon. In *Bell Beakers Today: Pottery, People, Culture, Symbols in Prehistoric Europe,* Franco Nicolis (ed.), pp. 59–75. Torento: Servizio Beni Culturali Ufficio Beni Archeologici.

Mylonas, G. E. 1957. *Ancient Mykene Capital City of Agamemnon.* Princeton: Princeton University Press.

———. 1964. *Grave Circle B of Mykene.* Studies in Mediterranean archaeology 7.

———. 1966. *Mykene and the Mykenean Age.* Princeton: Princeton University Press.

Needham, Stuart. 2005. Transforming Beaker Culture in North-West Europe: Processes of Fusion and Fission. *Proceedings of the Prehistoric Society* 71: 171–217.

———, and Claudio Giardino. 2008. From Sicily to Salcombe: A Mediterranean Bronze Age Object from British Coastal Waters. *Antiquity* 82: 60–72.

Nelson, Max. 2005. *The Barbarian's Beverage: A History of Beer in Ancient Europe.* Abingdon, Oxon: Routledge.

Netting, R. McC., R. R. Wilk, and E. J. Arnould (eds.). 1984. *Households: Comparative and Historical Studies of the Domestic Group.* Berkeley: University of California Press.

Nilsson, Martin P. 1932. *The Mykenean Origin of Greek Mythology.* Berkeley: University of California Press.

Nordström, Hans-Ake, and Anita Knape (eds.). 1989. *Bronze Age Studies*. Stockholm: Statens Historika Museum.

Osgood, Richard, Sarah Monks, and Judith Toms. 2000. *Bronze Age Warfare*. Stroud: Sutton.

Pallottino, Massimo. 1950. *La Sardegna Nuragica*. Rome: Edizioni del Gremio.

Panagiotaki, M. 2007. The Impact of the Eruption of Thera in the Central Palace Sanctuary at Knossos, Crete. *Mediterranean Archaeology and Archaeometry* 7: 3–18.

Papadopoulos, G. A., and F. W. McCoy. 2011. Modelling of Tsunami Generated by the Giant Late Bronze Age Eruption of Thera, South Aegean Sea, Greece. *Geophysical Journal International* 186: 665–680.

Parkinson, William A., and Michael Galaty. 2007. Secondary States in Perspective: An Integrated Approach to State Formation in the Prehistoric Aegean. *American Anthropologist* 109: 113–129.

——— (eds.). 2009. *Archaic State Interaction: The Eastern Mediterranean in the Bronze Age*. Santa Fe: SAR Press.

Peroni, Renato. 1996. *L'Italia alle soglie della storia*. Rome: Editori Laterza.

Piazza, Alberto, and Luigi Cavalli Sforza. 2006. Diffusion of Genes and Languages in Human Evolution. In *The Evolution of Language: Proceedings of the 6th International Conference on the Evolution of Language*, Angelo Cangelosi, Andrew D. M. Smith, and Kenny Smith (eds.), pp. 255–266. Rome: World Scientific.

Preziosi, Donald, and Louise Hitchcock Preziosi. 1999. *Aegean Art and Architecture*. Oxford: Oxford University Press.

Price, T. Douglas, Gisela Grupe, and Peter Schröter. 1996. Migration in the Bell Beaker Period of Central Europe. *Antiquity* 72: 405–411.

Pruneti, P. 2002. Palafitte a Poggiomarino sul Sarno: Protostoria ai piedi del Vesuvio. *Archeologia Viva* 94: 72–76.

Pryor, Francis. 1989. Look What We've Found: A Case-Study in Public Archaeology. *Antiquity* 63: 51–61.

———. 1996. Sheep, Stockyards, and Field Systems: Bronze Age Livestock Populations in the Fenlands of Eastern England. *Antiquity* 70: 313–324.

———. 2001. *The Flag Fen Basin: Archaeology and Environment of a Fenland Landscape*. Archaeological Reports. London: English Heritage.

———. 2004. *Britain BC: Life in Britain and Ireland before the Romans*. London: Harper Collins.

———. 2005. *Flag Fen: Life and Death of a Prehistoric Landscape*. London: Tempus.

———. 2006. *Farmers in Prehistoric Britain*. London: History Press.

———, C. A. I. French, and M. Taylor. 1986. Flag Fen, Fengate, Peterborough. I. Discovery, Reconnaissance, and Initial Excavation. *Proceedings of the Prehistoric Society* 52: 1–24.

Pulak, Cemal. 1988. The Bronze Age Shipwreck at Ulu Burun, Turkey: 1985 campaign. *American Journal of Archaeology* 92: 1–37.

———, and D. A. Frey. 1985. The Search for a Bronze Age Ship-Wreck. *Archaeology* 38(4): 18–24.

Randsborg, K. 1993. Kivik: Archaeology and Iconography. *Acta Archaeologica* 64: 1–147.

———, and Kjeld Christensen. 2006. Opening the Oak-Coffins. New Dates—New Perspectives. *Acta Archaeologica* 77.

Renfrew, Colin. 1972. *The Emergence of Civilisation: The Cyclades and the Aegean in the Third Millennium B.C.* London: Methuen.

———. 1987. *Archaeology and Language: The Puzzle of the Indo-European Origins*. London: Jonathan Cape.

Rowland, Robert J. 2001. *The Periphery in the Center: Sardinia in the Ancient and Medieval Worlds*, BAR International Series 970. Oxford: Archaeopress.

Sahlins, Marshall. 1972. *Stone Age Economics*. Chicago: Aldine-Atherton.

Samson, Alice V. M. 2006. Offshore Finds from the Bronze Age in North-Western Europe: The Shipwreck Scenario Revisited. *Oxford Journal of Archaeology* 25: 371–388.

Schliemann, H. 2010 (1880). *Mykene: A Narrative of Researches and Discoveries at Mykene and Tiryns.* Reissue. Cambridge: Cambridge University Press.

Schmidt, Mark. 2002. Von Hüten, Kegeln und Kalendern oder Das blendende Licht des Orients. *Ethnographisch-Archäologische Zeitschrift* 43: 499–541.

Schofield, Louise. 2007. *The Mykeneans.* Los Angeles: J. Paul Getty Museum.

Schortman, Edward M., and Patricia A. Urban. 2004. Modeling the Roles of Craft Production in Ancient Political Economies. *Journal of Archaeological Research* 12: 185–226.

Schultz, Milert. 1993. *Borum Eshøj—en gravplads fra bronzealderen: Oversigt over bronzealdergravene ved Borum Eshøj før og nu.* Aarhus, Denmark: Moesgård Museum.

Service, Elman R. 1971. *Primitive Social Organization: An Evolutionary Perspective.* New York: Random House.

Sherratt, Andrew. 1981. Plough and Pastoralism: Aspects of the Secondary Products Revolution. In *Pattern of the Past: Studies in Honour of David Clarke*, I. Hodder, G. Isaac and N. Hammond (eds.), pp. 261–305. Cambridge: Cambridge University Press.

———. 1983. The Secondary Exploitation of Animals in the Old World. *World Archaeology* 15: 90–104.

———. 1998. The Human Geography of Europe: A Prehistoric Perspective. In *An Historical Geography of Europe,* Robin A. Butlin and Robert A. Dodgson (eds.), pp. 1–25. Oxford: Clarendon Press.

———. 1994. The Emergence of Elites: Earlier Bronze Age Europe, 2500–1300 B.C. In *The Oxford Illustrated Prehistory of Europe*, B. Cunliffe (ed.), pp. 244–276. Oxford: Oxford University Press.

———. 2000. Circulation of Metals and the End of the Bronze Age in the Eastern Mediterranean. In *Circulation of Metals in Bronze Age Europe*, C. F. E. Pare (ed.), pp. 82–98. Oxford: Oxbow Books.

Sørensen, M. L. S. 1995. Reading Dress: The Construction of Social Categories and Identities in Bronze Age Europe. *Journal of European Archaeology* 5: 93–114.

Taylor, Maisie, and Francis Pryor. 1990. Bronze Age Building Techniques at Flag Fen, Peterborough, England. *World Archaeology* 21: 425–434.

Thrane, Henrik. 1993. Otte fynske bronzealderlurer og nogle lerstumper. *Fynske Minder 1993: 44–56.*

———. 1999. Bronze Age Settlement in South Scandinavia: Territoriality and Organisation. In *Experiment and Design: Archaeological Studies in Honour of John Coles,* A. F. Harding (ed.), pp. 43–58. Oxford: Oxbow Books.

Tykot, R. H., and T. K. Andrews (eds.). 1992. *Sardinia in the Mediterranean: A Footprint in the Sea.* Sheffield: Sheffield Academic Press.

Tylecote, Ronald F. 1986. *The Prehistory of Metallurgy in the British Isles.* London: Institute of Metals.

Vander Linden, Marc. 2006. *Le phénomène campaniforme dans l'Europe du 3ème millénaire avant notre ère: synthèse et nouvelles perspectives.* Oxford: Archaeopress, BAR international series 1470.

Vandkilde, Helle. 1997. *From Stone to Bronze: The Metalwork of the Late Neolithic and Earliest Bronze Age in Denmark.* Aarhus, Denmark: Aarhus University Press.

———. 2011. Bronze Age Warfare in Temperate Europe. In *Sozialarchäologische Perspektiven: Gesellschaftlicher Wandel 5000–1500 v.Chr. zwischen Atlantik und Kaukasus,* Svend Hansen and Johannes Müller (eds.), pp. 365–380. Berlin: Deutsches Archäologisches Institut, Eurasien-Abteilung.

———, U. Rahbek, and K. L. Rasmussen. 1996. Radiocarbon Dating and the Chronology of Bronze Age Southern Scandinavia. In *Absolute Chronology: Archaeological Europe 2500–500 BC,* pp. 183–198. *Acta Archaeologica* supplementa I.

Vasilakis, Antonis Thomas. 2000. *The 147 Cities of Ancient Crete.* Heraklion: Kairatos Editions.

Ventris, Michael, and John Chadwick. 1973. *Documents in Mykenean Greek: Three Hundred Selected Tablets.* Cambridge: Cambridge University Press.

Verlaeckt, K. 1993. The Kivik Petroglyphs: A Reassessment of Different Opinions. *Germania* 71: 1–29.

Vermeule, Emily. 1964. *Greece in the Bronze Age.* Chicago: University of Chicago Press.

Voutsaki, S., and J. Killen (eds.). 2001. *Economy and Politics in Mykenean Palace States.* Cambridge: Cambridge University Press.

Wailes, Bernard (ed.). 1996. *Craft Specialization and Social Evolution: In Memory of V. Gordon Childe.* University Museum Symposium Series, Volume 6 University Museum Monograph UMM 93. Philadelphia: University Museum of Archaeology and Anthropology.

Wardle, K. A., and Diana Wardle. 1997. *Cities of Legend: The Mykenean World.* London: Duckworth.

Warren, P. M. 2006. The Date of the Thera Eruption. In *Timelines: Studies in Honour of Manfred Bietak,* E. Czerny, I. Hein, H. Hunger, D. Melman, and A. Schwab (eds.), pp. 305–321. *Orientalia Lovaniensia Analecta 14.* Louvain-la-Neuve, Belgium: Peeters.

Webster, Gary S. 1991. Monuments, Mobilization and Nuragic Organization. *Antiquity* 65: 840–56.

———. 1996. *A Prehistory of Sardinia 2300–500 BC.* Sheffield, UK: Sheffield Academic Press.

———. 2001. *Duos Nuraghes:. A Bronze Age Settlement in Sardinia. Vol. I: The Interpretive Archaeology, BAR International Series 949.* Oxford: Archaeopress.

———, and M. Teglund. 1992. Toward the Study of Colonial-Native Relations in Sardinia from c. 1000 BC–AD 456. In *Sardinia in the Mediterranean: A Footprint in the Sea—Studies in Sardinian Archaeology Presented to Miriam Balmuth,* R. H. Tykot and T. K. Andrews (eds.), pp. 317–346. Sheffield: Sheffield Academic Press.

Webster, G. S., and M. R. Webster. 1998. The Duos Nuraghes Project in Sardinia: 1985–1996 Interim Report. *Journal of Field Archaeology* 25: 183–201.

Wells, R. Spencer. 2001. The Eurasian Heartland: A Continental Perspective on Y-Chromosome Diversity. *Proceedings of the National Academy of Science* USA 98: 10244–10249.

———. 2002. *The Journey of Man: A Genetic Odyssey.* Princeton: Princeton University Press.

Whitelaw, T. 2001. Reading Between the Tablets: Assessing Mykenean Palatial Involvement in Ceramic Production and Consumption. In *Economy and Politics in the Mykenean Palace States,* S. Voutsaki and J. Killen (eds.), pp. 51–79. *Proceedings of the Cambridge Philological Society*: Supplementary Volume 27. Cambridge: Cambridge Philological Society.

Chapter Six   Centers of Power, Weapons of Iron

Arnold, Bettina. 1990. The Past as Propaganda: Totalitarian Archaeology in Nazi Germany. *Antiquity* 64: 464–478.

———, and D. Blair Gibson (eds.). 1998. *Celtic Chiefdom, Celtic State: The Evolution of Complex Social Systems in Prehistoric Europe.* Cambridge: Cambridge University Press.

Asingh, Pauline, and Niels Lynnerup (eds.). 2007. *Grauballe Man: An Iron Age Body Revisited.* Aarhus, Denmark: Moesgaard Museum.

Avery, Michael. 1993. *Hillfort Defences of Southern Britain.* Oxford: Tempus Reparatum.

Banti, Luisa. 1973. *Etruscan Cities and Their Culture.* Berkeley: University of California Press.

Barker, Graeme, and Tom Rasmussen. 1998. *The Etruscans.* Oxford: Blackwell.

Biel, Jörg. 1980. Treasure from a Celtic Tomb. *National Geographic* 157: 428–438.

———. 1981. The Hallstatt chieftain's grave at Hochdorf. *Antiquity* 55: 16–19.

———. 1982. Ein Fürstengrabhügel der späten Hallstattzeit (Württemberg). *Germania* 60: 61–104.

———. 1985. *Der Keltenfürst von Hochdorf.* Stuttgart: Theiss.

———. 1996. *Experiment Hochdorf: Keltische Handwerkskunst wiederbelebt.* Stuttgart, Germany: Keltenmuseum Hochdorf/Enz.

Bispham, Edward. 2009. *Roman Europe: 1000 BC–AD.* Oxford: Oxford University Press.

Bonfante, Larissa (ed.). 1986. *Etruscan Life and Afterlife: A Handbook of Etruscan Studies.* Detroit: Wayne State University Press.

———. 2011. *The Barbarians of Ancient Europe.* Cambridge: Cambridge University Press.

Bossuet, G., C. Camerlynck, C. Brehonnet, and C. Petit. 2001. Magnetic Prospecting of Diachronic Structures (Antiquity to First World War) on the Site of the Sanctuary of Ribemont-sur-Ancre (Somme, France). *Archaeological Prospection* 8: 67–77.

Brendel, Otto J. 1995. *Etruscan Art.* New Haven, CT: Yale University Press.

Brunaux J.-L. 1988. *Les Gaulois, Sanctuaires et Rites.* Paris: Editions Errance.

———. 2000. La mort du guerrier celte: Essai d'histoire des mentalités. In *Rites et espaces en pays celte et méditerranéen,* S. Verger (ed.), pp. 231–251. Rome: Ecole française de Rome.

———. 2000. Un trophée monumental à Ribemont-sur-Ancre. In *Les religions gauloises,* J. Brunaux (ed.), pp. 101–112. Paris: Editions Errance.

Brunaux, Jean-Louis. 1996. *Les Religions Gauloises.* Paris: Editions Errance.

———, M. Amandry, V. Brouquier-Redde, L.-P. Delestree, H. Duday, G. Fercoq, T. Lejars, C. Marchand, P. Meniel, B. Petit, and B. Rogere. 1999. Ribemont-sur-Ancre (Somme): bilan préliminaire et nouvelles hypothèses. *Gallia* 56: 177–283.

Brunaux J.-L., P. Meniel P., and F. Poplin. 1985. Gournay-sur-Aronde I: Les fouilles sur le sanctuaire et l'oppidum (1975–1984). *Revue Archéologique de Picardie,* n° spécial.

Carneiro, Robert L. 1970. A Theory of the Origin of the State. *Science* 169: 733–738.

———. 2000. The Transition from Quantity to Quality: A Neglected Causal Mechanism in Accounting for Social Evolution. *Proceedings of the National Academy of Science* 97: 12926–12931.

Chadwick, Nora. 1970. *The Celts.* London: Penguin Books.

Champion, T. C., and J. R. Collis (eds.). 1996. *The Iron Age in Britain and Ireland: Recent Trends.* Sheffield: J. R. Collis.

Chaume, Bruno. 1997. Vix, le Mont Lassois: État de nos connaissances sur le site princier et son environnement. In *Vix et les éphèmères principautés celtiques: Les VIe and Ve siècles avant J.-C. en Europe centre-occidentale,* P. Brun and B. Chaume (eds.), pp. 185–200. Paris: Editions Errance.

Coles, B., J. Coles, and M. S. Jørgensen (eds.). 1999. *Bog Bodies, Sacred Sites, and Wetland Archaeology.* Exeter: Wetland Archaeology Research Project.

Collins, Roger. 1999. *Early Medieval Europe. 300–1000.* Basingstoke: Macmillan.

Collis, John R. 1984. *Oppida: Earliest Towns North of the Alps.* Sheffield: University of Sheffield.

———. 1997. *The European Iron Age.* London: Routledge.

———. 2003. *The Celts: Origins, Myths, and Inventions.* London: Tempus.

Cunliffe, Barry. 1983. *Danebury: Anatomy of an Iron Age Hillfort.* London: Batsford.

———. 2000. *The Ancient Celts.* London: Penguin.

———. 2000. *Iron Age Britain.* London: B. T. Batsford.

———. 2003. *The Celts: A Very Short Introduction.* New York: Oxford University Press.

———. 2003. *Danebury Hillfort.* London: History Press.

———. 2008. *Europe Between Two Oceans: 9000 BC–AD 1000.* New Haven, CT: Yale University Press.

———, and John Koch (eds.). 2010. *Celtic from the West.* Oxford: Oxbow Books.

Dannheimer, Hermann, and Rupert Gebhard (eds.). 1993. *Das keltische Jahrtausend.* Mainz, Germany: Philipp von Zabern.

Davis-Kimball, Jeannine, V. A. Bashilov, and L. T. Yablonsky (eds.). 1995. *Nomads of the Eurasian Steppes in the Early Iron Age.* Berkeley: Zinat Press.

Edward, James. 2009. *Europe's Barbarians AD 200–600.* London: Longman.

Egg, Markus. 1996. *Das hallstattzeitliche Furstengrab von Strettweg.* Maoni: Römisch-Germanisches Zentralmuseum.

Ehrenreich, Robert M. 1985. *Trade, Technology, and the Ironworking Community in the Iron Age of Southern Britain.* Oxford: British Archaeological Reports 144.

Ellis, Peter Berresford. 2003. *The Celts: A History.* Philadelphia: Running Press.

Geary, Patrick J. 1988. *Before France and Germany: The Creation and Transformation of the Merovingian World.* Oxford: Oxford University Press.

Gebhard, Rupert. 1995. The Celtic Oppidum of Manching and Its Exchange System. In *Different Iron Ages: Studies on the Iron Age in Temperate Europe,* J. D. Hill and C. G. Cumberpatch (eds.), pp. 111–120. BAR International Series 602. Oxford: British Archaeological Reports.

Geselowitz, Michael N. 1988. The Role of Iron Production in the Formation of an "Iron Age Economy" in Central Europe. *Research in Economic Anthropology* 10: 225–255.

Glob, P. V. 1977. *The Bog People: Iron Age Man Preserved.* New York: New York Review of Books Classics.

Graham-Campbell, James, and Magdalena Valor (eds.). 2007. *The Archaeology of Medieval Europe: The Eighth to Twelfth Centuries AD.* Aarhus, Denmark: Aarhus University Press.

Green, Miranda J. (ed.). 1995. *The Celtic World.* London: Routledge.

———. 2004. *The Gods of the Celts.* London: Sutton.

Hachmann, Rolf, Georg Kossack, and Hans Kuhn. 1986. *Völker zwischen Germanen und Kelten.* Neumünster: Karl Wachholz.

Harding, D. W. (ed.). 1976. *Hillforts: Later Prehistoric Earthworks in Britain and Ireland.* London and New York: Academic.

Haynes, Sybille. 2000. *Etruscan Civilization: A Cultural History.* Los Angeles: J. Paul Getty Museum.

Hedeager, Lotte. 2011. *Iron Age Myth and Materiality: An Archaeology of Scandinavia AD 400–1000.* London: Routledge.

Holloway, Ross R. 1996. *The Archaeology of Early Rome and Latium.* London: Routledge.

Jakobson, Esther. 1995. *The Art of the Scythians: The Interpenetration of Cultures at the Edge of the Hellenic World.* New York: E. J. Brill.

James, Simon. 2005. *The World of the Celts.* London: Thames and Hudson.

Joffroy, René. 1954. *La tombe de Vix (Côte-d'Or).* Vol. 48, fascicle 1. Paris: Monuments et Mémoires (Fondation Eugène Piot).

———. 1962. *Le trésor de Vix.* Paris: Fayard.

Jones, Prudence, and Nigel Pennick. 1997. *A History of Pagan Europe.* London: Routledge.

Knudsen, Lise Roeder. 1994. Analysis and Reconstruction of Two Tabletwoven Bands from the Celtic Burial Hochdorf. In *Archäologische Textilfunde—Archaeological textiles. Textilsymposium Neumünster* 4.–7.5.1993. Neumünster, pp. 53–60.

Knüsel, Christopher J. 2002. More Circe Than Cassandra: The Princess of Vix in Ritualized Social Context. *European Journal of Archaeology* 5: 275–308.

Koch, Julia K. 1999. *Der Wagen und das Pferdegeschirr aus dem späthallstattzeitlichen Fürstengrab von Eberdingen-Hochdorf (Kr. Ludwigsburg).* Dissertation, Christian-Albrechts-Universität zu Kiel.

Kostrzewski, Józef. 1936. Osada bagienna w Biskupinie w pow. Żnińskim. Poznań.

Krämer, Werner. 1960. The Oppidum at Manching. *Antiquity* 34: 191–200.

Kristiansen, K., and J. Jensen (eds.). 1994. *Europe in the First Millennium B.C.* Sheffield,: J. R. Collis Publications.

Kromer, Karl. 1959. *Das Gräberfeld von Hallstatt.* Florence: Sansoni.

Laing, Lloyd, and Jenifer Laing. 1992. *Art of the Celts.* London: Thames and Hudson.

Lawrence, D. H. 1932. *Etruscan Places.* London: Secker.

Lejars, T. 1998. Des armes celtiques dans un contexte cultuel particulier: le charnier de Ribemont-sur-Ancre (Somme). *Revue Archéologique de Picardie* 1–2: 233–244.

Macnamara, Ellen. 1991. *The Etruscans.* Cambridge, MA: Harvard University Press.

Marcus, Joyce. 2008. The Archaeological Evidence for Social Evolution. *Annual Review of Anthropology* 37: 251–266.

Megaw, Ruth, and Vincent Megaw. 2001. *Celtic Art from Its Beginnings to the Book of Kells.* London: Thames and Hudson.

———. 2005. *Early Celtic Art in Britain and Ireland*. Princes Risborough: Shire.

Millet, Martin. 2003. *The Romanization of Britain*. Cambridge: Cambridge University Press.

Moscati, Sabatino, Otto-Herman Frey, Vencelas Kruta, Barry Raftery, and Miklós Szabó (eds.). 1991. *The Celts*. New York: Rizzoli.

Müller-Scheeßel, N. 2000. *Die Hallstattkultur und ihre räumliche Differenzierung: Der West- und Osthallstattkreis aus forschungsgeschichtlicher Sicht*. Rahden, Germany: Verlag Marie Leidorf.

Musset, Lucien. 1993. *The Germanic Invasions, the Making of Europe 400–600 AD*. New York: Barnes and Noble.

Nørbach, Lars Christian. 2002. *Prehistoric and Medieval Direct Iron Smelting in Scandinavia and Europe*. Aarhus, Denmark: Aarhus University Press.

Pallottino, Massimo. 1975. *The Etruscans*. Harmondsworth, UK: Penguin.

Payne, Andrew, Mark Corney, and Barry Cunliffe. 2007. *The Wessex Hillforts Project: Extensive Survey of Hillfort Interiors in Central Southern England*. London: English Heritage.

Piotrovsky, B., L. Galanina, and N. Grach. 1987. *Scythian Art*. Oxford: Phaidon.

Piotrowska, Danuta. 1997/98. Biskupin 1933–1996: Archaeology, Politics and Nationalism. *Archaeologia Polona* 35–36: 255–285.

Pleiner, Radomír. 1980. Early Iron Metallurgy in Europe. In *The Coming of the Age of Iron*, Theodore A. Wertime and James D. Muhly (eds.), pp. 375–415. New Haven, CT: Yale University Press,

Pohl, Walter. 2002. *Die Völkerwanderung. Eroberung und Integration*. Stuttgart: Kohlhammer.

Rajewski, Z. 1970. *Biskupin—osiedl obronne sprzed 2500 lat*. Warzaw: Arkady.

Rankin, H. D. 1998. *Celts and the Classical World*. London: Routledge.

Reeder, Ellen, and Michael Treister. 1999. *Scythian Gold*. New York: Abrams.

Ridgway, David, and Francesca R. Ridgway (eds.). 1979. *Italy Before the Romans: The Iron Age, Orientalizing, and Etruscan Periods*. London: Academic Press.

Rieckhoff, Sabine, and Jörg Biel. 2001. *Die Kelten in Deutschland*. Stuttgart, Germany: Konrad Theiss.

Rolle, Renate. 2011. The Scythians: Between Mobility, Tomb Architecture, and Early Urban Structures. In *The Barbarians of Ancient Europe,* Larissa Bonfante (ed.), pp. 107–131. Cambridge: Cambridge University Press.

Ross, Anne. 1986. *The Pagan Celts*. London: B. T. Batsford.

Rostoker, William, and Bennet Bronson. 1990. *Pre-Industrial Iron: Its Technology and Ethnology*. Archaeomaterials Monograph, no. 1. Philadelphia: University of Pennsylvania.

Scarre, Chris. 1998. *Exploring Prehistoric Europe*. Oxford: Oxford University Press.

Sharples, Niall M. 1991 *English Heritage Book of Maiden Castle*. London: B. T. Batsford.

———. 1991. *Maiden Castle: Excavations and Field Survey 1985–86*. London: English Heritage.

Sjoestedt, Marie-Louise. 1982. *Gods and Heroes of the Celts*. Berkeley: Turtle Island Foundation.

Sowerby, Robin. 2009. *The Greeks: An Introduction to Their Culture*. London: Routledge.

Spivey, Nigel J. 1997. *Etruscan Art*. New York: Thames and Hudson.

———, and Simon Stoddard. 1990. *Etruscan Italy: An Archaeological History*. London: B. T. Batsford.

Sprenger, Maja, and Gilda Bartoloni. 1983. *The Etruscans: Their History, Art, and Architecture*. New York: Abrams.

Stevens, Rhiannon E., Emma Lightfoot, Julie Hamilton, Barry Cunliffe, and Robert E. M. Hedges. 2010. Stable Isotope Investigations of the Danebury Hillfort Pit Burials. *Oxford Journal of Archaeology* 29: 407–428.

Stika, Hans-Peter. 1996. Traces of a Possible Celtic Brewery in Eberdingen-Hochdorf, Kreis Ludwigsburg, Southwest Germany. *Vegetation History and Archaeobotany* 5: 81–88.

Stoddert, K. (ed.). 1985. *From the Lands of the Scythians.* New York: The Metropolitan Museum of Art.

Stødkilde-Jørgensen, Hans, Niels O. Jacobsen, Esbern Warncke, and Jan Heinemeier. 2008. The Intestines of a More than 2000 Year Old Peat-Bog Man: Microscopy, Magnetic Resonance Imaging and ^{14}C-dating. *Journal of Archaeological Science* 35: 530–534.

Tacitus. 1970. *The Agricola and the Germania* (trans. H. Mattingly and S. A. Handford). London: Penguin.

Thurston, Tina L. 2009. Unity and Diversity in the European Iron Age: Out of the Mists, Some Clarity? *Journal of Archaeological Research* 17: 347–423.

———. 2010. Bitter Arrows and Generous Gifts: What Was a "King" in the European Iron Age? In *Pathways to Power*, T. D. Price and G. Feinman (eds.), pp. 193–254. New York: Springer.

Todd, Malcolm. 2004. *The Early Germans.* Oxford: Blackwell.

Torelli, Mario (ed.). 2001. *The Etruscans.* New York: Rizzoli.

Tylecote, Ronald F. 1992. *A History of Metallurgy.* London: Institute of Materials.

Vandkilde, Helle. 2007. *Culture and Change in Central European Prehistory.* Aarhus, Denmark: Aarhus University Press.

Wainwright, G., and Barry Cunliffe. 1985. Maiden Castle: Excavation, Education, Entertainment. *Antiquity* 59: 97–100.

Wells, Peter S. 1981. *The Emergence of an Iron Age Economy, The Mecklenburg Grave Groups from Hallstatt and Sticna.* Cambridge, MA: Harvard University Press.

———. 1984. *Farms, Villages, and Cities: Commerce and Urban Origins in Late Prehistoric Europe.* Ithaca, NY: Cornell University Press.

———. 1999. *The Barbarians Speak: How the Conquered People Shaped Roman Europe.* Princeton: Princeton University Press.

———. 2001. *Beyond Celts, Germans and Scythians: Archaeology and Identity in Iron Age Europe.* London: Duckworth.

———. 2002. The Iron Age. In *European Prehistory: A Survey,* S. Milisauskas (ed.), pp. 335–383. New York: Kluwer Academic/Plenum.

———. 2011. The Ancient Germans. In *The Barbarians of Ancient Europe,* Larissa Bonfante (ed.), pp. 211–232. Cambridge: Cambridge University Press.

Wertime, Theodore A., and James D. Muhly. 1980. *The Coming of the Age of Iron.* New Haven, CT: Yale University Press.

Wheeler, Mortimer. 1943. *Maiden Castle, Dorset.* London: John Johnson.

Wilkinson, C. M. 2004. *Forensic Facial Reconstruction.* Cambridge: Cambridge University Press.

Wilson, David M., and Christine E. Fell (eds.). 2003. *The Northern World: The History and Heritage of Northern Europe AD 400–1110.* London: Thames and Hudson.

Wolfram, Herwig. 1997. *The Roman Empire and Its Germanic peoples.* Berkeley: University of California Press.

Epilogue: Past and Present—Lessons from Prehistoric Europe

Bingham, Paul M. 1999. Human Uniqueness: A General Theory. *The Quarterly Review of Biology* 74:133–169.

Guttmann-Bond, Erika. 2010. Sustainability Out of the Past: How Archaeology Can Save the Planet. *World Archaeology* 42: 355–366.

Hoffman, Barbara T. 2005. *Art and Cultural Heritage: Law, Policy and Practice.* Cambridge: Cambridge University Press.

Lipe, W. D. 1974. A Conservation Model for American Archaeology. *The Kiva* 39(1–2): 213–243.

Sagan, Carl. 1980. *Cosmos.* New York: Random House.

PICTURE CREDITS

CHAPTER ONE

Fig. 1.1. Wikimedia, Creative Commons Attribution/Share Alike 3.0 Unported, Map by San Jose

Fig. 1.2. Figure 6, Geology and Nonfuel Mineral Deposits of Greenland, Europe, Russia, and Northern Central Asia, by Warren J. Nokleberg, Walter J. Bawiec, Jeff L. Doebrich, Bruce R. Lipin, Robert J. Miller, Greta J. Orris, and Michael L. Zientek. Open File Report 2005–1294D. U.S. Department of the Interior, U.S. Geological Survey

Fig. 1.3. Wikimedia, GNU Free Documentation License, photo by Petr Novák

Fig. 1.4. Wikimedia, Creative Commons Attribution/Share Alike 3.0 Unported, map by San Jose

Fig. 1.5. T. Douglas Price

Fig. 1.6. Wikimedia, Public Domain

CHAPTER TWO

Fig. 2.1. Wikimedia, Creative Commons Attribution/Share Alike 3.0 Unported, map by San Jose

Fig. 2.2. T. Douglas Price

Fig. 2.3. T. Douglas Price

Fig. 2.4. T. Douglas Price

Fig. 2.5. © Nature Publishing Group, 2008 E. Carbonell et al. The first hominid of Europe. *Nature* 452: 465–470. Permission granted

Fig. 2.6. Courtesy of Eduard Carbonell, Jordi Mestre/IPHES

Fig. 2.7. Science Photo Library

Fig. 2.8. Javier Trueba/Madrid Scientific Films/Photo Researchers, Inc. Images and Text Copyright © 2011 Photo Researchers, Inc. All Rights Reserved

Fig. 2.9. Courtesy of Mark Roberts and the Boxgrove Project

Fig. 2.10. Courtesy of Mark Roberts and the Boxgrove Project

Fig. 2.11. Courtesy of Mark Roberts and the Boxgrove Project

Fig. 2.12. Wikimedia Creative Commons Attribution/Share Alike 3.0 Unported, photo by Didier Descouens

Fig. 2.13. Courtesy of the Research and Development Centre Schoeningen, © NLD

Fig. 2.14. Courtesy of the Research and Development Centre Schoeningen, © NLD and J. Lipták

Fig. 2.15. Courtesy of Boudewijn Voormolen

Fig. 2.16. Courtesy of the Research and Development Centre Schoeningen, 1997 © Peter Pfarr NLD

Fig. 2.17. From Sawyer and Maley 2005. Photo courtesy of Blaine Maley

Fig. 2.18. © Natural History Museum London

Fig. 2.19. Courtesy of Peter K. A. Jensen

Fig. 2.20. © Böhlau Verlag

Fig. 2.21. Courtesy of Sabine Gaudzinski-Windheuser and the *Journal of Human Evolution*

Fig. 2.22. Courtesy of Joe McNally

Fig. 2.23. Courtesy of Jean-Louis Hussonnois

Fig. 2.24. ArScAn équipe d'Ethnologie préhistorique, Nanterre, France, photo by Leroi-Gourhan

Fig. 2.25. Open Access, Creative Commons. Caron et al. 2011

Fig. 2.26. Courtesy of David Frayer

CHAPTER THREE

Fig. 3.1. Wikimedia, Creative Commons Attribution/Share Alike 3.0 Unported, map by San Jose

Fig. 3.2. Courtesy of McGraw-Hill Higher Education, Images of the Past

Fig. 3.3. © Musée d'Archéologie national de Saint-Germain-en-Laye

Fig. 3.3. © Mircea Gherase

Fig. 3.4. © Mircea Gherase

Fig. 3.6. © Mircea Gherase

Fig. 3.7. Courtesy of Tjarko Evenboer

Fig. 3.8. Courtesy of the French Ministry of Culture and Communication, Regional Direction for Cultural Affairs—Rhône-Alpes region—Regional department of archaeology, photo by Jean Clottes

Fig. 3.9. Courtesy of the French Ministry of Culture and Communication, Regional Direction for Cultural Affairs—Rhône-Alpes region—Regional department of archaeology

Fig. 3.10. Courtesy of the French Ministry of Culture and Communication, Regional Direction for Cultural Affairs—Rhône-Alpes region—Regional department of archaeology

Fig. 3.11. Courtesy of the French Ministry of Culture and Communication, Regional Direction for Cultural Affairs—Rhône-Alpes region—Regional department of archaeology

Fig. 3.12. Courtesy of Michel Girard

Fig. 3.13. Google Earth/T. Douglas Price

Fig. 3.14. Courtesy of Jiri Svoboda

Fig. 3.15. Redrawn from Klima 1962

Fig. 3.16. Courtesy of Jiri Svoboda

Fig. 3.17. Courtesy of Jiri Svoboda

Fig. 3.18. Courtesy of Don Hitchcock, www.donsmaps.com

Fig. 3.19. After Galli 2008

Fig. 3.20. Courtesy of Don Hitchcock, donsmaps.com

Fig. 3.21. © Musée d'Archéologie national de Saint-Germain-en-Laye (France), photo by Loïc Hamon

Fig. 3.22. Courtesy of Gerhard Bosinski

Fig. 3.23. Drawing by Dietrich Evers, Bosinski 2007. Courtesy of Gerhard Bosinski

Fig. 3.24. Courtesy of Gerhard Bosinski

Fig. 3.25. Courtesy of Dieter Schmudlach

Fig. 3.26. Courtesy of Stig A. Schack Pedersen

Fig. 3.27. Courtesy of Jonathan Adams, from Adams and Faure 1997, http://www.esd.ornl.gov/projects/qen/

Fig. 3.29. Courtesy of James Enloe

Fig. 3.30. Drawing by T. Douglas Price

Fig. 3.31. Drawing by T. Douglas Price

Fig. 3.32. Courtesy of Wim van Vossen

Fig. 3.33. After Alley 1995

Fig. 3.34. Wikimedia, GNU Free Documentation License, Photo by 5telios

Fig. 3.35. Wikimedia, GNU Free Documentation License, Photo by 5telios

Fig. 3.36. Courtesy of Tammara and W. L. Norton

Fig. 3.37. Courtesy of Peter Woodman

Fig. 3.38. Courtesy of Peter Woodman
Fig. 3.39. Courtesy of Peter Woodman
Fig. 3.40. Courtesy of Pedro Alvim
Fig. 3.41. Drawing by T. Douglas Price, after van der Schriek et al. 2007
Fig. 3.42. Courtesy of Leendert Louwe Kooijmanns
Fig. 3.43. Courtesy of Leendert Louwe Kooijmanns
Fig. 3.44. Courtesy of Leendert Louwe Kooijmanns
Fig. 3.45. Courtesy of Leendert Louwe Kooijmanns
Fig. 3.46. Courtesy of Anders Fischer
Fig. 3.47. Courtesy of Søren Andersen
Fig. 3.48. Courtesy of Søren Andersen
Fig. 3.49. © Flemming Bau
Fig. 3.50. Courtesy of Søren Andersen
Fig. 3.51. Redrawn from Albrethsen and Petersen 1977
Fig. 3.52. Courtesy of the National Museum of Denmark, photo by Lennart Larsen
Fig. 3.53. Courtesy of Knut Helskog
Fig. 3.54. Courtesy of Trond Lødøen

Fig. 3.55. Modified with permission from Peter Rowley Conwy

CHAPTER FOUR

Fig. 4.1. Wikimedia, Creative Commons Attribution/Share Alike 3.0 Unported, map by San Jose
Fig. 4.2. T. Douglas Price, drawing by Randy Law
Fig. 4.3. Courtesy of Jean Guilaine, fouilles J. Guilaine; photos P. Gérard
Fig. 4.4. Courtesy of Jean Guilaine, fouilles J. Guilaine; photos P. Gérard
Fig. 4.5. Courtesy of Jean Guilaine, fouilles J. Guilaine; photos P. Gérard
Fig. 4.6. Courtesy of Jean Guilaine, fouilles J. Guilaine; photos P. Gérard
Fig. 4.7. Courtesy of ArchAtlas, http://www.archatlas.dept.shef.ac.uk/; after Gallis 1992
Fig. 4.8. Reproduced with the permission of the British School at Athens
Fig. 4.9. Courtesy of Catherine Perles, drawing by Gerard Monthel
Fig. 4.10. Courtesy of Catherine Perles
Fig. 4.11. Courtesy of Miha Budja, drawing by Gerard Monthel
Fig. 4.12. Courtesy of Catherine Perles, drawing by Gerard Monthel
Fig. 4.13. Wikimedia Public Domain
Fig. 4.14. Courtesy of Dusan Boric
Fig. 4.15. Courtesy of Dusan Boric
Fig. 4.16. Drawing by J.G.H. Swagger, Courtesy of Dusan Boric
Fig. 4.17. Courtesy of Dusan Boric
Fig. 4.18. T. Douglas Price
Fig. 4.19. Courtesy of Muzej grada Beograda, Arheološko nalazište u Vinči
Fig. 4.20. Photo by Adam Woolfit © National Geographic
Fig. 4.21. Wikimedia, GNU Free Documentation License, no author
Fig. 4.22. Courtesy of B. Jovanovic
Fig. 4.23. © Copyright British Photographers' Liaison Committee/Finers Stephens Innocent as agreed by BAPLA, AOP, NUJ, MPA and the BFP
Fig. 4.24. Wikimedia, GNU Free Documentation License, photo by Yelkrokoyade
Fig. 4.25. Courtesy of E. Volpe, University of Foggia
Fig. 4.26. T. Douglas Price
Fig. 4.27. With kind permission from Springer Science+Business Media B.V., *Journal of World Prehistory* 17, ©2003, The Italian Neolithic: A Synthesis of Research, Caroline Malone, Fig. 8, p. 254

Fig. 4.75. Wikimedia, GNU Free Documentation License, photo by Locutus Borg
Fig. 4.76. Wikimedia, GNU Free Documentation License, photo by Jose Mª Yuste
Fig. 4.77. T. Douglas Price, after Molina and Cámara 2005, p. 32
Fig. 4.78. Wikimedia, GNU Free Documentation License, photo by José-Manuel Benito Álvarez
Fig. 4.79. Courtesy of Domingo Leiva Nicolas
Fig. 4.80. © Museo Arqueológico Nacional, Madrid
Fig. 4.81. Courtesy of Daniel Cilia
Fig. 4.82. T. Douglas Price
Fig. 4.83. © Heritage Malta. The Main Hall of the Hypogeum is situated at Hal Saflieni Paola, the Islands of Malta. Heritage Malta is the National Agency of the Government of Malta set up in 2002 under the provisions of the Culture Heritage Act and entrusted with the management of National Museums and Heritage Sites and their collections in Malta and Gozo, including seven UNESCO World Heritage Sites.
Fig. 4.84. Wikimedia, Creative Commons Attribution/Share Alike 3.0 Unported, photo by Hamelin de Guettelet
Fig. 4.85. Courtesy of Oreto Garcia and Valentin Villaverde. ©Departament de Prehistoria i Arqueologia, Universitat de Valencia
Fig. 4.86. Courtesy of Cambridge University Press. From Beltran, Antonio. 1982. *Rock Art of the Spanish Levant*. Cambridge: Cambridge University Press. Plate 33
Fig. 4.87. © Nature Publishing Group. Dams, M., and L. Dams. 1977. *Nature* 268: 228–230. Figure 2

CHAPTER FIVE

Fig. 5.1. Wikimedia, Creative Commons Attribution/Share Alike 3.0 Unported, map by San Jose
Fig. 5.2. Courtesy of Christoph Hormann
Fig. 5.3. J. Wilson Myers, Eleanor Emlen Myers, Gerald Cadogan, eds., *An Aerial Atlas of Ancient Crete*. ©1994 by the Regents of the University of California. Reprinted by permission
Fig. 5.4. Courtesy of Sydne Pruonto
Fig. 5.5. Courtesy of John Bennet
Fig. 5.6a. Wikimedia, Creative Commons Attribution/Share Alike 2.0 Generic, photo by Claire H.
Fig. 5.6b. Wikimedia GNU Free Documentation License, photo by Satyr
Fig. 5.7. Wikimedia, GNU Free Documentation License, photo by Wolfgang Sauber
Fig. 5.8. Courtesy of Harry Schuler
Fig. 5.9. Courtesy of Klearchos Kapoutsis
Fig. 5.10. Wikimedia, GNU Free Documentation License, by Maximilian Dörrbecker
Fig. 5.11. http://www.imagefree.org/default.aspx (visited 08/121/2011)
Fig. 5.12. Courtesy of Daniel Skoog
Fig. 5.13a. Courtesy of Amy Christensen
Fig. 5.13b. Wikimedia, GNU Free Documentation License, drawing by Anton
Fig. 5.14. Courtesy of Walter Shandruk
Fig. 5.15. Wikimedia, GNU Free Documentation License, Photo by Xuan Che
Fig. 5.16. Wikimedia, GNU Free Documentation License, photo by παρακάτω
Fig. 5.17. © Shutterstock
Fig. 5.18. Wikimedia, GNU Free Documentation License, no photographer
Fig. 5.19. Courtesy of Nicola e Pina Europa
Fig. 5.20. Courtesy of the Institute of Nautical Archaeology
Fig. 5.21. Courtesy of the Institute of Nautical Archaeology
Fig. 5.22. Courtesy of the Institute of Nautical Archaeology

Fig. 5.23. T. Douglas Price

Fig. 5.24. Wikipedia, GNU Free Documentation License, photo by willow

Fig. 5.25. © Landesamt für Denkmalpflege und Archäologie Sachsen-Anhalt, photo by E. Hunold

Fig. 5.26. T. Douglas Price, map by Randall Law

Fig. 5.27. Courtesy of Andras Czene and the Directorate of Pest County Museums

Fig. 5.28. T. Douglas Price, map by Randall Law

Fig. 5.29. Courtesy of Andrew Fitzpatrick and Wessex Archaeology

Fig. 5.30. Courtesy of Andrew Fitzpatrick and Wessex Archaeology

Fig. 5.31. Pasquale Sorrentino/Photo Researchers, Inc. ©2011 Photo Researchers, Inc. All Rights Reserved

Fig. 5.32. Courtesy of Mauro Antonio Di Vito

Fig. 5.33. © National Academy of Sciences, U.S.A., 2006

Fig. 5.34. © National Academy of Sciences, U.S.A., 2006

Fig. 5.35. Wikimedia, GNU Free Documentation License, photo by Dbachmann

Fig. 5.36. Courtesy of the National Museum of Denmark. Photo by John Lee

Fig. 5.37. From Randsborg and Christensen 2007, with permission of Klavs Randsborg

Fig. 5.38. Courtesy of Gerhard Milstreu, Tanums Hällristningsmuseum. Tanum Rock Art Museum, Underslös

Fig. 5.39. Wikimedia, GNU Free Documentation License, photo by Philip Pikart

Fig. 5.40. © Shutterstock

Fig. 5.41. Courtesy of Gary Webster

Fig. 5.42. © DeA Picture Library / Art Resource, NY

Fig. 5.43. Courtesy of Gary Webster

Fig. 5.44. T. Douglas Price

Fig. 5.45. © Shutterstock

Fig. 5.46. Courtesy of Cristiano Cani

Fig. 5.47. Courtesy of Dave Goby http://www.flickr.com/

Fig. 5.48. Courtesy of Mads Holst

Fig. 5.49. Courtesy of the National Museum of Denmark

Fig. 5.50. Courtesy of the National Museum of Denmark, watercolor by A. P. Madsen 1875

Fig. 5.51. Courtesy of the National Museum of Denmark, photo by Robert Fortuna/Kira Ursem

Fig. 5.52. Courtesy of the National Museum of Denmark, photo by Robert Fortuna

Fig. 5.53. Courtesy of the Antiquarian-Topographical Archive at the Swedish National Heritage Board, Stockholm, Sweden, photo by Bengt A. Lundberg

Fig. 5.54. Courtesy of the Antiquarian-Topographical Archive at the Swedish National Heritage Board, Stockholm, Sweden, photo by Bengt A. Lundberg

Fig. 5.55. Courtesy of the South West Maritime Archaeological Group

Fig. 5.56. Courtesy of the South West Maritime Archaeological Group

Fig. 5.57. © Sarah Wilson, Flag Fen

Fig. 5.58. Courtesy of Chris Robinson

Fig. 5.59. Courtesy of Chris Robinson

Fig. 5.60. Courtesy of Johan Ling

Fig. 5.61. Courtesy of Paula-Soler Moya

CHAPTER SIX

Fig. 6.1. Wikimedia, Creative Commons Attribution/Share Alike 3.0 Unported, map by San Jose

Fig. 6.2. T. Douglas Price

Fig. 6.3. T. Douglas Price

Fig. 6.4. libreria@delucaeditori.com

Fig. 6.5. Musée du Pays Châtillonnais, Côte d'Or, France
Fig. 6.6. Courtesy of Simon James
Fig. 6.7. Courtesu of Libor Balák
Fig. 6.8. Courtesy of the National Museum of Denmark, photo by Roberto Fortuna
Fig. 6.9. Wikimedia, Free Domain, photo by Д. Колосов
Fig. 6.10. © Flemming Bau
Fig. 6.11. Wikimedia, GNU Free Documentation License, photo by Andrzej Łuczak
Fig. 6.12. Courtesy of the Archaeological Museum in Biskupin
Fig. 6.13. Courtesy of the Archaeological Museum in Biskupin
Fig. 6.14. Wikimedia, GNU Free Documentation License, photo by Fazer
Fig. 6.15. Wikimedia, GNU Free Documentation License, photo by Francesco Gasparetti
Fig. 6.16. T. Douglas Price
Fig. 6.17. Wikimedia, Public Domain, photo by Pufacz
Fig. 6.18. Wikimedia, Creative Commons Attribution/Share Alike 3.0 Unported license, photo by I. Sailko
Fig. 6.19. © Unesco Photoban
Fig. 6.20. Wikimedia, GNU Free Documentation License, photo by B. Matteo
Fig. 6.21. Wikimedia, GNU Free Documentation License, photo by pipimaru
Fig. 6.22. Pubic Domain
Fig. 6.23. Wikipedia, GNU Free Documentation License, photo by Detlef Meissner
Fig. 6.24. © Landesmuseum Württemberg, Stuttgart
Fig. 6.25. Courtesy of Thilo Parg
Fig. 6.26. Musée du Pays Châtillonnais, Côte d'Or, France
Fig. 6.27. McGraw-Hill Higher Education, Images of the Past
Fig. 6.28. Musée du Pays Châtillonnais, Côte d'Or, France
Fig. 6.29. Musée du Pays Châtillonnais—Trésor de Vix, Châtillon-sur-Seine, Côte d'Or, France
Fig. 6.30. © Lastrefuge.co.uk
Fig. 6.31. Courtesy of Barry Cunliffe
Fig. 6.32. Wikimedia, GNU Free Documentation License, photo by Rhys Jones
Fig. 6.33. Courtesy of Karen Margrethe Boe, Silkeborg Museum
Fig. 6.34. Courtesy of Moesgård Museum, Pauline Asingh
Fig. 6.35. Courtesy of Moesgård Museum, Pauline Asingh
Fig. 6.36. Wikimedia, photo by Anja Mößbauer
Fig. 6.37. Wikimedia, photo by Anja Mößbauer
Fig. 6.38. © Lastrefuge.co.uk
Fig. 6.39. Drawing by Paul Birkbeck. Copyright © Paul Birkbeck
Fig. 6.40. Courtesy of the Dorset County Museum
Fig. 6.41. Courtesy of J.-L. Brunaux
Fig. 6.42. Courtesy of J.-L. Brunaux
Fig. 6.43. Courtesy of J.-L. Brunaux
Fig. 6.44. Courtesy of J.-L. Brunaux
Fig. 6.45. © Landesmuseum Joanneum
Fig. 6.46. T. Douglas Price
Fig. 6.47. © Shutterstock
Fig. 6.48. Courtesy of Henrik Schilling and Sagnland Lejre

EPILOGUE

Fig. E.1. © Shutterstock

INDEX

Page numbers written in bold refer to photos or illustrations.